1

Ted Smith

Contact
ted@readfiction.co.uk

ACKNOWLEDGEMENTS

There are a number of people I owe a huge debt of gratitude to with some in particular putting up with a great deal during the often painful yet exhilarating process.

A special thanks goes to Caroline Gardiner, my long suffering partner, sounding board and reader. Deborah Hardwick, my sister for her invaluable contributions. My children, Theo, Lily, and Isadora for humouring me along the way. My great friends Mr Keppie and Mr Knight for their consistent support and reassuring talks over far too many beers.

Also, more recently, my friend Louis *'not a nutter'* Netter, who not only did the splendid illustrations, but also put Blotto up for me.

I could never have done any of this on my own.

I would also like to thank a number I have met on various writers' groups including the now defunct Authonomy group - you know who you are.

Finally, a posthumous thank you to Serafina Clarke, the indomitable literary agent who signed me all those years ago but, sadly, a little too late. Still, she was instrumental in inspiring me with a degree of confidence and pushing me along, and for that I can only thank her.

Chapter 1
Bristol, UK
November 2004
Late Friday Afternoon

She's stamping her feet, the small girl in front in the fur rimmed hood. She's stamping her grimy trainer feet on the sticky mini-mart floor. 'But you promised,' she's whining.

Beside her, a skinny young woman and little more than a girl herself pulls her in by her quilted sleeve. 'Not now. D'ya hear me?' she hisses like some end o' the pier ventriloquist.

Standing directly behind, he can see the tops of her studded ears flushed pink - red even - her hair pulled back tight and flat and bleached to her scalp. Idly, he wonders whether the two of them might, in fact, be sisters.

'But you said,' continues the girl.

'Wha' d'I say?'

'That you'd get me one.'

'One o' what?'

'One o' them!' squeals the girl, pointing. 'They're on special offer. Over there. Look!'

'What? Silly bits o' plastic? You gotta be jokin' me!'

'They're not silly! Everyone's got one!'

'Yeah, sure they 'ave.'

'They have! They're only one-ninety-nine!'

'Two quid? You must think I'm made o' money. The answer's no!'

'Mu-um! *(It's her mum he reasons. He's clever like that)* That's so unfair!'

'Life's unfair,' she says, 'an' the sooner you get used to it, the better.'

'If you didn't smoke so much,' risks the daughter very dangerously. 'They must cost tons.'

'Come 'ere, ya cheeky little cow!' her mother snaps, snatching her by the hand and squishing it bunched fingers tight.

'Ow! Get off me! That hurts!'

'Hurts, my foot!'

Twisting, the girl manages to pull herself free, folding her arms high up past her chin then dropping them down hard onto her belly. 'I hate you,' she mouths.

'Wha' d'you just say? I heard that!' her mum barks before giving her a quick backhander to the side of the head - no real damage, but … you know … vicious.

Wincing, he can't but help mirror the girl's flinch.

'Shut-it!' the mother hammers home, staccato fashion. 'Do-you-hear-me? Shut-it.'

The girl shuts it. She knows the score. But he, he can't hold back. 'Steady up, love,' he starts off gently enough in his late afternoon slur and like he might be chewing a toffee.

-

Elsewhere in the city, at the New Horizons Nursing Home near Ashton Gate, Margaret, a healthcare assistant, is gesturing pitifully. 'I think Mrs Dando needs sorting out,' she's saying.

'Who d'ya say?' asks Sheryl - the senior of the two by way of age and rank - miles away, the last bite of a Jaffa Cake in hand, her eyes idly scanning a well-thumbed celebrity magazine.

'Ellen, over in the corner,' informs Margaret. 'Think she might have had a little accident.'

'Has she now?'

'Shall I get her then?'

-

'Wha' the hell's it gotta do wi' you?' the mother demands, immediately aggressive.

'Just take it easy on the littl'un, that's all I'm sayin',' he says.

'S'none o' your business, ya daft ol' piss 'ead. Look at the state o' ya! Get lost!'

'Oi! Less o' the old,' he says, trying to make light of it.

She looks him up and down, blatant and sneering. 'You're mistakin' me for someone that gives a shit what ya think, mate,' she bats back.

'Nice to meet you too,' he says.

'Nice to meet you too,' she apes him before turning her back to kiss her daughter on the top of her hooded head - a double peck, kiss-kiss, closed ranks, end of.

-

Sheryl leans back and glances up at the clock on the wall. 'Ah, leave her, Maggie,' she says, popping the last of the biscuit into her mouth, 'the next lot can do her. They'll be here any moment.'

'We can't leave her like that… surely?'

'I told ya before, stop calling me Shirley.'

'Ha-ha! Very funny… well? Shall we then?'

'She won't hurt for five minutes. She opened her bowels earlier, didn't she?'

'Well ... yeah.'

'Then it'll only be a bit o' piddle then, won't it?'

'But ...'

'But don't make work for yourself,' Sheryl stops her, her long-term engagement ring now tapping an intermittent and impatient rhythm on her cold and empty coffee mug. 'You'll get it in the end. You'll see.'

-

Clearly unsteady on his feet, he looks to others in the queue for a cursory sign of approval that he'd said or done the right thing, but he's well out of luck. No, they simply don't want to get involved and look into the middle distance like butter wouldn't melt or find sudden interest in the rows of thick cut loaves to their left. 'Fuck ya, then,' he says, but not so loud as to cause serious offence.

You see, dressed in his time-honoured Levi jacket, frayed collar forever turned up over his pony-tailed greying mullet and like some wannabe but ageing rock star, and positively reeking of the pub, Derek, or Dekko to his mates, cuts an ominous looking figure to the uninitiated and certainly not someone you would want to meet in a dark alley late at night - but, in reality, it's all a façade. For the best part, he's as soft as shite, a woolly sheep in wolf's clothing.

-

Hovering uncertainly and somehow feeling like she was the one being obstructive and out of order, Margaret can't let it go. 'I don't mind, Sheryl,' she persists.

'Bloody hell, Maggie. I've just said, haven't I? Why won't you listen?'

'It won't take us two minutes, if we get our skates on.'

-

However, Derek can't leave it alone - never could, never can.

Instinctively, but unwisely, he reaches out to place a conciliatory hand on the young mother's shoulder. 'I was only tryin' to be nice, love,' he offers.

It's a bad manoeuvre all 'round.

-

Sheryl sighs heavily, juddering her chair back across the linoleum floor as if it were some great and Herculean task. 'What are you like?' she reluctantly agrees. 'Wheel her in then, if you must ... then I'm off.'

-

As soon as she feels his touch, she spins, coiling up as if she were a snake about to strike. 'Get your filthy fuckin' hands off o' me!' she near yells at him, a globule of spit jettisoning out from in between her tombstone and precarious looking front gnashers.

'Whoah! Easy tiger!' he says, holding up his hands in mock submission and with those on either side now at last reacting - taking a half step away into the blue corner you might say, into the red.

'I've had it up to 'ere with the likes of you stickin' your bleedin' nose in!' she continues to rant, repeatedly karate chopping her forehead to leave short-lived little bloodless lines.

Derek laughs uncertainly - a chortle. 'You'll do yourself an injury if you carry on like that,' he tries.

The young woman then clenches her fist and stiffens her body. 'Don't you fuckin' laugh at me, ya stinkin' gobshite!' she says.

OK.

Joke's over.

'Now, that's enough!' he tells her firmly.

'I ain't even fuckin' started yet!'

'Bloody 'ell, girl, there's just no talkin' to you is there? All I'm sayin' is that you can't just smack a kiddie round the 'ead like that anymore. Tha's all!'

'Sez who?'

'Sez everyone! It's all over the papers. TV. Everywhere. Ain't you see it?'

'All I ever get nowadays - watch your language 'ere, mind the kids there, don't do this, can't do that,' she reels off like it was a story of her life. 'Bollocks to 'em! An' to you, ya wankah!'

'Hey! Tha's enough I said!'

Then, bizarrely, and as quick as a flash, she clatters her basket to the floor and squares up to him like a sinewy bantam weight boxer - face on, drop jaw, fists up.

''Ere, what ya playin' at?' Derek shouts as she starts to pummel at his chest. 'Are you bleedin' mental or summat, ya daft bint!'

Alerted by the kerfuffle, a middle-aged woman from behind the tills calls out. 'Oi, you lot back there! Behave yourselves or else!' she shouts, her turquoise tabard in shocking contrast to her sunbed skin and hair of a similar hue. 'I don't wanna call the police again ... but I will,' she warns.

'Not again, mum,' the girl pleads. 'Please stop!'

With that, the young mother's demeanour changes in an instant, her eyes moving wildly from side to side like she'd just realised she'd left the kids at home with a box of matches, but, in truth, reminded of the hidden monitor strapped to her ankle.

8

'You wanna learn to chill out,' says Derek, slightly ruffled, patting himself down, rearranging his collar.

'Come on you, we're off,' the woman instructs her daughter, 'before I do summat I regret.'

'But what about our stuff?' the girl bawls as she finds herself being dragged side-shoe towards the exit. 'We got Monster Munch in there!'

'I'll gi' you fuckin' Monster Munch! Now, come on! Out!' the mother orders as they swiftly head out into the soft drizzle of the already darkening street and are gone in an instant.

'I'm not stoppin' ya gettin' your shoppin' nor nuthin',' he calls after them.

-

Margaret doesn't need to be told twice and walks briskly to the window on the far side of the room where the old lady sits, day in, day out. 'Come on, Ellen,' she whispers into her ear, 'let's get you cleaned up, shall we?'

'I can't help it, I'm ever so sorry,' she apologises, covering her lap with an old, crocheted doll that rarely leaves her side.

'Don't you worry yourself, my love. That's what we're here for.'

'I'm ever so sorry,' Ellen repeats.

'Hush yourself now. Off we go,' says Margaret as she releases the brake on the chair and wheels her towards the large utilitarian bath-cum-treatment room next to the kitchenette.

-

As relative peace and harmony returns to the store - well, other than the coughs, blows, and sighs of impatience and virulence together with the all too infrequent 'beep' of a bar code scanner and the rasp of the lottery machine churning out its all too slim potential - Derek, still shaking his head in exaggerated disbelief, pushes the abandoned basket aside with his foot and takes a welcome moment to admire his new Texan style cowboy boots. 'Good ol' PG,' he mutters to himself as he turns them out, turns them in, checking for early marks and scuffs.

But then, irritatingly, he spots a sticky label or somesuch protruding from under one of the soles. He can't be having with it, but he knows he daren't bend down - not with several pints on board and his bladder filling by the second, he can't - he'd go arse over tit, sure as eggs are eggs.

So, much to the further consternation of those standing either side of him, Derek now begins to teeter like someone first time on roller skates, dragging his angled foot across the floor like he was smearing shit onto grass - but all to no avail - it sticks like shit to a blanket.

9

'You sure know how to make our life difficult, don't ya, you little minx?' says Sheryl as Margaret pushes Ellen in through the double swing doors.

'What's that you say? You'll have to speak up,' says the old lady. 'I haven't got me hearing in.'

Behind the tills, of the three members of staff, only one, a tall and gangly pot-marked youth deigns to serve whilst 'Tango' woman, seemingly oblivious to the unmoving queue, studies loose leaf pages in an A4 ring binder like it was of utmost importance and her badge of rank. The other, a young black girl, is burning time restocking the brightly lit shelves behind with packs of cigarettes.

As Derek continues to try to dislodge the sticker on the metal edge of a low-level display unit, someone finally shouts out from the back. 'Oh, come on!' the voice yells. 'Can't we get a bloody move on 'ere!'

'We ain't got all day!' adds another. 'Can't someone else serve?'

'Yeah, an' I'm gonna piss meself 'ere if you don't hurry up!' Derek joins in and to a genuine ripple of laughter this time.

At last, reacting to the shouts of complaint, the girl aligns the last of the packets and saunters towards the till at the far end and taps in her code. 'Next,' she says.

Margaret gently squeezes Ellen's shoulder from behind. 'Let's get you out of them wet things, shall we?' she reassures her.

'And let's get rid of that old dolly of yours too?' adds Sheryl. 'Smelly ol' thing.'

'No! My mother made it for me!' reacts Ellen, holding onto it for all it's worth.

'Let's stick it in the washing machine at least.'

'No! It's got her hands on it.'

'It's not hurting, Sheryl,' interjects Margaret as they both now stand either side and slip the hoist into position to lift the old lady up onto the vinyl couch.

'I can still stand, you know,' Ellen complains. 'I only need a bit of help.'

'Quicker this way,' Sheryl rejects the idea.

No-one complains as Derek seizes his opportunity and brazenly leapfrogs two or three others to be first in line. 'Just these few bits, love,' he says urgently, 'and this,' he adds, pulling out a folded lottery docket from the bulging breast pocket of his jacket. 'It's a big rollover tomorrah, so someone was sayin'.'

'Can I do these first?' she answers tetchily, reaching into his basket.

'Sure, whatever ya like,' he says. 'But get a move on, yeah? I'm gettin' a bit desperate 'ere.'

As ever, Derek is short on funds, but he'd worked it out. He's enough for two ready-made meals - a Macca with Cheese and a Spag Bog - together with a sliced loaf, half a dozen eggs, a tin of Italian peeled tomatoes, some rashers of bacon, a newspaper, a tin of light tan shoe polish, a pound for the lottery, oh, and in reserve, enough for one more pint, the price of face-saving pub entry level.

'But it is though, yeah?' he repeats. 'A rollover I mean?'

She points him towards a handwritten poster stuck on the back of the till displaying its life changing message. It's a rollover alright with a colossal jackpot of more than eleven million pounds.

'Jeezus!' he says, laughing and rummaging in his jeans to locate the last of his change, 'that'd pay a few bills, girl, wouldn't it?'

He always plays the same numbers does Derek - various family birthdays, those of his three children, his mother's, and even that of his ex-wife, Marion (he daren't change it, it'd bound to come up. Sods' Law) and finally, making up the six, 29, his dad's all too young age when he'd lost his life. He keeps a single snapshot of him in his wallet, his only reminder - grainy, faded, indistinct.

Having scanned his shopping, the girl finally takes his docket and smooths it out on the counter. She threads it into the machine, but it doesn't read. She tries it again. It goes in, comes out - no result. 'You'll have to re-do it,' she says, gesturing to the red plastic lottery stand over in the corner by the greeting cards rack.

'An' get back in that great big queue again? Give us a break, love,' he pleads.

She shrugs like there was no other option.

'An' you don't want me to embarrass meself, now do ya?' he warns her whilst shifting his weight from one leg to the other for added effect.

Rolling her eyes towards the ceiling in some show of teenage disgust and embarrassment, she reaches under the counter and takes out a new slip.

'See, wasn't so difficult, was it?' he says as she quickly copies and marks the numbers using a betting shop sized pen. 'I'll tell ya what,' he then adds, winking at her, 'if they all come up, I'll make sure I see you alright. Alright?'

She offers him an insincere smile, like she hadn't heard or had heard it all before. 'That's seven-twenty-nine,' she says.

'Seven-twenty-nine, eh?' he repeats as he hands over his money. 'They're two o' me numbers. We might get lucky, you and me,' he adds as the girl slides a penny in change over the counter and looks across and behind him. 'Next,' she says.

-

'So, seen that son of yours recently?' asks Sheryl with barely concealed contempt, lifting the old ladies skirt above her waist.

Seemingly unaware of the nuance, Ellen smiles, a twinkle in her eye. 'He'll be here to see me shortly,' she twitters.

'Yeah, he'll be here when he wants something,' says Sheryl under her breath.

'What's that you say?' asks the old lady.

'If only she knew. You got the wipes, Maggie?'

'He's ever so busy you know, my Derek,' Ellen then tells them. 'Works all over he does.'

'Yes, he'll visit you soon enough, Ellen,' coos Margaret as she goes over to the dressing's cupboard.

'Oh yes, visits me regular he does.'

-

Derek cowers in the doorway like a dog unwilling to get wet and, setting his carrier between his legs, takes out his tobacco.

He peels off a Rizla and holds it up to the light to be sure of the gummed edge and deftly rolls himself a cigarette, shielding himself in his jacket to light up. Drawing deeply, he takes the plunge and dashes to the kerb to finally scrape the gummy label from off the sole of his boot. 'Get lost!' he says as it drops into the gutter.

It's decision time - Left, home. Right, to the pub. It's a no brainer, and, after all, nature calls.

And so, with roll-up cupped in hand and head down, Derek legs it up the precinct and past Bombay Nights, as yet unlit but still wafting out the all-pervasive aromas of food being prepared. Next to that, the now defunct and boarded up ironmongers, its covered doorway strewn with flattened cardboard boxes, a sleeping bag folded neatly alongside the collected litter of its vortex corners. Then, opposite Rub-a-Dub-Dub, the launderette, he crosses the street and towards the bookies where he acknowledges the ever-present security guard standing overweight and corseted in the entrance. 'Alright then, mate?' he greets him.

'Yeah, all considerin', Dekko,' the guard answers him. 'Nice night if you're a duck, I s'pose.'

Derek laughs. 'Quack-bloody-quack!' he says.

'Not 'avin' a little flutter tonight then?'

'Nah, not tonight.'

'Dogs are up soon. Walthamstow an' Swindon.'

'Maybe tomorrah.'

'What? On a mission, are ya?' guesses the man, wavering his hand like he was holding a pint glass.

Derek grins.

'Lucky bastard!'

'Ha! If only!' he replies. 'If only!'

Chapter 2

Purpose built in the early sixties, The Traveller's Rest to give the pub it's full yet seductively misleading name is a near symmetrical brick-built job that sits elevated and squarely in its own marked out car park, now chock-a-block with its regular Friday evening trade.

The very sight of it looming large and warmly lit through the incessant drizzle cracks Derek's face into a broad and boyish grin. He bloody loves it, he does.

OK, for sure, the façade's seen better days and in need of a bit of TLC, as does the interior, but none of that bothers him, not one tiny bit.

For example, the initial letter T had long gone from its name such that, now, nearly all simply refer to it as the 'Ravellers' - which is rather apt as most of its clientele do go there to get 'ravelled' or 'unravelled' as the fancy may or may not take them.

Directly underneath, a drooping flag of St George is lashed to the paint-peel drainpipes, and, below that, a wide plastic banner that proudly announces, *Open All Day - Live Sports on Sky.*

Next to the main entrance there's an A-framed blackboard chained to the metal railings, written in permanent chalk marker - hand script, drop shadow, like a greengrocer's market stall - *Full Sunday Roast ONLY £3.95!* - it reads, and, drawing-pinned to the bottom, an almost illegible and waterlogged laminated sheet - ♪*Live Music Every Tuesday*♪

In his overwhelming desire to get back in, Derek launches himself up the steps two at a time, catching the carrier bag between the doorframe and his knee in the process. He feels the unmistakeable crack of an egg or two. 'Ah bollocks!' he says, laughing. 'Scrambled it is then!'

-

Julie is sitting at the kitchen table still dressed in her school uniform - white blouse, black skirt, white socks, black shoes, cropped short red tie.

Her sweet smelling pencil case lies unzipped and open - her pens, pencils and crayons, and rubbers of various shapes and sizes spilling out onto the wipe-clean tablecloth.

She's doing her homework - Life Sciences - cell division, mitosis, and meiosis. She's copying from a textbook, annotating the cell parts, the nucleus and mitochondria in accurately drawn red biro lines.

She's in her element, is Julie. She's a studious girl. Neat.

-

The air is thick as Derek crashes back in, his noisy re-entry greeted with cheers and jeers in equal measure.

'Hey up! Watch out! 'Ere he is! Back again!' shouts out a voice from amongst the many sozzled faces now turned expectantly in his direction.

'Yeah, give us one o' ya turns, Dekko!' yells another. 'Come on, gi' us all a giggle!'

So, despite his full to bursting bladder and never being one to disappoint, Derek performs a slightly less elaborate version of one of his Shakespearian style bows - one leg stuck straight out, the other bent at the knee whilst sweeping his free hand, spread fingered, towards the floor. It's a party piece when he's lit up and in full flow. 'A pint, a pint, my kingdom for a pint!' he then booms like he was Brian-bloody-Blessed or something.

He's alight.

As ever, the bar shouts and whoops its approval. It would be fair to say that, in his local boozer at least, Derek is a legend in his own lifetime.

'An' about all it's worth,' shouts yet another of the drinkers populating the heaving bar. 'Yours 'ould barely stretch to 'alf o' fuckin' shandy!'

'Ha-har! You may say that,' retorts Derek, quick as you like, 'but you don't know what I got squirrelled away in me offshore accounts, now do ya, ya fuckin' fuckwit!'

On fire.

'What? You? Offshore accounts? You a secret bleedin' Tory or summat?'

'Never know, might be,' Derek taunts and teases. 'Property, investments, got the lot, me!'

Piping hot.

'You been playin' at that bloody Monopoly again, ain't ya?'

'We all like a bit o' Piccadilly ev'ry now an' then,' quips Derek, smirking lasciviously.

'Yeah, an' watch you don't end up in Pentonville too, ya weirdo!'

'More like the Old Cunt Road!' shouts out another, the bar now erupting into even greater and raucous laughter.

'See you been doin' your shoppin' then, Dekko?' observes one more, nodding at his bag. 'Meal for one again, is it?' he adds snidely.

'Nuthin' wrong wi' the ol' *à la ping*!' Derek comes back yet again, raising the carrier bag aloft like he'd won the FA Cup for the Rovers.

Incandescent.

'Besides, you all know me - I never eat on an empty stomach!' he proclaims and to which there is a moment's silence as glasses are raised in solemn drinkers' solidarity.

'Drink to that, Dekko!' says one. 'Bottom's up,' says another.

But Jimbo, the landlord in all but name, his sausage meat complexion forever glistening under the fluorescent strip lights behind the bar, his two-sizes-too-small nylon shirt stretched tight over his distended belly, has heard enough. He attempts to quieten them all down. 'Alright, you lot, alright!' he yells as best he can with his pronounced lisp caused by his undershot bulldog jaw. 'Cut the volume, yeah?'

'Fuck me, Jim,' says Derek as he begins to weave his way through the jostling crowd towards the end of the bar where they always stand -

Crackers Corner they call it with its all-year-round multi-coloured fairy lights - 'didn't know we wuz in a fuckin' library! I'd o' brought me bifocals had I o' known.'

'That means you too, Dekko. Behave, or else!' he instructs, but still, picking up a clean glass to pull him a pint of his usual.

Derek, scrunching his face at him in defiance, addresses his best mate, Phil, instead. 'You gettin' this or what, ya tosser?' he says, more by way of a demand than a question.

-

Even with the door pushed to, Julie can still hear the television blaring out in the sitting room with her mum and sister calling out wrong answers to an all too familiar game show.

'Jules, will you leave that now?' Marion, her mum, calls out. 'Your tea's getting cold 'ere.'

'I need to finish this first,' she complains.

'It's not all about books ya know.'

'Yes, it is.'

'No, it's not. You got to eat.'

-

'Do I 'ave a choice?' says Phil, slapping Derek on the back, his shirt sleeve lifting to further reveal his heavily tattooed forearm, a relic from his Royal Navy days, that had blued and bled over the years such that any design or wording is now pretty much lost or indecipherable.

'Nah, you don't. Just stick it in!'

'Bit short again, are we? Was told you were bein' a good boy an' on yer way 'ome.'

'You're kiddin' me! On a Friday? I ain't dead yet!' says Derek as he dumps his shopping on the bench underneath the cigarette machine. 'Anyway, you'll 'ave to gi' me a minute. I am dyin' for a piss 'ere!'

'Make it quick then. I got summat that might put a smile back on your face.'

'Like what?' asks Derek, intrigued but knock-kneed, he starts to scurry out towards the Gents.

'It can wait. Go on,' Phil calls after him.

'Tell me! What?'

'Go!' orders Phil before turning back to Jimbo. 'I'll get that, Jim, an' stick another in for me while you're at it, yeah?'

Manning the bar all on his own as usual, Jimbo shakes his head with a mixture of knowing disbelief and inevitability. 'Knew he'd be back,' he says, 'ain't made double figures yet - piss 'ead.'

-

'Come on, Julie! I'll not tell you again,' her mum shouts to her once more. 'I haven't done all this for nothin', ya know.'

'Yeah, come on, swot features,' agrees Janice, Julies' sister, her eyes fixed to the television, fork in hand. 'We need your help. You're good at this.'

Julie at last relents, replacing the cap to a felt tip pen, putting her ruler back in her case. 'OK! OK! I'm coming!' she says.

'Halle-bloody-lu-yah!' says Derek, exhaling forcibly and resting one hand on the tiled wall for support.

'That you, Dekko?' enquires a twitchy sounding voice from inside one of the two cubicles behind him.

'Who the fuck's that?' Derek asks as he now takes aim at a disintegrating cigarette butt and fires it past a blue disinfectant block and towards the drain hole.

'Who d'ya think it is? It's me, ya wazzock. You know how it is.'

'Oh, delirious Dave!' Derek recognises. 'What you up to, me ol' mucker?'

'Keep it down, yeah?'

'Thought me luck was in for a minute,' jokes Derek, camping it up.

'You should be so lucky.'

'Not my type I'm afraid, y'ugly cunt.'

'Very funny. So, you out on the razz tonight as usual?' asks Dave.

'Nah, can't I'm afraid, bit low on funds,' Derek bleats expectantly. 'Just a couple more then that'll be me lot.'

'Shut up! I'll get you a bloody beer,' Dave offers. 'Just been paid.'

Result!

'I gotta hand it to ya, mate, you're a good 'un, despite what every other fucker sez,' jokes Derek by way of acceptance.

'There's gratitude for ya.'

'So, what ya got? Charlie, or just a bit o' whizz?'

'Fuckin' 'ell! Keep it down, Dekko! Jim's got me on a warnin' as it is!'

'I ain't stupid, David. There's no-one 'ere.'

'OK, as long as you're sure. I'm down to me last squidgin', else you could have 'ad a bit,' Dave lies as he slips a two-gram wrap into the back pocket of his paint bespattered tracky bottoms.

'Nah, not for me, mate. I've done with all that shit nowadays. You wanna knock it on the head an' all if you 'ad any sense. Save your money. It fries your brain - not that you got any.'

'Oi! D'you want that beer or not?' says Dave before moaning with pleasure as the icing sugar sweetness hits the back of his throat.

'Better?' Derek asks.

'Better,' confirms Dave, cuffing his nose.

'See you in a bit, Dave,' says Derek as he shakes and zips up. 'Thanks.'

'No, problem, mate. Sure you'd do the same for me.'

'I would,' confirms Derek as the sprung loaded door twangs noisily shut behind him, 'ya little twat.'

Both her mum and older sister are perched on the edge of their two-tone Dralon settee, steadying their plates on their laps as Julie finally comes in to join them.

Her meal sits cooling on the coffee table, her knife and fork nestled in between a couple of sausages and some potato croquettes swimming on a bed of baked beans.

'Dunno why I waste my time,' her mum tells her.

-

'So, wha's new, Dekko?' asks Phil, passing him his pint.

'Cheers. Had a bit of a two-an'-eight down the shops just now, but not a lot. So, what ya got for me then?'

'What d'ya mean, a bit of a two-an'-eight?'

'Nuthin', just some young girl smackin' her little kid, tha's all. She had a right go at me when I tried put her straight. Tried to punch me she did, the mad bint! So, what is it?'

'Poor kids nowadays,' says Phil, stabbing at a copy of the Sun, sodden and dishevelled on the bar. 'Make's ya fuckin' sick wi' all them paedos about.'

'Don't think she was a kiddie-fiddler nor nuthin', Phil,' Derek puts him straight, 'just a bit wired, tha's all. Anyway, forget it, wha's the surprise?'

'Mind you, a lot o' these young uns could do with a good wallop,' Phil carries on. 'My mum used to gi' me what for, an' me Dad. Didn't do me no 'arm.'

'Fuck me! Did you get outa the wrong side o' the bed or summat, ya miserable ol' sod?' says Derek, laughing. 'Spit it out!'

'Some sponduliks,' reveals Phil as he reaches into his pocket to hand him fifty quid in fivers and tenners. (They'd help do a bit of house clearance a couple of days back, the pair of them - cash in hand, drinking tokens) 'The blokes not long dropped by and waded us in a bit early.'

Derek, delighted, licks his fingers, counting, the evening now panning out very nicely in front of him. 'Good man!' he says.

'Happy now?'

'Pig in shit!' says Derek, kissing the notes and looking skywards. 'Thank you, God! Thank you!'

-

'Where's Jez,' asks Julie as she picks up her plate. 'Isn't he in yet?'

'What do you think?' groans their mum as if she didn't care. 'An' I'm buggered if I can be at his beck and call all the time neither. His is still in the oven.'

'I saw him on my way home,' Janice informs them, 'him and his so-called mates' actin' like they're all gangsters or somethin'. Have you seen what they're all wearing?'

'What? With their arses hangin' out their trousers ya mean?' complains Marion once again. 'Looks bloody ridiculous!

'Couldn't even bring himself to say hello he couldn't,' continues Janice.

'You'll have to watch him, Mum,' warns Julie with genuine sisterly concern. 'He'll get himself put on an ASBO if he doesn't watch out. Half them he hangs out with are on one.'

'Ah, he won't listen to me. An' you know your father's bloody useless. I've told him I 'ave, but he just thinks it's funny. Anyway, I'm not going to ask you again. Eat your tea.'

-

Jimbo, never one to miss a trick, had seen the money change hands and makes his move. 'Hey, Dekko, as you're wedged up, how about knockin' out some of your tab, eh?' he asks with little or no expectation.

'Not just now, Jimbo, eh?' pleads Derek. 'Next week, yeah?'

'Look, I can't keep subbin' ya all the time. I ain't a bloody bank.'

'You'll have it all by closin' as it is.'

'That's not the point, Dekko.'

'OK, OK, but next week, yeah?' he repeats. 'When I pick up me giro.'

Jimbo rolls his eyes up into his head. 'Don't let me down again, but while we're at it, I'll still 'ave your lottery money off ya,' he insists.

There's twenty-three of them in the syndicate. They've never won anything of any consequence - four numbers, a hundred quid or so, tops, certainly not much when it was all divvied up. They'd written up a contract when the Lottery had first started up years back. Jimbo held the original and had given them all copies - Equal share of all winnings. Miss your payment (which was frequently ignored) then you've lost your chance to claim on any win. No arguments. Landlord's decision is final. That was about it - signed, done, and dusted.

'No problem there,' says Derek, fishing out a pound coin from his pocket and handing it over with great aplomb. 'Here y'are.'

'No, no, no! That'll be three please, Derek. You've missed the last two weeks too, remember? I've got it all written down.'

'Money, money, money, that's all you think about innit?'

'I'm not a bloody charity neither!'

'Never mind, Dekko,' says Phil. 'When our numbers come up we'll buy his effin' pub! That'll shut 'im up.'

'You lot come out wi' the same ol' guff every week,' says Jimbo and at last raising a smile as he drops the coins into the tin next to the till and marks the book. 'In your dreams, lads, in your dreams.'

-

On the television 'The Weakest Link' is showing in lurid colour, their telly is on the blink and Anne Robinson, whose ginger hair is now flaming vermillion, is abusing some poor unfortunate as is her style.

'You should go on this, Jules,' suggests her sister. 'You could win it, I reckon.'

'I hate that bloody woman!' Marion shouts at the screen. 'She's so rude all the time!'

'Go on, why don't you?' continues Janice. 'I'll write off for you if ya like.'

'I'm not old enough!' says Julie, cringing but feeling flattered all the same. 'You'd have to be at eighteen at least.'

'Lie. They'd never know, not with a bit o' make-up.'

'What is the alliterative name for the artist that was known for his blue period?' Anne is heard to ask.

'Rolf Harris!' sputters their mum, her mouth full of sausage.

'It's Picasso, Mum. Pablo Picasso had a blue period,' Julie tells her.

'No, Pablo Picasso,' corrects Anne (the contestant having offered Prince, or the artist formerly known as).

'Bloody clever clogs!'

'We did him at school, that's all.'

'But I thought he was a bloke?' asks Janice, a cheeky glint in her eye.

'Who?' asks Marion.

'That Picasso geezer.'

'He was,' says Julie, quizzically.

'Then how come he had a period then?' says Janice, smirking and twiddling a strand of her highlighted and straightened hair.

'Hey, I'm tryin' to eat 'ere!' her mum reprimands her.

'What are you like, Jan?' squeals Julie as both girls now begin to giggle hysterically.

Marion watches them in transfixed bemusement, stopping mid chew. 'Stop it, the pair o' you,' she says, raising her knees and rocking herself to and fro out of the low, soft, sofa and reaching for her packet of cigarettes. 'You'll end up chokin' yourself to death like that, Julie.'

'Mum! I haven't finished eating yet!'

'One little ciggie won't hurt ya.'

'I'll have one in a minute,' says Janice, 'when my little sis is done.'

'Have you ever heard of passive smoking?' asks Julie indignantly.

'Never did me any 'arm. Your gran was a smoker an' she almost got a telegram from the Queen. You'll just 'ave to open the window a bit if it bothers you that much.'

'Please Mum!'

'And as for you, Janice,' she adds, turning her attention, 'when are you going to cough up for some of your own?'

'Stingy cow.'

'You're not too big to get a slap y'know.'

'You wouldn't dare,' Janice answers playfully.

'Oh, wouldn't I now?'

'I'd get the Social on ya.'

'Be the last thing you ever done.'

'Deep vein thrombosis,' Julie then answers yet another of Anne's questions.

'No. Deep vein thrombosis,' she sarcastically corrects another contestant.

'That's what my sister just said!' Janice shouts at the screen. 'See! You really should go on this. You'd be brilliant!'

'I could o' swore she said DVD,' says Marion.

'So did he,' says Julie, pointing to the shame faced man on the television.

-

Dave at last reappears and walks over to join them all on Cracker's Corner. 'You ready for that beer then, Dekko?' he garbles, his eyes like saucers, his jaw clenching and grinding.

Derek necks his near full pint like he was pouring it down a sink. 'Never been one to look a gift horse in the mouth,' he says, belching and wiping his lips.

'That even touch the sides?' observes Phil, laughing.

Dave then leans up against the bar and, foolishly, holds out the curled up note he'd just been using, flipping his wrist to catch Jimbo's attention. 'Beers all round, Jim,' he says before offering a reluctant afterthought, 'an' one for yourself.'

'Cheers, Dave. I'll put one in for later if that's alright?' thanks Jimbo.

'Fine,' he says. (Bollocks, he thinks)

Taking the money and curiously unfurling the note, Jimbo gives Dave a double take. 'Ere, you haven't been doin' what I think you been doin' 'ave ya, Davey boy?'

'What? Doin' what?' he squeals his innocence.

Derek, feeling strangely complicit, turns his back and tries to drain a little more beer from his empty glass.

'Sniffin', snortin', whatever you call it,' says Jimbo, unsure of the terminology.

'Give it a rest, Jim,' Dave denies. 'Gave up that palaver a long time since. You know it, I know it. after you'd warned me that time.'

Still, Jimbo doesn't look convinced.

'Straight up!' Dave insists.

'Well, you make damn sure, not in my pub. You've seen the signs. Zero tolerance, no exceptions. If I find out that you're tellin' me porkies, then you're out, permanent. Geddit?'

'Keep your hair on, Jimbo! I wouldn't take the piss, just bought ya a fuckin' pint haven't I?'

'Yeah, an' you know where you can stick it if I catch you out again,' says Jimbo as he moves off towards the sound of glasses being rattled at the other end of the bar. 'Wait a minute! I'm comin', I'm bloody comin',' he shouts.

But he means it, does Jimbo. Only just recently, they'd had trouble with a couple of dealers doing business in his pub and using the car park as a rendezvous point. They'd had plain clothes in through the door, watching the comings and goings, nursing their half pints for an eternity, playing far too many games of darts. They were put on an official warning he and Reenie, Jimbo's wife. She'd come within a gnat's breadth of losing her licence, her name above the door.

'Twat,' hisses Dave when Jimbo is well out of earshot and flicking him the V's below the level of the bar.

'You're seriously pushing your luck, me ol' son,' warns Phil.

'Nice boots, Dekko,' says Dave, rapidly changing the subject. 'They look the right dog's bollocks they do.'

'He will ban you for good, ya know,' Phil continues.

'What they set you back? Much?' says Dave like he hadn't heard.

'A score. I've seen 'em over a ton, ton-twenty, in the shops,' answers Derek looking pleased as Punch with himself.

'Is that all? I'll 'ave a pair for that!'

'Oh yeah?' Phil twigs. 'Where d'you get 'em?' he asks.

Derek doesn't answer.

'Don't tell me you been buyin' stuff off that fuckin' tea leaf PG Tips again?'

'No!' Derek tries to deny.

'Why don't I believe you?'

'Well, not direct, one of his boys. You know 'im. Clappie? He's sound.'

Phil shakes his head in disbelief. 'You've paid 'im up front I take it?'

'Not as yet, didn't 'ave it, but I will,' says Derek, tapping his wallet. 'I didn't want to miss out, tha's all.'

'You twat, they'll end up costin' ya twice that!'

'No they won't.'

'Oh yes they will unless you settle up! We've all the heard stories despite all his airy-fairy poncing about. He surrounds himself ya know, muscle an' that. There's plenty who've got a hidin' for messin' 'im about.'

'He's alright, I've had plenty off 'im!' dismisses Derek.

'Pay up and stay clear, yeah? Tha's my advice to you.'

'Come on, I know he looks like a bit of a twat in all his tweeds an' that, but he can get ya anything you want if you just ask. He's into containers o' the stuff now, off the ships at Avonmouth. You can save yourself a fortune, 'specially in the run up to Christmas.'

'Your ol' man worked in the port, didn't he?' remembers Phil.

'Yeah, Bristol Docks in the late fifties when I was just a baba,' confirms Derek.

'Sad.'

'Yeah. He's taking orders right now, PG that is, and he's chuckin' in a box o' crackers for anythin' over fifty quid. Nice ones, proper toys. No shit.'

'Ooh, that's good of 'im,' says Phil sarcastically. 'You're a bloody fool if you're taken in by all that crap, Dekko. He's a shark an' you know it.'

'It's only a pair o' bloody boots!' says Derek.

'Don't matter. Besides, how could you give your family knocked off gear for Christmas?'

'Don't remind me. Bloody Christmas!'

'Be the first year, won't it?'

Again, Derek doesn't answer.

'You'll be alright, mate. Where you spendin' it?' asks Phil.

'Down 'ere with all the other sad wankers, I expect, crying in me beer wi' the rest of 'em.'

'Not seein' all your lot then?' asks Phil disbelievingly.

'Wha'? All playin' happy families an' paper hats? Don't think so, not with that fuckin' Nigel on the scene,' says Derek, involuntarily clenching his fists.

'But you always come down 'ere, Dekko,' points out Dave. 'Besides, I'll be here. Why break the habit of a lifetime, eh?'

'But it won't be the same,' says Derek morosely, the harsh reality beginning to sink in.

'How's that then?'

'How's that?' repeats Derek. 'I only ever came down for a couple of bevies before dinner while Marion was whackin' in the turkey.'

'A couple? A gallon more like! No wonder the poor woman had enough o' ya!' says Phil, trying to make light of it. 'You'd go 'ome pissed as a fart!'

'Oi! I never let her touch the washing up after,' reacts Derek and appearing to swallow hard and cuff an eye like no-one would notice. 'I always let her put up her feet, watch the Queen an' that.'

'An' wha' about your ol' mum? You not seein' her, then?'

'Might pop over. I hate that home she's in.'

'She'd like to see ya.'

'S'pose.'

'Look, you can come to ours after if needs be. I'm sure you'd be welcome,' Phil offers but the uncertainty palpable in his voice.

'Yeah, right!' says Derek with an exaggerated laugh. 'Think your Betsy might 'ave other ideas. She can't stand the sight o' me.'

'She's alright wi' ya,' Phil answers, punching him lightly on his upper arm. 'I could talk 'er round, ya daft bugger.'

Derek takes a good swig of beer to compose himself. 'Nah, I'd rather be on me own to be honest, or down here, thanks all the same.'

'Look on the bright side,' Dave pipes up again. 'They always do a good spread for the regulars down here, all the trimmin's an' that.'

'Well, the offers there if ya want, Dekko,' reaffirms Phil. 'I'm bein' serious.'

'An' if ya play yer cards right,' continues Dave, 'Reenie might give you a snog after she's had a Snowball or two!'

'Give it a rest!' says Derek, guffawing and pretending to retch.

'Yeah, enough!' agrees Phil, laughing along. 'I mean, Reenie, what's she like?'

'I'll tell ya what she likes … Shaggin' n' bingo!' cracks Dave, grinning from ear to ear.

'Be like kissin' an owl in them bleedin' glasses!' hoots Derek before rapping his glass down onto the bar. 'So, who's round is it?' he asks.

Simultaneously, both Phil and Dave shake theirs in his face, gurning at him. 'Yours!' they both chorus.

And so, inevitably, it begins. The very serious business of a Friday night out down at the 'Raveller's is about to unravel.

It could, and does, take several hours.

Chapter 3

She'd had a difficult time of it, Ellen, in the perfecting beauty of her mid-twenties and the subsequent radiance of her bloom - very difficult indeed.

Unwed and still living at home with her parents in their straitlaced neighbourhood of washing line envy, twitching curtains, and scrubbed doorsteps, it had carried a huge stigma, back then, when she'd fallen pregnant.

It was in the June of 1956, a Saturday, on a day trip to Weston-Super-Mare, that Ellen had first set eyes on the man who would become the father of her one and only child.

She and her friend, Joyce, had been saving their money for weeks and had merely been awaiting a spell of good weather before taking the day-tripper train from Bristol Temple Meads and over to the coast.

With the promise of that hot and sunny day finally in the offing, they'd taken the plunge, literally, and in what seemed like no time at all had found themselves hurrying arm in arm towards the seafront, excitedly making their way down onto the already bustling sands.

Luckily, or so they thought, they'd found themselves a suitable yet surprisingly uncrowded spot and, with towels held straitjacket tight, had helped each other change into their skirted bathing costumes to take a brave dip in the gently lapping but mud-murky waters of the Bristol Channel.

Shrieking with laughter and splashing each other as they'd soon ran back out however. It was still quite chilly in there and they'd resigned themselves to dry off, settle back, and hopefully catch a bit of a tan in the breezeless warmth of that wonderfully sunny day.

However, they were soon to discover why there were relatively few others sat around them as, suddenly assaulted by an acrid smelling stench drifting over them, they'd found themselves far too close to a tethered line hang-head donkeys traipsing by on their perpetual and monotonous route. It almost made them wretch but, still laughing uproariously, they'd quickly got dressed again, drawn, in any case, to the sudden buzz of activity up on the esplanade as the huge and glittering carousel started to blast out its rousing organ music for all to hear.

They'd treated themselves to a ride on it and, such was the thrill, stayed on for a second go, feigning a bout of exaggerated giddiness as they'd clambered off. Then, succumbing to the allure of the many noisy and clunking penny arcades, had wasted far too much of their money there. But again, neither could care less. Hang the expense they'd said. It was simply a joy, a relief, to escape their otherwise controlled and humdrum existence back at home.

Their extravagant and frivolous sense of fun had continued throughout the day as, after gorging themselves silly on fish and chips sat in the Winter Gardens, they'd each bought a postcard and second class stamp from one of the many souvenir shops along the front. 'Wish you were here, x', was all they'd written on each before sticking them in the nearest post box, imagining the dumbfounded reaction they would likely receive when they'd at last dropped onto the doormats and long after they'd got back home. 'What a waste of money!' they could hear their parents exclaim. 'You were only gone for the day!' If only they'd plucked up the courage to buy a couple of the saucy ones they'd seen! What a talking to they would have got then! It didn't bear thinking about! It was all just too hilarious!

But, like all good things, it was soon to come to an end and they'd agreed to savour their last moments from the giddy heights of the Grand Pier and take a final look out along the broad and expansive beach towards Brean Down.

To the sound of the waves kicking up more energetically at the turn of the tide and the distant squawking of the four-thirty Punch and Judy show in full swing, they'd entertained themselves by watching the hordes of people still busy at their leisure, the mass exodus yet to begin in earnest.

Gleefully, they'd pointed out the squealing children burying each other neck deep in the sand or waiting impatiently for their moated castles to fill. They'd laughed uproariously at one particularly sunburnt man, lobster red, with knotted handkerchief on his head becoming increasingly incandescent as he'd tried to adjust his snapping deckchair. Then, directly below them, they'd caught sight of a pair of very buxom women, straight off one of the postcards they'd so very nearly bought, paddling ankle deep on the shoreline, their bright floral dresses tucked high into their knickers, their more than ample and gleaming bosoms clear for all to see, not least by various men alerted to the spectacle and taking a sneaky peek before their wives could notice or had yanked them away in anger and disgust.

It was right then, right there, as Ellen had turned her back to lean into the balustrade and tilt her face towards the late afternoon sunshine that she'd first set eyes on him. He'd been sat on one of the central benches that extended the length of the pier, his legs stretched out, one arm clasped behind his head, a bright pink candy floss held in the other. Despite the fact that he was wearing sunglasses, she could easily tell he was looking intently in their direction.

As ever, Ellen was convinced his attention was almost certainly directed at her taller, more willowy friend and not towards her at all. But no, that wasn't to be the case this time, as, smiling and dipping his forehead to reveal his pale blue eyes, he'd clearly fixed her gaze, and hers alone.

Immediately, she'd flushed almost the same colour as the confection in his hand, her knees all but turning into jelly as he'd stood to cut across the steady stream of sauntering people to stand almost within touching distance of her.

He'd held out the candy floss, inviting her to help herself and, brazenly and extremely unlike her, she'd reached forward to tear off a piece, popping it sticky-fingered into her mouth.

Then, intriguingly, and like some sort of mime artist using gestures alone, he'd conveyed to her to remain exactly where she'd stood and had hurried to the nearby kiosk to buy her one all for herself. And neither did she move, not an inch, despite her friend prodding and pulling her to find out what was happening and who on earth he might be.

Their subsequent attempt at conversation had been particularly awkward and not helped by Joyce who, becoming increasingly agitated at being forced to play gooseberry for once, had repeatedly suggested that it was time for them to go and that they might miss their train. But that wasn't the half of it. No. Ellen had also found it difficult to understand this beautiful young man's strangely evocative accent. She'd heard it before, in the cinema, but she couldn't quite place it.

Then, as the crowds on the beach finally began to stir with towels and blankets being shaken and deck chairs snapped shut and stacked by the attendants, she'd pointed out the imposing Grand Atlantic Hotel dominating sea front and, without thinking, had said how lovely it would be to go there one day but that it must be very expensive. As soon as the words had left her mouth she'd flushed with embarrassment once again and had wished that the wooden slats of pier would open and drop her deep into the sea. Smiling cheekily, he'd raised his eyebrows, gently mocking her, and had suggested that, if she was lucky, one day, he might take her there.

But time was truly beginning to run short and with Joyce then suggesting she might have to leave without her if they didn't get a move on, Ellen had quickly reached into her handbag for a piece of paper and pen to hurriedly exchange names and addresses.

Then, just as they were about to part, she'd done something else quite unlike her and had slipped the blue ribbon from her hair and had pushed it tight into his hand. That first skin to skin contact had been nothing short of electric for her.

Then, to her astonishment, he'd offered the ribbon to his nose, inhaling deeply, taking her in.

It was right then that she knew.

He was the one.

She was smitten.

He her too.

It was almost six months later that her suspicious and probing mother had first noticed the tell-tale signs - her glowing complexion, the lustre of her hair, her early morning lack of appetite and poorly hidden nausea, together with the fact she seemed uncharacteristically tearful and emotional.

Of course, at first, Ellen had tried to deny it, nervously dismissing the searching questions but, eventually, she'd cracked. At two and a half months gone and her baby growing by the day, what else could she do?

'I knew it! I could tell!' her mother had yelled as soon as she had confirmation of what she already knew to be true. 'How could you bring shame into this house, you dirty little hussy!'

'It's not like that!' Ellen cried, wanting to explain.

'Let's see what your father has to say when he gets home then, shall we? Heaven help you, young lady! Your life won't be worth a light!'

That very evening, terrified and shaking, Ellen had thought she was going to be thrown out onto the street such was the fury, the incandescent rage, of her father.

'So, who is 'e?' he'd yelled. 'Do I know 'im? I'll knock 'is ruddy lights out if I get my 'ands on 'im, so 'elp me God, I will!'

'But he wants to meet you, Dad!' Ellen exclaimed.

'Yeah, an' I'd like to meet 'im too!' said her father, punching the air.

'He wants to do the right thing!'

'Too late! The 'orse 'as bolted, an' the church won't 'ave ya. We should stick you in the workhouse where you bloody belong!'

'You'll just have to get rid of it,' her mother had wickedly suggested, 'I know someone, Jack. I'll find out,' she'd told her husband.

'No! Never! I'll never do that!' Ellen had screamed like she'd never screamed before dashing up to her room, sobbing and alone for what seemed like an eternity.

At seven o'clock, with her life and that of her unborn baby in the balance and armed with a purse full of coins, she'd managed to escape out of the back door of the house and into the alley to make one of their regular phone calls from the nearby telephone kiosk. In floods of tears, hyperventilating, and barely able to string the words together, she'd told him of her father's reaction and her mother's awful suggestion.

Feeling utterly powerless and desperate living at such a distance, he'd tried to calm her down and had reassured her that nobody, not even her family, would divide them and stop them from being together. As planned, they would be married he'd told her. He would provide a home for them to raise their baby and they would spend the rest of their lives together. He loved her more than anything in the world, he'd said, and at the very first opportunity he would come into Bristol to see her father to ask for her hand in marriage.

-

There were no pleasantries that very next Sunday afternoon when he'd arrived, no cups of tea in the best china cups or fairy cakes arranged neatly on crocheted doilies to welcome him. No, he didn't even receive a greeting or even offered a seat and was just left standing in the middle of the sitting room in silence, dressed in his best shirt and tie, nervously riffling his hair, his chin held as firmly as he could manage.

'Well?' had asked Ellen's father, gruff and rude. 'Wha' d'you come here for?'

'I'd like to ask for your permission to take your daughter's hand in marriage,' he'd said, coming straight out with it.

For what seemed like an eternity, Jack Owen had simply sat rigid in his armchair, looking to all intents and purposes like he'd been clattered around the head with a cricket bat. He was absolutely dumbfounded. Not for one moment had he considered that his only child, his own little girl, would put him in such an invidious position, a predicament that was far more unpalatable than he'd first understood or could possibly have imagined. But he was cornered, and he knew it, wedged firmly between the prospect of social disgrace and his profound and innate rejection at the very idea.

'Well, Jack?' his wife had prompted him. 'What's it to be? A yay or a nay?'

After much huffing and puffing, he'd finally acceded with a grunt before levering himself out of the chair to leave the room, closing the door hard shut behind him.

Ellen had not fully explained, you see.

Her handsome young man was named Detlef. Detlef Otto.

He was a foreign boy - worse - a German, a throwback from the bloody war.

In short, a Kraut.

-

As a seventeen-year-old boy and soldier in the German 7th Army, Detlef had been captured just outside Rouen in the August of 1944 by Canadian Forces during the Battle of Normandy and had been sent to England as a Prisoner of War.

Initially, he and others of his regiment (well, the relative few that had not been killed or severely injured that is) had spent the first few weeks in the relative ease of a detention camp in Oxfordshire, but it was only to be temporary.

At first he was quietly relieved to be away from the dehumanising horror and exhaustion of warfare. He had seen and experienced some terrible things that would haunt him for the rest of his life, but his allocation to a remote and ramshackle dairy farm in rural Somerset as a lowly farmhand, general dogsbody, and whipping boy had put even that thought into doubt and his desire to fight and escape had been reignited.

Alone and unable to speak the language, he foresaw had a new battle on his hands and his natural and youthful patriotism had manifested itself into anger and shame at his continued incarceration and with the feeling that any effort on his behalf was simply helping the enemies war effort, not his own. It made him feel like a traitor, but his resulting aggressive and truculent behaviour was met with varying degrees of punishment, from near starvation to outright brutality liberally dished out by the other indigenous workers on the farm and as if he'd simply jumped out of the frying pan and into the fire.

Eventually, and in the depths of despair and with his spirit all but broken, he'd come to realise, for his own sanity's sake if nothing else, he had no other option than to acquiesce to their continuous and exhausting demands, knuckle down, bide his time, as difficult as it might be. After all, even if he could not escape, the war couldn't last forever it, could it?

So, with his change of attitude and newfound resolve, he'd actually surprised himself as, day by day, he began to take some pleasure in the tasks he had been set, and not least the begrudging respect it ultimately afforded him as a diligent and hardworking farmhand.

'I thought we 'ad a right lil' basturd on our 'ands first orf, Mother. But bugger me, he's turned out alroight', fer a Nazi,' had conceded the farmer, Old Man Ogden in his heavy West Country burr. ''Ard worker an' all…... but oi've still got me eyes on 'im, duncha worry. Bu' oi've told the boys to lay off 'im fer a bit, see how us all goes wi' 'im. Yeh?'

'Tha's nice o' you, O,' Nancy, his wife, had agreed. ''E's only a young un after all. Seen some terrible things, no doubt.'

As weeks turned into months, Detlef was at last given some degree of freedom and even allowed to leave the confines of the farm so long as he was in the company of others, even enjoying an occasional beer with them in the tap room the Fleur de Lis in nearby Norton St Philip, or sometimes the George, but more often than not, Tucker's Grave, the cider house and the one within easiest walking distance - so long as he kept his trap shut. 'He's a mute,' they'd explained to the various landlords and landladies.

But still, ever desperate for news of his family, he'd asked for, and had been given a pen and some paper and envelopes and had set about writing letters back home. However, with no replies forthcoming, he'd even started to try friends of friends, old acquaintances, in fact to anyone whose address he could vaguely remember and who might possibly give him some information, but, still, there was nothing.

Like so many thousands of POW's in Britain at the time, Detlef was not offered repatriation until 1947 and it was only shortly before then that he'd finally discovered the awful truth.

Although the much awaited reply to one of his letters had been delivered in the early morning post, old man Ogden had waited until Detlef had finished his supper before handing it to him; an envelope with a German stamp and postmark on it, his name written in a flowing hand - *Herr Detlef Otto* it read, a thin letter that he could immediately feel contained no more than a single sheet of paper.

'Oi thenk yoo've bin waitin' fer this, Detlef,' had said Ogden, 'an' oi 'ope its good nooz for yuz, lad.'

With his heart in his mouth and retreating to the security of his small gas lit room and sitting nervously on the edge of his bed, he'd turned it over and over in his now rough and calloused hands before carefully slicing it open with the pen knife, a gift he'd received from his father on his sixteenth birthday and that he'd somehow managed to avoid losing or being confiscated for all this time.

Unfolding it like it was some delicate ancient artefact, he'd glanced to the signature at the bottom. He immediately recognised the name. It was from an old family friend and neighbour.

Mouthing the words as he read, it had simply confirmed his worst fears, the news that he had dreaded the most. '*Es gibt keine einfache Möglichkeit, dies zu sagen, Detlef...*' it had said - there is no easy way to tell you this, Detlef .... He had lost the remaining members of his immediate family. All of them.

His father he already knew about, killed in action in North Africa much earlier in the war, but also the death of his mother, sister and younger brother. They had all lost their lives in one single night in the February of 1945 during the fire-bombing of his beautiful home city of Dresden.

Everything, but everything, had then changed for him.

There was nothing and no-one to go back to.

He'd spent the rest of the night unable to sleep and staring blankly at the wall, the sharp blade of his knife pressed to his wrist, to his neck, and vomiting.

Early the following morning, even Ogden could not help but notice Detlef's upset - his red eyes, his posture, his very defeat.

'The boyz's looked loik 'e'd bin croiyin' 'e 'ad,' he'd explained to Nancy when he'd gone in for his breakfast. 'Oi told 'im, oi did, 'e b'aint no good to man nor beast loik tha', so oi sent 'im back to 'is room an' told 'im to stay there.'

'Tha's kind of you,' she'd said. 'Not good readin' I daresay. Poor lad.'

'No, s'peck not, Mother,' he'd agreed, pulling up a chair, rolling back his sleeves.

'Bes' leave 'im be, then,' she'd advised, pressing two slices of bread into the pan with the back of a wooden spatula and frying them to a crisp.

And that's where they'd left him, huddled in the corner of his windowless room in part of a poorly converted stable, holding his knees tight to his body and rocking to and fro for the whole of that seemingly interminable day. It was not until the evening that he was disturbed by a thudding knock-knock at his door.

'Grub up fer yer, young un,' had growled Ogden. 'Oi'll leave it out y'ure by the door. Dun let it spoil now. An' oi'll see yuz broight an' early in th'mornin'. We'll be needin' ya fu' the milkin'. Don't let me down, ya hear?'

'*Ja,*' had said Detlef almost inaudibly.

'Wass tha' yoo say?'

'Yes,' he'd repeated more loudly.

'There's a good lad,' had replied Ogden before hesitating for a moment. 'Chin up now,' he'd added before shuffling away. 'Things'll get better. They always do.'

-

They were duly married, Detlef and Ellen, as quickly as was humanly possible and before her belly had really started to show.

To say the least, it was a very low-key affair with many of the family's friends and relatives finding various excuses not to attend or with others being even less polite than that and just giving a flat refusal on receiving their 'off the cuff' verbal invitation.

'German, you say? Forget it. I'll 'ave nuthin' to do with 'em,' had said Gordon, the youngest of Ellen's uncles, adding, 'Dougie would turn in his grave, he would.'

Dougie was one of her mother's brothers who'd been killed on exercises on Salisbury Plain before he'd even been deployed, let alone seen any action. He'd suffered a sad and ignominious end. He'd always been a bit on the clumsy side, all arms and legs, even as a child, and he'd tripped in a waterlogged rut running alongside and too close to the crushing caterpillar tracks of a Vickers six-tonner. Squished he was. Dead in an instant. Still, the family had all agreed that he would still be alive were it not for that 'bleeding Hitler and his bunch of murderous black shirts'.

Fortunately, for Detlef and Ellen, the vicar of the local church, a forward thinking man and a conscientious objector himself, had agreed to marry them despite her condition.

So, walking up the aisle, wearing her cousin's old bridal gown and smelling everso slightly of moth balls and lavender, Ellen had to hold on tight to her father's arm for fear of him walking on ahead such was his desire to get the whole sorry affair over and done with. But even more hurtfully, having consented to give her away, he had refused to have anything more to do with them, not even joining them for a celebratory drink in the function room above their local pub afterwards. 'They've made their bed,' was all he would say.

No, it was not what you would call a joyous occasion but little more than a perfunctory one. The newlyweds, Detlef in particular, had tried their best to put on a brave face and jolly it along but there was no real sense of celebration. It had felt more like a wake than a wedding.

However, remarkably, and thankfully for him, Detlef did have some guests in his own right. Old Man Ogden, his wife, Nancy, Dick, their son, and another farm hand, Frankie, who'd become Detlef's friend over the years and had even agreed to be his best man, had made the effort, and had travelled all the way into Bristol in their old flat-bed lorry.

They'd even brought the newlyweds a couple of gifts, an amber coloured Carnival ware glass sugar bowl with an EPNS silver spoon and a handmade crocheted coverlet for a baby's cot together with a shawl and bonnet. Sadly, other than a small set of saucepans from Ellen's friend, Joyce, these were the couple's only presents but still,

Detlef had put them in pride of place on a table by the door for all to see, but rather like the couple themselves, they looked painfully lonely and forlorn.

They had set up home, the new Mr and Mrs Otto, renting a very modest and sparse top floor flat in a three storey Victorian terraced house in Brislington on the outskirts of the city.

Detlef had wanted to return to the countryside and go back to the relative tranquillity of village life and continue working on the farm. Ogden had assured him that he still had a job there if he wanted and that he and his family would be more than welcome. But Ellen couldn't face it. 'I'm no country girl, Detlef. I wouldn't know where to start. I'd end up trying to milk a pig knowing me!' she'd tried to make light of it.

No, in truth, she couldn't bear to be far from her family and had held onto the desperate hope that they would soon come around, lured by the birth of their first ever grandchild, a beautiful baby boy they had named Derek.

But it was not to be, and things only became progressively more difficult for them, not least financially.

Way back then, in 1957, finding employment wasn't at all easy for Detlef. Bristol was still rife with anti-German prejudice with much of the city still bearing the scars of the colossal damage inflicted by the Luftwaffe only sixteen or seventeen years previously (an irony not entirely lost on him).

Ellen tried her best to help make ends meet, of course, taking in some washing and ironing, a bit of sewing, but it was just pin money, literally, and never nearly enough.

As life became ever more difficult, and in his desperation to provide for his young family, Detlef had inadvertently but inevitably fallen in with the wrong crowd.

It proved to be his downfall and the beginning of the end.

The knives really came out for him then.

The poor man never really had a chance.

Chapter 4
Hannover, Germany.

Some weeks back, Detlef Otto had received some life changing news - life threatening in fact.

His doctor had told him that, yes, as his symptoms might suggest, the results of his blood test had confirmed that he did, indeed, have Type 2 Diabetes and that his blood pressure was a little high, but, unfortunately, there was more to reveal.

'I'm sorry to have to tell you this,' the doctor said, looking at him directly and in the eye, 'but we have uncovered something a little more serious.'

Detlef's face had dropped instantly, pitiful and questioning, a raw hollowness suddenly manifesting itself in the pit of his stomach. 'What is it, Herr Doktor?' he'd beseeched. 'Please. You must tell me.'

'Herr Otto, I am sorry to inform you that we have discovered you have Leukaemia,' he'd answered him, straight and to the point.

'But that's cancer isn't it?'

'Yes, it is, of the blood, but I will explain ... Look, may I call you Detlef, Herr Otto?' the doctor had asked politely.

Detlef nodded in acceptance, steeling himself for the worst.

'Thank you, but first, can I enquire? Do you have anyone with you?'

'Yes, my wife, Gisella. She is in the waiting room.'

'Perhaps you would like her to join us? It would be better for both of you to hear this together.'

With his mind racing, Detlef had been very unsure that it was a good idea and had not answered at first. He didn't think he could face her upset as well as his own and was already considering glossing over it and keeping it all to himself.

'To make sure we get the facts straight,' suggested the doctor, gently insistent, 'it would be for the best. I'll call her through, yes?' he'd said before picking up the telephone and asking reception to bring Frau Otto through to his consulting room.

'But, Herr Doktor,' had said Detlef, his voice catching as the physician had replaced the handset, 'before she arrives, you must tell me, am I about to die? I must know. It could be too much for her to take.'

'Detlef, please calm yourself. It's not quite like that,' he'd said, walking towards to the door and opening it in readiness. 'Shall we wait until she gets here?'

Gisella had hurried along the corridor with a young receptionist taking her by the arm and had entered the consulting room already looking very distraught and apprehensive. 'Detlef, what in heavens is it?' she'd asked, reaching out for her husband's hand, her papery skin ruching under the pressure of his anxious fingers.

'Frau Otto, please, take a seat,' said the doctor, pulling up a chair.

'The doctor is about to tell us, my love,' Detlef had said to his wife. 'We must listen to what he has to say,' he'd told her quite calmly, mustering a level of stoicism that had completely masked his own terrifying fears.

Addressing Gisella in the first instance, the doctor had briefly repeated what he had already said.

'Oh, Detlef!' she'd cried, her lips quivering, her eyes filling, as she'd searched in vain for a handkerchief from her handbag. Quickly, the doctor had offered her some tissues from the box on his desk before he'd continued. 'Now, please, before you become unduly upset, let me explain further. As you may well know, Leukaemia is a type of cancer of the white cells in your blood,' he'd said, softly spoken and professional.

At that moment Detlef could no longer keep up his pretence and had bent forward, his elbows on his knees, his head dropping, his hands clasped in a white knuckle fist.

'Detlef?'

'Herr Otto? Are you OK?'

Detlef looked up, releasing his hands. 'Please continue, Herr Doktor. I am listening,' he'd said, reassuring them both.

'If you are certain? We can take some time if you wish. Would you like some water?'

'No, no. Please carry on.'

'Very well. Now, specifically, you have a condition called Chronic Myeloid Leukaemia, but thankfully, it would appear you are in the relatively early stages of the illness and nowadays, with modern medicine and treatment, we can usually control the condition quite effectively.'

Detlef had looked up. 'What does that mean? Effectively?'

'What I am saying, Detlef, is that although you must prepare yourself and it is a very serious condition, it might not be as bad as you might have thought,' had replied the doctor. 'We will need to start you on a course of chemotherapy, in the form of pills, which you will need to take for the rest of your life I'm afraid. But I must say, given your state of health, which is otherwise very good, I suggest that that we should be able stabilise the condition for some considerable time to come.'

'Stabilise? That's not a cure, is it?'

'No, you are right, there is no cure at present. Control. However, to emphasise, the prognosis is good in many cases and we would expect to hold it in check for a number of years, providing there are no further complications of course. Naturally, we will continue to monitor your progress with regular tests to be absolutely sure once you are in remission.'

'There is hope then?' Gisella had looked to confirm whilst ineffectively dabbing her nose with her sodden tissue.

'Of course, of course. There is always hope. But you must be aware, Detlef, that you are likely to feel quite poorly in the early stages.

Some flu like symptoms can develop, general tiredness and headaches. More latterly you may experience some discomfort in the abdomen and sometimes in the bones but, as I suggest, these symptoms may not occur for some time, if at all. In addition, there is also the option of a bone marrow transplant, although this is not the normal practice in people of your age, but we will cross that bridge as and when we come to it. Do you understand what I have said so far?'

The doctor had sat patiently waiting for a response.

'Possibly years you say?' Detlef had answered, his head craning back to the top row of bound journals on the bookshelf behind the doctor's desk.

'Yes, yes, quite possibly.'

'And I'm an old man already,' had said Detlef, 'so, as long as I don't rattle with all the pills you will expect me to take, let's get on with it!' he'd then tried to make light of the situation.

'Excellent, Detlef, that's the spirit. A good mental attitude is very beneficial in these circumstances, vital in fact,' the doctor had said, smiling.

'Yes, my love,' had agreed Gisella, pulling his hand toward her and kissing it. 'You are strong. You've always been strong.'

'Ha! It is just another hurdle, everything I have been through, it is just another fight. I must, we must, remain positive, Gisella.'

'And we will do our part,' had stressed the doctor. 'So, in conclusion, we will be in contact over the next few days to give you the schedule of treatment we will need to undertake. You will be pleased to know there will be no need for hospitalisation for this, you will be treated as a day patient so will be able to go home afterwards.'

'That's good, but please, tell me Herr Doktor, how soon will this all begin and how will it affect the quality of my life in the short term?' Detlef had asked rather candidly.

'Oh, we will get started almost immediately and you will be in good hands. The hospital has a very good team and we will send you details of all the support that is available to you,' he'd said, 'and as to your ability to live a normal life, you will be able to carry on pretty much as you have up to now, once your condition has been stabilised of course.'

'Really?'

'Yes, really, Detlef. We will do everything in our power to ensure that. I have a small booklet here that will give you answers to some other concerns that may occur to you over the next few days, but please do not hesitate to contact us whenever you need.'

Gisella had taken the information and slipped it into her handbag. 'That's wonderful, thank you,' she had said.

'So then, Herr and Frau Otto,' had said the doctor, placing both hands on his desk and drawing the appointment to a close. 'I shall be seeing you very, very shortly. Please take care, both of you.'

Outside, hand in hand and in silence, the couple had started to walk their way back home before Detlef had stopped and had gently held his wife back.

'Gisella, you know we will need to talk about this,' he'd said.

'Yes, of course, my love, but it's so much to take in. Not just now maybe.'

'We will need to break the news to the family, this weekend, when they visit. They will need to know,' he'd carried on.

'So soon? Would it not be better to leave them, just for a little while, until we have had time to come to terms with it all ourselves and you begin your treatment?'

'We can't be in denial, and Renata will suspect something. I know she will.'

'You are right, but please, can we at least keep it from the grandchildren, they are too young. It would upset them too much to think that their Papa is unwell.'

'Certainly, but Renata and Oskar should know. Are we agreed?'

'If you wish.'

'Thank you,' had said Detlef before looking more intently into his wife's eyes. 'But there's one more thing, something that has been playing on my mind for far too long now.'

'What?' she'd said, knowingly.

'Gisella, it is now far more pressing.'

'Oh, Detlef, must you think of him now?'

'I know what I'd asked of you, but I must find him. I have left it too long. There are things he needs to understand.'

'But you must think about yourself right now, your own wellbeing must come first.'

'No, I have been too weak for too long. This is my wake-up call. Somehow I must find him and hope he will listen.'

'Is that wise, after all these years?' she'd then asked with anxiety rising in her voice. 'You don't even know where to begin or even if he is still alive and well.'

'Oh, Gisella, please,' Detlef had continued pointedly, 'I don't know how, but I am sure Derek is still alive. Besides, why should he not be? He is still a relatively young man. It is something I simply must do.'

'Detlef, if you make yourself worse in all of this, I will kill you!'

'My darling wife,' he'd said, managing a laugh. 'I just want one chance to explain before it is too late.'

Chapter 5

Despite having been a good friend over the years, Derek and Marion's long-standing neighbour, Nigel, had ultimately proved himself to be a right snake in the grass.

Shamefully, and whilst simultaneously offering them both solace and support when their marriage had all but had it - a trusted 'pint down the pub' mate to Derek and a shoulder to cry on for Marion - he'd been manipulating them for his own ends all along.

'Don't be so bloody stupid, Nige!' Derek had dismissed him over one of those very beers when he'd suggested that, maybe, it really was all over between the pair of them. 'She'll 'ave me back soon enough,' he'd insisted. 'All I gotta do is bide me time, tha's all.'

'I hope for your sakes you're right,' Nigel replied, 'but it's not as if she's relegated you to the sofa for just a couple o' nights, now is it, me ol' mate? It's been nearly two months now. Long time in the scheme of things.'

'So?'

'Well ...'

'Well, what?' Derek had pushed him.

'Well, it might be for the best.'

'Piss off! For the best, my arse!'

'I'm only trying to offer ya a bit of advice - a bit o' help.'

'Yeah, some help,' Derek answered sarcastically.

Nigel had paused for a moment, watching Derek take the very last draw on his roll up and pinch it dead into the ashtray. 'But seriously, mate, maybe it is time to stop crucifyin' each another, yeah?' he'd said. 'For the sake of the kids if nuthin' else. They don't need the continual arguments all the time, the shoutin', now do they?'

'Oh, I get it,' Derek scoffed, 'she told you to tell me that, did she?'

'No, she didn't! Definitely not!'

'It'll all blow over, you'll see,' Derek repeated whilst edging his already empty glass into the centre of the table.

'You're like one o' them birds with their head stuck in the sand. Wha' d'ya call 'em?'

'Ostriches.'

'Yeah, that's it, an ostrich.'

'Tha's as maybe, Nige, maybe I am,' Derek admitted, uncharacteristically lowering his guard for a moment, picking up a beer mat and tearing it into tiny pieces. 'But I still care about 'er, an' the kids. Christ knows we've 'ad our ups and downs, who ain't? But I never played away nor nuthin', tried me hardest to provide.'

Nigel had coughed in barely concealed disbelief at that.

'Oi! Don't take the piss ... I did!'

'Alright, alright, keep yer hair on. I'm not sayin' you didn't!'

'All I do know is I can't stick that poxy flat I'm in for much longer, that's for sure. What am I goin' to do, eh? Where am I goin' to end up?' Derek had continued, now wallowing in self-pity.

'But it ain't all about you, Dekko.'

'She's got the house, I ain't! It was my 'ome too!'

'I know it was. I feel for ya, but when all's said and done, Dekko, what you've got to ask yourself,' said Nigel, steeling himself before going in for the kill.

'As meself what?'

'Do you still love her? I mean really *love* her?'

Derek chose not to answer that, not immediately at least, and had started to reassemble the beer mat like pieces of a jigsaw puzzle. 'We go back,' he said at last. 'I mean, what's she gonna do wi' two kids still at school, eh? How's she gonna manage?'

'Well, she's done OK so far, Dekko. Credit where credit's due.'

'Hang about, who's side you on, ya wanker?'

'I'm not on anybody's side!'

'OK, but can I ask ya somethin'?' said Derek, rolling his head on his shoulders like a boxer preparing to get in the ring.

'Yeah, yeah, I'll get ya another,' said Nigel, misunderstanding and picking up Derek's glass.

'No, not that, but I wouldn't say no.'

'Thought as much. What then?'

'Bit awkward.'

'I'm all ears. Spit it out.'

'Has she, like, sort of, met someone else d'ya reckon?'

'Not that I know of,' Nigel had said before rapidly finishing the last of his own drink and standing to make his way to the bar. 'Just let me get these in, yeah?'

'Cheers, mate. You're a good 'un. I'll pay ya back.'

With that, Nigel had forced a quick laugh, a laugh to somehow let him off the hook. 'When 'ave I 'eard that before?' he'd said. 'Same again?'

-

They'd moved onto the estate, Nigel, his parents, and older brother years ago when he was in his late teens.

Even way back then he'd had a thing for her, lusted after her in fact, his racing adolescent hormones summoning up erotic fantasies from the very first time he'd copped eyes on her. He'd watch her making her way to the shops or pushing little Janice along in her pram from the privacy of his bedroom. Often she would be in the company of a gaggle of other young mothers, but to him she was the best of the bunch by a country mile - sassy, trim, laughing, and full of it. Unseen behind curtains, he'd mouth her name.

Now, in his late forties and still single, he finally had his chance and he wasn't about to pass it up. Of course, he didn't feel great about it, not at all. Scared too, but faint heart never won fair woman as his father used to tell him, often, when he'd worried that his forever girlfriendless son might, in fact, be gay.

Still, he was dreading the inevitable backlash, however Marion might react to his manoeuvres.

He didn't have to wait long.

-

It was a couple of weeks later that Derek first began to sense that others were nudging each other when he came into the pub but, typically for him, he'd failed to put two and two together. It was not until one pissed and smirking buffoon had asked him direct that the penny had finally dropped.

''Ere, Dekko, was that that Nigel I saw leaving your place early this mornin?' he'd asked snidely before adding, 'she didn't 'ang about, did she?'

Derek had half a mind to punch the guy's lights out there and then for even suggesting such a thing but someone else had then chipped in. 'Yeah, just so you know, Dekko, I'm sure my missus mentioned something about seein' 'em shoppin' down Broadmead together last week,' he'd added in a more conciliatory tone but twisting the knife all the same. 'Buying her a dress or summat so she said.'

Whack!

Poor Derek had instantly felt like he'd been punched in the stomach but, defensively, had chosen to laugh it off, saying he couldn't give a shit what she got up to and had just carried on drinking but even more copiously than usual.

However, as the afternoon had dragged on, his normal ebullient behaviour had all but disappeared as the very idea and the images it had conjured up had finally got the better of him until, angry, taciturn, and feeling like he was under a very dark cloud, he'd made his excuses and left.

On his way home, he'd seen Phil go into the Chippy and had followed him in. ''Ave you heard anything about 'im stayin' over, Phil?' he'd asked him on the QT, wanting but not wanting to know all at the same time. 'Every other fucker seems to know, 'cept me,' he'd slurred.

'Pass. News to me, fellah..., yeah, cod an' chips twice, a battered sausage, an' two fishcakes, please,' he'd said and doing his utmost to avoid Derek's blurry gaze.

'Come on, ya bastard, you gotta tell me! I would you!'

'Fuckin' 'ell, Dekko, you know how it is,' said his mate.

Right then, Derek had his answer.

That night, lying in bed, sobering up fast, and unable to sleep, he'd made his plans.

Early that following morning, very early, he'd set about watching the house from the obscurity of his beaten-up old Rover. He'd tucked it around the corner in the opposite direction to the school and bus stop and almost entirely obscured behind a high sided Transit van that hadn't seemed to have moved in weeks. He'd wanted to make sure the kids were well out the way before making his move and had slumped low in the seat, puffing fags like some old-school private eye, watching, waiting, biding his time.

At last, when he had seen all three children leave and was certain that the coast was absolutely clear, he'd jumped out of the motor, marched up the path and rapped on the door under the pretext of picking up some of his things.

'Now's not a good time Derek. You can't just turn up like this,' objected Marion, still in her dressing gown, alarm already rising in her voice. But he was having none of it, and, with his skin strangely taught and the colour all but drained from his face, he'd barged his way past her. 'Out the way!' he'd demanded.

In all their years, she'd never seen him like that before, not with that degree of ferocity and intent she hadn't, and, realising what was about to happen, she'd called out to Nigel in warning, but already, it was too late.

Derek had found him in the sitting room, sat in *his* chair, watching *his* television, and looking like a hare in headlights. 'There you are!' he'd bellowed. 'You two faced fuckin' bastard! I trusted you, you cunt!'

'Dekko! Listen to me! It's not what you think,' Nigel tried to explain before the inevitable physical assault began.

Screaming, Marion had tried to pull Derek off as Nigel had curled up tight into a ball, covering his head in a vain attempt to avoid the rain of blows thundering down on him from above, a flurry of hard but indiscriminate punches lasting nothing more than a few seconds.

Derek did some damage though, cracking Nigel's nose and cutting his ear, an injury inflicted, poignantly enough, by Derek's wedding ring that he'd not, as yet, taken off. But he couldn't follow through, he couldn't knock him out and finish the job. He didn't have it in him. No, all of a sudden, like a snotty-nosed schoolboy in a playground fight, he was suddenly unwilling to carry on. Speechless and pumped with adrenalin, he'd simply ended the assault by jabbing his finger into thin air as if to tell him that he should thank his lucky stars.

He left as quickly as he'd arrived.

He didn't pick up any of his things.

-

'Don't get me wrong,' Marion had explained to her mother, Florrie, on the phone later that evening, 'he never hit me nor nuthin', he just gave Nigel a bit of a poundin', that's all. You should see the state of him, poor thing. Think his ear might need a stitch or two.'

'Well you can't blame him, love, can you? Nigel and him go back years. And don't forget, your Derek's lost everything - you, the house, the kids,' said her mum.

'He's not *my* Derek anymore, Mum. It's over.'

'Don't be silly, o' course he his. By the way, where were they when this all kicked off? The children? I hope they didn't see.'

'No, they were all gone, lucky enough, off to school, Janice at work.'

'You know, they can't find it easy, a new man in the house.'

'No mum, it's hasn't been easy.'

'There you go then.'

'What do you mean, 'there you go then'? Anyhow, the girls seem to be coming 'round to it, but I'm worried about our Jez, he can't be in the same room, he can't.'

'There you go then.'

'Will you stop saying that?'

'Well!'

'Nigel tries his best, of course. Offered to take him to the Multiplex to see some film just last weekend.'

'And?'

'Jez just told him to 'eff' off, the little bugger.'

'There you go, ya see. He misses his dad.'

'For the umpteenth time, will you give it a rest, Mother!'

'Sorry, Marion, but if the cap fits…'

'Arrgh! Now look here, Jez and his sorry excuse for a father never did anything together in any case, so what's so new? It's no wonder he's forever gettin' into trouble.'

'Boys will be boys. He'll grow out of it.'

'Like his father you mean? He never 'grew out of it'. Besides, he only lives five minutes away. All he's got to do is call. I ain't stoppin' him seeing them.'

Florrie didn't answer straight away and there was just a prolonged pause.

'You still there, Mum?'

'Yes, I'm still here. You two need your heads banging together, that's all I know.'

'Just like that, eh? Bang our heads together? Brush it all under the carpet and pretend nothing ever happened, that what you're sayin'?'

'Sometimes you have to take the rough with the smooth, love. Life's like that.'

Even from day one, Florrie had had a soft spot for Derek. He reminded her of her own husband, Marion's father, and always referred to him as 'my bonny lad.' It was the Geordie in her and she wasn't about to let her daughter give up on him that easily.

'How about marriage guidance? Have you tried them?' she'd continued.

'I asked him loads of times. He just laughed it off.'

'I'll have to have another word with him then, see if I can get the two of you to see some sense.'

'What do you mean you'll have *another* word with him? Have you seen him then?'

Again, Florrie pauses before answering. *'Yes, he pops round,'* she admits. *'He came round the other day, hell of a state. I felt right sorry for him I did, gave him a couple o'quid so he could get himself a bit of something to eat.'*

'You are kiddin' me, aren't you? Did he ask you for it?'

'No, no, no. I put it in his pocket, on his way out. I couldn't see him going short, now could I? He's promised it back.'

'You'll be lucky.'

'I told him to go and get something decent inside him.'

'Yeah, and he would o' done. Beer!'

'Well, that's up to him. A man needs a pint every now and then.'

'Every now an' then? He drinks like a fish, each an' every day.'

'You still care for him though, don't you?' Florrie had deflected.

'Yes, of course I do! Nobody'd get married if they didn't, would they? I just couldn't take it anymore, Mum! Nigel and I talk, I mean really talk. He's interested in me for who I am. He's lovely.'

'Oh, do stop it. You sound like a lovesick teenager.'

'What if I do? Can you remember what that feels like? How nice it is?'

'Marion, all relationships start off all lovey-dovey. You wait and see what it's like in a few month's time. It'll all wear off - you mark my words.'

'What if it does? I'm enjoying myself now. I feel alive, wanted.'

'Do you... really?'

'Yeah, I do! Look, it's over between Dekko and me, has been for years if the truth be told, and the sooner he gets it into that thick head of his, the better, and the same goes for you too.'

'You'll be the death of me.'

'Don't start all that again.'

'I just hope you know what you're doing, that's all.'

'Let's get one thing straight shall we? Let me remind you. Derek was never there for me, not really. I'm amazed I stood it for as long as I did, never going out, never any money. Livin' on the dole ain't great y'know! It don't leave much room for luxuries.'

'Luxuries! I never had luxuries!'

'Ooh, get the violins out, shall we? He'd take odd jobs here and there o' course, but then he'd be off with his mates down the pub, or to the footie. I hardly ever saw him, neither did the kids. I never bargained for that, Mum. I never got married to raise a family pretty much on my own.'

'But he never had a father figure of his own, did he?'

'No Mum, he didn't, but for cryin' out loud, stop making excuses for him! He's a grown man now! Or s'posed to be!'

For way too long, Marion had held onto the memories of the wonderful times they'd had together all those years ago and the trips they'd had to Minehead and Weston on his old Norton Speed Twin - the dances, the parties, the alfresco sex, their marriage, and the birth of their first, Janice. The good times.

But by the time Jez had arrived, some five years later, with Julie, who had been a mistake, arriving very soon after, the cracks were well and truly beginning show such that the last of their twenty-three or so years together had been little more than a misery for her.

It had all come to a head the previous Christmas. She was having a terrible time of it yet again, what with one thing and another - the inevitable lack of money, being left to sort out all the preparation and shopping (which even included her having to buy her own present from him. 'I don't know what to get you, love, now do I?' his annual excuse. 'Just tell me how much it cost. I'll give ya the money') and his incessant drinking such that on New Year's Eve, as they were preparing to go out, the shit had well and truly hit the fan.

Derek had been getting all fidgety and was keen to get back down to the pub, albeit he'd already been there most of the afternoon, whilst Marion was going through the motions and umming and ahhing over what to wear. 'Dekko, just go by yourself if you can't give me another five minutes,' she'd said.

'Why is it always such a palaver with you?'

'Always? Always, you say? Don't go there, Derek, just don't.'

'What?'

'How many times have you and I been out together this year? I could count 'em on the fingers of one hand, prob'ly less!'

'Not that again! I'm takin' ya out now, ain't I? Everybody'll be down there. Just get yer skates on, yeah?'

'You might be OK lookin' like a tramp, but I'm not.'

'Thanks! You look fine wi' what you've got on.'

'And how are we going to afford it, Dekko?' she'd added.

'I've got a few quid tucked away.'

'Oh, have ya now? We got better things to spend money on than down that bloody pub!'

'Better things to spend our money on,' he'd mimicked her. 'You're turning into a right boring cow nowadays, you are.'

'That's it!' she'd snapped, unbuttoning her best cardigan and chucking it back down onto the bed.

'Come on, don't be silly,' he'd tried to backtrack. 'You'll enjoy it when we get down there.'

'Boring cow am I?'

'I didn't mean it like that.'

'Get out of my sight, Dekko.'

'Come on, Mar,' he'd pleaded.

'I said, get out of my sight!'

'Oh, suit your bloody self! If that's the way you wanna be, then so be it,' he'd said as he turned to head downstairs.

As she heard the front door latch open, she had shouted back down to him. 'I've had it with you I have, Derek. Either you get yourself somewhere else to live or I will!'

'An' how many times 'ave I 'eard that?' he'd shouted back up. 'You know you won't! You can't!'

'Oh, can't I now?'

'So, you're not comin' then?'

'No, I'm not!'

'You know where I'll be when you change your mind,' he said assumptively, dismissively.

'Get out!' she'd yelled as she heard the door close shut behind him.

Predictably, the following day, almost lunchtime, he'd woken up, still fully dressed and on the sofa. Even in his befuddled brain, the house seemed strangely silent to him save the distant sound of mumbled voices talking quietly in the kitchen - but no TV, no radio. After he'd taken himself upstairs to the bathroom, he became vaguely aware that some of her stuff seemed to be missing - her make-up bag no longer on the top of the cistern, her toothbrush not in the glass. Then, walking through into their bedroom, he couldn't help but notice that the bed didn't look as if it had been slept in and that there was an unfamiliar void above the wardrobe where the suitcase always were, unmoved and gathering dust.

Going back downstairs, he'd found his three children sat around the kitchen table. They barely acknowledged him, and Jez had shrugged him away when he'd tried to scruffle his hair.

'Happy New Year you three,' he'd said almost as a question. 'Where's your mother then?'

None of them answered him.

'Hello-o. Someone bloody died, 'ave they?'

'Are you thick or something?' said Janice, sharply.

'Wha' 'ave I done?' he said, high pitched and already pleading his innocence.

'Too much, Dad,' Julie had joined in, the rims of her eyes red with tears.

'And not enough!' Janice added.

'Why? What?'

'She's not coming back until you've gone, that's what! And I can't say I blame her. Look at the state o' ya, lunchtime, and you're still pissed as a fart!'

'I am not,' he'd protested, holding out and steadying his hand as if to prove it.

'Can't you see we don't want you here anymore!'

Even within the ravages of his pounding headache and his churning guts, that comment cut him to the very quick, but still, he retaliated.

'You button your lip, Janie. I'm your dad, an' don't you forget it!'

'Dad? Dad?! Well start acting like one then!'

'Oi! Tha's enough. So, where's she gone?' he then asked.

'Where do you think?'

'Don't tell him,' Jez chipped in.

'Oh, he speaks! Get the bloody flags out!'

Jez had then bounced his head off the kitchen table, slopping tea, angry, upset, frustrated.

'What are you playin' at, ya little idiot?'

'Please, Dad! Leave him alone,' Julie pleaded.

'Her mother's,' Derek had then twigged. 'Don't take much workin' out does it? Don't worry, I'll call her.'

'If you've got any sense left in that pickled brain o' yours, you'd leave her alone!' yelled Janice. 'You're a waste of fuckin' space!'

Ouch.

Sobering up by the second and with panic beginning to set in, he'd pulled out his phone and tried calling her at her mother's, two, three, four times he tried before Florrie finally picked up. She'd sounded very apologetic when she told him that Marion, point blank, refused to come to the phone. 'I'm sorry, bonnie lad,' she'd said, 'but she's adamant. You're going to have to give her a bit of space this time. Leave it with me, eh?'

And that was it.

His wife didn't want him, neither did his kids and so, belittled and choked up, he'd reluctantly gone to see if Phil could put him up for a couple of nights or so. He could think of anyone else. There was no-one else. 'Only a day or two, mate, I'll keep meself scarce,' he'd pleaded. 'Reckon it might be the menopause or somethin',' he'd tried.

Betsy, Phil's wife, then appeared behind him. 'Alright, Dekko. Problem?' she'd asked but sounding very unsympathetic.

'Could say that, love.'

'He just needs a bed for the night,' explained Phil, wincing a little at the expected reaction.

'Oh, right,' she said, smiling but, unseen, prodding her husband in the back and disappearing back inside. 'I'll leave that for you to sort out, Phil,' she added, ominously.

'She alright?' asked Derek.

'Yeah. You'll have to find yourself something more permanent though, Dekko,' he reluctantly agreed and knowing full well he was putting his own wellbeing and that of his family on the line.

'As long as I ain't landin' you in it?'

'It'll be alright. Just a night or two though, yeah?'

'Thanks, mate, appreciated... hey, I don't s'pose you fancy a hair o' the dog, do ya?'

'Fuck me, no, Dekko! Ain't you had enough?'

'No, not the way I'm feelin', I ain't. I could murder one,' he tried again.

'Dekko, please, gimme a break. I got the little ones to think about 'ere. Why don't you just come in, get yer head down, and sober up?'

'You reckon I should?'

'Yeah, I do. You'll feel all the better for it, see things a bit more clearly, eh?'

So, after going back home and picking up a few essentials, he'd holed up in their tiny and crowded box room like some wounded animal.

Unable to sleep, sweating and trembling, and aware of the sound of slightly raised voices below him, he'd sat for what seemed like an eternity on the edge of the bed with an old vacuum cleaner and a battered game of Twister placed awkwardly under his feet until, finally, fatigue had got the better of him and he'd drifted off.

The following day, the second of January, Phil, had been very busy on his behalf. In no uncertain terms, Betsy had put him under orders, she wanted Derek out, like straight away. 'Have you smelt that room he's in after just one night? Even from the landing!' she'd said incredulously. 'Out, today, do you understand me?'

Miraculously, after a bit of asking around and checking out ads in the local free press, Phil had managed to find a semi-furnished flat in one of the tower blocks behind the precinct.

'It's not much, mate, but it'll have to do you for the time being,' he'd explained when he'd taken him there to have a look that very afternoon.

'She'll have calmed down by now. I'll just go an' see 'er, talk some sense into 'er,' said Derek, clutching at straws.

'Don't be a damn fool, mate. A break might even do the pair of you a power of good. You know what they say? Absence an' all that.'

'You think?'

'I think.'

So, very unhappily, and tapping Phil up for the price of the deposit, Derek had moved in.

-

In the months that followed, Marion kept all necessary contact between them to over the phone. She went out of her way avoid seeing him and would even cross the road or nip into a doorway if she so much as caught sight of him on the street.

But still, she got his post, brown envelopes and credit card companies and began opening one or two out of curiosity. Heaven knows how he intended to pay them all back. It was thousands.

Advised and encouraged by Nigel, she'd begun to mark them *Not known at this address. Return to sender.* It would affect her credit rating he'd told her and that if she wanted to put her life back in order, she needed total separation.

And so, with something of a heavy heart, she'd started proceedings.

Chapter 6
Saturday Morning

'Right, for starters, Derek,' Marion begins when she phones him, 'you need to get your post redirected. I'm sick to the back teeth with it all. I don't wanna have to ask you again. D'you hear me?'

'Not hurtin' ya are they? S'only a few bits o' paper. Chuck 'em in the bin if it bothers ya that much,' he dismisses her.

'Chuck 'em in the bin? What sort of answer is that, you fool? Do you want me to give them your new address? Cos I will if you push me,' she threatens.

Derek doesn't answer her.

'You've got another think comin' if you reckon I'm goin' to sit by an' 'ave the bailiffs bangin' on my door,' she continues angrily.

'I pay 'em off a bit every now and then, keep 'em off me back. Relax, will ya?'

'Relax? Have you seen how much you owe? You'll never be rid of it, not as long you live.

''Ave you been openin' my mail, ya nosey cow?'

'You call me that once again, Derek! See what happens!'

'Oo-ooh! Get out o' the wrong side o' the bed, did we? All cuddled up next to that bastard, Nigel?'

'Gimme strength! And there's the last of your junk to sort out as well. I'll throw that out an' all if you don't get 'round and pick it up, like pronto.'

'Do what ya like, woman. I got pretty much everything I need. Besides, I don't suppose you want a repeat performance if I lay my hands on 'im again, now do ya?'

'Oh, grow up! What's that gonna to prove, eh? And you remind me, we need to have talk about maintenance.'

'Wha'? Money ya mean?'

'Yeah, what else d'you think? Chocolate buttons?'

'I've 'ad a lot of expenses since 'avin' to move in 'ere, Mar,' says Derek, adopting a more conciliatory tone. *'It all mounts up ya know.'*

'Hooray! He gets it at last! Anyhow, that's your look out. You don't want me to call me in the CSA, do ya?'

'You wouldn't.'

'Wouldn't I now?'

'Ah, do as you soddin' well like! They can't get blood out of a stone.'

'They're still yours, Derek! You can't expect Nigel to keep shellin' out to support *your* kids all the time - food on the table, clothes on their back!'

Wallop! That hurt. Right smack between the eyes.

'Yeah, they are mine, an' don't you forget it!' he reacts, shouting back.

'Well, grow some then! And you need to have a word with your boy. We've had the community copper around again. He's been caught drinkin', an' right below where you live. Don't you never see him?'

Derek puts the phone down on the table and starts to roll himself a cigarette but can still make her out.

'Are you listenin' to me, Derek?'

'Not really,' he says but picking up the phone and holding it into his neck as he lights up.

'Well, you'd better! If you spent less time down that stinkin' pub then you could help your family out a bit more.'

'Wha', an' sit in front of the box in this poxy flat of mine night after night? You're 'avin' a laugh, ain't ya?'

'I've had to, Derek! For bloody years, I had to! Don't try an' make me feel guilty. It won't wash. You brought this all on yourself, and you bloody well know it!'

'I can hardly swing a bleedin' cat.'

'Fucking hell, Derek! When are you going to man up for once in your life?'

'You really are a heartless cow, ain't ya?'

'Right, that's it! If you want a fight, you got it! You're not walking over me no more. Do you hear me? So, these letters ....'

Derek's heard enough and cuts her off mid tirade - *click.*

Instinctively, he looks back at his phone to check the time - it's just about early doors, time for a top up, a laugh and a joke, the inevitable and regular post-mortem from the crazy night before.

He checks the contents of his wallet. ''Kin' 'ell! Is that it?' he says as he all finds is a solitary manky fiver plus a few bits of shrapnel in his jean's pocket.

It's barely enough for three pints.

He'll just have to think on his feet.

Even through the early wisps of layering cigarette smoke, the bar is particularly bright as Derek lollops in with near horizontal shafts of late autumnal sunlight penetrating the stale and acetic air.

As ever, he doesn't need to ask - Jimbo had seen him coming, his familiar head bobbing above the net curtains and is already pulling him his pint. 'Usual?' he asks irrelevantly and by way of a greeting.

Derek nods in acknowledgment, pulling up a stool and sitting down like a man twice his age. 'Jim,' he says, groaning.

At this time in the morning, it's eerily quiet too, save the *chunk-a-chunk-a-chunk* from the fruit machine giving some old biddy a much needed pay out and a couple of gnarled old cider boys puffing and harrumphing over on the bench seats behind the pool table.

'Feelin' a bit rough, are we?' Jimbo asks him.

Derek doesn't reply, ignores him in fact, he's still not fully engaged and, like a lizard bathing himself in the first heat of the day, warming himself to the prospect of his first drink.

'Well, you bloody well oughta be,' Jimbo continues, gently chastising him.

Derek shrugs it off. 'Phil or Dave in yet?' he asks.

Jimbo raises his hand to his head like the peak of a cap, scanning the near empty room, peering under the bar, lifting up a drip mat. 'Not as far as I can see,' he says sarcastically.

'Alright, ya cheeky cunt.'

'You lot were well and truly plastered last night, fuckin' blotto in fact. Surprised you're even out and about as yet - and as for Phil, wha' a liability he was!'

Derek looks at him with a vacant expression. He doesn't have a clue.

'Don't you remember?'

'Pass.'

'Intent on goin' to drive into town for a kebab? Yeah?'

'Did he?' Derek laughs. 'What a twat!'

'No, he didn't! I managed to get his keys off him or else he'd o' got done again. Made 'im walk home.'

'Not as if he's got far to go is it?' colludes Derek, pleased for once that the heat was not aimed directly at him. 'Lazy bastard.'

'What you lot don't understand,' continues Jimbo as he squeezes the head onto Derek's pint, 'is that it's muggins 'ere that could end up takin' the rap with punters drivin' away shit-faced. The police take a very dim view.'

'You'll have to 'ave a word with 'im again then, won't ya? Explain.'

'Don't you worry, I will, for all the good it will do,' says Jimbo, handing him his drink, 'and don't let me forget, you left your bits o' shoppin' 'ere last night too. I put the bacon in the fridge though most o' the eggs were smashed to fuck. I had to bin 'em. I'm sure we got a few more you can 'ave."

'Very kind o' ya, I'm sure.'

'There's gratitude for ya! Shan't bother next time. Anyway, get that down your neck, fresh out a new barrel. That'll be one-eighty-five.'

Derek leans forward and without touching the glass slurps the top off of it. 'What a very fine pint you keep, landlord,' he then says, buttering him up. 'How *do* you do it?'

'Ne'er mind all the soft soap shit, Dekko. Just give me the bloody money. I know your little game.'

'Stick it on me tab would ya, Jim?' Derek implores him, scribbling in the air. 'You know how it is.'

'What? You already spent all that money Phil gave you last night?' asks Jimbo, his voice rising in disbelief. 'Fifty notes?'

'You should know,' says Derek accusingly, 'you took most of it.'

'And you drank it! Still, the answers no. I'm sorry,' says Jimbo firmly. 'I'm tryin to run a bloody business 'ere, and as I said to ya, it's creepin' up, you owe nearly sixty quid as it is. I can't do it no more, Dekko.'

Miserably, Derek sticks his hand in his pocket to retrieve his coins. 'Thanks for nuthin',' he says.

Jimbo leans in towards him. 'Look, don't take it personal, Dekko,' he says, almost apologetically. 'Most in 'ere are on the never-never, you know it, I know it, but, between you an' me, I'm getting it right in the neck.'

'Reenie?' Derek guesses.

'Shush! Shut up, ya bloody idiot!'

'But I've never let you down yet 'ave I? Always paid up.'

'Yes, you have, me ol' cocker, but I got to put me foot down somewhere.'

Like a little boy lost, Derek sprinkles his coins onto the bar and starts to count.

'Oh, put it away, ya daft bastard,' relinquishes Jimbo, waving him away but looking nervously over his shoulder. 'But that's yer lot. After this, you're on stop.'

'Stop?'

'Yeah, stop. No more tick.'

'But…'

'Stop, I said.'

Despite Jimbo's generosity, Derek feels strangely belittled and is about to react but, right at that moment, the door clatters open as a bar snacks rep struggles in with boxes of crisps stacked high above his chin. 'Alright there, Mr Beazer,' he calls out chirpily, peering over the top.

'About time too,' says Jimbo tetchily. 'We're completely out o' Cheese an' Onion … an' Dry-bloody-Roasted.'

'The bloody money I spend in 'ere!' Derek is thinking to himself.

'Sorry, it always goes a bit mental in the run up to Christmas,' the rep offers his excuse.

'Wha' d'ya mean? It's only the beginning o' November!'

'Ungrateful bastard!'

'I won't let it happen again. Promise.'

'Fuck 'im'! Fuck 'is pub!'

'Make sure as you don't. I'm losing money here. There are other suppliers ya know.'

Derek now watches as the flustered rep rushes back and forth to get yet more boxes of crisps, boards of nuts and pork scratchings from his van before Jimbo re-appears behind the bar, muttering. 'A word, Jim,' he says, beckoning him aggressively and foolishly just about to cut off his nose to spite his face.

'Not now, Dekko, yeah?' says Jimbo, looking with horror at the invoice in his hand.

'Why? What's that?'

'Bills, Derek. Wha' d'ya think? More bloody bills! It's gettin' really fuckin' serious.'

Derek picks up his pint and takes an uncharacteristic and less than enthusiastic mouthful.

'So, sorry. What is it you want?' asks Jimbo, sliding the invoice alongside others next to the till.

'Nuthin',' says Derek. 'Forget it.'

Soon, in dribs and drabs, the bar begins to fill as a succession of battle-weary but hardened drinkers drift in. 'Alright then, Dekko?' the majority greet him. 'Yeah, no worries, you?' he replies to each and every one as he idly flicks through the pub's copy of the Bristol Evening Post.

'Where's ya mates then?' asks one.

'They'll be in,' Derek assures him, slowly sipping the end of his fourth pint, the last he can afford, and keeping a hopeful eye out for someone who might step in and bail him out.

In desperation, he tries calling Phil, tries him a few times, and Dave, but all to no avail - *the person you are calling is not available, please try later* - says their voicemails. 'Switch on your bloody phone, mate!' he hisses. 'Wha's the fuckin' point?!'

So, wringing his glass for all it's worth, Derek acknowledges he is well and truly out of luck and out of options. Quietly, he places the glass on the bar so as not to draw attention to himself. He hates it, he does. It feels just like he was being kicked out of his home all over again, and, to make matters even worse, as he stands up to leave, his intended discreet exit is foiled as Jimbo calls over to him. 'Hold on a minute, Dekko, I got your shoppin' out the back. Remember?'

'Leave it.'

'Don't be daft, only take me a second. It's yours.'

Derek's humiliation is now complete as he is forced to wait, his shoulders noticeably hunched, his hands in his pockets, and with the demeanour of a whipped pup.

'Bloody hell, you off already, Dekko?' questions one fellow drinker, genuinely surprised. 'Not like you. Summat up? Feelin' ill?'

'Things to do, people to see,' he lies.

'What, on a Saturday? Get a few more down yer neck, ya daft bastard!' says the man cheerily, holding up his full pint to admire. 'Look at that. Nectar o' the Gods that is.'

'Here y'are,' says Jimbo, reappearing and handing him his carrier. 'I popped a couple of eggs in too, so be careful.

Derek takes it, avoiding both hand and eye contact.

'Sorry, mate,' Jimbo mouths, genuinely feeling for him. He'd been there himself you see, potless and out on his jack, before he'd met Reenie. But he can't go back on his word, not now. Besides, the bar is filling up to capacity, there's a big match coming up on Sky - Man U versus The Arsenal and there's work to be done. 'Get a bit o' scrunch down ya, yeah?' he advises as Derek takes his leave. 'Do yourself a favour.'

So, at just after two o'clock on a Saturday afternoon, he finds himself unlocking his door at the top of the echoing concrete stairwell - an all-time first for him.

His flat is basic to say the least with his only concession to brightening the place up a bit was to stick up a couple of posters with Blu-Tac, a team photo of Bristol Rovers and a very faded alpine scene - you know the type of thing, snow covered mountains, blue sky, a picturesque red roofed chalet perched cosily in a meadow. He'd had it years, always liked it, and had promised he'd take himself and the family there one day.

Fat chance now.

Unsurprisingly, he has little or no appetite as he searches in the cupboard next to the sink for his one and only pan and starts to knock up a meal of sorts.

With the electric ring on the cooker starting to warm and spatula in hand, he can't help himself as a wave of self-pity envelops him. He'd never thought for one moment his life would come to this, all on his own, totally skint, and, fiercely, he cuffs his eye with the back of his hand. 'Bastard!' he says.

His daughter Janice had been right, hadn't she? He really was a waste o' fuckin' space. There was no escaping it. It was the truth.

He barely touches his food and, after scanning yesterday's paper, he is soon fast asleep, flat out and snoring in front of the TV and misses a call from Phil. It goes straight to his answer phone.

- You have reached the voicemail service for 0-7-7-8... - please leave your message after the tone - if you want to re-record your message please press one at any time…… beeeeep. 'Oi, Dekko, you want a beer or not? Heard you're brassic. I'm in the chair. Get your hairy arse down here right now, ya stupid wazzock!'

It's gone half-past-eight by the time he begins to stir, his face and neck wedged awkwardly into the corner of the sofa-bed, the metal frame hard and unforgiving through the thin upholstery, a stream of saliva dribbling from the corner of his mouth.

On the other side of the room, the telly is still playing away to itself and in his semi-consciousness state he becomes aware of the sound of an audience cheering together with a series of strangely familiar numbers being called out, but, still half asleep, he turns his back and nestles back down.

However, as he hears yet another of his numbers, he turns, looking over his shoulder through a single half open eye.

Displayed at the bottom of the screen, he can just about make them out and, now rubbing his eyes frantically and dropping his stockinged feet to the floor, he accidentally steps into the cold and greasy remains on his plate.

They <u>are</u> his numbers!

He reads them over, backwards and forwards, forwards and backwards, slowly, quickly. He knows them off by heart!

They Really Are His Fucking Numbers!

He'd imagined how this moment might feel so many times in the past - how he'd react, how he'd scream and shout, but he can't. No, with his mouth is as dry as a Jacobs Cream Cracker, his heart beating as fast and as hard as any pneumatic drill, he can't move. Pole-axed but feeling like he's about to explode in one immense and fantastic physical reaction.

Then it hits him.

BANG!

Crying out in unbelievable and immense release, he simultaneously feels like he's floating on air, like an eagle in a red hot thermal, then like a man shot out of a cannon as the weight of the world is miraculously lifted from his shoulders and to be replaced with a feeling of absolute and joyous ecstasy.

He punches the air, the wall, the door, the lampshade and his very own chest to connect himself to the wonderful reality of it all.

Nothing hurts anymore.

Not a bloody thing!

HE'S A WINNER!
For the first time in his life, he's a fuckin' winner!

'But how much? How much? How fuckin' much?' he suddenly yells at the screen.

Alan Dedicoat then gives him his answer, he's saying it out loud. The jackpot is......

Eleven Million, Three Hundred and Fifty-five Thousand Pounds!

He can't think straight, he's all over the shop - sixes and sevens, eights and nines. Millions in fact!

'Where's me jacket? Where's me fuckin' jacket? Fuckin' hell!' he yells, repeating it like a mantra before finding it hanging over the top of the kitchen door and, snatching it down, almost ripping the collar clean off as he does so.

'The ticket! The ticket! Where's the fuckin' ticket?'

Frantically, he pulls out his wallet and for a few terrible seconds, he can't find it, sandwiched as it is between a couple of receipts and his kidney donor card (though who'd want his kidneys is anyone's guess).

'Is it right?' he then worries. 'Did the girl get them right?' He hadn't checked when she'd copied them for him. He didn't check, the bloody idiot!

He reads the numbers, over and over, eyes agog.

'It's right! She got it bloody right!'

F'WHOAAR!

He can't hold it in, he has to share it, got to share, but who? His ex? His family?

Nah, don't be stupid! His ex ain't getting a fucking bean. He knows that, but the clock on the wall says there's still time.

So, yanking on his boots, stamping them down to force in his feet and with the ticket held firmly in a vice like grip, he can't get out of the door quickly enough and leaps down the stairwell two and three at a time, twisting his ankle but feeling no pain as he heads out and onto the street at break-neck speed.

It's party time.

It's bloody party time … and he needs a drink, fast!

Chapter 7

Sinking low into his wingback Chesterfield, PG is settling down for a rare night in front of the TV. It's not really his thing, television, but tonight he's making an exception.

In one hand he cradles and swirls a leggy glass of claret whilst securely resting the other on a hardbound and well-thumbed A5 notebook, his current trusted ledger. It never leaves his side.

He'd been looking forward to it, the TV programme, a documentary entitled 'The World's Greatest Art Forgeries' on BBC2 as he'd only just recently acquired a few pieces himself; a nice little Raoul Dufy oil on canvas complete in a heavy ormolu frame, a damaged but passable Derain picturing the London skyline, and possibly the star of the show, a simple but bold charcoal sketch of a ram signed 'Picasso'.

They were a steal of course, and each of dubious provenance, but after a little restoration work, a tweak here, an embellishment there, and adding a couple of convincing bills of sale, they could prove to be very tidy little earners indeed.

Cocooned in the sumptuous leather of his chair and thrumming his book, he considers this initial foray into the prestigious and lucrative Art Market to be long overdue and an essential and desired career progression. Idly, he flicks the book open to remind himself of how much, or how little, the artworks cost and/or owed him. Having a near photographic memory, he doesn't really need to look, but PG likes to be sure. He's a belts and braces, dot the i's and cross the t's type and likes to have everything in its place and a place for absolutely everything.

He'd amassed over two hundred of these notebooks of his over the years with each one filled with meticulously written entries, all of which he keeps neatly aligned and in chronological order on a single high shelf in his otherwise impressive antiquarian library. In many ways, they were equivalent to his diaries and through them he could pinpoint where he'd been and what he'd bought, received, or sold for over four decades or more.

You see, growing up as an only child in a family that had absolutely no desire or aptitude for reading or writing of any sort, it had become an obsession of his - keeping books and keeping record.

It had all started in earnest soon after he'd found himself in the unruly mayhem that was his secondary school. Way back then, he'd quickly come to realise two things. One, that his parents were a crucifying embarrassment to him, illiterate and living on benefits (but often topped up with the selling of stolen goods that they would shoplift themselves or get from the back of a van) and, two, that the education he was receiving at school was so woefully inadequate that, if he was to make anything at all of himself at all, he needed to take matters into his own hands.

And so, quite remarkably for someone so young and from such a background, some might say impressive, he'd set about reinventing himself.

For starters, he'd joined the local library before progressing to the awe-inspiring Bristol Central Library on College Green. He liked the grandness of it and its location adjoining the affluent Clifton area of the city and such a far cry from his own council house sprawl.

There, he would immerse himself in the Encyclopaedia Britannica in particular, where not only did he discover that he could readily acquire knowledge on a broad and far-reaching scale - Science, History, Geography, Art, Literature, the lot, but he also took great pleasure in their size and weight, despite the fact it made them near impossible to steal.

Such was his desire to rise above his lowly born status, he'd even taken to wearing wire rimmed spectacles perched on the tip of his nose (although he didn't actually need them) and dressing in a burgundy whale-cord jacket and accompanying moleskin waistcoat and trousers. Even more curiously, he began to affect a clipped version of an upper-class accent that did not, and still doesn't, entirely conceal his strong Bristolian vowels.

But make no mistake, his bizarre metamorphosis came at a price.

As a rather weedy adolescent growing up in and around the estates of Bristol in the mid to late seventies, PG cut a very peculiar figure indeed. As one might imagine, his change in appearance and character was greeted with varying degrees of mockery and outright derision from numerous and various quarters, violence even. But he didn't really give two hoots, not one bit, as it merely served to confirm what he had known all along - he was a cut above the rest and superior to all those around him.

However, that said, he soon came to understand that he was missing one key and vital ingredient to complete his magnificent transformation. Money, and lots of it.

So, utilising his keen and newly honed intellectual vigour and ever the opportunist, it dawned on him that there was a temporary solution of sorts staring him right in the face - the 'family business' so to speak. He could see it had potential.

To the welcome astonishment of his parents, who quickly struggled to keep up with his voracious demand, PG was soon busy supplying more or less anything that anyone could possibly have wanted - cigarettes, alcohol, cosmetics, sports gear, records, tapes, even general household items - all knocked off and at knocked down prices.

It was a result and lined his pockets very handsomely indeed. Moreover, as a very welcome spin off, it gave him clout and afforded him much needed protection as people now actively sought out his company. After all, there was stuff to be had and serious money to be saved.

For the young Peter Green, it was a no-brainer, and he developed the whole concept with unbridled determination.

-

With his man-tits moving in a wholly independent rhythm to his belly, and his rasping breath clouding in the cold night air, Derek holds his winning ticket hard and flat against his thigh in his pocket as he hurriedly lopes and limps towards the 'Ravellers.

Strangely, he suddenly becomes aware of an old but familiar *'zizzing'* noise as he hears the denim of his jeans rubbing vigorously together. It takes him back, back to his long-lost youth, racing to see a long-forgotten girlfriend, on a Saturday night, on a promise, and he's as late, as ever.

Dangerously, he's close to collapsing from hyperventilation as the rush of oxygen only adds to his already sky-rocketing sense of delirium and euphoria.

-

With the programme at last about to begin, PG pours himself another small glass.

No, other than a couple brief spells in Pucklechurch Remand Centre in his late teens, caught out while he was learning the ropes so to speak, life has turned out well for him, very well indeed with a fine Edwardian pile in Cotham, a leafy suburb of the city, complete with live in housekeeper, a top of the range Jaguar and Range Rover parked on the gravelled driveway outside, and plenty of money in the bank and squirrelled away here and there.

But despite his obvious material wealth, there was always one intangible prize that had continued to elude him despite all his best efforts .... he could never quite seem to gain full acceptance in the more elevated circles of society and amongst those whose company he had always so desperately craved. It was like they saw him coming, shunned him almost, despite all of his clever lies and fabrications.

This is where the Art would come in. It was to be his steppingstone into greater things. You see, for him, it isn't really about the money anymore.

-

After what seemed like an eternity, Derek finally makes it to the pub and falls in through the double doors, almost sprawling flat out on the floor.

'Hey, Dekko! Got me text then, ya silly sod?' Phil immediately calls out from over on Cracker's Corner.

Panting and gasping for breath, Derek can't answer and promptly creases up with a stitch.

'Wha's the problem? Got withdrawal symptoms or summat, 'ave ya?'

'I've done it, Phil,' he says hoarsely as he hobbles over. 'I've gone and bloody done it.'

'Done what?'

'It!'

'It? What are you bloody on about? Done Nigel in good an' proper this time? Invented a cure for the common cold? What!?'

With his sweat laden hair now hanging in rattails around his face, Derek leans hard forward and places both fists on the bar, the winning ticket hidden tight in his right hand.

''Ere, you're startin' to freak me out 'ere, Dekko,' worries Phil as he now notices the torn collar on his jacket. 'Have been in a fight? Who was it? We'll 'ave 'em!'

Derek shakes his head, coughing. 'You'll 'ave to gimme a minute,' he catches.

Even by his own unique standards, this particularly dramatic entrance is already attracting the attention of the other punters lined up along the bar and those sat down at the tables behind him. They're nudging each other, gesturing with intrigue and laughter. More than a little curious himself, Jimbo ambles over to have a nose. 'He alright, Phil?' he asks.

'Pass. Your guess is as good as mine, Jim. Be a good chap an' pour 'im a pint will ya?' he asks insistently, somehow fearing the worst and cocking his head towards the pumps to steer him out of the way and clear of earshot.

Derek pushes himself back up, hands on hips, arching his spine.

'Well?' asks Phil urgently. 'Spit it out, man. Wha's occurred?'

'You wouldn't believe me if I told ya.'

'Try me.'

'It's me numbers,' says Derek but still grimacing as if someone's now twisting a blade into his side.

'Wass-e-say?' asks Jimbo, straining to hear and leaning back from the pump.

'Me fuckin' lottery numbers,' explains Derek, matter of fact, and opening his hand to reveal his now crumpled ticket. 'They've come up.'

'Bleedin' hell, Derek!' says Phil in hushed tones. 'You positive?'

'Well, yeah,' he answers a little unconvincingly.

'What? All six?' asks Jimbo, his lip already twitching. 'It was a rollover, weren't it?'

'Yeah.'

'How much then?'

'Eleven million, or so they're sayin'. I'm a fuckin' multi-millionaire!' Derek at last shouts out.

'Oi! Zip it up, mate!' Phil tries to quieten him, but it was already too late. Suddenly, it was as if there was a glowing celebrity standing in their midst having mistakenly dropped in for a quick pint. With all eyes upon him, you could almost hear a pin drop as a reverential hush descends over the place and as the words 'eleven' and 'million' are fully digested.

Then, in as little time as it takes Derek to slip the ticket into his top pocket and tap his jeans to search for his baccy, the pub starts to hum with whispered comments and intrigue.

'Wha's 'appened?'

'Dekko over there, he's gone and won the bloody lottery!'

'Nah? You're jokin'!'

'I'm not!'

'How much?'

'Over eleven million, or so he reckons.'

'Eleven fuckin' million?'
'Yeah.'
'Nah!'
'Yeah!'
'Alright for bloody some, innit?'
'Yeah, makes ya bleedin' sick, dunnit?'
'Too fuckin' right it does!'
'I give up!'
'Lucky bastard!'

For sure, there are one or two standing nearby that slap him on the back and offer him words of congratulations, but only for a few seconds at a time. It's like he's somehow off limits with nobody wanting to be seen toadying up to him and trying to ingratiate themselves. No, except for Phil, who is grinning broadly and looking as happy as Larry, the vast majority are simply wrestling with the green-eyed monsters that now burble furiously away inside them. It is not until one of the wags from down the bar attempts to crack the ice that something like normality returns. 'Seems like the drinks are on you then, Dekko, ya rich cunt!' he shouts out.

'Yeah, get 'em in! Or ain't we good enough for ya anymore?' howls another to the rumblings of agreement.

'Hey, I would if I could, lads,' Derek replies apologetically, drawing on his roll-up and closing one eye against the smoke, 'but,' he hisses on inhalation, 'believe it or not,' another drawer, 'I ain't got a fuckin' bean on me!'

'Yeah, right! Why don't that surprise me? Always got an excuse, ain't ya?'

Derek exhales a great plume of smoke and roars with laughter. 'Check me pockets if ya don't believe me! Ask Jimbo! He's put me on stop! It's why I had to fuck off earlier! I'm fuckin' brassic!'

Looking a little embarrassed and with the distinct feeling he's probably already blown it, Jimbo quickly disappears out the back to find Reenie.

'Ah, bollocks to ya!' then spits another of the punters and a member of the pub lottery syndicate. 'You'll always be a fuckin' tight-arse! Forever on the cadge!'

'Oo-ooh! Bit jealous, are we?' says Phil, putting him in his place.

'Well, I hope he's gonna give us all a pay day seein' as we've all been in it together?' the bloke continues. 'Don't forget your mates, yeah, Dekko?'

'Why the fuck should he, ya daft git?' defends Phil. 'It's got nuthin' to do with the syndicate. Dekko's won this off his own bat, fair an' fuckin' square! Ain't ya, mate?'

'I'll get the drinks in when I got the money in me hand,' offers Derek, genuinely taken aback at the sudden and unexpected aggression. 'I'll get you all properly pissed, 'ave no fear 'bout that.'

'That it? Drip feedin' us wi' a few beers 'ere an' there to make yerself the big I am!' the man continues to rant.

'Oh, piss off, ya sad bastard,' Phil tries to slap him down once again. 'If you think…'

'You wanna know what I think?' the man cuts him short. 'I'll tell ya what I fuckin' think. Fuck ya! Fuck the lot o' ya!' he shouts before necking his pint and storming off out the door.

'Jeezus,' says Derek, 'what's got into 'im? I don't want no 'ard feelin's nor nuthin'!'

'Forget 'im, Dekko. You're bound to get some stupid twats with their noses put out o' joint,' says Phil loudly and as a warning for all to hear. 'What's more important is that you call the Lottery people an' stake your claim, Dekko. Have you done it yet?'

'No. Haven't had a chance yet, come straight down 'ere, ain't I.'

'An' you wanna write your name and address on the back of it while you're at it, be on the safe side.'

'You reckon?'

'Fuckin' right I do! Plus, you need to get it somewhere safe, like double quick before you lose it, or someone tries to nick it off ya!'

At that very moment, Reenie strides briskly through to the paying side of the bar. 'Jim tells me you've got some great news, Derek,' she says, peering at him through her glass bottom spectacles that magnify her eyeballs such that they look like two giant pieces of frogspawn.

She makes Derek feel uneasy, always has. The last time she'd said anything of any consequence to him at all was to tell him to cut out the noise and behave or get out. 'Um, yeah, Reenie, seems like it,' he answers.

'Got yourself a drink?' she then asks, all saccharin like. 'One on the house, with us, to celebrate your good fortune,' she insists with a thin smile.

'Phil's already got me a pint in, ta,' he declines uncharacteristically.

'No, no, no! A proper drink, Derek. A malt perhaps?' she suggests. 'Mind you,' she adds conspiratorially, 'I don't know why we bother stockin' it with this lot in here.'

'Er, yeah, OK, thanks very much,' he accepts but not sure whether he should feel flattered or insulted.

She looks over to her husband. 'A Glenfiddich, James,' she instructs him.

'You what?'

'You heard. And make it a large one.'

''Ere, that's favouritism that is,' someone else shouts out.

'Yeah, what about us?' adds another.

'What about you?' she bites back. 'It's not you I'm talking to.'

Derek then seizes his opportunity, chancing his arm. 'Look, Reen,' he starts off, 'I know I'm on stop an' all that, but all this makes me feel, you know, a bit….'

'A bit what, Derek?' she says already one step ahead, or so she thinks.

'Look, what I'm sayin' is can I add to me tab? I mean, it's not every day is it?'

Jimbo places the whisky on the bar.

'I don't think we'd have a problem with that, under the circumstances,' says Reenie, handing him the glass but looking towards her husband. 'He wants to buy a few drinks, Jim.'

Jimbo shakes his head, he knows what's going to happen, the flood gates are just about to open and it's all about to get very messy.

Now grinning like a Cheshire cat, Derek knocks back the malt in a single swig and bangs the empty glass back down on the bar. 'Right then! The lot o' ya! Whatever you want!' he announces, shouting. 'The nights on me! Fill yer fuckin' boots!'

Collectively, the bar erupts, now whooping its approval. For the time being at least, they know exactly how to react as glasses are quickly emptied and noisily thrust across the bar.

But Jimbo stands back, holding his hands up and suddenly looks very suspicious. 'Hang on a minute, hang on,' he says. 'Tell me, Dekko, this isn't some silly ruse o' yours, is it? You're not pullin' my plonker after this afternoon, are ya?'

'No! Wha d'ya take me for?' Derek squeals and looking to show his ticket again. 'Course not! It's real!'

Right then, someone yells out from down on the other end and pointing at the TV bracketed high up on far wall. 'Here's yer answer! The Lottery Update, it's on right now!'

Jimbo scrambles for the remote control from under the bar and points it towards the set, his arm extended, his forefinger pressed hard on the button sending the lime green volume bands racing across the screen.

'And finally, here are tonight's Lotto results,' blares out the voice. *'The numbers are 5 - 9 - 17....'*

'They right, Dekko?' someone calls out.

'Bloody listen will ya!' Phil shouts as a small crowd now gather around Derek, casting their gaze from TV to ticket, ticket to TV.

'.... And, finally, 29. The bonus ball is 34. Early indications are that there is one lucky winner scooping a whopping eleven million, three hundred and fifty-five thousand pounds.'

'There ya go, Jim!' shouts Phil, shaking his fist. 'I think you owe 'im an apology, don't you?'

As Derek stands immobile, bathing in the glory, his arms outstretched, his eyes closed, and his face turned up like some beatific religious icon, Jimbo shuffles uneasily. 'Fair do's, Dekko,' he says, red-faced. 'I'm sorry I doubted ya, mate. Honest, I do.'

Raising her voice above the cacophony, Reenie instructs her husband. 'Just pour the bloody drinks, Jim,' she says. 'Go on!'

-

Not so far away, Jez is hanging out with his mates down at the precinct and, as ever, they are making a nuisance of themselves and creating a general mess of the place.

Earlier they'd got an older lad to sort them out with a few bottles of cider and forty Lambert and Butler. Now, at just after ten o'clock, with the shutters rattling down and the drink and smokes all but gone, they are getting bored, jostling each other, and looking for something else to do.

Enticingly, a couple of them had spotted a souped up Renault 5 turbo parked up around the corner and are jealously admiring its flared arches and oversized exhaust. To them, it was as sweet as.

'What d'ya think then, Jez?' asks Boiksy, one of his friends and in the year above him at school.

'What?'

'The car? Wanna give it a go?'

Jez hadn't thought about it. Macks had though, his other mate, he'd had his eye on it all night. 'I fuckin' do! I'm well up for it,' he says.

'It'll be alarmed to fuck,' warns Jez, uneasy at the idea.

'So? You shittin' it or summat?'

'Nah, course not! But we'll never get in.'

'You're lookin' at the master 'ere,' boasts Boiksy, cracking his fingers. 'You fuckin' watch me. There's no such thing as never.'

-

With everyone topped up, Jimbo leans over to Derek as best as his stomach allows and speaks into his ear. 'Hope there's no hard feelings?' he says, contritely.

'Nah, no problem, Jimbo, reckon I would o' said the same had I o' been in your shoes. As you say, you got a business to run,' replies Derek but laughing hysterically.

'Thank you, Dekko. Appreciated. But as Phil said, you wanna watch that ticket o' yours. You don't wanna go losin' it, now do ya?'

'Be alright. I got it tucked away.'

'You sure?' questions Jimbo. 'You really sure?'

'OK, so wha' d'ya reckon?'

'Well, I can put it in the safe if you want?' he offers.

'Good thinkin', Batman. Great idea.'

'Yes, Dekko, not a bad idea at all,' agrees Phil. 'Just sign the back so that Jimbo 'ere can't do a midnight flit with it, yeah?'

'I'll ignore that,' says Jimbo, annoyed by the very suggestion.

'Just sayin', just sayin',' jokes Phil. 'Not every day you got millions in yer safe, now is it? I mean, there's probably fuck all in there at the moment.'

'Don't take the piss, Phil. So, what d'you wanna do, Dekko? Stick it in there or not? I'm not twistin' your arm nor nuthin'.'

'No, no, makes perfect sense,' agrees Derek.

'But, still, you'd better call em' first, stake your claim,' advises Phil, 'it'd only take ya a couple o' minutes.'

'Ah, leave it, Phil. I'm gettin' pissed already. Tomorrow'll do. It ain't goin' anywhere, is it?'

'Come through the hatch with me then an' we'll put it under lock and key,' says Jimbo, adding, 'an' you can come too, Phil, hold yer mates' hand, if you don't fuckin' trust me, ya wanker.'

So, as both men disappear behind the bar with Derek waving his ticket aloft, one of the revellers breaks into song. 'If I was a rich man!' he sings in a mock guttural Jewish voice with others immediately joining in. 'Yoddle-iddle-oddle-yiddle-oddle-iddle-oddle-um. If-I-were-a-iddy-biddy-rich, if I-was-a-wealthy-man! Oi! I wouldn't have to work hard, yoddle-iddle-oddle-um ......'

-

True to his word, Boiksy is into the car in no time at all and already busy knocking the ignition off with half a house brick. 'Get in,' he says.

Quickly, Macks squeezes into the back, Jez into the passenger seat, as Boiksy then hotwires the engine into life. 'Let's see how this baby goes, shall we?' he says, laughing, slapping the car into gear, and snaking it out onto the street.

-

With Derek and the landlord temporarily out of the way, the jungle drums begin working overtime with phone calls and text messages being sent out all over the place.

'Who d'you say's won it?'
'Derek.'
'Derek?'
'You know, bloody Derek!'
'Can't place him.'
'Grey mullet! Ponytail. Always in a denim jacket!'
'You got me there.'
'Big drinker!'
'Ain't we all!'
'Bloody 'ell! On Cracker's Corner!'
'Oh, Dekko ya mean!'
'Yeah, fuckin' Dekko! He's in the chair an' shellin' out like a good 'un!'

'You should 'ave said in the first fuckin' place! I'll get me bloody coat!'

Chapter 8

And so, and as if by magic, the 'Raveller's is soon full to bursting with many characters it hadn't seen for some weeks, months even.

Some are a little shame-faced and awkward as they sidle in, others totally brash and brazen, but all are looking for the self-same thing - a free piss-up.

With his face twitching uncertainly, Jimbo tugs at his wife's sleeve, pulling her to one side. 'You sure we're alright wi' all this?' he asks her again as a veritable army of loud and raucous drinkers rattle and bang their emptied glasses back down onto the bar, baying for more.

'Why? What's the problem?'

'What's the problem?' he repeats. 'Are you serious? Look!'

'Just think,' she hisses, sounding exasperated. 'He'll spend his money somewhere or other and it might as well be in here. No point in keepin' him on a tight leash an' upsettin' him, now is there?'

'No, s'pose not,' Jimbo agrees doubtfully, 'but so long as we don't have to wait too long for him to settle up, that's all.'

'He will, soon enough. You saw the ticket.'

'Yeah, but 'ave you seen his tab? It's over three-hundred and fifty quid already an' there's bugger all in the till to show for it!' worries Jimbo.

'Oi! There's thirsty people here!' interrupts one of the many drinkers now waiting impatiently. 'Get your skates on, yeah?'

'Could cripple us once and for all. Might be weeks he has to wait for his money,' he continues.

'Gaspin' we are!'

'Just shut up and serve, Jim,' Reenie orders him, 'just shut up and serve. I'll not tell you again.'

-

Out on the ring road, the emergency services are out in force with the blues and twos noisily lighting up the cold night sky.

There'd been a car chase. A Renault 5 had hit a barrier and is now mashed up and on its side in the centre of a roundabout.

-

As a still fretful looking Jimbo nods towards the door at yet more new arrivals, Derek, perched atop his barstool, a permagrin fixed upon his face and surrounded by countless people vying for his attention, replies with a magnanimous sweep of his hand. 'Yeah, *yes*, whatever they want, James,' he insists in a put-on plummy accent. 'Just keep it flowin, will ya? Can't ya see I'm in a conversation 'ere!'

And indeed, he is. Well, if you can call being bombarded with questions from all and sundry about what he will do with such a colossal sum of money a conversation that is. He can hardly get a word in edgeways, not that it bothers him. He's simply revelling in it. Besides, the questioners have all the answers. In their minds eye, they already know, already spent it.

Going to buy yourself a lovely new house then, Dekko? Course y'are!
You'll wanna get away from this shit 'ole that's for sure. I would. Get
some o' that money o' yours into bricks an' mortar, that's what I say! ...
Look, word to the wise, they're building some right stonkers up near the
motorway, executive type homes they are ... goin' like hot cakes! I read
about 'em in the Evening Post, there were some pictures in the property
section. Huge they are, ginormous! Gert big stone pillars 'round the
front door wi' them bushes that look like lollipops on a stick on either
side. You know, like the ones you might see in Bath ... very la-di-dah!
Built to a very high standard too, no shit ... an' for a bit extra, you can
get a free fitted kitchen! You know, one o' them with an island in the
middle, an' I'm not talkin' about the Isle o' fuckin' Wight! No, them
where you can sit an' chop yer onions, peel your spuds, whatever, an'
'ave a glass o' your favourite tipple all at the same time! ... Wha'd'ya
think o' that? Fantastic, eh? ... Yes, all the latest mod cons... Double
glazin', security cameras, dimmer switches, you name it, they got it! An'
none of 'em have less than four bedrooms, five, some, with the main one
'en suite'... an' that don't mean they come with a box o' fuckin' Quality
Street neither! Ha! What am I like?! Joke a minute, me! No, that's the
bathroom to the likes o' you an' me, with a proper walk-in shower, not
one o' them useless things on the plugs at the end o' yer bath, I barely
get a dribble out o' mine!... Useless... An' they probably got one of them
bidet whatchamacallits to wash your you-know-what when you're done!
... Disgustin' habit if you ask me. I mean, what's wrong with a bit o' bog
paper, eh? Never did us any harm ... except that Izal shite o' course...
ha! Remember that stuff? Like wipin' yer arse wi' a piece of greaseproof
paper! ... good for tracin' though, when we were kids ... Anyway, where
was I? Yeah, tha' was it... the gardens! Lovely bit o' deckin' 'round the
back they got, you know, for entertainin' an' that, barbecuin', plus a
decent bit o' grass too ... an' a good size considerin' how they squeeze
'em all in nowadays ... besides, you won't wanna spend all your time
mowin' the fuckin' lawn, now will ya? No! Neither would I! Not with all
that dosh! You'll want all your time for livin' it up! Minimal
maintenance, that's what I say! Modern! New! Not damp ol' shit like we
got 'round 'ere an' always summat needin' doin'. I'll tell ya, Dekko, I
can't sing their praises enough. Just go and have a look at the show
home for yerself, you'll be well impressed! ... I'll come along wi' ya if
you like, always love the smell of a fresh bit o' distemper, me. An' by the
way, cheers for the beers, you having another one yourself? ... Yeah?
Top man! I'll stick 'em on yer tab, shall I?

'Yeah, it's an idea innit? A fuck off house,' agrees Derek in
genuine wonderment that he can if he wants to. 'Hadn't thought about it
to be honest, but, yeah, you carry on. Shout 'em out. Jim!'

-

Whilst a team of paramedics stand in as close as they dare, holding a
single saline drip aloft, the Fire Brigade are busy cutting the roof off the
mangled car with powerful hydraulic pincers which, momentarily,
drowns out the groans and cries of pain.

Hey, Dekko, thought about a new motor yet? *I got loads of magazines if ya wanna 'ave a borrow? ... Yeah? No problem ... It's gotta be an Aston Martin though, mate, duncha think? When shit comes to shove, what else is there? ... A Vantage ... rag top ... tha's what I'd 'ave ... no question of a doubt! Top down on a sunny Sunday afternoon, wind in yer hair, what more could you want? Var-oom-bloody-oom! Definitely! An' it's not as if you can't afford one is it, ya lucky sod? Yes, that's what I'd get ... British Racing Green... Quality ... mind you, red if you were to get yourself a Ferrari ... Bloody 'ell! ... Now there's a thought ... with all that money you could easily get yourself a Testarossa too! Shit off a fuckin' shovel, them bastards! ... Decisions, decisions, eh? ... Then there's yer Bentleys an' yer Rollers o' course, can't discount one o' them buggers, now can ya? ... Hey, bollocks to it! You could 'ave one of each! ... An' a top o' the range Merc or a Beamer for yer day to day potterin' about, to the shops an' that. Mind you, what a hoot takin' the Aston to Tesco's. I would! Just for a bag o' doughnuts or summat! That'd show 'em all! ... You could 'ave as many or whatever ya want, couldn't ya? Mind, you'd need a bloody gert big garage to keep 'em all in! Be like that Beaulieu museum ... went there once, motors as far as the eye could see. You wanna take a trip. Petrol 'eads' 'eaven it is! ... And don't forget them big Yankee jobs neither! Fuck me! What d'you call 'em again?... Not a Humber, me Dad had a Humber when I wuz a kid... No, a Hummer! That's them! Awesome! Total respect behind the wheel o' one o' them monsters! Get out of my fuckin' way, ya cunts! Scare the livin' daylights out o' them at the supermarket wi' one o' them! What a laugh! ... Not many miles to the gallon though, none of 'em, but you wouldn't give a flying fuck, would ya?... No ... An' you can ignore all that global warmin' shite an' all! You take a leaf out of that Jeremy Clarkson's book, he don't give a toss! Get yourself a big fat guzzler an' sod the fuckin' planet! You're only 'ere once! ... As it 'appens, I got me own motor outside, an' I'll tell ya, Dekko, she can be a bit thirsty when I give 'er a bit o' the ol' wellie! Two an' a 'alf litre injected see ... front an' rear spoilers, dropped suspension, upgraded shockers, sound system as bassy as fuck, exhaust the size of an elephant's dick! Beautiful! I spent a lot o' time on 'er, I 'ave ... days, weeks, months! It's been a labour o' love! I'll gi' ya a spin in 'er if ya like, bu' ya'd need to buckle up! ... Anyhow, the drinks well appreciated. Your good health. I'll not take advantage though, just a couple more, you can't be too careful can ya, wha' wi' drivin' an' that?*

'Yeah, I could get anythin' I like, couldn't I?' realises Derek, grinning broadly, 'but you just ask Jim, he'll sort you out somethin' for the road, no problem. An' ask 'im if he's got any Polo's while you're about it. You might need 'em if you get stopped by Policeman Plod.'

Some seventy-five yards away from the Renault's final resting place, now illuminated by searingly bright white arc lights, an Accident Report Unit are trying to identify the skid marks and points of collision and marking them out with a tin of yellow spray paint. One of the officers finds a shoe and carefully puts it in a specimen bag. It had been a very serious incident and serious questions would need to be asked.

-

You gonna take a nice holiday then, Dekko? Take my advice, fellah, first thing you'd wanna do ... give yerself time to think. Yeah? Tell ya what, you got family, why don't ya take the kids to Disneyland? Be great, that. I would wi' mine. The one in Florida is best. Better than bloody Paris ... not only would ya be sure of the weather, but they don't speak all that froggie French neither! Bloody 'ho-hee-hon' all the time! Gobble-de-fuckin'-gook if you ask me! ... Oh yes, my nippers, love that they would - Donald Duck, Mickie Mouse, Plato ... all of 'em, just wanderin' about large as life they are, meetin' an' greetin'! Some o' the real littl'uns can get right freaked out, mind. Happened to a mate o' mine, his little lad pissed himself standin' next to Dumbo with his fuck off ears! It's all the excitement see. Christ, they must sweat to high heaven in them costumes, the poor bastards! Still, you know what they say? Disney's for kids of all ages! You'd have a right laugh! And apparently, they got some lovely hotels on site too, all included ... but that reminds me, don't get caught by them there mini bars though. Steep or what! Our sister's neighbour got charged the over seven fuckin' quid for one o' them tiny cans o' lager an' a bar o' peanut brittle! Rip off or what!? She 'ad no bleedin' idea, the daft bint! Thought it was free! Not that you'd be bothered. You could eat an' drink the lot an' not even think about it. Small change to the likes 'o you now, innit? So, your tab, still open is it? Parched, as a budgies cage I am.

'Yeah, I'll definitely be takin' the kids away somewhere, sure as eggs are eggs,' says Derek, throwing his head back and laughing uproariously. 'But you carry on. You wet your whistle, mate!'

-

Tragically, with one body already removed, strapped and covered onto a stretcher and in the back of one of the waiting ambulances, a second young lad is being eased out of the vehicle and onto a PAT Slide, his neck in a brace, unconscious, whilst, clattering overhead, a police helicopter is scouring the area, it's probing searchlight seeking out a third, who, miraculously, had managed to extricate himself from the carnage and done a runner.

-

Dekko! Ever thought of moving abroad? I don't mind sayin' we 'ave, me an' the missus. I'll tell ya, you can lead the Life o' Reilly down on the Costas, me ol' mucker - Blanko, Bravo, Sole ... Dogger, German Bight. Yeah? You got it... Not only 'ave they got all that lovely sunshine, but decent pubs and proper English grub too! None of that foreign muck... An' there ain't too many Spaniards left there to bugger it up neither. No, it's mostly just us good ol' Brits... OK, I'll grant ya, you do get the occasional Kraut nickin' all the sunbeds an' the odd Swede, but that aside we go there as often as we can. Yes! Love it there we do. And here's the thing, you... YOU!... could easily afford one o' them serious fuck-off type villas. You know the ones, big bastards wi' their own swimmin' pool. Lovely places they are, all painted white, tiled roofs, marble floors, shutters for your siesta in the afternoon, although I can never work the buggers... No, shangri-bloody-la it is! ... An' flowers everywhere! Beautiful! Wha' do they call 'em? ... Bougainvilleas! That's them!... An' that Jasmine! Stinks to high heaven that does! What a pong! 'Specially at night!... Goes straight to her head it does, the missus, when she catches a whiff. Like a bitch on heat she goes! You don't believe me, do ya? I 'ave to stick her in a cold shower, I do ... I do! Tie her down! Honest! You wouldn't credit it, lookin' at her, would ya? No, that's where we'd live - Spain - definitely - you wouldn't see us for dust! ... Don't agree wi' that bullfightin' though, do you? No! ... Cruel bastards! ... We went to that Ronda once, hell of a ring that is. We had a bite to eat there once, a toasted sandwich an' a jug o' sangria sat above this valley. Funny that, don't ya think? Ronda in Spain 'avin' a valley? Like Rhondda but spelt different. We did. Laugh! Yakky-dah! Us bloody Welsh boyos get everywhere, don't we? ... Yeah ... we like that sangria we do. To be fair, it's only a bit o' red plonk an' lemonade with a bit o' fruit an' veg thrown in for good measure, but fuck me, does it pack a punch! Olé! You could kill a fuckin' bull yerself after a few pints o' that stuff!... But right now, Dekko, me ol' mate, me ol' pal, I'd 'appily settle for another Scrumpy Jack. That alright wi' you?

'Yeah, wakin' up every day to bit o' sun would be nice,' Derek thinks aloud but already slurring heavily. 'I'm sure Jimbo's got a bit o' wine lurkin' about somewhere or another, an' plenty o' lemonade. Ask 'im. He'll do you an' ya missus one. Tell 'im I said.'

-

In the grounds of an industrial estate, a police dog, an Alsatian, is in hot pursuit of the escapee, his handler holding on tight to the leash with another bringing up the rear, panting and breathless. Simultaneously, with its lights full on and flashing but siren turned off, the first of the ambulances is leaving the scene.

-

So then, Dekko, what about gettin' yourself a nice dolly bird, eh? You'll have no trouble there, ya dirty ol' dog, you! You can fill yer size tens there, no bother, what wi' all that money! I should bloody co-co! They'll be 'round ya like flies 'round cow's arse, you mark my words! Yes, by buggery they will! An' there's some right corka's from Eastern Europe let me tell ya - Russia an' that! Wha'd they call it? ... Ukraine. Tha's it. You wanna see 'em! Phwoar! Legs right up to their 'airy bleedin' armpits! ... Not that that bothers me. You? No? I like a bit o' natural. me! Gimme the ol' short an' curlies any day o' the week! Mind you, them Orientals lop it all off though, don't they? Clean as a whistle so I've seen ... only pictures an' that! ... I'm not a perv nor nuthin'! Yeah, I always enjoy a Chinkie on Friday night! Ha! Listen to me! ... A bit o' sweet an' sour, a bit o' crispy duck! ... Even daft ol' bastards, ugly fucks like me, come away with some right stunnas. And they're taught how to please men, not like your average British bird lyin' back an' thinkin' o' fuckin' England! No, not on your nellie! Wash you with their fannies they do, the 'airy ones! I saw a video! Scrub-a-dub-dub, three men in a tub! Straight up! You don't believe me do ya? I'm tellin' ya, I've seen blokes even 'round 'ere walking about wi' 'em on their arm. You must 'ave seen 'em! Shagged out they are, the poor fuckers ... but 'appy though! Talk about the cat who got all the fuckin' cream! ... But you'd wanna get one of them pre-nuptials though, see a solicitor an' that. They'll fleece ya good an' proper given 'alf a chance. It's the passport they're really after, see. But hey, 'ave a bit o' fun in the process, tha's wha' I say. I'm what you call a silver surfer, see. I've done me homework. There's thousands on the internet, millions probably. But I'll have to give it a rest, I'm giving meself the bleedin' horn 'ere just thinkin' about it! ... Ha!... thirsty work though, don't ya think? All that pussy? Bu' I don't wanna be greedy nor nuthin', just another Stella'll do for me. You good wi' that, Dekko? You gotta push the boat out, me ol' son, ain't ya? Tonight of all nights?

'You're not wrong. I could do wi' a bit o' female company,' drawls Derek with exaggerated lasciviousness, 'but you carry on, mate. You fill ya size tens.'

-

The dog is now barking furiously at a row of wheelie bins where, tucked in behind, they find the third occupant cowering - his head covered with a large piece of sodden cardboard in a ridiculous attempt to conceal himself, his legs and feet sticking out, one trainer missing, clearly visible in the powerful torchlight.

As the police move in to pull him out, he doesn't put up any resistance, practically gives himself up in fact. He is in a state of shock with blood covering his face and jacket from a sizeable gash to his scalp and holding his arm awkwardly.

-

And, finally, there were the inevitable come-ons.

You and Marion still living apart then, Derek? *- Yeah? I heard. Your ex will be kickin' 'erself now, won't she? Silly cow. Still, must have been everso hard for you after all them years together, bringin' up a family an' that, gettin' your house all nice an' the way you want it ... an' then what? Poof! You poor, poor, thing you ... but not poor with all that money! No, I'm not sayin' that! Just 'avin' the rug pulled out from under your feet, that's what I mean. But life carries on ya know. I been there meself, splittin' up. Havin' said that, best thing I ever done to be honest. Right bastard he turned out to be ... No, reckon I'd better pull me finger out an' get me skates on if I'm gonna stand any chance wi' a handsome man of means like you ... Ha! What must you think o' me?! I'm not a gold digger nor nuthin' ... But seriously, you can come 'round any time, for a coffee an' that? ... No, <u>no</u>! Not 'that'! ... I'm diggin' a right hole for meself 'ere, ain't I? What must you think? Fur coat an' no knickers, eh?... Stop it! Besides, I got me M&S's on tonight! Best place, so they say. But, seriously, the offers there if you want, Dekko. You know where I live ... the doors always open if you get lonely or anythin'... I tell ya*

what, I'll knock you up somethin' to eat if ya like. Way to a man's heart
so they say, don't they? Bit o' grub? I do a mean pasta I do, all the
shapes an' sizes – curly ones, them shells, and I do me own Bisto ...
what am I talkin' about?! Idiot! I meant pesto! I make me own pesto! *...*
Listen to me, tipsy I am already thanks to you, you naughty boy! ...
Anyhow, the offers there, you gotta keep your strength up, fine figure of
a man like you. And remember, none of us a getting any younger, are
we? Come on, give us a great big cuddle, you lovely, lovely man!
Anyway, don't suppose you'd like to get a girl another vodka and tonic
if she asked nicely, would ya? ... Yeah? Course you would. An 'ouse
double 'ould go down a treat as you're so flush. Got to help you
celebrate ain't we, my luvver?

'Yeah, I might take you up on that,' says Derek, unable to take his
eyes from her thrusting her bosom, 'you can have a bloody treble if you
want, love! 'Ere, Jimbo, look lively! There's a lady waitin' over 'ere!'

-

Sound asleep in their bed, Marion and Nigel are disturbed by a late-night
phone call.

'Who the hell's that at this time?' moans Nigel, flicking the bedside
light on and looking at the alarm clock. 'It's gone midnight!'

'How should I know?' says Marion, picking it up.

'Well?' he asks.

She covers the receiver. 'It's the police,' she says.

Nigel tuts, rubbing his eyes with the palms of both hands. 'What's
he been up to now?' he asks.

'He's been hurt,' she whispers, ashen faced, her lips trembling.
'He's on his way to hospital right now. Southmead.'

-

Ding-Ding!
It's well after time when Jimbo finally rings the bell. 'Drink up plee-
ease!' he yells only to be met by a wall of boos and jeers. 'No, no, no!
Fun's over!' he repeats. 'Tha's yer lot!'

'Ah, fuck off, Jim, ya wet fuckin' blanket, ya!'!' remonstrates
Derek, thoroughly sozzled and almost entirely unintelligible. 'It's only
just got started!'

'Gimme a break, mate. There's fuck all in the cellar as it is.
You've almost drunk the place out!'

'But I wanna stay 'ere! This is where I belong!'

Jimbo pauses for a moment. 'Look, just sit tight, yeah?' he says
conspiratorially. 'You an' Phil can 'ave a couple more after I clear this
lot out.'

'Is the right answer!' slurs Derek, relaxing at the thought.

'Time for ya beds! Off ya go!' Jimbo then continues to shout.

-

'Right, come on!' says Nigel, urgently jumping out of bed and throwing
on some clothes. 'Let's get you over there, like now.'

'We're on our way,' she says before putting the phone down.

'What's he done?'

71

'Car accident.'

'Car accident? Is he alright?'

'I'll have to call Dekko.'

'At this time? He'll be in no fit state,' dissuades Nigel, hurriedly buttoning his shirt.

'But he needs to know,' she says, beginning to cry.

'Just tell the girls. They'll wonder where we are. They're what's more important right now.'

-

As the vast majority sup the last of their drinks and slowly start to make their way out, a couple of the local constabulary make an unwelcome appearance in the doorway, their towering presence a sudden and sobering influence as they make their way in against the flow of blind drunk and tipsy people on their way out. 'Busy night tonight, landlord?' observes the more senior of the two and tapping his wrist to his non-existent watch.

'They're all just leaving. I'm clearin' 'em,' says a now panic stricken Jimbo as he rapidly begins to clatter pint pots together in the grip of his stubby fingers. They're in for it and he knows it. He and Reenie had already been put on a warning when they'd had dealers on the premises and told in no uncertain terms to clean up their act. Surreptitiously, he turns to Derek and Phil. 'Another time, lads, yeah? Sorry,' he says before hurrying back down the bar to collect more glasses.

'Ere, I ain't finished that!' complains one old soak who hadn't seen the police looming up behind him but had been keeping his head down in hope, his innate sixth sense telling him that there was definitely a lock-in in the offing.

'Oh yes you have,' says Jimbo, snatching the last of his drink and pouring it down the sink.

'Oi! I paid...,' then correcting himself, 'Dekko's paid good money for that,' he complains as, unseen, the older policeman moves in close, bends forward, and speaks gently into his ear. 'I'd listen to what's being said if I was you, sir,' he advises.

Spinning on his stool, the old sot finds himself confronted with a row of shiny buttons and the hiss and crackle of a two-way radio. 'As I was saying, Jim,' he says, immediately playing the game, 'I'd love to stay, but I must be on me way.'

With that, an equally worried looking Reenie then appears. 'Sorry about this, officers. It's a bit of one off you see,' she starts to explain.

'Oh, yes?' says the constable, disbelieving.

'Yes. As you know, we always like to run a tight ship here at the Travellers, but Derek here, a very old and valued customer of ours,' she says, pointing, 'he's had great reason to celebrate.'

'Oh really, why's that? Won the lottery, has he?' jokes the younger PC sarcastically.

'Yeah!' sputters Derek, laughing. 'How d'ya know? Is nuthin' a secret?'

'What? You?' questions the copper, momentarily backfooted.

'Tha's wha' I said.'

'Tonight's rollover, you mean?'

'Yep. All eleven million, four hundred, no, three hundred. What was it again, Phil?'

After a second or two as they take it in, the older policeman continues. 'Please accept our congratulations, sir,' he says convivially enough, 'but as they say, rich or poor, the laws the law. So, as you've just been asked, it's time you were on your way.'

'Tell ya what,' tries Derek, 'how about I buy you both a couple of vodkas each an' you can forget all about it.'

'Dekko! Please! Stop! They're on duty!' Reenie speaks over him. 'We'll see you in the morning, yes?'

'How about a couple of hundred quid each then? To keep schtum?'

'We'll ignore you said that, sir.'

'Five 'undred then!'

'Let's just get you on your way, shall we?'

Derek then attempts to stand, his legs buckling beneath him. 'Hey, Phil! We could always bugger off into town!' he suggests as he falls back down onto his stool. 'There's always somewhere open. Bound to be!'

'I don't think you should be going anywhere, sir, other than to your bed,' advises the constable before reaching forward to take his arm.

'Oi! Get off me! I'll do wha' I like! None o' your business!'

'I think you'll find it is, sir. Drunk and disorderly, an arrestable offence. You've had enough.'

'You my dad all of a sudden?!'

'We're asking you nicely,' he says, now taking Derek more firmly.

'Oi, I told ya, get your hands off me! I ain't done nuthin, ya wanker!'

'And watch your language too, or we'll nick you for breach of the peace too,' adds the younger copper as they both now turn him and point him towards the door.

'Ow! Police fuckin' brutality!' shouts Derek. 'You're breaking me bastard arm, ya' fuckin gorillas!'

'That's your last warning!'

'Come on, Dekko, do us a favour, mate,' pleads Jimbo. 'Please!'

'An' thanks for fuck all to you too!' Derek then shouts at him. 'I know where I'm not fuckin' wanted!'

'Don't be silly, Derek,' says Reenie, 'you're always welcome.'

'Yeah, right! You're just after me fuckin' money! I know your game!'

'Shut up, Dekko!' says Phil, now jumping in. 'Look, I'll take him home right now. He'll be as good as gold, promise,' he tries to reassure them all.

'Make sure as you do then, sir,' instructs the senior policeman, 'or else.'

But Derek isn't finished. 'Me lottery ticket! I want me lottery ticket!' he demands, the sound of his mobile phone going off in his pocket.

'Leave it, Dekko! It'll be alright left 'ere. Jimbo's got it locked up safe and sound. We'll see you tomorrow, guys,' Phil bids them goodbye as, unsteadily, he guides Derek out.

-

With Nigel driving, Marion is still on her mobile. 'He's not answering,' she says.

'Now there's a surprise,' says Nigel. 'You're wasting your time, love.'

'But I have to keep trying. He needs to know!'

-

As the cold night air hits them, and with Derek reeling, the two men almost fall down the steps.

'That would o' been a great fuckin' way of spending your first night as a millionaire, ya lairy arse, banged up in the cells an' pissin' in a bucket!' says Phil as the clatter of a helicopter's rotor blades can be clearly heard somewhere above. 'After some poor bastard, I expect,' he observes.

'So, where's your motor?' Derek asks.

'Give it a rest, Dekko! With the rozzers in there? You out o' your tiny mind?'

'Thought we were going into town?'

'It's stayin right here where it is. An' no, we ain't. Ain't you had enough already?'

'As it 'appens, no,' says Derek, belching. 'Reckon the Offie might still be open?'

'You seen what time it is?'

'No.'

'It's gone half past twelve, ya wazzock!' Phil says, then, hesitantly, adding, 'look, I think I got a bottle o' red from last Christmas and best parts of a bottle o' whiskey at home. You can come back if you promise to behave.'

Derek turns to his friend with a great big grin. He doesn't need to be asked twice. Moreover, he doesn't want to be left alone. 'I love you, I do,' he says and attempting to give him a kiss.

-

'He's bloody useless, that bloody ex o' mine,' says Marion, 'never there when you need him, ever!'

'Don't worry, I'm here now,' says Nigel. 'We'll be there shortly.'

-

With Derek holding on to his mate for support, the pair of them stagger up the alleyways into the back of a cul-de-sac and, upon opening the Phil's back gate, they can clearly see his house is in complete darkness.

'Quiet as a mouse, d'ya hear me. They're all sparko,' instructs Phil whilst fumbling for his keys, snagging on a loose thread in his trouser pocket lining.

'Still OK though, ain't we?'

'Yeah, course,' he answers uncertainly as he snaps his fob free, ripping a hole and allowing some loose change to spill out and down the inside of his trouser leg, tinkling out onto the path.

'There's one just there by yer foot!' says Derek, overloud and setting the next-door neighbour's dog off. 'Fifty pee piece!'

'Shut up, Dekko!' says Phil as he slides the key around the lock, trying to locate the hole. 'Bloody animal!'

'I'll take me boots off if ya like,' offers Derek, but still eyeing the ground for lost coins - old habits dying hard.

-

'No wonder our Jez is such a little tearaway,' Marion continues as Nigel pulls into the car park of the A&E department, 'with a waste o' space dad like that.'

'Here we are,' Nigel announces unnecessarily.

'I do hope he's OK?'

'To be honest, Marion, I don't really care.'

'I beg your pardon?' she asks, uptight and incredulous.

'You were talking about Dekko...'

'No. Jez!'

'Sorry.'

'Do you ever listen? There's a spot there, just over by the entrance!'

-

As Phil creeps in, closely followed by Derek and like a pair of hapless housebreakers, they are suddenly illuminated by the landing light as Betsy stands atop the stairs in dark silhouette, hands on hips, her form clearly visible through her nightie. 'Oh, come on Phil! Not again! It's much too late,' she complains. 'You'll wake the kids.'

'But love, listen, you don't understand,' says Phil, stuttering.

'No buts, you're pissed, both of ya, and I got an early start tomorrow. Work. Remember?'

'Betsy, will ya listen to me?' Phil tries again.

'Not tonight, Derek. Sorry.'

'Betsy! He's gone and won the bloody lottery, tonight's jackpot!' says Phil.

'No-o,' she resonds, putting her hand up to her neck in disbelief.

'So, look, we'll keep it down. You won't even know we're here, OK?'

'Really, Dekko? Have you, love? The rollover?'

'Yeah Bets, looks like it,' he says, trying very hard to sound as coherent as possible.

'Much?

'Eleven million, three ... What was it again, Phil?'

'Eleven million,' repeats Betsy. 'Bloody hell, in that case I think I might have to come and join you.'

'You've changed yer tune all of a sudden!' says her husband. 'What about your early start?'

'I'll put something on,' she simply replies.

'Yeah, I would if I was you,' says her husband, 'you can see your knickers an' everything through that.'

'Phil!' she squeals, quickly turning on her heels. 'Stop it!'

-

'Take this,' instructs Marion, handing Nigel a carrier bag.

'What's that?'

'What do you think?'

Nigel shrugs.

'Toothbrush, pants, clean shirt. You men really are useless.'

-

Within no time at all, Betsy comes downstairs having thrown on a dress and brushed her hair, splashed her face. 'So, what you going to do with all that money then, Dekko?' she asks him almost immediately.

'Dunno, love, just enjoy it I s'pose, buy some shit.'

'I know what I'd do.'

'Don't you start,' Phil stops her. 'The world an' 'is wife 'ave been givin' 'im their opinions tonight, and you know what they say 'bout opinions duncha?'

'I know, I know! No need to be crude! I was only asking. It's, you know, exciting, just thinking about it.'

'She's alright, Phil. I quite enjoy bein' asked to be honest,' says Derek, eyeing the bottle of whiskey that his friend has in his hand. 'There's been some good ideas. House, car, 'olidays, you know the type o' thing.'

'S'up to you. Anyway, we got any decent glasses in this place, Bets?' asks Phil.

'In the cupboard. You'll have to watch yourself, Dekko, whatever,' she continues. 'You'll have all sorts crawling out of the woodwork, you mark my words. I was reading about it. So, how much was it again you say,' she enquires, wanting to hear the words again.

'Christ Almighty! Eleven million, three hundred and fifty-five thousand,' says Phil, trying to shut her up.

'I wouldn't mind the three hundred and fifty-five!' says Betsy. 'There's some tumblers in the back of the cupboard, Phil. That's a fortune alone, Dekko!'

'Reckon I might o' spent that in the pub tonight, Bets,' he says, laughing about the very idea of it.

'I can see,' she agrees, laughing in return. 'Still, I don't blame you for celebrating, not under the circumstances.'

'Where are they?' asks Phil. 'Can't see a bloody thing.'

'Come out the way,' she says, going over. 'Look, there, right under your nose.'

'And where's that bottle o' wine we had?

'Out on top of the boiler. Give them here, I'll give them a rinse.'

Right then, a phone goes off once again. 'It's yours, Dekko,' says Betsy, 'it's coming from your jacket.'

Derek pulls it out, looks at it for a few seconds, then switches it off.

'Someone on the cadge already?' asks Phil knowingly.

'Who d'ya think?' Derek groans.

'Ah.'

'Look, loads o' missed calls from her - surprise, surprise.'

'Word travels fast, eh?'

'Yeah, but she'll be getting' jack shit from me, if you'll excuse me French.'

Chapter 9
Sunday

The following morning, Derek wakes with the mother of all hangovers - confused, too, to find himself sprawled out on a settee in a dark and unfamiliar room, a child's Teenage Mutant Ninja Turtles duvet wrapped around his legs, his jacket rolled up under his head as a makeshift pillow, an empty bottle of whiskey still held tight in his grasp.

As a rule, he didn't get hangovers, but he'd broken the golden rule, hadn't he? The muppet. The grape and the grain and all that. And bloody Teachers - always the bane of his life!

But that said, strangely, weirdly, he can't help but feel wonderfully elated too and for a few short seconds he couldn't quite suss it out ... but then the penny dropped ... big time!

Ker-bloody-PLUNK!

He'd won the Lottery, hadn't he?

Yeah!

The bloody LOTTERY!

And this was Phil's house.

He remembered it all now!

Phil's, and he'd won fucking millions!

So, despite his face creasing up with a ball of pain centred just behind his left eye socket, together with the excruciating stabbing sensations in his upper gut, he manages to pull on his boots (odd, as he didn't remember taking them off), throw on his jacket, and hurriedly slips out the back door, stopping only to bend down and pick up two or three coins glinting invitingly in the early morning light.

-

Detlef Otto, too, is already up and about and rummaging in his loft. He needed to retrieve his suitcase but is also searching out an old and battered Huntley and Palmers biscuit tin.

Finding it, he eases the lid and prises it open. Inside, on the top, there is a stack of old letters tied together with the now faded blue ribbon, the one that Ellen had given him all those years ago on the pier in Weston-Super-Mare. He'd always kept it in his wallet, well, up until his second marriage, he had. Untying it, he picks up the letters, riffling the edges as if they were a deck of playing cards, ashamed to see the unmistakable but fleeting glimpse of one or two that were clearly stamped HMP Horfield or 'Return to Sender' in amongst them.

Underneath and loose in the bottom, he paws through some of his other keepsakes and fingers them each in turn as if they were priceless museum artefacts, offering them to his nose, smelling their mustiness and remembering - a couple of 'lucky' pebbles with holes in them threaded onto a piece of string and some sadly disintegrating seashells, a few old British coins, a key to a door, old bus and train tickets, a house rental agreement marked 'Deposit Paid', a frilly garter, a knitted baby's bonnet, and a half a dozen or so small black and white photos of

Ellen and Derek as a babe in arms, and, the one he was looking for in particular, that of him cradling his son, proud and beaming.

Directly below, down in the bedroom, Gisella is busying herself laying out his freshly ironed clothes. 'Detlef?' she calls. 'Are you still up there?'

'Here, I have it,' he says, shaken from his reverie and quickly slipping the ribbon into his pocket along with the baby's bonnet, sliding the photos into his wallet.

'Hurry up then,' she says rather tetchily. 'We're not nearly finished as yet.'

And it was true. Early tomorrow morning, Detlef is due fly to Bristol in England, and he can ill afford to dwell. There was more to be done.

Gingerly, he lowers the case back down through the hatch and onto the ladder. 'Can you take this, my love?' he asks.

'What did your last slave die of?' she replies with continued and uncharacteristic sharpness as she slips a pair of his highly polished shoes into a cloth bag.

-

Back in Bristol, down by the steep and glutinous banks of the River Avon, the cold and dreary weather is taking a turn for the worse despite the pale and insipid sun trying it's damnedest to break through.

In stark contrast, inside Packet Café, it is brightly lit and so warm that the large plate glass windows are all but covered in condensation such that the towering masts of the S.S. Great Britain directly over the road and on the opposite bank appear broken and twig-like through the rivulets that run down and collect in mercury like pools on the gloss white painted sills.

It's eight o'clock on the dot and PG, dressed incongruously in his ubiquitous country tweeds and cravat, his notebook and pen at the ready, is sitting across a Formica topped table from a tall and rangy man dressed in counterfeit Adidas sports gear and a knocked off pair of genuine Nike trainers. 'Can I get you a little something, Clappie?' he asks as he meticulously butters a piece of toast.

'Just a can o' coke'll do me, ta,' says Clappie in reply, slightly taken aback by PG's atypical generosity.

'Heavy night?' he asks as he clicks his fingers towards the woman behind the coffee machine

'No, not at all! I just don't do breakfast, tha's all. Don't go on already, yeah?'

'Very silly. Anyway, to business. What's to report?' PG continues as if it were of great concern to him, which it is not. Chicken feed in fact. It's just what he does, that's all. He's been holding these various little meetings of his over a bite to eat with various gofers, minions, and minders since the early days - usually breakfast, sometimes lunch or, rarely, an afternoon tea. He simply likes to keep his finger on the pulse, on the off chance, and this particular meeting was about to reveal a very juicy morsel indeed. 'Everything ship shape and Bristol fashion, I trust?' he asks, his standard presumptive question and before turning his attention to the ceramic teapot, cup, and saucer.

'Yeah, I've sold a bit,' reassures Clappie, 'got most o' the money in.'

'Good. Make sure you get the rest. Tell them there's interest to be paid. Ten per cent per day, compounded.'

'Yeah, yeah. I know! But, first of all, you'll never guess what?'

'No, probably not,' replies PG, pouring the milk, 'give me a clue.'

At that moment, the woman brings Clappie his can of drink together with a glass and places it in front of him. 'Cheers,' he says before pulling the ring and drinking straight from the tin.

'I do wish you wouldn't do that,' chastises PG.

'What?'

PG nods towards the glass. 'We're not apes, you know,' he says.

Dutifully, Clappie pours the rest out. 'Pardon me for breathin'!' he apologises.

'So, you were saying?'

'Yeah, last night,' Clappie picks up the thread, 'I was out walking me bitches, see.'

Melodramatically, PG grabs the edges of the table. 'Are you trying your hand at a bit of pimping, dear chap?' he says and pretending to look aghast.

'Bloody Hell, PG! Me greyhounds! Dogs an' bitches ain't the same thing!'

'Aren't they?'

'No. An' you 'ave to give 'em a good run every night. It's a must wi' racin' dogs, after they've eaten.'

'Please spare me the lesson in canine husbandry, Clappie. Just get to the point.'

'I will if you'll gi' me a bloody chance! ... So, I was just headin' home when I bumped into this bloke I know. In a right hurry he was, on his way to the pub.'

'Really?' says PG, now continuing with his air of sarcastic indifference. 'A man hurrying to the pub, eh? Whatever next?'

'Give it a rest! An' I'd 'ave gone there meself if it wasn't for the girls. They don't let 'em in, see, an' they howl something chronic if I leave 'em alone outside.'

PG rolls his eyes, stirring the pot to enhance the flavour.

'Anyhow, you've heard me mention Derek Dando, ain't ya? You know, people call 'im Dekko?'

PG taps his notebook but doesn't need to look. 'Much to my chagrin,' he says.

'Your 'sha' what? Swallowed a dictionary again, 'ave ya?'

'Imbecile.'

'Won't tell ya then!'

'Just spit it out.'

'Right. He had a pair of them boots off us just recently?' says Clappie, looking to confirm. 'Yeah?'

'Yes, yes, I know who you mean. I make it my business to know - a dipsomaniac and frequenter of the Traveller's Public House, I believe.'

'Yeah, that's 'im.'

'The one in downtown Beirut as I like to call it.'

'Oi! I live thereabouts too! It ain't as bad as people make out!'

PG waves his hand by way of an insincere apology.

'We ain't all hoity-toity like you in your leafy suburbs, PG. But you got 'im alright, that's Dekko,' says Clappie, allowing himself a chuckle. 'Right piss 'ead. Drinks for England he does.'

'So, has he not settled for that dreadful footwear as yet?'

'No, but I don't think you'll have any problems when I tell ya!' says Clappie now looking genuinely animated and excited.

'How so?' says PG, taking a little more interest.

'Well,' hushes Clappie, leaning in over the table, 'he's gone and won the bleedin' lottery, ain't he!'

'Much?'

'Too bloody right! Eleven million plus, or so I heard.'

PG picks up the teaspoon, tinkling it on the rim of the cup. 'Mmm, interesting,' he acknowledges. 'Nice one, Clappie. Well done.'

'Thought you'd be pleased,' he says, now jiggling his leg like one of his hounds having her belly scratched.

'You'll have to fix it for me to meet him properly then, won't you?'

'A fool and his money, eh? I can see where you're goin' with this, PG,' says Clappie, winking and tapping his nose. 'Great minds, eh?'

PG ignores the comment. 'Just tell him I've got something for him, a nice little gift to celebrate his good fortune. I'll think of something. Let him have the boots gratis too. That means for free. All you have to do is get him to me. Do you think you could manage that?'

'Is the Pope a Catholic? Do bears shit in the woods?'

'Please! I'll also thank you to keep your crude metaphors to yourself.'

'There you go again, meta what?'

'Just do as I ask.'

'OK, OK, I'll do me best,' he says, guzzling back the last of his drink. 'So, any chance of that bit o' brekkie you offered then? I'm feelin' proper hungry now.'

'You know where the counter is, Clappie,' says PG before opening his book and peering down over his spectacles. 'But before you do, let's get down to other business, shall we? How much money do you have for me? Cash.'

-

Understandably, things had been very stressful for Gisella and Detlef, the treatment for his illness almost the least of their concerns. There had been their daughter, Renata, to consider. She had needed to be told about it, and much more besides.

Detlef had only ever spoken of his war years, his first marriage, the birth of his son, and the subsequent disastrous turn of events to Gisella, and had done so shortly after they'd met. He didn't want any secrets between them, but neither did he want his past to overshadow the rest of their lives and had asked that the subject not be mentioned again. She'd agreed, somehow believing that they were then free to forge a new and seemingly uncluttered future together and, over the years, they'd barely spoken of it again.

As a result, and quite shamefully for them both, Renata had grown up oblivious to the truth and never having any reason to consider herself anything other than an only child and the sole recipient of her parent's doting adoration. *'Du bist der Apfel meines Auges'* her father would continue to say to her to this very day.

However, with his illness now inexorably driving the agenda, and the desperate search for his son about to begin, he simply could not hide it from her any longer.

He was not looking forward to it.

It would hit her like a bombshell.

-

As hugely elated as he feels, Derek is exhausted and still suffering such that, upon his return home, he crawls back into bed and promptly falls into a fitful sleep. It is not until midday that he finally re-awakes.

Still in discomfort, he reaches for his phone and switches it back on. Immediately he can see that he'd missed loads of calls and texts from all over - Marion mostly, but also Phil, Dave, the pub, and a fair few from numbers and names he doesn't recognise or had long forgotten.

He rolls himself a cigarette and lights up. He knows he needs to get his winning ticket safely back in his hand and, as a starter for ten, he calls the pub.

-

They'd invited their daughter and Oskar, her husband, over for lunch shortly after they'd received the news about Detlef's leukaemia and, intentionally, when they knew the grandchildren were out of the way and staying with Oskar's parents.

As ever, Gisella had prepared a delicious meal for them all, but Detlef could not enjoy it. He simply had no appetite and terrified about the potential consequences of what was about to unfold.

Sat directly opposite him over the dining table, Renata had looked very concerned and had questioned him. 'Are you alright, Papa?' she'd asked. 'You've hardly touched your food.'

'I know,' he'd said. 'I'm sorry, but I'm a little preoccupied.'

'Oh? Really? What about?'

This was it. It was now or never.

'Papa, you are worrying me. Tell me, what is it?'

'There are some things we need to talk about,' he'd said, swallowing hard, his mouth at once dry. 'There is no easy way to say this but, firstly, I have to tell you, I have been to the hospital,' he begins.

'Traveller's,' says Jimbo's voice.

'It's me, Jimbo. Dekko.'

''Bout bloody time. Did ya get me text?'

'Just got up.'

'Lazy bastard. Thought you'd be down here crack o' sparras,
make sure Reen and I hadn't legged it wi' your ticket.'

'You'd better not! I'd track ya down!'

'Don't be daft. Anyway, you've got a right fan club down 'ere.
'Ave a listen,' says Jimbo, holding up the phone for people to shout and
jeer.

'Who's there then?'

'Loads, everybody, and hey, we got a right roastin' cos' o' you, ya
silly sod.'

'What?'

'Them coppers, remember?'

'Vaguely,' Derek lies.

'An' somebody tried to break in last night too, tried to force the
back window, lucky they scarpered when I hit the lights. Thought it was
you for a moment. Wasn't, was it?'

'What the fuck you on about?'

'Just get down here and get your ticket will ya? I'll be glad to see
the back of it, it's a bloody liability.'

'Give us half an hour. Mine's a pint.'

'He's gonna be half an hour,' Jimbo calls over his shoulder.

'Tell 'im he's late on parade, fuckin' lightweight!' Derek can hear
one voice call out.

'Yeah, blotto on the fuckin' lotto!' shouts another, laughing.

''Ere, ask 'im if his tab's still open!' demands yet another.

'D'ya hear all that?' asks Jimbo.

'Yeah, fuckin' idiots. So how much do I owe ya?'

'I'll show you when you get down here, you might need to sit
down.'

'Why? I can afford it.'

'I know, I know. And, hey, before you go, your Marion's been after
ya an' all. She even called by earlier, right upset she was.'

'Yeah, thought she might be.'

'She'll be on to you now, Dekko, you mark my words.'

'She can go swing. Look, I'll be there shortly, OK?' says Derek
hitting the off button.

It had been a huge amount of information for anyone to take in in such a
large and single dose, overload in fact, and Renata had suffered what
could only be described as a panic attack such was her disbelief and
level of distress, crying and hyperventilating. 'You were married to
someone else?' she'd cried, clasping her hands to her face and pulling
her eyes slant down either side in horror. 'And you tell me I have a
brother? An older brother?'

'Yes, I was, and you do,' her father had repeated shamefacedly.

'And you knew about this all along, Mama!' she'd shouted, addressing her equally distraught looking mother.

'Oh, Renata, please try to understand,' she'd started to explain and trying to reach out, only to be rebuffed and forcibly pushed away.

'Renata, please! It is not your mother's fault! I asked her not to talk of it. It is me you must blame, not her!' pleaded Detlef.

'I don't care! How could you? How could you both?!'

-

Within seconds of putting the phone down to the Traveller's, it starts ringing. It's Dave.

'Dave,' he answers.

'Hey, Dekko, it's Dave.'

'I know, I just said that. What can I do you for?'

'I'm down the pub an' just heard your fantastic news!'

'Yeah. Pretty good, innit?'

'Looks like I missed out on a fuckin' good night, ya lucky git!'

'Should o' been down there then, shouldn't ya?'

'Got tied up, you know how it is. No, I just wanted to offer me congratulations, that's all. You comin' down?'

'Didn't Jimbo just tell ya?'

'No. I'm in the car park 'avin' a crafty smoke.'

'Ah, thought as much. So, if you get off the fuckin' phone and give me half a chance, I'll be there.'

'OK, but before ya go, I just thought we might, you know, 'ave a chat, on the QT like, somewhere quiet, when you get here.'

'What for?'

'Hold up a minute, there's a fuckin' lorry.'

Derek can hear what sounds like a large wagon rumbling past.

'Bleedin' lorries on a Sunday morning! Look, to cut a long story short, me ol' chuffer, I'm onto something an' wondered whether you might be able to help?'

'Help wi' what?'

'Cash-wise.'

'Fuckin' 'ell, Dave, I ain't got the bleedin money yet!'

'I know, but when ya do, I was wonderin' if you could bung us a couple o' grand?'

'A couple of grand?'

'It's important.'

'What for?'

'Business.'

'What sort o' business?'

'You know.'

'What? Drugs? No fuckin' way, Hosé!'

'Don't be hasty, mate. There's methadone in me madness, ya know,' Dave tries to make a joke of it.

'What part of 'no' don't you understand, ya wanker?'

'It's not for fuckin' personal, ya twat! It's an investment! I could make a serious killin'! We could make a serious killin'.'

'Just fuck off, Dave.'

'I'd cut you in.'

'Dave, off and fuck.'

-

Detlef had then steeled himself for his final revelation. 'Renata, there is one more thing I must tell you,' he'd said.

She'd cleared her throat, her eyes wide and agog in woeful anticipation. 'What?' she'd asked him, fiercely. 'There's more?!'

'Yes. I am going to England to find him. I am going to England to find your brother.'

'Come, Oskar, we are going,' is all she'd said. 'We need to get our children.'

-

Derek is shaking his head in disbelief. Dave, *fuckin' Dave,* had just asked him for two grand! But he can't help liking the sensation. Somehow it makes him laugh. He'd only ever found himself in a position to bung a mate a fiver here, a tenner there, tops. Now, he'd just been asked for thousands. It felt weird, wonderful but weird. 'Cheeky cunt!' he says as he walks into the bathroom, chuckling.

Standing at the sink, his mouth now full of toothpaste, his phone rings yet again. This time it's Marion. 'Here we fuckin' go, she's got wind alright,' he says to himself as he hits the cancel button.

It rings again.

She isn't going to stop.

Snarling, he picks up.

'Marion,' he answers curtly. 'Not a good time right now, yeah?'

She's not listening. She sounds hysterical.

'Where have you been? I've been trying to get hold of you since last night! I even came looking for you.'

'Yeah, thought you might.'

'What are you talkin' about?'

'You bloody know?'

'No, I don't bloody know! Oh, I can't be bothered with your stupid games right now. It's Jez, he's in hospital and under arrest!'

'You what?' says Derek, dropping the brush into the sink and spitting out the toothpaste.

'He's been in an accident, a car accident.'

'Is he alright?!'

'Sort of.'

'Wha' d'ya mean? Sort of!'

'He's OK. A bit of concussion and a badly broken arm, which is more than you can say for one of his mates.'

'What? Who?'

'Some lad called Mackie.. He's been killed, Derek. He's dead. Jez is in a right state, he is.'

Derek is momentarily struck dumb.

'You still there, Dekko?'

'Yeah, I'm here. How the fuck did it happen?'

'They'd nicked a car. Gone joyriding.'

'When?'

'Late last night. The coppers are waitin' to interview him. They're tryin' to work out who was driving.'

'He wasn't, was he? He can't drive!'

'I bloody hope not,' she says tearfully, *'he says not.'*

'How many were there?'

'What d'you mean?'

'In the bloody car!'

'Three altogether, including the lad that got killed.'

'So, it might not 'ave been 'im.'

'No.'

'But where the hell were you? Why didn't you make sure he was home safe?' says Derek accusingly.

'Don't you dare! Where were you? Pissed again? Too damn late to play the responsible father now!'

'Ah, whatever!' he says, backing off. 'So, where is he now?'

'Southmead, they're keeping him in to be on the safe side.'

'Have you seen him?'

'Course I've bloody seen him! Unlike you I been down there since the early hours!'

'I'll get down there right now, quick as I can.'

'I'll have to see you there later. I'm back home. I've got to get him a change of clothes, his are covered.'

'How you gettin' there?'

'Nigel's driving me.'

'No he fuckin' isn't! I don't want him there, he's my bloody son, not his. You get his kit together an' I'll pick you up, no if's, no but's. Besides I don't know what ward he's on.'

'In that car o' yours, are you having a laugh. Get a taxi! I'll see you there.'

'I'll not tell you again.'

Derek can hear a muffled conversation as Marion speaks to Nigel.

'OK then, but you screw up an' I'll kill you. Have your guts for garters.'

'It'll be fine.'

'You'll have to give me ten minutes.'

'I'll be there.'

'I'll look for you out the window.'

'You do that.'

Marion is already out waiting by the kerb, a holdall at her feet, and disbelief clearly written across her face as she sees Derek turn the corner in his clapped-out and smoking car. He pulls alongside, revving the engine to keep it alive. 'Jump in then,' he says. 'Quick!'

It's rust bucket of a vehicle on an A-plate that had originally and conveniently been painted fudge brown with matching velour trim. Its nearside passenger door lock is broken too with the window missing and taped up with a black bin bag such that he keeps it tight up against a wall behind his block of flats, not that there's anything in it worth nicking of course, even the car itself. Neither had he been able to afford to insure it, although it did have a colour-copied tax disc sellotaped to the windscreen. 'At a glance, Dekko, nobody'd tell,' Clappie had assured him.

'If you think I'm getting in that thing you got another think coming!' screeches Marion. 'I don't care what you say, I'll get Nigel to drive us.'

'No, you bloody won't! You're getting' in! Anyway, I'll be gettin' a new one soon.'

'Oh, will ya now?' she dismisses him. 'With what?'

'Bloody hell', he thinks, she really doesn't know, does she?

'But you'll have to get in the back an' jump over,' he says, pointing to the taped-up window before reaching around to clear the seat of sandwich wrappers, a dirty old work coat, and a defunct and keyless crook lock. 'The door's knackered.'

'No, I'm not 'jumping over'. I'll sit in the back, thank you!'

'Your choice,' he says.

As Marion reluctantly slides herself in, Nigel, who had been peering out from behind the living room curtains, plucks up the courage to go to the front door and opens it. 'You OK there?' he calls out before taking a few tentative steps out onto the path and into what suddenly feels like no man's land to him.

'Wondered when that twat'd show his face,' says Derek as he drops the clutch. 'Swivel!' he shouts, throwing him the finger, his arm held out high above the car roof and as they lurch and judder off down the road.

'Grow up, Dekko,' says Marion. 'Just grow up, will you?'

'Ah, he deserves it,' is all Derek says as they head off the estate and onto the dual carriageway. 'So how is he then?' Derek speaks over his shoulder as the bin bag begins to flutter wildly as he builds up speed.

'You'll have to speak up! I can't hear a bloody thing!'

'What? Hang on a minute,' says Derek, leaning over to rip the piece of plastic clean out. 'That's better. What d'you say?'

'Whoah! That's bloody freezing now!'

'Stop complainin', thank yer lucky stars it ain't rainin'. I said, how's my boy?'

'What d'ya think? Not great, Derek. He's in a state o' shock,' Marion is still forced to shout.

'Do the girls know yet?'

'Yeah, o' course they do. Janice had to go to work but Julie's up there with him. Nigel paid for a taxi.'

'Did he now?' Derek growls.

'Yes, he did! She's waiting with him in case he gets the results of his blood test, he was well over the top on the breathalyser.'

'I thought you said he weren't drivin?'

'That's what he says, but the Police are taking no chances. As I said, there was another lad in there too, they're takin' all the prints.'

'Boys, eh? Mad buggers.'

'Boys! Is that all you can say? Do you realise how serious this is? There's one poor lad lying dead, and Jez could end up in a Young Offenders this time! You make me sick!'

'We'll 'ave to see about that,' says Derek, confidently.

'You seem very upbeat, considering. Still pissed are we?'

'I'll ignore that. It's not cut and dried, never is, that's all I'm sayin'. Not 'til the fat lady sings.'

'Fat lady sings? What *are* you on about? Come on, what's going on?'

'I'll just 'ave to get him top notch brief then, won't I?' he says, toying with her.

'How's that, Derek? On Legal Aid? Don't make me laugh.'

'I'm not.'

'An' I'll not ask Nigel, he shells out more than enough as it is.'

'I don't need his fuckin' charity, believe me!'

'We'll have to go and see ol' Jefferson in the precinct,' she suggests. 'He'll have to do.'

'That old duffer? He should o' been put out to grass years back. He's well past it. I'll get somebody better.'

'Do stop it, Dekko, you fantacist,' she says, leaning forward and suddenly catching a whiff of him. 'You stink like a brewery! You can't go into a hospital smellin' like that!'

'I had a few sherbets last night, so what? Why shouldn't I? My life.'

'I'd like to know where you get your money from all the time! You need to pay for your kids first and foremost.'

'I will,' he continues to tease, 'an' sooner than you might think. But there'll be nuthin' for you or that shithead of a partner o' yours.'

'He doesn't need or want your money!' she says. 'Anyway, you need to watch yourself, there's coppers on the ward. You don't want to be put on a drink drivin' charge as well!'

'You really haven't heard have ya?' he says, unable to hold back any longer.

'Heard what?'

Derek laughs and raps the steering wheel.

'What?'

'I won the lottery!

'Yeah, right. Pull the other one.'

'Hello-o! Last night, I won the lottery. The rollover!'

'You telling me the truth? I can still tell ya know.'

Derek turns his head and grinning broadly into her now searching face. 'Ever had the feelin' you might o' backed the wrong horse?' he says.

Chapter 10

'They gi' me the right heebie-jeebies, bleedin' hospitals,' says Derek as he and Marion walk briskly towards the main entrance. 'An' nearly two friggin' quid to park! Rip off or what!'

'Hey, I paid it, not you,' she sharply reminds him. 'Besides, why should you worry, mister-moneybags-all-of-a-sudden?'

'I'll gi' it back to ya soon enough, woman.'

'Oh, you will, Derek. Trust me, you will.'

'An' wha's tha' supposed to mean?' he demands, curling his top lip and tapping for his baccy as he attempts to head over towards the ever-present huddle that, despite the 'No Smoking' signs, stand shoulder to shoulder in their foot-stamping fug.

'Oh no, you won't! You ain't got time for none o' that,' she stops him.

'Just a quick drag before we go in!'

'Jez'll be waitin',' she tells him, pulling him back. 'And yes, I will be having my fair share. You watch me if I don't.'

'You bloody won't! The kids will, but you'll be gettin' jack shit! You seem to forget summat, you and me ain't nuthin' to do wi' each other anymore!'

'An' you seem to forget something too.'

'Like what?'

'We ain't divorced yet.'

Whack!

Momentarily, he looks like he's been hit around the back of the head with a bit of two-bi'two. 'Wish I hadn't fuckin' told ya now!' he says.

'I'd have found out sooner or later, you bloody idiot,' replies Marion as they enter through the automated doors and, by stark contrast, are wafted by the antiseptic warmth of the reception area.

'If you think for one moment tha' I'm gonna let that wanker Nigel get his dirty little mitts anywhere near it, then you've got another think comin'!' Derek continues as the doors slide shut behind them. 'D'you 'ear me? Not a fuckin' bean!'

'Now you listen up, and you listen good,' says Marion, beginning to bristle. 'As I told you before, he doesn't want your money.'

'He will when he hears I got bleedin' millions!'

'No, he won't, and as I told you, he regularly sticks his hands in *his* pockets to put food on *your* kids' table. You should be ashamed of yourself.'

'Why? He fuckin' engineered it!'

'Bullshit. You owe him.'

'I owe him fuck all!'

'Besides, it's not about him, you tight-fisted arse!'

'Not true!'

'What d'ya mean, not true?'

'I am *not* tight-fisted,' complains Derek.

Marion rolls her eyes. 'Just an arse then,' she says, allowing herself a laugh.

'Har-har! Ain't you just the funny one?'

'No, but down that stinkin' boozer buying drinks for all an' sundry all night, you'll be generous to a fault there,' she carries on, 'but you haven't given *me* so much as a penny since you up and left.'

'Since I left?' he squawks. 'That's fuckin' rich!'

'Shut up, Derek. I can't be doin' wi' all this right now,' she stops him again. 'Just think about your son for a moment, he's what's important right now.'

'I know! I know! It's why I'm 'ere, innit? I can't be doin' right for doin' bloody wrong wi' you, can I? ... Never could.'

'No Dekko, you can't,' she says, laughing again.

'Ah, I give up! So, come on then, where is he?'

'Up this way. Follow me.'

-

Detlef is sat at the kitchen table doing his final checks - his passport, hotel reservation, flight tickets, and medications. Then, opening the plastic 'Bureau de Change' wallet, he counts out his money once again - just over a thousand pounds in crisp and pristine banknotes. 'All seems to be in order,' he calls out to Gisella who is in the sitting room reading quietly, or so he thinks. 'Tea?' he then asks. 'Coffee?'

She doesn't answer.

-

As the two of them walk briskly along what seem like endless corridors, Marion breaks their echoing footfall silence. 'So, are you gonna tell 'em?' she asks. 'Or am I?'

'Tell who what?'

'The kids! 'Bout your win, o' course! What else?'

Derek stops dead in his tracks. 'Oh no you bloody won't! Don't you dare! I will! I'll tell 'em!' he demands, fiercely. 'An' in me own good time. I just might wanna surprise 'em. Got it?'

'Whatever you say,' she says in a tone that says she doesn't mean it. 'Anyway, we're here now,' she warns as they turn a sharp left onto the ward. 'Now, watch yourself,' she warns.

Immediately, Derek spots two policemen sitting outside one of the side rooms, their hats lodged underneath their seats, and, as they near, and by an extraordinary coincidence, one of them, the younger one, recognises him from the night before. 'Alright then, sir?' he says knowingly and like he might be a long lost friend. 'Still in one piece, I see.'

Marion gives Derek a sideways glance, but he simply quickens his step and pretends he hasn't heard.

'Excuse me, sorry,' the copper continues, standing, 'but are you here to see Jeremy Dando?'

'What if I am?' replies Derek through tightened lips so as not to breathe too heavily. 'I'm his bloody dad, ain't I?'

'He is,' Marion confirms with an ill concealed grimace. 'He's my ex.'

'Ah, OK, just so long as we know,' the copper relaxes, re-taking his seat. 'Back again then?' he says, addressing her.

'Yeah. Back an' forth. Clean clothes,' she explains like it was an everyday occurrence, lifting the holdall.

'Of course. You alright?' he then asks her.

'Yes thanks,' she answers. 'They got you two a cup o' tea yet?'

'Machine,' he moans, pulling a face. 'Downstairs.'

'Keeps ya fit, I s'pose,' she says, smiling as she and Derek brush past him and disappear into the room.

The PC then leans into to his colleague. 'What are the chances of that, eh?' he whispers.

'What?'

'That's the fellah I was telling you about from last night!'

'What, the one that won the lottery?' scowls the other, craning his neck towards the small paned window to try to get another look. 'You're bloody joking, ain't ya?'

'I'm bloody not.'

'Where's the justice in that, eh?'

The first shakes his head in agreement.

'I mean, what's a bloke like that goin' to do with all that money?' continues the other. 'Eleven million quid so you said?'

'Yep. Eleven million. Up against a wall, I expect. Did you smell him? He'll be broke within the year, you mark my words.'

-

'Here you are, *meine liebe,* I've made us some coffee,' says Detlef, passing his wife the hot mug, handle first, but she doesn't reach up for it. 'Are you alright? What is it?' he asks her rather clumsily.

As she lifts her head, he can see that she has been crying, her cheeks wet and glistening. 'It's this book,' she lies before folding the corner of the page and setting it down beside her.

Derek is visibly taken aback, shocked even, when he sees his son looking so battered and bruised, sat in a hospital bed, his arm in a plaster, his bloodied and unwashed hair sticking up like the leaves of a pineapple above the wraparound bandage on his head. 'Jules, love,' he greets his younger daughter first.

'Dad,' she answers him, quietly.

'So, what you got yourself into now, ya blinkin' twit?' he then asks his son, trying his best to sound upbeat but Jez just closes his eyes and clenches his fists, saying nothing.

'You gotta talk about it,' continues his dad, clumsily.

Jez then covers his face in his hands, but still clearly screwing up his face like he might scream or burst into tears.

'Look, I'm sorry to hear about your mate an' all that, really sorry,' Derek carries on before gesturing out towards the waiting constabulary, 'but they're gonna want some answers, mate.'

Again, Jez doesn't answer but, this time, kicks his feet under the covers in combination of anger, frustration, but most of all, crushing guilt.

'Stop it, Derek! You're like a bull in a bloody china shop! Can't you see he doesn't want to talk about it?' Marion berates him, shoving him aside and placing the holdall down beside the bedside cabinet. 'Here y'are, love,' she then coos, 'some lovely clean clothes for you, all nice an' fresh. Ignore him.'

'There's no point beatin' about the bush, now is there?' Derek continues to steamroll. 'This is serious. All I want to know is, was he drivin'? Yay or nay? It's not that difficult a question.'

'Dad, ple-ease?' pleads Julie.

'But….'

'You heard her!' Marion slaps him down yet again. 'Enough!'

'But….'

'Please, Dad!' his daughter repeats.

'Not when we crashed, alright!' Jez suddenly blurts out.

'So, you had been then?' says his father, smirking at his ex at having got something of an answer.

'I had a go, yeah, but just for a few minutes.'

'But not when you crashed?'

'No!'

'Honest?'

'Yeah!'

Derek thinks for a moment. 'OK. Not clever,' he says. 'Your dabs will be on the steering wheel, but that's all you need tell 'em, nuthin' else,' he then advises him under his breath so as not to overheard. 'An' I don't want you to worry. I'll sort it, d'ya hear me? In the meantime, you'll need a duty solicitor.'

Julie looks up at him in surprise. 'How are you going to sort it then, Dad?' she asks rather cynically. 'How?'

'Go on then, Dekko, here's your chance,' says Marion, unable to suppress her eagerness to let the cat out the bag.

'Oi, you! Wha' did I tell ya?'

But Marion carries on regardless. 'Your Dad's got some news. Great news,' she informs them.

'What?' asks Julie, now acutely aware of her mother's animation and her father's obvious irritation. 'You're both acting really strange.'

'I was goin' to surprise ya, book a holiday or summat,' says her dad, flatly. 'Thanks for nuthin', Mar.'

'Holiday? What holiday?' asks Julie.

Marion grins broadly. 'Go on then,' she says. 'Tell 'em.'

Even Jez now appears a little more engaged, perking up and eyeing him quizzically.

With a dramatic sigh, Derek draws the bright, patterned curtain around them in a futile attempt to afford them some added privacy in the otherwise empty room and pulls up a chair. Sitting down with his hands on his knees like he was going to tell them a bed-time story for the first time in his entire life, he starts off. 'Right … now… look, you's two,' he says slowly and deliberately, building up the expectation. 'There's summat I got to tell ya … but keep it to yerselves, yeah?' he continues. 'D'ya promise?'

'Oh, get on with it!' urges Marion, exasperated and excited all at the same time.

'Will you shut up an' gi' me a minute?' says Derek before cupping his hands to his face like a loudhailer. 'What would you say if I was to tell you that your ol' man's a multi-millionaire?' he says to them. 'Would ya like that, would ya? A multi-millionaire!'

-

Now back in the comfort of his own home, PG wants to be doubly sure that his emerging idea will go exactly to plan and is making an important call. He doesn't want any setbacks or mistakes and is about to implement 'the pitchfork' as he likes to call it, his preferred two-pronged attack when the stakes are a little more interesting, as you might say.

'So, there you have it, Brian,' he finishes explaining. 'You know where he drinks, you've got his number, now all I want you to do is get him to me. Tell him that I could help.'

Brian, a no-nonsense Scot and bit of a hard man, is by far and away PG's star performer, offering a rare combination of wile and brawn. His 'extracurricular' services, however, don't come cheap and PG only uses him for such things only when absolutely necessary.

'Yeah. Fo' sure. I can manage tha',' he answers in his broad East coast accent.

'Just give him one of those Rolexes as a little sweetener, the likes of him will never know the difference. You've got some left I presume?

'One or two.'

'Four to be precise.'

'Ha-har! Nae flies on yoo, PG!'

'No, I think you'll find there's not. Just make it so.'

'Message received loud an' clear. Leave i' wi' mi. I'll deliver 'im tae ya, nae bother.'

'Just pin him for a time and date so I can set it all up.'

'So, wha's the big idea?'

'None of your business. But nicely now, don't frighten him, Brian.'

'I'll put mi' kid gloves on then, shall I?' he says with an unseen and wry smile.

'You do that, and don't forget Clappie, use him if needs be.'

'Tha' wee streak o' gnats piss? I'll pass if it's all the same tae you?'

'The pitchfork, Brian? The carrot and the stick. You know the way we do things.'

'I dinnae need no carrot..'

'No, I'm sure you don't, but OK, the ball's in your court, just don't let me down. Usual terms?'

'Mmm - I mi' be wantin' a bonus fae this one.'

'A bonus?'

'Aye.'

'Why? What for?'

'Why? Because we're talkin' real money here, pal, an' ya dinnae wanna see it slippin' through ya fingers, now do ya?' answers Brian, shrewdly.

'I only want him bloody delivered, not gift wrapped.'

'Nice talkin' tae ya, PG. Bye,' says Brian, ready to put the phone down.

'Wait! Stop! Don't be so hasty.'

'Well then, a bonus, on results,' Brian repeats assertively. *'You know the way we do things,'* he mimics him.

'You drive a very hard bargain. So, what are you looking for?'

'Let mi see, ... you'll be fleecin' this poor bastard fo' a king's ransom, tha's fo' sure. It'll 'ave tae be five big ones.'

'Five thousand! Never! You're pricing yourself way out of the market! Clappie might come up trumps yet, and for little more than a slap on the back.'

'Clappie? Dinnae make mi laff! He could'nae knock tha skin off a rice puddin'! An' in tha' meantime, some other bastard will be in tae this Derek character big time. Your choice.'

PG falls silent for a moment. 'Two,' he then offers.

'Four.'

'Two thousand, five hundred, Brian, absolute tops.'

'Wi' five hundred up front fae expenses.'

'You don't want much, do you?'

'S'up to you.'

'Drop by. I'll have it for you.'

'A pleasure doin' business wi' ya, mister Green. I'll be on mi way over poste haste. 'Ave it ready.'

\-

'You'll 'ave to let Janice know yerself,' Derek tells Marion as he stands to leave. 'I'll catch up with her later after I've dropped Jules off.'

'Bloody hell, Dekko, can't you wait a bit?' she complains. 'She'll only be half an hour. She's coming here straight after work. She'll be over the moon.'

'No, you tell her, that's what you want innit? Tellin' people?' he says, still miffed at having his once-in-a-lifetime news whipped out from under his feet. 'Besides, I got things to do, stuff to sort.'

'Oh yeah? Like what?' says Marion, viewing him suspiciously. 'Off down the pub again, are we?'

'No!' he denies, 'about our Jez 'ere! Tha's what!'

'Who on earth are you going to be able to talk to today, Dekko? It's a Sunday in case you hadn't noticed!'

Derek ignores this inconvenient truth. 'I've got a couple of ideas,' he says unconvincingly.

'Don't gi' me that. I know you like the back of my hand.'

'So, what if I am?' Derek snaps. 'Can do what I bloody well like!'

'Please don't shout, you two,' pleads Julie. 'We should all be happy as anything when Jez is OK.'

'Sorry, love,' her dad apologises to her. 'Besides, I got no choice. I gotta go down there,' he continues more gently.

'I knew it,' says Marion. 'Why?'

'Nuthin',' says Derek rather sheepishly.

'Why?!' she demands.

'I left the ticket there last night for safe keepin',' Derek reluctantly admits.

'You what?! You left an eleven-million-pound lottery ticket in the pub? Are you effing serious? Talk about shit for brains!'

'Mum!' Julie complains again.

'It's in Jimbo's safe, ya daft bat!' explains Derek. 'Safe as houses!'

'Are you sure?'

'Yeah! Course I'm sure! I put it in there meself!'

'I flippin' well hope so. I never thought I'd hear myself say this, but you go there right now and get it!'

'Thanks for your blessin',' says Derek, sarcastically, before turning to his daughter. 'So, let's get you home, young lady, before yer mother blows another gasket, eh?'

'And you take it steady with her, Derek,' Marion then warns him so as not to be heard by the police. 'Do you hear me?'

'I'll watch him, Mum, he'll be alright.'

'It's not him I'm worried about, love.'

Derek then puts his hands on his daughter's shoulders and steers her out. 'You just leave it wi' me, Jez,' he says to his still stunned looking son. 'It'll be alright.'

'Thanks, Dad,' he says.

'No problem, son. What dads are for,' says Derek without any sense of irony and allowing himself a little sneer towards the waiting police.

'Are you planning on driving, sir?' asks the one copper suspiciously, having pretty much caught the entire gist of their conversation.

'Who? Me? Nah! Taxi,' Derek bare-faced lies. 'In fact, I might just buy the whole damn rank while I'm at it,' he adds. 'It's great bein' rich. You should try it sometime. It's brilliant.'

-

With her head leant back on the sofa and her eyes closed against the imminent inevitability of it all, Gisella finally speaks. 'I worry I might never see you again, Detlef,' she says, her voice catching.

'Nonsense. Of course, you will,' he gently reassures her, sidling up alongside. 'Don't be silly.'

'But what if…?'

'What if, nothing,' he says, hushing her lips. 'It is only for one week. The time will pass quickly enough. I'll be back home before you know it.'

-

Walking out with his daughter, arm in arm, Derek cannot help but feel wildly exuberant and tries, but fails, to jump and click his heels.

'World's our lobster now, girl, innit?' he says, guffawing and stumbling.

'I hope so, Dad,' says Julie, laughing along and trying to catch his weight.

'You bet your bottom dollar it is, girl! We can do anythin' now, you an' me!'

'So long as Jez is going to be alright,' she cautions again.

'I'll get him the best legal beagle money can buy, you see if I don't!' says her father, pulling her in close and nuzzling into the top of her head, kissing her.

As she catches the acrid stench of stale alcohol and tobacco on his breath, Julie recoils a little. 'You need to start looking after yourself a bit better, Dad,' she then says. 'You want to be able to enjoy it, don't you?'

'Whadya mean, ya daft a'peth? I am enjoying it! Look a' me!'

'But you drink much too much, Dad, and smoke. You could make yourself seriously ill if you don't watch out. What would be the point then?'

'I'm not tha' bad, am I?' he says, again holding his hand out flat for her to see.

'You are, look, you're shaking!'

'Solid as a rock,' he dismisses but, still, flexing his fingers to have a better go.

'Seriously, Dad, you could end up killing yourself. Heart disease, lung cancer, anything.'

'Bloody 'ell, love, give it a rest!' he says jocularly enough. 'You're beginning to sound just like your mother.'

'I get worried, that's all. We all do,' she says, adding, 'and you should definitely get your liver function checked out as well.'

'Liver function? Blimey, you a doctor all of a sudden?'

'I want to be. I want to study Medicine,' she announces.

'What? Like a *real* doctor you mean?' he asks, genuinely surprised.

'Da-ad! I've told you loads of times!'

'Sorry, Jules, must o' missed that one,' he answers her with an embarrassed and apologetic smile. 'I'll make it up to you. Promise.'

'But that's if I even get in. It's everso hard, you know.'

'What is?'

'University!'

'You'll smash it! A girl o' mine!' he encourages her. 'Besides, you know what they say, if it was easy, every bugger would be doin' it.'

'I'm trying my best at school.'

'That's it, you stick at it. I'll back you all the way. No student loans for you, eh?' he says. 'Paid all the way!'

'Thanks, Dad! That'd be brilliant!'

'That's what us dads are for, supportin' their kids,' he repeats and liking the sound of it. 'What a difference a day makes, eh? Soon to 'ave millions in the bank, an' now a daughter who wants to be a doctor,' he adds, puffing himself out, making her laugh.

'Have you told Nan yet?' she then asks.

'Uh, no. Ain't 'ad chance yet. I'll have to get over to see her later. Tomorrow maybe.'

'You must. Although she doesn't complain much, she really hates that home she's in.'

'Yeah, yeah, I know… Hey! Perhaps I can sort her out a little place of her own, get her some carers in,' he says with even further amazement.

'Oh Dad, she'd love that! Somewhere closer. You must!'

'I could. I really could, couldn't I? Get her a little bungalow!'

Suddenly, Julie pulls him in by the arm.

'What is it?' he asks. 'Forgot somethin'?'

'Can I ask you a question?'

'Why don't I like the sound of this?'

'Do you think you and Mum might get back together now?' she asks, looking at him directly and straight in the eye.

Thoroughly back-footed, Derek coughs out loud. 'You don't 'alf come out with 'em, don't ya?' he says, stumbling over the words.

'Well?'

'Give us a break, love,' he squirms. 'It's difficult. Your mum's made her decision. It's her you should be askin', not me.'

Right then his phone beeps in his pocket as a text comes in. 'Sorry, love. Give us a minute, will ya?' he says, quietly relieved at the diversion. *CALL ME ASP. CLAPPIE,* is all it reads.

'Important?' Julie asks.

'Dunno, probably not,' he dismisses as they exit the hospital and into the car park.

'It would be lovely, living all back together again,' she tries once again.

'Feelin' strong?' is all he says, pointing to his motor. 'She might need a little bit of a push.'

Cradling her face, Detlef pushes an invisible hair aside as Gisella begins to weep again. 'Gisella, my love,' he says, softly but deliberately, 'you know it is something I must do. We have discussed it. I will be fine. *We* will be fine. I even have Renate's blessing now, remember?'

And it was true. Detlef did finally have his daughter's approval after those stressful and angst filled days immediately after he'd revealed all to her.

Despite her terrible sense of betrayal and previously unknown feelings of competition for her father's affection, she couldn't help but become intrigued at the notion that she had a half-brother, and more than a little curious at the snapshot it had given her into her father's early life. She found herself wanting to know more, needing to know more in fact.

When, at last, she'd come back to visit, with both being immediately emotional and apologetic, hugging each other and crying on the doorstep, she'd even brought a photograph of herself and her family together with a card and message written in her schoolgirl English to give to him should he be fortunate enough to find him. Overjoyed and relieved at her sudden support, and at this touching gesture, Detlef had kept them safe on his bookshelf before placing them, together with the ribbon and the bonnet, flat within the folds of a towel, now packed securely in his suitcase.

He might have been forgiven for thinking that everything had slotted itself neatly into place, but nothing was ever quite so simple. No, the focus of his attention and concern had rapidly shifted toward Gisella. Increasingly, she was struggling with the whole idea.

The worry and anxiety of it all had obviously become all too much for her and her previous and apparent stoicism uncovered to be little more than a brave façade. She'd began to fret, hugely, not only with regard her husband's health and his ability to take on such a journey, but also, and more tellingly, with regard Ellen, his first wife. What if she was still alive, she'd asked him? What might happen then?

After having dropped Julie safely back at home, Derek re-parks his wreck of a vehicle up around the back and takes out his phone.

'Hey, Clappie, it's me, Dekko. I got your text. If it's about them boots….?'

'Christ, don't worry 'bout them, ya jammy bastard!'

'Might o' guessed.'

'No secrets 'round 'ere, my baba. Jungle drums. Smoke signals.'

'So, wha' d'ya want then?'

'Nuthin', just to offer my congratulations. I've not long spoken to PG an' he's made up for ya too. He's asked me to touch base.'

'Oh yeah? Why's that?' Derek asks suspiciously.

'Don't be so bloody negative! Just to thank ya for bein' such a good customer, that's all. Them boots are on him for starters!'

'Nah, I'll pay for 'em. Be better,' says Derek recalling Phil's earlier advice.

'Don't be like that! He's told me he'd like to see ya, help ya, give ya a few pointers. You need to have your head screwed on wi' all that money, Dekko - an' PG's definitely yer man for that. He understands it. Oh, an' while I'm at it, he said he's got a little summat extra for ya too, a little gift. Ain't you just the lucky one?'

'Oh yeah? Like what?' asks Derek, unable to suppress his interest.

'That's more like it! Dunno, be somethin' nice though, special. He wants me to sort out a time you two could meet up. How would tomorrow suit? I can pick you up an' get you back, no trouble.'

'Don't think so, Clappie. I got too much on. Look, I'll call when things settle down a bit, yeah?'

'Day after then, my baba? Tuesday?' asks Clappie, now sounding rather desperate.

'Clappie, as I said. I'll let ya know.'

'Help us out here a bit, Dekko. He only wants a chat. You know how it goes.'

'Look, I don't wanna be rude nor nuthin', mate, but fuck off, yeah?'

'I can't twist your arm nor nuthin'?'

'Clappie.'

'You'll accept the boots?'

'If it keeps ya 'appy, but tha's it. Now, I gotta go. It's important.'

'Laters?'

'See ya, Clappie.'

'Would you call me?'

'Maybe. We'll see.'

-

With the obvious distress he'd caused his family, Detlef had come very close, and on several occasions, to abandoning his plan altogether. But he couldn't, not then, and not now.

He was fully aware that his decision might be seen as being ultimately very selfish, foolish, irrational, but he simply had to see it through. It was like he was attempting to find the one missing piece of the jigsaw before it was too late.

He simply had to try, despite the exacting and unknown price he might likely be asked to pay.

-

Very apprehensively, Clappie rings PG to explain. He knows he's not going to be best pleased.

'I tried me 'ardest, PG,' he starts off.

'I could have put money on it. You really are quite useless, aren't you?'

'He told me he'd call as soon as an' when he got a chance.'

'Not enough.'

'He will, he's good like that. He's just busy. Bound to be.'

'So am I, Clappie, so am I. Anyway, things have moved on, I've already got someone else on the case.'

'Who?'

'Brian.'

'Brian? Wha', *Brian,* you mean?'

'Yes, Brian. He might call you too, although I doubt it. Just make yourself available if necessary.'

'Fuckin' 'ell, PG! Will I be gettin' anythin' for the nod at least?'

'No, not unless you prove useful.'

'There's gratitude for ya!'

'Then you should have done what I asked. Now, on your way, and keep busy.'

-

'Watcha, you lot!' shouts Derek as he finally careers in through the door to deliver a mini version of one of his bows and anticipating a tumultuous reception. He's not disappointed, but he is surprised to see Phil standing behind the bar, drying up cloth in hand. 'What the hell are you doing back there?' he asks. 'Jimbo given you a job or summat?'

'Nah, he had to pop out. Cash n' carry or so he said. Reenie had to go out an' all for some reason. They've asked me to cover for 'em.'

'Weird,' says Derek. 'I only spoke to 'im earlier, he never mentioned anythin'. So, where's he put that ticket o' mine then, eh? Don't suppose he left it with ya, did he?'

'Nope, still safe in the safe, I s'pect.'

'Bloody 'ell! I gotta get on with it. I need it, like now. Make that phone call to the lottery people, like you said.'

'Can't help ya, Dekko. You'll 'ave to wait 'til they get back. Anyway, what's the hurry all of a sudden?'

'You don't wanna know,' he answers, pulling a face.

'What?'

'Family stuff, I'll tell you about it later. They say how long they were goin' to be?'

'Well, they *said* half an hour, but that was well over an hour ago now by my watch. I'll have to start askin' for wages at this rate.'

'Fuckin' 'ell!'

Dave is standing over on Crackers Corner. 'Dekko,' he greets him, but sounding a tad peevish after this morning's conversation.

'Dave,' acknowledges Derek similarly.

'That's not what I saw,' Dave then says, 'they were both gettin' in the back of a mini cab just as I was comin' back in. Round the back they were, an' carrying couple o' bags, suitcases by the look of 'em. Said summat about droppin' some shit off at the charity shop.'

'Really?' says Phil looking astounded. 'News to me.'

'She had sunglasses on too, Reenie, in this weather!' fuels Dave, straight-faced as you like.

'Suitcases?' asks Derek, swallowing hard, his guts already falling out of his arse.

'Well, yeah. Looked like it.'

'Jeezus Christ, Dave! Couldn't you o' let me know?' says Derek, taking the bait.

'Don't blame me, Dekko! Only tellin' ya what I saw.'

Derek is hooked and everyone in the bar is now watching in joyous anticipation as Phil and Dave set about reeling him in.

'Bloody 'ell, Dekko! I had no idea!' gasps Phil, feigning total surprise. 'You're not thinkin' what I'm thinkin' are ya?'

With the adrenalin now pumping like a good 'un and looking like he might throw up at any moment, Derek is on the verge of total panic. 'I wouldn't trust that bloody Reenie as far as I could throw her!' he shouts. 'But not fuckin' Jimbo, I've known him for years! What a cunt!'

'Ring 'em', quick!' suggests Dave, urgently. 'I got Jim's number 'ere somewhere.'

'I got it in mine I think,' says Derek, whipping out his phone and scrolling down to J. 'Here, here it is! Bloody Jimbo!' he says as he stabs it with his finger. 'You wait 'til I get my hands on the theivin' bastard!'

After just a few seconds a phone rings on the back shelf by the empty ice bucket. Phil picks it up and offers it for Derek to see. 'Fuckin' 'ell,' he says. 'Why would he leave it? He's always got it on 'im.'

'They've up an' had it-a-bloody away! Pound to a pinch o' shit'! says Dave, barely able to stop himself from cracking up. 'An' wi' your ticket! I reckon you ought to get yourself down to Bristol Airport,

Dekko, like pronto. Catch 'em up before they end up in fuckin' Rio de Janeiro!'

Derek paces up and down on the spot, frantically rubbing his face and kicking the bar. 'Bastards!' he shouts. 'Cunts! I fuckin' knew it!'

'I warned ya, Dekko, now didn't I?' chastises Phil, feigning anger. 'But would you listen? No Would you hell as like! You should o' phoned it in and staked your claim when I said, you twat!'

'Hey, Dekko!' interjects another of the drinkers from down the bar and keen to get in on the act. 'I'd get onto the police and get all the airports blocked if I was you. Get 'em on red alert! I'm serious!'

'You reckon?' says Derek, his mouth now agape and as dry as the bottom of a budgerigar's cage, the colour all but drained from his face.

'Yeah, I do! An' phone Interpol while you're at it!'

Derek starts to hyperventilate, panic stricken, dropping to his knees.

But Phil can hold the pretence no longer as tears of hysteria begin to squirt from the corner of his eyes.

'Ya silly wanker!' screeches Dave, slapping the flat of his hand flat on the bar with a loud resounding smack. 'Gotcha, ya cunt,' he says. 'Hook, line, and bloody sinker!'

With the flood gates now open the whole pub erupts in yells and uproarious laughter. Then, right on cue, through the door to the back of the bar, Jimbo appears closely followed by a very tight-lipped looking Reenie. In his hand, he's waving the ticket. 'So, I'm a cunt, am I?' he asks.

-

'I shall need to have a very early night tonight,' Detlef, tells his wife. 'Will you join me?

'I don't think I shall sleep,' she says.

'Nonsense,' he says. 'Come with me. Please. I need a cuddle from my beautiful wife.'

-

'Family stuff, you said earlier?' Phil asks Derek after everyone's nicely topped up and things begin to settle down.

'Yeah, you could say that,' he says, pulling a face.

'What? All after their pound of flesh already, are they? Crawlin' out o' the woodwork?'

'Nah, well, yeah, but that's not it.'

'What then?'

Derek looks awkward. 'It's our Jez,' he says, 'he's got himself in a spot of bother an' I got to try an' sort it out.'

'Oh-ar? What's he been up to now?'

'Nothing to do with that kiddie getting 'imself killed in that pile up last night then?' asks Dave, accidently hitting the nail on the head.

'How d'you know?' asks Derek almost angrily.

'Only a fuckin' guess, mate! Don't get all pissy! Fuck me!'

'But not your Jez?' asks Phil, shocked.

'No, no! One of his mates!'

'We heard the sirens last night, remember?' reminds Phil. 'The 'elicopter?'

Derek can barely recall a thing, but his blood runs cold all the same.

'It's been all over the local news, Dekko, and on the telly,' says Dave trying to justify himself. 'Didn't you see it?'

'No. I been up the hospital,' says Derek, more conciliatory.

'Is he alright then?' Phil asks.

'Bust his arm, smacked 'imself up a bit, but he's alright, considerin'.'

'So, wha's the story?'

'Nicked a car, the bleedin' idiots. 'Twockin' they call it, don't they? Flipped it on one of the roundabouts and, bingo, some kiddie gets killed.'

'Bloody hell, Dekko!' says Jimbo, earwigging as ever 'I'm really sorry to hear that. We'd never 'ave taken the piss if we'd o' known, mate.'

'Nah, no problem, you weren't to know. Trouble is, they ain't sure who the driver was. Jez's sayin' it weren't 'im when they crashed it, but he had been, the twat. The police are up with 'im right now. They got 'im under arrest.'

'He had driven it then?' Phil looks to confirm.

'Yeah, at some point, or so he says. I need to sort 'im out a brief.'

'What about ol' wassisname, Jefferson, down on the parade?' offers Jimbo.

'You been talkin' to Marion?' questions Derek. 'No, no, no, I can afford to get someone better than 'im now. He's well past it. Got any ideas? I ain't got a clue.'

'Don't write him off, Dekko,' offers Dave. 'He does a lot with kids, so I've heard. I should know, years back. Be right up his street. You don't want to waste your money for the sake of it, do ya? Be worth a chat at least.'

'Now, you listen to me, Derek,' Phil stops them, taking control. 'First things first, I'm gonna stand over you 'til you ring the fuckin' lottery people. Then we'll get our heads around your Jez. OK? We'll help ya sort it.'

Derek nods in agreement and with Phil reading the numbers off the back of the ticket, he dials.

'Welcome to the National Lottery Helpline,' it says. *'Please press any button on your telephone now to hear available the options ... if you are a major winner or wish to talk to an operator, please press one.'*

Derek presses it.

'Hello, you're through to the National Lottery Helpline. My name's Asif, how can I help you?' says a real human voice at the end of the phone.

'Yeah, hi,' answers Derek. 'Think I got the winning ticket,' he says.

With that, and despite Jimbo trying to quieten them all down, the bar turns into a pack of baying hounds, shouting and yelling once again.

'Great! Sounds a bit noisy where you are,' says Asif. *'Are you celebrating already?'* he asks knowingly.

'Yeah, sorry,' says Derek, 'I'm in me local boozer and I can't hear meself bloody think. I'll go somewhere a bit quieter, gimme a mo.'

'No hurry. When you're ready.'

So, outside, in the car park, and to a backdrop of a row distorted and gurning faces pressed hard up against the windows and with hands and knuckles rapping on the glass, Derek carries on with the call, pacing up and down and fiddling with various car aerials and wing mirrors, as he does.

After a good five minutes or so, he finally walks back in.

'So come on, what they say?' Phil shouts out above the racket.

'Staked me claim ain't I,' Derek tells them. 'Now I just got to wait for one of their other people to call me back, see what I want to do.'

'They goin' to send someone, then?' asks Jimbo.

'Yeah, they can do, or I can pick it up apparently. Oh, an' he wanted to know if I wanted to go public?'

'You wouldn't!' says Phil. 'You'd be mad! You'd get all kinds o' shit.'

'Might do, might not? Couple o' dolly birds on me arm an' holdin' a fuckin' great big cheque. Could be a laugh.'

'What you thinkin', ya daft bastard! You'll 'ave all an' sundry onto ya!'

'You don't wanna wait either,' cautions Dave. 'Pick it up! Get the bloody money in yer hand an' in the bank! I would!'

'You could do it 'ere,' suggests Reenie who, unusually, is still loitering behind the bar. 'The presentation I mean.'

'Hey! That's a thought, love!' says Derek excitedly. 'We could have a party!'

'I'd put on a lovely spread for you,' she adds.

'Where would you 'ave to go to pick up the cheque?' interjects Phil and introducing a note of seriousness.

'Watford, apparently,' Derek informs him. 'Head Office.'

'Hey! I used to live near there,' says Dave.

'Why, got a Nick there, 'ave they?' asks Jimbo.

'Fuck off!'

'I s'pose I could make a trip out of it,' Derek then thinks out aloud. 'A day out o' Bris'ol would make a change.'

'I could take ya, if ya want,' offers Phil. 'Give you a lift.'

'Yeah! Great! Quite like the idea of being chauffeured,' says Derek. 'Let's do it, shall we?'

'I'll come along for the ride,' Dave jumps in. 'I could show ya me ol' stompin' ground.'

'No! She's only a little Fiesta!' Phil immediately objects

'We'd all get in!' overrides Derek, 'Got four seats innit?'

'Wha' d'ya mean, four seats?'

'Jim too!'

'Chance 'ould be a fine thing,' Jimbo quickly counts himself out. 'Chained to this place, I am.'

'You can go if ya want,' says Reenie quite uncharacteristically. 'I am capable, you know.'

'Whoah, whoah, whoah!' stops Phil. 'Think o' the weight! It'll knacker the suspension!'

'Relax, Phil! I'll buy ya a new bugger if the bloody wheels fall off!' says Derek, bursting into near hysterical laughter.

Chapter 11
Monday Morning

Detlef finds himself distracted by a twinkly eyed and snotty nosed little girl peering back at him from in between the seats. He smiles at her, wiggling his fingers Laurel and Hardy style, but, despite her obvious delight, she only serves to remind him of his own grandchildren back at home. It had only been a couple of days ago that he'd kissed them both goodbye and, ridiculously, he misses them already.

It had been years since he'd flown and with the enormity and the reality of the task that he's finally undertaking truly beginning to sink in, Detlef is finding it very difficult to settle and had treated himself to a miniature bottle of red wine in the vain hope that it might relax him, even enable him to catch a little sleep. It doesn't. Along with the altitude, it only serves to make him feel even more uneasy and not a little bilious too.

With the girl still trying to play peek-a-boo (well, up until her mother had gently pulled her away with an apologetic smile that is) he tries flipping through his newly bought English phrasebook in an attempt to rekindle some of his previously good command of the language, but that too had been years and very little, if anything, seemed to be going in.

But at least he'd been allocated a window seat, so, despite the near homogenous cloud cover, he resigns himself to look down past the wing on the off chance of catching a glimpse of a town or city below, a meandering river perhaps, a glistening lake, anything but anything that might give his racing mind a moments respite.

-

At just after eight o'clock in the morning, Phil is rat-a-tat-tatting on Derek's door at the top of his echoing stairwell, a spritely knock that would suggest the presence of a friend, not a loan shark or a bailiff, as if it mattered now. However, despite their arrangement and promises made the previous evening, there's no sign of an answer.

Crouching down, he pushes open the spring-loaded letterbox and peers into the hallway and through into the insipid light of the sitting room beyond. 'Where are ya, ya lazy bastard?' he calls through the flap as it snaps sharply back onto his thumb, drawing a little blood. 'Fuckin' ouch!' he curses before knocking again but this time with a thundering and thumping fist. 'Oi! Dekko! We're s'posed to be goin' over to bloody Watford! Remember?'

Nothing.

He's just about to try ringing him in some a last-ditch attempt when he senses movement from within and hears the unmistakable slap of bare feet upon laminate floor. Derek opens up, dressed only in his underpants.

'There you are! Still alive then?' observes Phil but recoiling at the unholy sight standing before him.

'Better come in,' invites Derek before heading back towards the kitchen.

'You really ain't a pretty sight first thing in the morning, are ya, ya ugly bastard?' says Phil, unable to avert his eyes from Derek's bloated and potbellied torso, miraculously supported, as it is, on a pair of white and sinewy legs. 'You look like shit.'

'I feel like shit. Cuppa?'

'We ain't got time for that now,' insists Phil, 'the others will be waitin'.'

'How d'ya take it?'

'OK, OK! I'll stick the bloody kettle on,' says Phil, resignedly, 'you just get your arse in gear an' get yourself dressed, yeah?'

'Yes, sir, whatever you say, sir, three bags full, sir,' Derek accepts his suggestion and makes an almost comedic about-right U-turn before padding his way into the bathroom.

Unfortunately for Phil, the thin stud walls of the flat leave little to the imagination and the sounds of Derek hawking and farting followed by the tell-tale rattle of the toilet paper holder make him shudder and grimace even more. 'S'no wonder your Marion kicked you out.' he calls out as he rescues a heavily stained mug from the sink. 'You're bloody disgustin'!'

'An' your shit don't stink, I s'pose?' retorts Derek, unable to find his toothbrush so squirting a blob of toothpaste directly into his mouth and rubbing his teeth vigorously with his forefinger. 'So, where are they then?' he sputters.

'You what you say?' misses Phil as the kettle cracks noisily into life.

'The boys? Dave, Jimbo?'

'Down the pub, where d'ya think?'

'Oh, alright. Thought they might be waitin' in your motor.'

'I got to give it to ya, me ol' mucker, you're pretty laid back, all things considered.'

'You're jokin', ain't ya?' says Derek as he emerges from the bathroom still in his pants but looking a little cleaner and fresher at least, his hair brushed back and dampened such that he looks like an old

Fifties Style Rocker. 'Can't get the little bleeder out o' me 'ead. Could easily o' been him dead on the road, not someone else.'

'But he's not. Just thank your lucky stars, yeah?'

'Yeah, you say that, but where was I, eh?'

'You'd won the bloody lottery, mate! You were down the pub, celebratin'. You had no idea.'

'S'pose,' acknowledges Derek, 'but he still might end up in a Young Offenders.'

'Dekko, as we said yesterday, just call ol' Jefferson to get the ball rollin',' Phil reminds him. 'You'll feel all the better for it. Trust me. I've even written his number down for ya.'

'You still reckon I should try him first then?'

'I do, as a starter for ten. You can always change your mind.'

Derek then mutters to himself. 'Useless cunt,' he's heard to say as he now goes into his bedroom.

'He ain't that bad, mate! Old, but not that bad.'

'Not bloody Jefferson, me!' explains Derek.

'Wha' ya talkin' about?'

'I'll tell ya wha' I'm talkin' about. Take yesterday for example, at the hospital. I told Marion that I'd get straight onto it, but what did I do? Got back an' got wankered as per usual. Even my little Julie's givin' me a hard time. She thinks I'm about to pop me clogs wha' wi' all the smokin' an' what I'm chuckin' down me neck.'

'We all drink too much,' agrees Phil, laughing it off.

Derek gives a little chuckle himself. 'Yeah! An' some! But I can't help thinkin' I've let 'em all down, mate,' he admits.

'Well, you can make it up to 'em now, can't ya?'

'Yeah, I can, and I will,' he says, firmly. 'Time to step up.'

'Is the right answer!'

'Don't suppose there's a pile o' washin' in there?' Derek then asks.

'Nope, don't look like it,' answers Phil, looking around the sparse kitchen. 'And perhaps your Julie's right? Perhaps you do need to clean up your act? A little bit at least.'

'True. As she said, the money's no good bein' dead, is it?'

'I wouldn't go that far, mate! You ain't dead yet! Let's just deal with the matters in hand first, yeah?'

'Yeah. OK,' agrees Derek. 'Tell me.'

'Right, 'ave you got your I.D. like you were asked? Drivin' license, utility bill, you know the type o' thing.'

'Yep, all sorted an' in me jacket. I did that last night when I got home, but fuck knows how. You sure there's nuthin' in there?'

'No, Dekko, there's not,' says Phil, squeezing the tea bag out with his fingers. 'An' don't forget the all-important ticket.'

'That's safe and sound, 'ave no worries 'bout that.'

'Sugar?'

'Don't think there is any.'

'Milk?'

'None o' that neither. Bloody hell! I know I've got some clean stuff somewhere!'

Phil opens the fridge and discovers for himself. 'How the fuck can you live like this, Dekko? You got fuck all in 'ere!'

'There'll be all sorts in there this time next week. Caviar, quail's legs, you name it, I'll 'ave it … where the fuck 'ave I put 'em?'

'It'll just 'ave to be black then.'

'So long as it's hot and wet, I couldn't give a stuff.'

'Just like your women, eh?'

'Here they are! Behind the bleedin' door!' shouts Derek as he picks out an un-ironed burgundy coloured shirt and runs it tight across his knee in a pointless effort to smooth it out.

'Here you go, a cup o' tea o' sorts,' Phil calls out. 'Now hurry up before it gets cold.'

It's not long before Derek at last reappears in the kitchen, a roll-up cigarette hanging in readiness from his mouth. As ever, he's dressed in jeans and his jacket (a safety pin now holding the collar in place) and wearing the clean but heavily creased shirt underneath, his boots buffed up with deep red oxblood shoe polish to match.

'You'll do,' says Phil, giving him the once over. 'Now, get all your bits an' pieces together an' let's get goin'.'

Derek lights up and, bizarrely, squinting against the smoke, pulls the cutlery drawer clean out and clatters it onto the worktop.

'What the fuck are you playin' at now?'

'Can never be too careful, not round here,' he says as he folds back his cuff and reaches right back inside to pull out an envelope. He opens it to double check.

'That what I think it is?'

'Yep,' says Derek, slurping back no more than a couple of mouthfuls of his tea before pouring the rest down the sink. 'Let's look lively then, shall we? We ain't got all day.'

'You really are a cheeky cunt sometimes,' says his mate, shaking his head and laughing.

'Motor, outside is it?'

'Yeah, all filled up and ready to go, price o' fuckin' petrol nowadays!'

'I'll sort you out. Don't worry.'

'Shut up, Dekko! I'm not saying that!'

-

Meanwhile, over in Ashton Gate, Ellen is already sitting in her day chair, propped up with pillows, when Margaret brings over her breakfast and places it on the detachable tray in front of her - scrambled egg on toast, a rasher of bacon, half a cooked tomato. 'Eat as much as you can, Ellen,' she says. 'Do you want me to cut it up for you?'

'I can manage,' replies the old lady.

'We've all got to keep our strength up, haven't we?'

'Yes, we have. Looks lovely,' she says overly politely.

'S'pect we'll be seeing your Derek soon, won't we?' Margaret then suggests hopefully.

Ellen nods. 'Oh yes, visits me regular he does,' she trots out her usual response.

'And your grandchildren, they come to see you too, don't they?'

'Only last week. Julie's such a lovely girl, and Janice. Always bring me something they do. They brought me a lovely bag of satsumas last time. Everso sweet they are. Do you want one? I've got some left.'

'Yes please! I do love a juicy satsuma,' accepts Margaret. 'I'll pop back when you've finished then, shall I?'

'Yes. Thank you. I'll try my best,' says Ellen, picking up her fork.

-

With her hips brushing past protruding shoulders, Detlef sees the stewardess making her way down the aisle and collecting empty drinks containers and food wrappers. As she reaches him, she leans over to speak. 'I'm sorry to rush you, sir,' she says noticing his unfinished beaker of wine, 'only we shall be preparing to land shortly.'

To his considerable amazement, he finds that he can understand her quite clearly and carefully hands it over together with the plastic bottle. '*Danke,*' he says, then quickly correcting himself, 'thank you. Thank you very much. I've finished. Careful not to spill.'

It is his first real spoken English in forty years or more.

-

''Ere the buggers are!' shouts Dave as he hears Phil's car pulling up outside, beeping the horn. 'Come on then, Jim, you ready?'

'I dunno, I might 'ave to bow out,' says the landlord uncertainly, looking at his watch. 'I told Reenie we'd be back early this afternoon. At this rate we'll never get back.'

'You a man or a mouse, Jimbo? We ain't gonna get all the way over to Watford, pick up his cheque an' come straight back, now are we? We're goin' to 'ave a have a sherbet or three.'

'That's what I'm worried about.'

'Shut up! We'll 'ave a ball! Don't be such a wuss, just don't tell 'er.'

Impatiently, Phil toots the horn again.

'So, you comin' or what?'

Jimbo walks behind the bar and calls up the stairs. 'We're off then, love,' he says more by way of a question than a statement.

'Have a lovely time,' they hear her call down. 'Go careful now.'

'We might be a bit later than I said,' he chances apprehensively.

'That's fine. I can manage. Just try not to get too drunk, yeah?'

''Kin' 'ell,' says Jimbo under his breath. 'What's come over her all of a sudden?'

'Let's 'op it then, before she changes her mind,' Dave urges him. 'Come on. Out!'

-

As Detlef feels the plane banking into its descent, he tugs at his earlobes and swallows hard - a trick he'd first been shown on his one and only parachute jump in the May of 1940. Back then, he'd been sat on a hard bench in the bowels of an unpressurised Junker, *ein Tante Ju*, behind enemy lines and flying over Holland, young and terrified. Right now, he feels pretty much the same, but older. Much, much older.

-

Standing next to his two-door Fiesta, Phil is holding the driver's side door as wide open as it will go. 'Jeezus, Jimbo!' he says, then sliding the seat far forward. 'You gonna be able to fit in there?'

'An' I ain't movin'!' says Derek, happily ensconced in the relative spaciousness of the front passenger seat. 'I'm stayin' right where I am!'

'No, there ain't many of 'im to the pound is there?' ribs Dave, sliding himself in first.

'Oi! Button it, you,' says Jimbo, already blowing hard in anticipation. 'I'll get in!'

'Got a shoehorn, Phil?' Dave continues to poke fun.

'Button it I said!'

'Hey! We should start callin' 'im Jumbo!'

'Stop it, girls, stop it,' Phil tries to calm them, 'and don't forget your seatbelts neither, we don't wanna all end up like Dekko's son's mate, now do we?'

'Fuck off, Phil!' says Derek but buckling up all the same. 'I don't wanna be reminded, thank you!'

Now dropping steadily through and below the clouds, Detlef is at long last rewarded with a clear view of the terrain below as the still very familiar landscape of the English countryside comes up fast to meet him. Blinking back sudden and unexpected tears, it takes him straight back, back to the end of his war and to his initial incarceration, back to the ramshackle farm and to old man Ogden and his family. Pulling out his handkerchief, he covers his nose and mouth to suppress the urge to sob out loud as his recollection of their curmudgeonly but genuine kindness gives him some much-needed sense of hope.

He cannot help but wonder whether any of them might still be alive? Ogden and his wife would surely be dead, he knows that, but what about their son, Dick? And his friend Frankie too? The one who had so kindly stepped in as his best man. After all, they were all of a similar age, were they not? They might still be about.

-

'Are you all done then?' asks Margaret, looking at Ellen's nearly completed plate, her knife and fork neatly aligned together. 'You've done well. Are you ready for your cup of tea?'

'Oh, yes please. One sugar, not too much milk.'

'I know,' says Margaret, smiling. 'I'll get it for you now.'

-

Thud! Thud!

Detlef is rudely jolted back into the here and now as the shuddering plane hits the runway, decelerating hard and thrusting him forward in his seat until it comes to a near standstill.

Then, as it turns and taxis back, he catches his first sight of the large and modern terminal building, a far cry from the near military airfield he'd been flown out from at the tail end of the 1950's. 'Welcome to Bristol International Airport' it proudly announces.

'Hier bin ich dann,' he says to himself as the sickly sharpness of acid reflux suddenly surges unwelcome into his mouth.

-

'Anyone got any objections if I light up?' asks Dave, flicking open a pack of Marlboro.

'Yeah, me!' says Phil, flicking the ignition.

'Better not be any o' that wacky-baccy, whatever you call it!' says Jimbo before reaching down in between his legs to rearrange his gonads and trying to find the best position for his knees.

'One won't hurt, Phil,' tries Dave again, ignoring Jimbo's comment.

'I said no,' reasserts Phil

'I can't go the whole journey without a ciggie either!' says Derek. 'Send me the valeting bill if it bothers ya that much?' he says, reaching back over his shoulder to take one of Dave's.

Realising he's on a hiding to nothing, Phil relinquishes. 'Bloody 'ell! Just try an' blow the smoke out the window, yeah?' he concedes. 'I got kids remember. But do yourself a favour, Dekko, before you light up, just call ol' Jefferson, yeah?' he insists, pulling out his wallet and handing him the piece of paper with the telephone number written down on it. 'Just do it.'

-

Detlef collects his case from the carousel and lifts it onto a trolley. Slowly, he pushes it out through the Customs Hall and into Arrivals where, unnervingly, he is confronted by a sea of expectant faces eagerly awaiting friends and relatives but not anyone for him, of course.

So, to the joyous squeals of recognition and excited laughter that make him feel even more isolated and alone, he eases himself out between two stony-faced and shiny-trousered drivers holding up scrawled names written skew-whiff on bits of old cardboard and walks over towards the ubiquitous coffee shops, burger bars, and car rental booths and in search of the exit.

-

'Ellen, if you don't mind me being nosey?' says Margaret as she brings her hot drink. 'Only I was wondering, when exactly did you lose your husband? You can tell me to mind my own business if you like?'

The old lady cradles the cup, warming her hands before speaking. 'Derek was only a baby,' she tells her. 'It was forty-seven years this September.'

'Oh, I'm sorry to hear that, Ellen. How terrible. I had no idea it was that long!'

'I don't mind.'

'It must have been very hard for you, and for little Derek.'

'Yes, it was. But I was one of the lucky ones, I had my family.'

'I can imagine, back then. So, what happened to him?'

Again, the old lady pauses. 'He was killed,' she then says, maintaining the family story such that, now, she almost believes it herself.

'How awful!'

'Yes, he worked in the docks, you know. It was a very dangerous place.'

'I can imagine. Oh, how sad!'

'I cried for a month, I did.'

'I bet you did.'

'I still miss him terrible.'

'Of course, you do!' commiserates Margaret. 'Of course you do.'

-

'There ya go. Not difficult was it?' says Phil as Derek ends the telephone conversation.

Derek shrugs it off like it was his idea all along, but he doesn't look entirely happy.

'So, you an' Jez off to see Jefferson tomorra then, Dekko,' says Jimbo from the back seat having had no option other than to listen to the conversation, as they all had done. 'Nice one. What time?'

'Ten o'clock.'

'You'll have to look a bit sharp then,' warns Phil. 'You don't wanna be late.'

'I'll get up, don't worry about that.'

'He's good, Jefferson. He'll help,' Dave chips in.

'We'll see, shall we,' says Derek. 'At least the police have released him pending their enquiries.'

'Have they?' queries Phil.

'Yeah, or so he says.'

'Jefferson? How did he know?'

'How d'you think? Marion. She's already been onto him this morning, the interfering cow.'

'She obviously didn't trust ya to get on with it then, did she?'

'What is this? Twenty fuckin' questions or summat?' Derek snaps, shutting them all up.

-

'So, there was never anyone else for you then, Ellen?'

'Oh, no! Nobody could replace my Detlef,' she says, accidently letting his real name slip for the first time since she could remember.

'That's an unusual name, Ellen. Where does it come from?

'I meant Derek,' she tries to correct herself. 'Derek was named after him.'

'Ah, OK. I just thought you said Detlef, or something like it.'

Hearing his name spoken, Ellen begins to cry quietly.

'Oh, I'm sorry, my love,' says Margaret, stroking the old lady's hairline. 'I should never have asked. Forget I said anything. Please, have a sip of tea.'

'I mustn't,' mutters Ellen.

'Mustn't what?'

'I'm never to mention his name.'

'Why ever not?' Margaret asks, now thoroughly confused.

'He wouldn't have it.'

'Who wouldn't have it?'

'Father,' the old lady now sobs. 'He wouldn't allow it.'

-

Staring out through the revolving doors and into the cold and wintery world beyond, Detlef holds on tight to the trolley for a moment and steadies himself.

In his head, he's counting down like he was that young paratrooper all over again - *Eintausendeins, eintausendzwei ...*

-

It's like a fuckin' sardine can, stuck in the back 'ere,' groans Dave. 'Can't you step on a bit, Phil?'

'No, I can't! She's strugglin' wi' four up as it is.'

'So how far have we got to go then?' asks Derek blearily, his head already back, his eyes closed.

'Gi' me a break, guys, we've barely been on the motorway five minutes!' answers Phil. 'This ain't the Starship bloody Enterprise ya know!'

'Yeah, beam me up, Scottie!' laughs Dave a little maniacally.

'Can we have a stop soon though, lads?' asks Jimbo and already sounding a little desperate. 'My knees are givin' me some serious gip back 'ere, an' to tell ya the truth, I could do with a wazz.'

'Didn't you 'ave one before you left?' asks Phil as if to a child.

'Yeah, but, you know how it is...'

'Me too. I could do with a visit meself,' adds Derek. 'That tea must o' gone right through me.'

'There's a Service Station soon,' Dave informs them, keenly. 'Leigh Delamare, Chippenham way.'

'Fuckin' 'ell!' Phil again acquiesces. 'I'll pull off as soon as I can, but then we gotta push on. Alright?'

-

Upon leaving the terminal building, Detlef is immediately overcome with a powerful sense of déjà-vu as the dank and wintery air of England invades his airways.

He remembers it all too well and it fills him with a peculiar sense of dread and homecoming all at the same time. 'This,' he thinks to himself, '*this* is it.'

So, pulling back his shoulders, he heads towards the marked taxi rank as briskly and as assuredly as he can.

-

'Do you want to talk about it, Ellen?' asks Margaret looking very concerned. 'We could get someone to help if you like? Someone trained?'

'No, I don't want to talk to a stranger,' says Ellen, wiping her eyes.

'Me then. I'll listen if you like?'

'Would you?'

'Yes, of course I would.'

'I've never spoken to anyone before.'

'Then you can start now,' Margaret gently suggests. 'I'm all ears.'

-

Eagle-eyed for his next fare, the driver of the first taxi in line (an older, square grilled Mercedes) jumps out and picks up his case before Detlef has even reached him and puts it into the boot, slamming the lid. 'Hi! You have good flight?' he asks, friendly and upbeat and a man that Detlef guesses can only be in his early to mid-twenties.

'*Ja, danke*, yes, thank you,' he answers, quickly correcting himself once again.

'Hey, you from Germany, yes? I can tell,' observes the driver, smiling broadly.

'Yes, I am,' acknowledges Detlef, taking some cheer in the young man's jovial demeanour and somehow detecting his own very un-English accent.

'So, where?' the driver asks.

Detlef pulls out his documentation tucked alongside his passport and begins to read from his hotel booking.

'No, no. I meant, where you from in *Deutschland*?'

'Oh, Hannover, I am from the city of Hannover,' replies Detlef, once again trying hard to expand on one or two-word answers.

'Nice. Very nice,' the driver repeats, pretending recognition but not knowing the city at all. 'So, now you can tell me, where do you want to go? I speak a little *Deutsch* if you like?'

'No, I must speak English,' says Detlef, holding the print-out for the young man to see.

'Redland Park Hotel, with post code! Excellent! I have super-duper new Sat-Nav, look,' the driver says proudly, pointing to it suctioned to the inside of his windscreen.

'Very good,' says Detlef he goes towards the front passenger door. 'I can sit here?' he asks.

The young man hurriedly runs around and opens it for him. 'Sure, go ahead! I help you brush up your English!' he says excitedly before getting in himself. 'And for you, I give lesson for extra special price!'

Detlef looks at the driver uncertainly.

'Ha! Don't worry, my friend, it's my joke!' says the young man, smiling and reaching across to shake Detlef's hand. 'I'm Maciej*,' he introduces himself, 'I can see you are kind man so, for you, it's free!'

'My name is Detlef,' replies Detlef, pleasantly amused.

*Pronounced Ma-chay

Chapter 12

It's not overlong before Phil is indicating to turn into the Leigh Delamare Service Station on the M4. 'But we can't 'ang about 'ere long, you lot,' he warns them before pulling into a parking space and yanking up the handbrake to emphasise as much. 'We got bloody miles to go yet!'

Still, all are relieved to get out of the cramped and noisy Fiesta and stretch their legs for a few minutes, particularly poor Jimbo who soon hurries himself into the building followed closely by the other three.

-

'I think you speak English great!' congratulates Maciej enthusiastically as they drive in towards the city.

'I was here before,' reveals Detlef, and relieved to discover that, yes, the English language seems to be flooding back to him.

'I knew it! I think to myself, this man, he has been here before.'

'Yes, but many, many years ago. I have forgotten much.'

'No! You know it! I have only been here eighteen months,' Maciej tells him.

'You like it?'

'Yeah, it's fantastic! Great country! I have beautiful wife, beautiful house, this beautiful taxi, what's not to like? So, tell me, where do you think I am from?'

Detlef has no real idea other than Eastern European perhaps and hazards a guess. '*Polska, vielleicht*?'

'Wow! Yeah! You got it in one! From Poland, near from Warsaw. You know it?'

'Maybe once.'

'Don't tell me! You were in the bloody war! Bang, bang!' Maciej grins boyishly, pointing two fingers over the steering wheel like a pistol.

Awkwardly, silently, Detlef brushes some imaginary flecks from his trousers, saying nothing.

'Maybe you were Nazi Stormtrooper!' adds Maciej with an innocent enough laugh, his eyes fixed on the road.

Detlef's continued silence alerts the driver who then turns to look at him. 'Hey, I'm sorry, I did not mean to upset. I joke too much!' he apologises profusely.

'Don't worry. I am just tired.'

'My mother, she tells me, one day, Maciej, she says, your stupid joking will get you into big trouble!'

'Please, don't' worry.'

'Thank you. You are nice man. Anyway, that's all gone,' continues Maciej with a sweep of his arm to suggest everything outside his vehicle. 'This is *Europa* now! One big happy family, yeah?'

'Yes, I hope so.'

'Hey! You *are* good! You understand everything! I have you speaking hind leg off donkey, like the Queen, no time!'

-

With Derek, Phil, and Jimbo lining up at the urinals, Dave slips into one of the back cubicles, locking the door.

'So, I wonder where we'll end up after I've picked up me cheque, lads?' asks Derek, already contemplating his next drink whilst absent-mindedly looking at a poster framed in front of his face about the early signs of prostate cancer. 'There's bound to be a decent pub somewhere thereabouts.'

'I used to know of a few good waterin' 'oles,' informs Dave from behind them. 'There's plenty.'

'Don't plan on makin' too a big thing out of it, guys,' complains Phil. 'Remember who's drivin' 'ere, yeah?'

Dave's voice is heard again. 'Don't be such a fuckin' wet blanket,' he says.

'Oi you! I'm buggered if I'm gonna 'ang around an' watch all you lot all get plastered whilst I'm left as sober as a judge.'

'I won't be plastered,' says Jimbo, now unable to empty his bladder and still worrying about the time, despite his wife's blessing. 'I'll 'ave stuff to do when I get back.'

'Give it a rest, Jim,' says Dave.

But Derek isn't listening to any of their concerns. 'D'you see this?' he says, reading. 'Do you have difficulty urinating?'

Jimbo zips up, pretending to have finished.

'It's already piss, what we get at the 'ravellers,' Dave calls out again. 'Ain't that right, Jim?'

'What *is* your problem, Dave?' he demands, 'Are you goin' to carry on like this all fuckin' day?'

'Will you two stop bleedin' bickerin'?' demands Phil, going to wash his hands. 'So, we all done then? Dave? You ready?'

'I'll see you outside in a mo,' he says. 'I ain't done yet.'

'Christ, you givin' birth to a python or summat?'

'Can someone buy me a few tinnies while we're waitin'?' Derek then asks. 'I could kill a can o' beer or two.'

'I thought you said you were going to take it easy?' questions Phil.

'Yeah, I will, mate, but not today, eh?' replies Derek a tad guiltily, his resolve disappearing by the second.

'An' while your at it, can ya get me twenty Marlboro's?' Dave calls out again followed by an almost indiscernible little sniff. 'You've smoked all mine, ya theivin' arse 'oles.'

'If you gimme me the money?' says Phil and feeling that the onus is on him somehow.

'I will, when I finished,' says Dave.

'Slip it under the door. I'll gi' ya your change!'

'Can't you wait?'

'No.'

'Ah, fuckin' hell!' Dave then says over dramatically.

'What?'

'Where is it?'

'Where's what?'

'Me wallet! I can't find me wallet!'

'Nice try. Gimme the money.'

'I must o' left it at 'ome!'

''Ave you dropped it in the car?' asks Jimbo. 'It might be in the back?'

'No, don't think so.'

'How d'ya know?'

'I just do.'

'You lyin' little shit,' says Jimbo. 'You're expectin' a free ride, aren't ya?'

'Fuck off, Jim!' Dave yells. 'I'm tellin' ya the truth! I definitely 'ad it this mornin'.'

'You must think we were born yesterday!'

'Now shut it, the lot o' ya!' Derek shouts them all down. 'Nobody's goin' to go short. D'you hear me? Nobody! Now, let's get some beer an' fags in an' get on our way!'

-

As the taxi continues to speed into the outskirts of the city, Detlef is at last pleased to see there are still many of the older Victorian style houses that were once so very familiar to him. 'Maciej, can I ask a question?' he says.

'Fire away, my friend, all ears open.'

'How far is Bris-ling-ton?' he asks, pronouncing the word in three distinct syllables.

'Brislington? Not so far. Why?'

'There is a house there. I would like to see it.'

'Now?'

'Yes, if we can?'

'Sure! Tell me, you lived there once perhaps?'

'Yes. I have written the address,' says Detlef, pulling out some more sheets of paper from his coat pocket. 'Will it take long?'

Maciej takes a quick look. 'Ten minutes, fifteen maybe?'

'Mmm,' says Detlef, pausing, 'is it possible there is a *toiletten*?'

'You must make piss? No problem,' says Maciej. 'There is somewhere near. We go.'

-

'So what ya gonna give us then, Dekko?' asks Dave a little over excitedly when they are all back in the car. 'Nobody'll go short you said.'

'You're fuckin' unbelievable!' Jimbo chastises him.

'Only askin'!'

'And keep yourself bloody still. It's like being sat next to a fuckin' ferret, sat next to you.'

All the same, Derek gives Dave an answer. 'You don't need to worry about money, any of ya,' he says, 'so just relax.'

-

Within just a few short minutes, the taxi is outside a large and daunting looking pub, The Raveller's Rest according to its name pinned high up on the wall.

Initially, Detlef appears reluctant to get out. He was not anticipating a place like this, so apparently down at heel with a large flag of St George draped over the front like a statement of deterrence to all things foreign. 'Will it be acceptable?' he asks uneasily.

'Sure! I know it. I take you in,' says Maciej, 'Come, they bark worse than they bite!'

Inside the pub, Reenie is busying herself behind the bar whilst talking with one or two of the older Monday lunchtime crew. 'Never seen so many,' she's saying. 'Heavin' we were.'

'Who'd o' thought it, eh? Bloody Dekko! Of all people!' says one before looking back as they hear the door swing open.

'Hi,' Maciej interrupts them, smiling, 'please, can my friend use toilet?'

'Yeah, if he must,' says Reenie, shaking her head but pointing towards the gents.

Detlef nods his thanks and disappears out through the back.

'You want a drink while you're here?' she asks.

'Sorry, I must drive.'

'Your friend?'

'No, thank you, he has to be somewhere. Next time, maybe?'

Reenie shakes her head again and returns to the two drinkers at the bar. 'Yes, Dekko had a right skin full over the weekend,' she picks up their conversation. 'Could barely stand.'

'Can't blame 'im though, can ya? Winning that lot? I'd o' got slaughtered too. How many million was it again? Five? Six?'

'No, no, well over eleven!' she says with the aloof air of someone in the know. 'That's where Jim is now, they've all gone over to Watford to pick up the cheque.'

'Watford? Tha's a fair 'ol fair jaunt.'

Hearing, Maciej tries to join in. 'Did someone here win the Lotto?' he asks excitedly.

'What's it to you?' one of the drinkers dismisses him.

'Sorry. I just try make talk, that's all,' Maciej apologises before retreating back over towards the pool table.

'They always say it won't change 'em, but it will,' continues the old punter. 'He won't wanna know us before long, you wait an' see.'

'More fool him if he thinks that,' says Reenie. 'This is where all his friends are.'

At that moment Detlef walks back into the bar rubbing and flicking his undried hands.

'All done, my friend?' asks Maciej rolling an un-potted pool ball into a pocket.

'*Ja, ich habe.* Thank you.'

'Great, let's go then,' he says then turning to the landlady. 'Thanks! You make an old man very happy!'

'Don't make a habit of it though, lads. This ain't a Public Convenience,' smirks one of the other drinkers as if on Reenie's behalf.

'Thank you,' repeats Detlef, oblivious to the remark and as the two of them make their way out.

When she is sure they are gone, Reenie tuts. 'There's them Eastern Europeans for ya, taking liberties,' she says. 'All over the place they are nowadays, can't move for 'em. I've seen the young one in here before, mind you. A taxi driver I think he is. A Pole. No bother though. Pleasant enough.'

'If my ears ain't deceivin' me, Reen, the old boy sounded more like a kraut to me, when he just spoke,' says the one.

'Funny that, I could o' swore I recognised 'im when he first walked in,' says the other.

'Yeah, now you come to mention it, he did look a bit familiar, didn't he?' agrees Reenie. 'Top up, you two?'

'Sorry about that,' Maciej apologises as they get back into his taxi. 'Not quite so friendly after all, eh?'

Detlef shrugs. 'It's OK. I know it.'

'I think they are not so happy because they are jealous. I hear them say someone just won the Lottery, you know, like Euro Millions.'

'Ah, yes,' acknowledges Detlef. 'My wife and I, we buy it sometimes, in Germany,' he says. 'Lucky person.'

'I would love to win lots of money!' exclaims Maciej.

'Too much is not so good I think,' Detlef cautions him.

'For sure,' agrees Maciej, 'you suddenly have many friends for the wrong reasons, eh?'

'Yes, I think so.'

Chapter 13

'If you don't mind me asking, why do you visit here now?' enquires Maciej as they crawl through busy streets of Bedminster. 'Not just to see a house, I think?'

'There is someone I must find,' Detlef offers by way of an answer.

'Must be someone pretty important.'

Detlef nods but is unwilling to elaborate.

'A friend?' Maciej continues to pry.

The old man shifts uneasily in his seat. 'No,' he says abruptly.

'I'm sorry. I shut up now,' apologises Maciej once again. 'My mother, she also tells me to keep my big nose out too!'

'Und vielleicht ist er gar nicht hier,' Detlef then whispers to himself, taking refuge in his native tongue and quietly exhausted at having to speak English.

But Maciej understands him it. 'But perhaps he is not here?' he repeats. 'You don't know? Do you not have address with postcode?'

'Nein, ... und nur eine Woche, um ihn zu finden,' Detlef continues and feeling more than a little ridiculous as the words leave his mouth.

'Just one week? You bite off a lot to chew I think, my friend!' says Maciej as they now head out on the Bath Road towards Arnos Vale where, once again, Detlef can see that the city has changed beyond all recognition and the enormity of the task looks ever more daunting. 'Hey! I know! If you want driver for few days, I'm your man!' Maciej then suggests enthusiastically. 'Here, take my number. You call me anytime,' he adds, handing him a business card from a stack wedged in the centre console. 'I would like to help. Would be nice to find who you are looking for.'

'That would be very kind of you,' says Detlef, grateful for the offer.

'And don't fret at the cost! I give you special price! How about seventy-five pounds per day, plus gas?'

Detlef thinks for a moment. 'Yes,' he agrees. 'That would be good.'

'Deal!' says Maciej and once again reaching across to take Detlef's hand. 'So, please, tell me, has it been a long time since you last see him?'

'Sechsundvierzig Jahre.'

'Wow! That's a long time, nearly twice my age! Is it perhaps your brother you look for?' Maciej attempts another guess.

Again, Detlef looks momentarily ill at ease, clicking the business card with his thumbnail before answering. 'No, it is my son,' he then reveals, his voice catching. 'I am looking for my son.'

'Your son?' responds Maciej with astonishment and pressing his foot a little harder on the accelerator. 'That's really important, Detlef! You must find him!'

'I hope.'

'I can call you Detlef?' the young driver adds politely.

'Yes, Maciej, *du kannst*.'

At long last, the four boys finally arrive at the National Lottery's Headquarters and pull up directly outside reception and into the visitors parking bay.

Immediately, Derek pulls the door lever to get out. 'See you all in a bit then, yeah?' he says. 'Wish me luck, not that I need it.'

''Ang about, mate, I'll come in with ya if you like?' offers Phil, sounding a little disappointed not to be asked to accompany him.

'Hey! What about us too?' asks Dave from the back seat and sounding increasingly agitated. 'What we s'posed to do? Sit 'ere like piffy?'

'We can't all go in,' Phil goes to explain.

'Why the fuck not?'

'It'd look stupid, that's why not. They'll wonder what's bleedin' hit 'em, all goin' in mob 'anded.'

'You sayin' I look stupid?' reacts Dave, irrationally.

'Hey, guys, remember what I said, yeah? Chill,' demands Derek once again. 'Trust me, I'll be in an' out in two shakes of a lamb's tail. No point in wastin' good drinkin' time now is there?'

'Gi' me a shout if there's a problem, Dekko?' Phil tries again as Derek exits the vehicle and swaggers towards the entrance, his arms held out from his side like a gunslinger on his way to a shootout.

'Pound to a pinch o' shite he'll be back out in a minute, lookin' for a bit o' moral support,' says Phil as Derek turns to perform one of his elaborate bows on the steps of the offices before disappearing inside.

'Meanin' you, I s'pose?' says Dave, taking a pop once again.

'What is your fuckin' problem?' demands Phil. 'Come on. Tell us!'

'You! I'll come wi' ya, Dekko? Make that phone call, Dekko. I've done this for ya, Dekko, I've done that for ya, Dekko,' mimics Dave, childishly.

'You'll be bloody walkin' home at this rate if you don't shut the fuck up,' warns Phil, stabbing at him with his finger.

127

'Ooh, touched a raw nerve, 'ave I?'

''Ere we bloody go,' groans Jimbo ominously.

'An' you can fuck off too!' rants Dave, turning his aggression. 'Don't tell me it ain't crossed your mind what you'll get out o' all this?'

'What are you on about?' says Jimbo like the thought hadn't even crossed his mind.

'Oi! I'll 'ave you know, you little shit,' growls Phil quietly but furiously, 'that I'm his best mate, an' 'ave been for years. I'm not after a damn fuckin' thing!'

'Ooh, I'm his best mate!' Dave apes him once again, thrusting his face forwards and grimacing. 'Like fuck, you are! A pig at the trough more like!'

Realising this is about to turn very ugly, Jimbo puts a hand on Dave's shoulder and tries to pull him back and force his bulk in between them both, but all to no avail.

'That's enough!' shouts Phil as he twists a full one-hundred and eighty degrees in his seat and launches a full-blown haymaker that lands full square on Dave's nose.

Splat!

It explodes on impact, blood everywhere, and sparking a mad free-for-all that rocks the car's suspension like there's a pair of lovers in there going at it hell for leather, not two grown men trying to knock seven bales of shit out of each another.

Shamefully, the short-lived spectacle is being watched with stunned horror and amazement by one or two faces at the office reception window and within seconds Derek comes running back out. 'For fuck sakes!' he yells, opening the door and seeing Dave's bloodied face. 'What the hell's goin' on in 'ere, you stupid bastards! Look at the state o' ya!'

'Don't look at me, Dekko,' says Jimbo, coughing and wheezing at the exertion of it all and trying to distance himself.

'Phil? Dave?' Derek then asks but fails to get a reply from either of them. 'Fuckin' behave yourselves, or else!' he warns them before slamming the car door almost off its hinges and hurrying back inside.

-

On reaching the Brislington area of the city and heading off into the maze of residential streets where he had once lived, Detlef is a little encouraged to find it feels less disturbed somehow and it doesn't take him too long to regain some sense of familiarity.

Soon, nearly every turn seems to evoke a dim and distant memory for him - where there had once been a fruit and vegetable shop, a newsagent and tobacconist, how he used to know the people that lived in that house (or was it that one?), and the bus stop, still there, where he, Ellen, and baby Derek used to travel into the city centre on the rare occasion when money had allowed.

'*Ich denke es ist hier auf der rechten Seite,*' he then announces, pointing, his voice cracking.

Detlef's heart literally skips a beat as they turn into the top end of his old street, looking down into the very jaws of it. This is where it had all happened, after all. This is where his life had changed irrevocably.

As the taxi slowly makes its way between rows of cars parked nose to tail on either side, Detlef is astonished to see how much busier the street appears, congested even. He recalls it being tidier too, more cared for, with the front gardens that were once so well-tended now looking unkempt and filled with countless wheelie bins awaiting collection or converted into parking places with their walls now long demolished. '*Halt!* Here, here!' he then says.

Maciej manages to pull into a single space directly opposite a rather imposing looking three storey semi-detached Victorian house built of large blocks of grey and red sandstone with white painted quoins. Amazingly, it really isn't too dissimilar from the way Detlef remembers it and as he looks up towards the steep gable end with its green painted filigree soffits, his gaze is inexorably drawn to a single sash window high up under the eaves on the right-hand side. It was there, in that very room, looking out, that he had held Ellen in his arms on their first night of married life together. There, cradling her distended abdomen, where he'd felt the baby kick for the first time and, with their heads touching, there when Ellen's soft tears had wet his shirt.

'You want to get out, have look around?' Maciej asks gently.

'No, I just wanted to see it, that's all,' Detlef replies, swallowing hard and coughing. 'Please, you can take me to the hotel now. I am very tired.'

'You sure?'

'I'm sure, Maciej. Thank you for bringing me here.'

'No problem, my friend. Let's go.'

-

With cheque in hand, but with a face like thunder, Derek finally emerges from the offices. 'You made me look like a right fuckin' twat in there!' he says, getting into the car. 'Wonder they didn't call the flamin' cops. They were bloody close an' all, 'til I explained!'

'But you've got it then?' says Phil rather sheepishly.

'Yeah, o' course I've bloody got it! But I want to have this out right here and now! This is supposed to be one of the best days in my life and you lot seem hell bent on fuckin' it up for me!'

'Go on, Philip, you tell 'im,' says Dave, holding his head back and pinching his nose like he is the aggrieved victim in all of this. 'Go on!'

'What's he on about?' Derek asks his friend.

Phil doesn't want to answer. 'You just watch you don't bleed all over my seats, you nasty little piece o' shit,' he says, addressing Dave.

'Come on. I wanna know. Spit it out!' Derek insists.

'Alright, alright!' says Phil. 'He reckons that I, we, all of us, are only here to get our hands on some o' yer money ... an' I reacted. OK?'

'Yeah? And?'

'An' nothing, that was it. Bit of a punch up,' says Phil, flushing red with embarrassment.

With that, Derek throws his own head back and roars with laugher. 'Course you are, you stupid cunts! You think I don't know that? I weren't born fuckin' yesterday!'

'It don't bother you then?' asks Jimbo.

'Course it don't bother me! I'd be like a rat up a bleedin' drainpipe demandin' money wi' menaces if it was one of you lot!'

'Let's 'ave a look then, Dekko?' asks Dave, very keen to see such a monumental cheque.

Derek holds it up for them all to see. 'There ya go, you bunch o' money grabbin' fuckwits!' he says, flapping it victoriously. 'Fuckin' millions!'

'Jeez! That sure is a sight for sore eyes,' says Jimbo, reaching forward to touch it like it.

'So, wha' do you reckon, Phil?' Derek asks his friend directly.

'Nice one, mate,' he says. 'I'm made up for ya. Honestly I am.'

'Good! Now, let's go an' find a fuckin' pub! I'm bloody gaspin'!'

'You need to get it into a bank first,' Phil cautions once again.

'Alright, dad,' says Derek, laughing, 'when we see one. But first things first, before I do, I want you all to kiss and make up or none o' ya are gonna get a fuckin' bean, d'ya hear me? Shake hands. Like now! I mean t!'

-

Mercifully for Detlef who is now beginning to feel very tired indeed, it is not too long before Maciej is driving onto the asphalt forecourt of the Redland Park Hotel - a Victorian Gothic building with a large and pointed turret rising majestically from one corner, the red leaves of its now nearly bare Wisteria carpeting the ground underneath. 'Hey, Detlef,

130

it's just like a Bavarian castle!' he says before jumping out to take the case from the boot. 'Today I look at more houses today than ever before. This one suits you, I think.'

-

At first glance, the aptly named 'Jackpot Bar and Grill', looks a bit too smart for their liking and obviously part of a restaurant chain, but, hey, it's open all day, there's a big sign outside that says as much.

'As long as it's got bloody beer, I don't give a toss,' says Derek, taking the decision and being obediently followed in by the others, their hands in their pockets, their heads down like they're on a very serious mission indeed.

-

With its highly polished brass handles and finger plates, Maciej pushes his back into the double wood and glass doors allowing Detlef to enter the dimly lit reception area that smells heavily of beeswax and lavender. It is eerily silent too, save the lazy tick-tock of a long case clock standing in the far corner.

'Wow, it's like a church,' says Maciej in reverential tones and pointing out an impressive lead glass chandelier glistening at the top of the wide and open staircase. 'Now, look, do you want me to wait with you until you are booked in?' he adds.

'No, I will be alright now, Maciej,' says Detlef, 'but first I must pay you. How much do I owe?'

'What's money between friends, eh?' Maciej pretends to dismiss, then, 'should be thirty pounds, but you give me twenty, *zwanzig*, and we call it quits, yeah?'

Detlef pulls out his wallet and hands Maciej a new fifty-pound note and refusing to take any change. 'Keep it, please. I will need you tomorrow.'

'You sure?'

'Yes. I cannot thank you enough, Maciej.'

'That's fantastic! I listen out for you, yeah?'

'Yes. I shall need an early start.'

-

Inside the cavernous bar-cum-restaurant, it is virtually empty with its busy lunchtime trade all but gone.

'What's it to be then, lads?' Jimbo is first to offer as they congregate at one end of the very lengthy bar.

'No, my shout,' insists Phil standing dangerously close to a teetering stack of dirty dinner plates still awaiting removal and whipping his wallet out before Jimbo has a chance.

'No, you done the drivin'. I'll get 'em in,' objects Jimbo.

'You can get the next one,' says Phil.

Still pinching his nose, Dave then chips in as they fall over each
to be as pleasant as possible. 'If someone can bung me a few quid, I'll
do the honours. I'll gi' it ya back, promise.' he says.

'Will someone just get the bloody ale in!' says Dekko, laughing.
'As I said, nobody'll be out o' pocket,' he adds, tapping his jacket to
where the cheque is now hidden.

'You really wanna be careful wi' that,' warns Phil again.

'I will. Stop worryin'.'

Phil doesn't look convinced. 'So, tell us, wha'd they say at the
offices?' he continues.

'Well, I gave 'em me ID, an' the ticket o' course, and that was
about it,' says Derek. 'They could see I was in a rush an' that, what wi'
you lot goin' fuckin' mental outside.'

'But, surely to God, they must o' given you some info or advice?'

'Yeah, o' course they did. Gave me a direct number, said I could
call 'em anytime I want an' told me there's plenty o' support if I need,'
answers Derek.

'Will ya?'

'Nah, I got it now, ain't I? Do what I like.'

'So, that was it?'

'Yeah, pretty much, other than to say they asked whether or not I
wanted to go public again or not.'

'And?

'I said yes.'

'No!'

'Yeah! And why not?' repeats Derek. 'I gave 'em the pub's
number, Jim. Alright?'

'Yeah. That'll keep Reen happy at least,' he says with a smile.

'Now,' continues Derek, 'is there anyone actually behind this
bloody bar?'

-

Detlef sees a small bell on the ledge by a split-door hatch marked
'Reception'. He picks it up and gently rings it.

'One moment, please,' says a disembodied voice from somewhere
inside before the doors slide open. 'Good afternoon, how can I help
you?' asks the proprietor, a man so tall that Detlef cannot see his face
and finds himself talking to his cardiganed chest. 'Otto, Detlef Otto, I
have a room booked,' he says.

'Ah yes, from Germany. We have been expecting you. I trust you
had a good journey,' says the man in a rather perfunctory manner whilst

running his forefinger down a small list of names in a well-thumbed and large desk diary.

'Yes, I did. Thank you.'

'Excellent. Right, here we are, room twelve. Welcome to the Redland Park Hotel, Mr Otto. I trust that you will enjoy your stay with us. Let me get someone to take your luggage.'

-

'Come on, lads,' says Derek, finishing his second pint after barely fifteen minutes. 'This place is like the bloody moon! A shit 'ole.'

So, decision unanimously made, they go in search of a more suitable watering hole - a proper boozer, they say, one with a bit of atmosphere, a pool table, or a darts board at very least and pile back into Phil's car.

-

Now sat at a small writing bureau in his room, Detlef sets about phoning Gisella on his new mobile telephone. He's never owned one before, but Oskar had programmed in the important numbers and had shown him the basics. He presses the appropriate keys. It rings.

'*Hallo,*' says Gisella's familiar but anxious sounding voice. '*Detlef? Is that you?*'

'Yes, it's me, my love. How are you?'

'*Are you there safely yet? I've been worried sick.*'

'Yes, everything is fine,' he reassures her. 'I am here, in the hotel, safe and sound.'

'*Oh, good.*'

'It's very comfortable and I've had a good journey. It just took a little longer than I thought, that's all.'

'*Thank heavens! I am so relieved, but tell me, have you eaten yet?*' she worries. '*You must eat, you must look after yourself.*'

'Don't worry, my love, I promise I will eat something soon,' says Detlef, smiling at her concern.

'*And your medication. Don't forget your medication! You did remember it didn't you?*'

'Of course.'

'*What time is it there?*'

'Half past two. I am going to try to get some sleep. I am a little tired.'

'*But you have not eaten yet! Oh, Detlef!*'

-

Following the signs out of Watford and towards the M25, Phil spots a branch of a bank. 'Is that yours, Dekko?' he asks.

'What?'

'The bank! There!'

'Yeah. It is.'

'Good! Well, go in an' pay it in then,' insists Phil, pulling over. 'We'll wait here. Just do it.'

So, looking a little dishevelled and smelling of booze already, Derek saunters in and pushes the cheque under the cashier's window. 'Can I just pop this in, love?' he says and like it was an everyday occurence.

As soon as she spots the logo on the cheque, her eyes widen, clasping her neck as she reads the huge amount written on it.

'Bet you ain't seen one as big as that, now 'ave ya, girl?' says Derek enjoying the double-entendre. 'A monster or what!'

Nervously, she beckons over an equally amazed work colleague to double check as she carefully taps in the figures in on her keyboard. She doesn't want any mistakes, an extra zero, a misplaced number could cost her her job she thinks.

After completing the transaction, she asks, as per her training, whether there was anything else she could do for him? But the question, and the very way she asked it, somehow gave it a whole new meaning and she can't help but colour up..

'Depends on what you're offerin'?' says Derek, grinning lasciviously. 'But now you come to mention it, any danger I can take a bit out now?' he asks.

'Of course, of course. What were you thinking?' she stutters.

'Not much, just a bit o' spendin' money, that's all.'

She then scans her screen and begins to frown. 'There don't appear to be any cleared funds at the moment, Mr Dando, just a few pence, I'm afraid,' she says, embarrassed and unsure what to do for the best. 'I can go and ask the manager if you like? How much are you looking for?'

'Just a hundred,' he says.

'Oh, fine, that shouldn't be a problem, I wouldn't think.'

'Thousand,' he adds.

'You want a thousand?'

'No, a hundred thousand,' he teases her.

'A hundred thousand pounds? I don't think we keep that type of money here.'

Derek lets out a great guffaw. 'Nah, just pullin' yer leg, love. I just wanted to say it,' he says. 'A couple o' hundred'll do. That should be enough. Just a few more drinkin' tokens.'

'I'll go and ask.'

'Wait!' he stops her. 'Make it four,' he says, changing his mind.

'Four hundred?'

'Yeah, four hundred. One each. That'd be perfect. You're a star.'

-

Despite his fatigue, Detlef simply can't settle. The events of the day had truly taken it out of him, and seeing the house where he had once lived had affected him more than he might have imagined. It plays on his mind and only serves to remind of the terrible and sorry events that led up to his forced departure all those year ago. But more than that, he now worries as to whether he has the strength or the stamina to achieve what he came here to do. He already feels extremely tired, and alone.

-

As was ever going to be the case, the journey home turns into a long-distance pub crawl and they squeeze in at least another five or six pubs along the way and are all pretty much seven sheets to the wind on the final leg home. But nobody's counting. Nobody can, not least the driver.

After having given them all a hundred pounds each whilst insisting there should be no more discussion or argument as to who gets the drinks in, in his cups and full of magnanimity, Derek had been promising them ever larger sums of money and upping the amount with every drink that they'd had.

Now standing at a very respectable but arbitrary thirty-five thousand pounds apiece, Dave, for one, is deliriously happy about it and chortling in the back seat. It means he is well and truly out of the shit and no longer fearful of someone breaking his door down in the middle of the night, or worse. Jimbo is so intoxicated that he does not understand the implication of it at all, other than to wonder whether it is to include Derek's bar tab or not. Phil, on the other hand, can't help but feel short-changed but refrains from saying as much. Yes, it was a hell of a lot of money, he knows that, but he was Derek's best mate, was he not? Surely, he was worth more than Jimbo, and certainly whole lot more than that idiot, Dave?

-

It is not until around half-past-eleven, and at about the same time that Derek and the boys finally arrive back at the pub, that Detlef finally succumbs and falls into a fitful sleep.

Phil, heavily under the influence and nearly asleep at the wheel, almost drives smack bang into the pub wall but manages to hit the brakes just in time, jolting the other three out of their drunken slumber.

'Er! Er!' yells Dave, alarmed.

'What time is it? You still open, Jimbo?' asks Derek but barely understandable.

'Yeah. Looks like she's still up an' about,' groans Jimbo, slumped in the back but seeing that the bar lights are still on. 'Nightcap?' he then adds, sensing, too, that he might be in need of a bit of moral support.

As they all stumble into the otherwise empty pub, Reenie rolls her eyes. 'Had a good time then, I see,' she says curtly but smiling all the same.

'Yeah, yeah. Look, love ...' Jimbo starts to make his slurred apologies.

'Save it, Jim, I can barely understand a word. You're in the back room tonight, don't even think about it, yeah? Tell me all about it tomorrow,' she says.

'Dekko's gonna go public,' he tries, knowing that it will please her. 'They're gonna call ya.'

'Are they, Dekko? Great,' she says, addressing him. 'I shall have to get me skates on then, shan't I? Oh, and before I forget, there was some bloke in here earlier asking for you. Big chap he was, a Scot, said his name was Brian.'

'Who?' says Derek, unable to think straight. 'Don't know a Brian.'

'Probably the newspapers on to ya already,' suggests Dave, now giggling.

'Anyway, I'm off to bed. Just keep it down, the four o' ya, yeah?' says Reenie before leaving them to it.

With the exception of Jimbo, who simple cannot stomach another drink, the other three seat themselves around Cracker's Corner as the landlord pours each yet another pint.

Derek, dipping his head, takes a sip. 'Right, listen up!' he starts, his largesse nowhere near finished as yet. 'This is me final offer!' he slurs, lifting his glass and banging it down like he was trying to buy something rather than give it away.

'What? You takin' us all on 'oliday an' all?' asks Dave. 'Somewhere nice an' sunny?'

'An 'oliday? Am I fuck as like! Get your own bastard 'oliday! No, I've decided, it's a hundred thousand pounds apiece and that's yer lot!'

'What, out o' eleven million quid, Dekko?' chances Dave without batting an eyelid. 'A piss in the ocean, ya tight bastard!'

'Two 'undred then!' shouts Derek like he was bidding at an auction and getting carried away.

'Make it a quarter of a mil' an' we'll all be 'appy!' says Dave, pushing his luck big time and laughing hysterically.

Derek looks at him for a moment, squiffy-eyed and barely able to focus. 'OK. Done!' he shouts. 'An' not a penny more!' he exclaims before falling clean off the back of his stool and landing with an almighty thud.

For a moment or two, the other three just look at each other in stunned silence.

'Did I hear right?' asks Jimbo, teetering behind the bar and holding onto the pumps. 'Two-hundred and fifty thousand? Each?'

'That's what he said,' says Dave, grinning.

'But is 'e alright?' worries Phil. 'He might o' smacked 'is 'ead!'

'He's alright. Look!' says Dave as Derek puts his hands under his head and curls up into a ball on the floor. 'Sleepin' like a baby.'

'Christ knows how he's gonna make it to the solicitor tomorra,' remembers Phil. 'I'll 'ave to take 'im home.'

'Leave ''im where he is,' dismisses Dave. 'We'll stick 'im on a bench. In the meantime, shall we all have a little chaser, gentleman?' he then suggests. 'It seems we are all as rich as fuck.'

Chapter 14
Tuesday

Despite his desire for an early start, Detlef nearly misses the nine-thirty deadline for breakfast. Unsurprisingly, he'd had a very poor night's sleep and felt nothing short of exhausted. For a split second, he'd even considered taking it easy for the rest of the day to recover, but he knows he can't. Time is short and there's none to waste.

So, fortified by a small coffee and as much of his generous 'Full English Breakfast' as he can manage, he takes Maciej's card from out of his wallet and makes the call.

'Hi, I wonder maybe you have forgotten me?' the young driver answers.

'I'm sorry,' Detlef apologises. 'Can you still pick me up or is it too late now?'

'It's never too late, Detlef!' Maciej reassures him, his joyful enthusiasm restored. *'I'm leaving right now, like Superman at the speed of light!'*

Understanding, Detlef smiles to himself. 'Thank you,' he says. 'That's very kind of you. I shall wait downstairs.'

'OK. Twenty minutes, maybe less!'

-

Yet again, Derek finds himself waking up somewhere other than his own bed. This time it's on the pub bench seat under the window, cold and shivering, with a broadly smiling Reenie gently nudging him and handing him a strong cup of tea. 'A little piece of toast?' she then offers, which he declines, of course, not ever having the stomach for food first thing in the morning. 'I've got some lovely homemade marmalade,' she tries again.

Her extraordinarily pleasant and generous demeanour is entirely attributable to the fact that, only moments earlier, she'd spoken to her even more ravaged and ill looking husband upstairs in the back bedroom. Ashen faced and grimacing, he'd furbished her with the basics - Derek's promise of a colossal sum of money, and the fact that he was going to go public and that the Lottery people would be calling her with regard to the presentation ceremony. 'Oh, an' remind him he's got a meeting at the solicitor's this morning with his lad,' he'd told her as an afterthought.

It was just as well, Derek had clean forgotten.

-

True to his word, Maciej arrives at the hotel in very little time at all.

'So, where to first, my friend?' he asks cheerily.

'I have it here,' Detlef replies, taking out a sheet of paper from a folder with various other half remembered addresses written on it. 'Thirty-nine Cabot Road,' he reads. 'It is where my ex-wife's parents once lived.'

'Ah, the in-laws, eh?' Maciej says, laughing. 'No problem. It's in Easton. I know it.'

'I hope that someone there might remember?' Detlef wonders aloud.

'You got to start somewhere,' encourages the young man. 'Maybe you might strike gold with first swing of hammer?'

Yawning and rubbing his eyes vigorously, Detlef doesn't look or feel at all convinced.

-

Effing, blinding, and berating himself, Derek dashes down to the precinct to where Jefferson has his first-floor offices above the Rub-a-Dub-Dub launderette. Outside, already waiting, are his son, the bandage still on his head, his plastered arm in a sling, with his irate looking mother standing impatiently alongside. 'Where the hell have you been?' she demands to know before he is barely within earshot. 'We've been here bloody ages!'

'Thanks a bunch for goin' behind my back!' he answers her. 'I could o' managed without you!'

'I'm one step ahead o' you, Derek,' she bites back. 'I don't want you sayin' nuthin' stupid.'

'Whichever, whatever,' he disregards her comment, 'let's get inside before it's too late, yeah? He'll charge us all the same.'

'Ha! Very funny! Why should you care?' she says, laughing at him. 'Besides, it's free, the first half hour, ya dope.'

'An' so it should be, money grabbing bastards,' he continues, coughing and sputtering.

'Are you still pissed?' she then asks but already knowing the answer.

'Might 'ave 'ad a couple,' he admits. 'What's it to you?'

'There's a surprise! You can't even stay sober for somethin' as important as your own son! You really hack me off sometimes, Dekko!'

'Only sometimes? Tha's summat at least.'

'And do something with that disgustin' mop o' yours! You look like Worzel bloody Gummidge dragged through a hedge backwards!'

'Gimme a break! We ain't got all day to stand here discussing how I look,' he says but smoothing his hair back down all the same. 'Let's just get on with it, yeah? I'm plannin' on gettin' over to see me Mum later, give her the good news.'

'Jeezus! Haven't you told her yet? She's your bloody mother for chrissakes!'

'I've just bloody well said, haven't I?'

-

For the second time in as many days, Detlef finds himself staring at another building that is indelibly imprinted into his brain, albeit he'd only ever seen the inside of it once and on the occasion when he'd asked for Ellen's hand in marriage. But he recognises the exterior of it alright, he'd seen more than enough of that in the past.

It's only an unassuming and typical terraced house built in the 1920's, but the very sight of it makes him feel particularly apprehensive and uneasy. After all, it was here that he'd been made to feel more unwelcome than at any other time in his entire life, even more so than in his days as a POW, or his later imprisonment and forced repatriation to Germany. It had been very different on that occasion. It had been personal.

Exiting the car, he takes the few short steps to the self-same front porch where, as a much younger man, he was made to wait for what seemed like an eternity before anyone had answered him. Gingerly, he presses the doorbell, but this time, almost at once, pixelated through the textured and coloured glass, he can see a figure move towards him.

A young woman opens up, eyeing him suspiciously. 'I'm not after anything,' she says on seeing the folder held in his hand.

Confused by this, he takes a polite step back but continues. 'I'm sorry to trouble you,' he starts, 'but I wonder if you can help me?'

'I don't want anything,' she repeats and begins to push the door back to.

'No, no, please, you don't understand. I am looking for a family that used to live here, in this house, many years ago,' he persists, explaining as clearly as he can.

'We've only been here six months, so, as I said.'

'Their name was Dando,' he tries again.

'No, sorry. Doesn't mean a thing to me.'

Within the house a child now begins to cry. 'OK, OK, mummy's coming,' she calls over her shoulder, then, turning back, she says, 'Look, you could always try Mrs Farnell down the road. She's been here forever, so I'm told.' The toddler then appears behind her legs, still crying. She picks him up, flipping him onto her hip in one fell movement. 'I've got to go,' she says.

'Which house is she, this Mrs Farnell?'

'Number fourteen, I think. That way,' says the woman, pointing down the street and with something of an apologetic smile and clicking the door shut.

-

PG is at home and on the phone to Brian.

'Any luck yet?' he asks him curtly.

'PG, I told ya, I'm on it! Dinna fash yerself.'

'Would you speak English please?'

'Fa' cryin' ou' loud, man! If ya must know, I went to his boozer last night, but he'd gone to ge' his cheque wi' 'is pals. I'll be goin' there again tonight. OK?'

'Don't forget the watch.'

'I'm not gonnae forget tha fuckin' watch!'

'Good. I need a result here, Brian. I don't want to let Sir Alun down.'

'Who tha' fuck's Sir Alun?'

'A business associate.'

'Just relax, will ya? I'll ring ya when I've something tae report. Now, ge' off my case, eh?'

'I will when you've done your job.'

'You're nae too important to gae a slap, PG.'

'Don't push your luck, Brian. You're being paid good money here. Now, just get on with it.'

—

Detlef repeatedly taps the solid wooden door of number fourteen but there's no answer. It's as if the house had long been deserted with letters and junk mail wedged into the vertically aligned and eye level letterbox, the curtains drawn in all the windows. He's just about to walk away when he hears an elderly woman's voice from behind. 'Yes,' she says, faintly. 'Who is it?'

'Mrs Farnell?'

'Who are you?'

'My name is Otto, Mrs Farnell. Detlef Otto. I wonder if you can help me?'

'Who do you say you are?'

'Detlef Otto.'

'I don't know of anyone by that name. Go away or I shall call the police.'

'Please, I mean you no harm, I am simply looking for the Dando family that used to live at number thirty-nine,' he continues swiftly. 'Do you remember them perhaps?'

'Who do you say you are?'

'The name's Otto, Mrs Farnell, I was once married to Ellen Dando, the daughter.'

Detlef can hear a key being turned and the latch being opened. The old lady then peers out from in between the gap afforded by the security chain, looking at him intently. 'Yes, I remember the Dando's,' she acknowledges. 'What about them?'

'You knew them?' he says in amazement but recoiling as the sharp and acrid stench of cats hits his nostrils.

'Yes. And you were married to Ellen you say?'

'I was. We had a son, Mrs Farnell. Derek, do you remember him at all?'

'Derek, yes. I remember little Derek, a sweet little boy.'

Staggered, Detlef is barely able to believe his luck. 'That is who I am trying to find! I am his father!' he says, the emotion immediate in his voice.

'I don't know,' the old lady worries.

'Please help me.'

'It's not my place.'

'Do you know anything of Ellen, perhaps?' Detlef tries.

'I don't know that I should,' the old lady continues to hesitate. 'You're that German, aren't you?' she then says. 'I can tell.'

'Yes Mrs Farnell, I am! How did you know?'

'Never you mind.'

'My name is Detlef Otto,' he repeats. 'I was Ellen's husband, that little boy is my son. I assure you I am telling you the truth. I just want to find him, that is all.'

'Maybe if you come back tomorrow? I shall have to think.'

'Please, Mrs Farnell, this is my last chance. As you can see, I am an old man, I don't have much time left,' he pleads to her, absolutely unwilling to let the opportunity pass or be delayed. 'I am begging you.'

The old lady doesn't reply at first, but neither does she close the door. 'You left her all alone with that baby,' she says. 'We were friends, you know, Ellen and I,' she then divulges.

'You were friends? Is she still alive? Please tell me!'

'We still send each other Christmas cards,' the old lady reveals. 'But it could be too much for her, like seeing a ghost. She might not want to see you. I knew all about it, you know.'

Again, Detlef is momentarily struck dumb. It is almost too much for him to take in and it's a few seconds before he is able to speak again. 'I do not wish to upset her, Mrs Farnell,' he then says. 'It is my son I wish to find, before it is too late. You must understand, life was difficult all those years ago and, yes, I got into trouble. I am not proud of what I did. You must believe me.'

'She thought you'd abandoned her.'

'Oh, no, no, no! I tried to stay in contact. I wrote many letters but never received anything in reply, not a single one.'

'I know, she told me.'

'She got them?'

'Well, yes, eventually.'

'I don't understand,' says Detlef, staring at her imploringly.

'Oh, I do so hope I am doing the right thing,' she says, pausing. 'All I can tell you is that Ellen had to move into a Nursing Home, here in Bristol. And as for young Derek, I don't know where he is. I haven't seen him in years.'

'Do you know the name of it? The Nursing Home?' asks Detlef urgently, the words tumbling from his mouth.

'I don't know that I should,' she says yet again, but, amazingly, releases the security chain and rattles aside the heavy velvet curtain that hangs behind the door on a heavy metal runner. 'You'd better step inside for a moment,' she says, 'but mind you don't let the cats out.'

Detlef edges his way in and into the darkness of the hallway and is aware of very many pairs of eyes watching him from along the hall, up the stairs, and every other conceivable nook and cranny.

'Wait here for a moment while I find the address,' she says as she shuffles into a room to her left.

After just a few minutes, she re-emerges and hands him a piece of paper on which she had written the name of the home - New Horizons, Ashton Gate, Bristol, it reads, together with the postcode.

Detlef takes her hand and even kisses her fingertips, he is so utterly grateful. 'You don't know what this means to me,' he says, welling up. 'I shall never forget you for this.'

'Say hello to Ellen for me if you see her.'

'I will, Mrs Farnell. Thank you.'

'Tell her it's Joyce.'

'Joyce?' Detlef repeats, suddenly making a dim and distant connection.

'Yes. Joyce. We nearly missed our train because of you,' she reminds him.

-

Standing under his portico and gently slapping a pair of fine kid leather driving gloves into the palm of his hand, PG is pondering on which of his vehicles to take. It's a very important decision as far as he's concerned, he wants to make the right impression and favours the Range Rover over the Jag. After all, Sir Alun lives in the country, does he not?

Decision made, he steps back inside to pick up his phone and the relevant set of keys from the Regency console table just inside his hallway. Then, walking back out onto the gravel drive, he gets in the vehicle, switches on the engine and picks up his phone.

'Yes,' says an abrupt and rather pompous sounding voice on the other end.

'Sir Alun?' says PG with his foot firmly on the accelerator of the otherwise stationary car.

'Who's this?'

'Peter Green, Sir Alun. Sorry, I can barely hear you,' he lies.

'Ah, Peter. Can I put you on hold for a minute?'

PG had met Sir Alun at a recent Private View for an up-and-coming London artist at the prestigious Brabazon Art Gallery in Clifton.

Mingling amongst the great and the good of the Bristol art scene and watching for a suitable target to offload his own works of art of a highly dubious nature, PG's attention had been drawn to him quite early on. He was right up his street, a distinguished upper middle-aged man dressed impeccably in a beautifully tailored tweed suit with mustard coloured waistcoat to match. To PG, he appeared the perfect well-to-do country gentleman ripe for the picking.

Biding his time, he'd waited until he'd seen him standing alone in front one of the large abstract pieces before making his manoeuvre.

Nonchalantly, he'd moved alongside him and, after a few moments of mutually silent observation of the work, had struck up a conversation. 'To be perfectly honest, I don't really understand this modern stuff at all,' PG had confided in him as a light-hearted opening gambit.

Sir Alun had smiled. 'But an interesting title though, don't you think?' he'd said.

Not knowing, PG then looked it up in his catalogue - a triptych entitled 'Urban Renewal' together with the price - £7,500.

'I'm a developer, you see, and considering buying it for one of my offices,' had said Sir Alun. 'I rather like it in fact. Modern,' he'd added before going on to describe a major new development and investment opportunity his company was building down in the docks.

Initially, PG had simply feigned interest and had tried to steer the conversation back to his 'family's' prized art collection and the valuable and classic works that he was considering putting up for sale. But then, as soon as Sir Alun had proffered his card, saying that he might possibly be interested and to give him a call, everything had changed in an instant. PG was smitten, so to speak. He was rubbing shoulders with a Knight of the Realm! A member of the landed gentry, and he had his direct line telephone number in his hand! For PG, life simply couldn't get any sweeter than this.

In the days that followed, despite a visit to Sir Alun's swish looking offices towards the bottom of Park Street and meeting up on a couple of occasions for coffee, Sir Alun had not, as yet, bought any of the works of art, but PG was already in the process of investing in Sir Alun's waterfront commercial and residential development. Two hundred thousand pounds worth to be exact, a considerable sum as far as PG was concerned, but little more than chicken feed with regard the figures Sir Alun would mention.

-

Smiling, Detlef waves the piece of paper excitedly as he walks as briskly back to Maciej waiting patiently in his taxi. 'Bloody hell, Detlef! I told you! You hit the jackpot already!' he congratulates him out of the open window. 'The Gods are with you, I think.'

Detlef beams. 'I cannot believe it. Do you know where this is?' he says, his hand shaking.

'Ashton Gate,' Maciej reads aloud. 'Yep, sure do, and you have postcode!'

'Can we go there now?'

'No fear! We will find it easily with this!' he says, immediately programming his prized SatNav still suctioned centrally to the inside of the windscreen.

-

'Yes, Peter,' says Sir Alun, returning to the phone. *'What can I do for you?'*

'I'm on my way back from Henley, Sir Alun, spot of business,' PG lies, trying to impress, and continuing to rev the engine for effect. 'I thought I might drop by into Bath on the way back through.'

'That's not convenient, I'm afraid,' Sir Alun had tried to dissuade him. *'I don't conduct business from my own home.'*

'Sorry, missed that, poor signal,' PG ignores him on purpose, 'only I've stumbled upon a very interesting prospect with regard the additional investment you might require?'

'Why can you not tell me over the phone?'

'I'd rather explain it to you face to face. I can easily drop down off the motorway.'

'Why all the cloak and daggers, Peter?'

'Because it's an unusual one, Sir Alun,' PG starts, 'but I am talking about very significant potential here. Millions quite possibly. I can be there within the hour.'

Sir Alun pauses for a moment.

'Henley, you say? That's pushing it a bit,' he says in a slightly more conciliatory tone and glancing at his watch.

'I'm already past Newbury,' PG qualifies himself quickly.

'Oh, right, OK. Look, I have a meeting at four. I could spare you half an hour, providing you get here by, say, one-forty-five?'

'I'll put my foot down,' says PG as, with phone in the crook of his neck, he begins to pull on his gloves, tightly interlocking his fingers. 'Now, how will I find you?' he asks.

-

'Wasn't so bad, was it?' says Derek, getting out his baccy as they descend the stairs and step back out into the shopping precinct.

'Can I 'ave one of those?' Jez simply asks.

'No, you can't!' objects his mum. 'You're only just fifteen!'

'Let 'im 'ave one if 'e wants! He's been under a lot of stress, poor lad,' Derek overrules her, handing Jez the pouch. 'You want me to make it for ya, wi' ya arm an' that?'

'No, Dekko!' continues Marion but astonished as she watches her son peal off a paper and roll himself a cigarette with consummate dexterity.

'So, OK, you'll have to go to court,' Derek carries on, 'although I don't get what they're gonna charge you with as you weren't drivin' at the time.'

'But that isn't what he said!' says Marion.

'Not what I heard. An' as they can't prove anythin' different, he'll probably just get away wi' just a slap on the wrist an' a bit o' community service.'

'He said he might face a custodial bloody sentence!'

'He's gotta say that, ain't he? Cover his arse,' Derek dismisses.

'But what if they *can* prove something?'

'Exactly! If! An' they can't.'

'And there's the small matter of the theft itself, don't forget!'

'First serious offence. It won't matter,' says Derek, casting that aside too.

'It won't matter?' shrieks Marion, watching her son as he now lights up and inhales deeply.

'Have a bit o' faith, woman.'

Marion shakes her head in disbelief. 'I don't reckon Jefferson's even up to it,' she then says. 'Seems a bit long in the tooth to me.'

'Yeah, bit of an antique, ain't he?' says Derek, chortling. 'But he seems to know his stuff. I was pleasantly surprised to be honest. I liked 'im.'

'Just hope he's got a decent flamin' suit when he goes to court,' Marion comments. 'Did you see the dandruff? His shoulders were white.'

'Will you stop bein' critical o' the way people look? He's just like somebody's funny ol' Grandad. It could work in our favour. Besides, half the bleedin' magistrates are the same, scruffy bastards.'

'I hope you're bloody right, Dekko.'

'I am. An' as he said, it's his bread and butter, young offenders. He does 'em all the time. It'll be a walk in the park.'

'I'll give you a walk you in the park if you're wrong!'

'Any way, I gotta go over to see me mum, so I'll 'ave to love ya an' leave ya,' says Derek.

'But it's not visiting time yet.'

'I know,' says Derek, 'but I got some things to do yet.'

'What's that then?' asks Marion suspiciously.

'Get myself tidied up,' he answers. 'Get her some flowers.'

'So, you've not got time for a quick cuppa then?' Marion then offers him out of the blue. 'Don't worry, Nigel's out at work.'

'Bloody 'ell! What's come over you all of a sudden?' says Derek, laughing suspiciously. 'Don't tell me. Let me guess?'

'Just thought you might fancy one, that's all. Only tryin' to be pleasant.'

'Another time maybe.'

'OK, but say hello to her for me, yeah? Send my love.'

'Will do. See ya, son,' his dad bids him farewell. 'An' chin up, it's all gonna be just fine.'

Chapter 15

As Detlef is about to enter the New Horizons Nursing Home, he is met by a nurse making her way out, a single cigarette and lighter hidden in hand.

'Can I help you?' she asks him.

'I am here to visit an old friend,' he tells her, seeing from the badge pinned to her tunic that her name is Sheryl.

'I'm sorry, but we don't allow visitors until after two o'clock,' she says, curtly. 'You'll have to come back a bit later.'

'I'm sorry, I didn't know,' says Detlef, looking at his watch and disappointed to see that it is not even yet midday.

'Feeding time, you see.'

'I understand, but perhaps, can you tell me?' he starts falteringly. 'Do you have a woman here by the name of Ellen Dando?' he asks. 'I'm not sure I have the right place.'

'And you are?'

'As I say, an old friend, I met her and her family when working near the city many years ago,' he offers by way of an explanation. 'I'm hoping to surprise her.'

'Thought you had a strange accent. Were you on the bridge when they were building it?' she randomly suggests, trying to suss him out.

Detlef looks confused for a moment, not knowing what on earth she is referring to.

'The Severn Crossing?' she says.

'Sorry, no. My English is not so good. I was at the old airfield, now the airport,' he tells her, quickly thinking on his feet.

'Ah, right. Big now, isn't it? Yeah, Ellen's here,' she then reveals.

Again, Detlef struggles to maintain control having found her already, and so easily, but he carries on. 'Does she see much of her family?' he asks. I knew them all, you see. I would so like to meet them again if possible.'

'Her grandchildren pop in from time to time with their mum.'

'Grandchildren?' he repeats, immediately considering whether they might possibly be related. 'I didn't know.'

'Yes. Three of them.'

'Girls? Boys?' asks Detlef with keen interest.

'Two girls and a boy, I think. And there's that son of hers, of course, when he can be bothered,' she adds, pulling a bit of a face. 'Anyway, I've got to get on. Come back later.'

'Her son? Would that be Derek?' Detlef stops her as calmly as he can.

'Yes, that's him. Dekko he calls himself,' Sheryl informs him. 'You know him then?'

'I did, when he was a baby,' he answers her truthfully. 'It would be nice to see him too. Do you know how I might find him?'

'You'll have to ask Ellen that,' she says, turning to walk away, 'but you could always try any of the pubs where he lives,' she adds very unprofessionally. 'Always drunk.'

Naturally, Detlef is dismayed to hear this, but he persists. 'Whereabouts in Bristol is that?' he enquires like it was only of passing interest. 'The city has changed so much since I was last here.'

-

As was always going to be the case, Derek slips back to the pub for a quick pint, knocking on the door to get Reenie to open back up for him. He's got more than enough time he tells himself, a good hour at least, and besides, a small hair of the dog wouldn't hurt, would it? Who'd notice?

-

'It's not open to visitors yet,' Detlef tells Maciej as he returns to the taxi.

'But is she there?' he asks. 'I saw you talking.'

'Yes, she is,' says Detlef leaning onto the roof for support.

'Wow! You really strike gold, my friend! And so fast!'

'Do you know Bishopsworth?' Detlef then asks, pronouncing it slowly and deliberately.

'For sure! We were there yesterday. Remember? You know, when you needed to take piss.'

'The pub?' recalls Detlef a little uncomfortably, getting in.

'Yeah, that's it.'

'Can we go there again, please?' he asks intuitively.

'What? You find your son as well?!' second guesses Maciej in astonished disbelief.

'I think he might be somewhere near there. I would like to ask.'

'We go right now!'

Detlef hesitates. 'Maybe later this afternoon?' he requests almost apologetically. 'I think I need to take a little rest. Perhaps I will try to see Ellen tomorrow.'

'Hey! Are you OK?'

Detlef shrugs and closes his eyes.

'I'll take you back right now,' insists the young driver. 'Get in! You must stay strong.'

-

'So, how'd it go, Dekko?' Reenie asks him as she pours him a pint. 'At the solicitors, I mean?'

'Yeah, fine thanks. I think it'll all be alright.'

'I do hope so, for everyone's sake.'

'Yeah,' Derek agrees. 'Still no Jimbo then?'

'No,' says Reenie but sounding uncharacteristically relaxed about it. 'He's well and truly poisoned himself - been throwing up all morning.'

'Ha! Bit of a lightweight for a big bloke, ain't he, your hubby?' says Derek with a chuckle.

Reenie laughs in return. 'Dekko,' she then says, 'sorry to ask, but Jim tells me that you are going to give us some of your winnings?'

'Did he now?'

'I hate to ask, but I've got plans for this place.'

'Oh yeah?'

'Spruce it up a bit. Sort the kitchen out, do some more food.'

'Not a bloody restaurant?!'

'No!' Reenie backtracks. 'Pub grub.'

'How much d'I say, then?' asks Derek, genuinely racking his brains.

'I don't like to mention.'

'I'm sure I'll sort you out wi' a few pennies,' he says, guzzling at his beer. 'In fact, I'd pay ya to keep it just the way it is,' he then adds, cuffing his lips.

Chapter 16

When, at last, Derek does finally make it over to his mum's nursing home, only mildly worse for wear, it had been a far cry from one of his usual short-lived and sporadic visits where he had little or nothing to say ... well, other than to steer the conversation around in the hope of cadging a bit of beer money before making his awkward and shamefaced leave. No, this time he'd stayed for well over an hour.

His dear old mum couldn't believe it when he'd told her his fantastic news and, in many ways, neither could he as he found himself telling her how he was going to buy her a lovely little ground floor flat, or a bungalow if she'd prefer, with a nice garden for her to enjoy a bit of sunshine as and when the weather allowed. He'd kit it all out, he'd said, with top of the range, brand new stuff and with a team of live-in carers to look after her every need. 'Would you like that, mum?' he'd asked her, feeling like a decent and proper son for the first time in his life. 'A place all o' your own again? People to wait on ya hand and foot? Somewhere to put all your little knick-knacks an' that? Have the grandkids over to stay? Would ya like that, mum, would ya?'

Ellen hadn't been able to answer him at first, but the sound of her little gasps and her fingers clutching at her handkerchief, dabbing her streaming eyes, had said it all. 'Don't cry, Mum,' he'd said to her. 'Things are goin' to be great from now on in! You wait an' see.'

Her tears were ones of happiness, of course. It was like all her birthdays and Christmases had come together at once. But it wasn't really about a new place for her, or all the new things in it, it was the sudden and wonderful realisation that she would soon be back home and living within the bosom of her family once again and not stuck out on a limb in an altogether different part of the city. That's what had really hurt the most over these past couple of years, her sense of forced isolation and abandonment, not the humiliating and debilitating effects of her age-related illnesses and resultant frailty at all.

-

Soon back in familiar surroundings and happy that he'd put such smile on his dear mum's face, Derek is already heading up the steps and about to reward himself the only way he knows how.

However, his usual blistering entrance is momentarily held in check by a trim and tidy woman in her forties following up closely behind him, a cased guitar slung over her shoulder, a keyboard and stand tucked under one arm. She's tonight's entertainment - *Now That's What I Call Music! With Roxxii!* She'd stuck up a couple of A4 posters only a few days back to advertise herself, a glamorous shot taken when she was much younger, less battle weary, still full of it.

Derek had seen her here before, watched her perform. She was a bit of alright he'd always thought, sassy in her rhinestone denims, a cowboy hat forever hanging down her back, her lacquered hair piled high like Tammy Wynette's. 'Here again then, love?' he asks as he steps back and reaches over to hold the door open.

'Yeah, yeah, I am,' she answers, distant and resigned, her voice coarse and gravelly through years of gigging in smoke filled bars and straining to be heard above the cacophony.

With his fingertips spread wide against the wire reinforced glass, his foot aligns parallel alongside hers, touching. 'Hey, look, we match, you and me,' he says, pointing down. 'The boots I mean.'

'Oh yeah, lovely,' she humours him.

'They're new, mine,' he says.

'Are they? Lovely, yeah,' she repeats whilst trying to manoeuvre herself in.

'Hey, what must you think o' me? D'you wanna hand wi' all that?' he asks.

'Nah, you're alright, I can manage.'

'I'll tell ya what though, you can play us a request later if ya like?' he suggests.

'Don't do requests as a rule.'

'Not even for a special occasion?'

'There's always a special occasion.'

'Not like this one, there ain't.'

'Look, sorry, I don't mean to be rude nor nuthin',' she says as she angles herself through, 'but I gotta set up, so, if ya don't mind?'

'Your show, love,' Derek backs off, letting the doors swing closed behind them. 'Your show.'

Despite fixing a smile and primping her hair, her appearance goes pretty much unnoticed as she flounces in. His, however, is greeted as raucously and predictably as ever, but now even more so.

'Here he is! Our very own mul-ti-fuckin'-millionaire!' shouts someone almost immediately.

'In the chair again then are we?' suggests another, hopefully.

'Yeah! Go on! You can afford it!' yells a third.

Almost imperceptibly Roxxii gives Derek a fleeting double take, her painted lips pursing just a tad, her eyes narrowing.

'Fuck off, the lot o' ya! Tab's closed!' he shouts back at them in jest.

Behind the bar, as ever, a still liverish looking Jimbo greets him, offering his hand. 'Watcha, mate,' he says before turning to the singer. 'Over there, love, in the corner, as per usual. I've cleared your space.'

Roxxii doesn't need to be told, she knows where she belongs, but this time she stalls, jiggling her guitar and adjusting the strap that separates her breasts like it was uncomfortable all of a sudden.

'How's it hangin' then, Jimbo?' asks Derek with a knowing grin. 'Still feelin' shit?'

'Don't think I got any bloody stomach linin' left,' he replies morosely. 'Oh, an' just so ya know, there's a couple o' blokes sat on the benches over there, asking after ya, been waiting a while,' he adds before gently clapping his hands to chivvy Roxxii along.

Derek doesn't even bother to turn and look. 'Oh yeah?' he says. 'No prizes for guessin' what they're after. So, you had the ol' multi-coloured yawn this mornin', did ya?' he continues, laughing.

'You could say that.'

'Any carrots were there?'

Transfixed and sitting completely motionless, his heart in his mouth, Detlef is in absolute turmoil as he watches his very own son standing only just a few short steps away.

Over the years, he'd literally ached for this moment, shed quiet tears over it, with not a day passing that he hadn't secretly yearned for it. But nothing could have prepared him for the reality of the situation and for the crippling high anxiety he now feels.

'You must have the constitution of a bloody ox!' continues Jimbo. 'I dunno how you boys do it night after night,' he adds before turning back to Roxxii. 'Are you goin' to play summat for us tonight, or what?' he demands, seemingly keen to get her out of the way.

'Course I am! Relax!' she says before addressing Derek. 'I just wanted to say sorry if I was a bit short just then. I'm just a bit cream crackered, that's all. Eight bloody nights on the trot this'll be.'

'No problem, love. You're forgiven,' says Derek before speaking to Jimbo once again. 'Years o' practice, me ol' mate, an' all paid for,' he says, tapping his paunch proudly.

'It's Dammo isn't it?' Roxxii interjects once again like she'd remembered him all of a sudden.

'Have another guess,' he replies, now a little sharply himself.

'Sorry, Dekko,' says Jimbo, 'but we ain't got time for all this. She's gotta set up. They'll all be in shortly.'

'That's it! Dekko!' Roxxii exclaims like she knew all along. 'Bloody close though, wasn't I?' she adds like she was prone to being a bit dippy.

'Glad you remembered,' says Jimbo sarcastically. 'Now, off ya toddle,' he insists.

But Roxxii isn't finished yet, nowhere near. 'Give us a minute, Jim,' she says. '*Dekko* here,' emphasising his name and like she hasn't got a clue what his celebration is all about, 'he was asking me if I'd do a few requests later? That'd be alright, wouldn't it?'

'Yeah, yeah, whatever ya like,' says Jimbo, confused at even being asked. 'As long as you don't run over time, I couldn't give a monkey's. I get enough complaints about the noise as it is. So, let's get on with it, yeah?'

'What were you thinking then, Dekko?' Roxxii persists. 'What's your favourite song?'

'Had a sudden change o' heart, 'ave we?' he says.

'Might o' done,' she purrs, coquettishly shifting her weight from one leg to the other.

Despite the forty-five years or so since he'd last seen him, Detlef had immediately recognised him as soon as he'd walked in.

He was his son alright. He could see it in an instant. The family resemblance is striking. You'd have to be blind not to see it.

Now, sat in this busy and raucous bar, he doesn't know what to do for the best but accepts that he must simply await a suitable opportunity. It is nothing short of agony for him.

'You don't do 'em as a rule, remember?' continues Derek as Jimbo hands him his drink.

'Aw, don't be like that, big boy. I'm offerin' now,' says Roxxii, smirking at her own innuendo.

With that, a few close by in the bar who have been watching and listening to every word, now begin to jeer lasciviously. 'You're in there, Dekko!' says one. 'Like a rat up a pipe!'

'But watch you keep yer hand on yer wallet!' adds another. 'She'll rinse ya good an' proper!'

'Oi! That's enough! Shut the fuck up, the lot o' ya!' Roxxii comes back at them as quick as you like and easily holding her own. She's had years of practice. 'So, Dekko, last chance, I won't ask again,' she then asks, hands now held defiantly on her hips. 'What's it to be?'

'Well…,' says Derek, softening to this highly spirited woman, 'just for a laugh, I was thinkin', 'Money's Too Tight To Mention', you know, by that carrot topped twat.'

'Simply Red, you mean?'

'Yeah, that's 'im.'

'Money's too tight to mention!' repeats Jimbo, now laughing along. 'You don't 'alf come out with 'em, Dekko.'

'OK. I'll see what I can do,' says Roxxii. 'It'll cost ya though.'

'Yeah, thought as much,' says Derek expectantly. 'What's the price?'

'Not much. Just a lager an' lime'll do,' she says, cleverly, 'but, as it's a special, you'll have to make it a pint.'

With his son so very close, Detlef can just make out his voice, something that he'd not even previously considered - what he might actually sound like - and, drifting, he recalls Derek's very first words. 'Da-da,' he'd said, still in nappies and only able to stand with the support of a chair or a table leg, 'Ma-ma', a crust of buttered toast held greasily in his hand, his mop of blonde hair and rosy-red cheeks and an image that Detlef had never ever forgotten.

He remembers, too, talking to Ellen about the wonderful potential of this glorious and vibrant little human being as they'd watched him explore the confines of that small one bedroomed flat in Brislington. 'What might he do?' they'd said. 'Who might he become?'

Now, in the harsh reality of this increasingly noisy and smoke-filled pub, he beholds a rather scruffy and ravaged middle-aged man drinking great mouthfuls of beer like his very life depended upon it. He couldn't help but feel greatly disappointed, not necessarily with the man standing before him, but in himself. If only he'd been there for him, he thinks, been a proper father. Things might have been very different indeed.

'Seen Phil? Dave?' asks Derek as Roxxii finally drops some of her kit in the corner.

'Dave dropped by earlier, forgot his coat. Ain't seen Phil though, not as yet' he informs him. 'Yours is over 'ere, Rox,' he then calls over to her. 'On the bar. But don't let it stop ya.'

'He'll surface soon enough,' says Derek hopefully.

'Fuck knows how we got home last night again!' says Jimbo, shaking his head. 'But yeah, he'll be in. He left his motor outside at least. Did you not see it?'

'Can't say as I did,' says Derek.

'He must be the one that won the Lotto!' whispers Maciej excitedly, piecing it all together. 'You have a very rich son, Detlef! Aren't you going to talk to him?'

Gently, Detlef places his hand on the young driver's forearm, quietening him.

Swallowing hard and mopping his brow with a bar towel, Jimbo moves to the very corner of the bar and leans over to beckon Derek forward.

'Problem?' asks Derek knowing exactly what is coming next.

'No, no, but look, I hate to ask,' starts Jimbo falteringly.

'What?'

'What you said yesterday? I just wanna know if you were bein' serious?'

'What was that then, Jim?'

'You know, last night,' he says almost inaudibly. 'When we got back.'

'Nope. You'll 'ave to remind me.'

Embarrassed, Jimbo doesn't feel he can carry on and backs off. 'S'OK. Forget it,' he says.

'Spit it out. What?' Derek repeats, continuing to toy with him.

'The money you mentioned.'

'I was too tight to mention money, Jim,' says Derek wittily.

'So, you don't remember then?'

'Not really, mate. No.'

'Sorry. Silly o' me. Forget I said anythin',' says Jimbo, unable to hide his disappointment and beginning to wipe the perfectly dry bar with the towel.

Derek lets him squirm for a tiny bit longer before roaring with laughter. 'Gotcha!' he then yells. 'I might o' been pissed as an 'andcart, but me 'effin memory still works, ya daft wanker!'

Jimbo then looks up in total amazement, but still questioning.

'Reenie even asked me about it this morning!'

'She didn't?'

'She did!'

'Silly cow! I told her not to say,' says Jimbo, not knowing whether to laugh or cry.

'Look at your face! What a picture! Worth every penny, Jim! Ev'ry penny!"

'As much as you said?' he then looks to confirm.

'Wha' d'I say?' Derek begins to tease him again.

'You know.'

'No, I don't know. Tell me.'

'Bloody 'ell, Dekko!'

'What?'

'It's embarrassin'!'

'Tell me. Go on.'

'You said two hundred and fifty thousand,' whispers Jimbo as quietly as he can, but suddenly feeling completely ridiculous at the very mention of such a large sum of money.

'Fuck me! Don't remember that bit! But if that's wha' I said, so be it! I'm nuthin' if I'm not a man o' me word!'

Jimbo then turns away and looks up at the ceiling, blinking. He can't help himself.

'What's up wi' ya now?' asks Derek. 'Ya daft prat!'

'You got no idea,' Jimbo answers, wiping his eye. 'No idea at all. It's been bloody 'ard. We been that close to losin' the lot between you an' me, what wi' bills an' that. I'll never forget you for this, Derek. Never.'

'Oi, it's Dekko to you! Now stop your fuckin' blubberin' an' get me another drink! An' while you're at it, you can open the bloody tab back up again! Drinks all 'round!' he shouts and to be greeted with whoops and cheers once again.

As Jimbo swiftly heads back to the pumps and the clamour for more drinks, Detlef stands up to make his move but is immediately thwarted as a booming Scottish voice calls out from behind him. 'Dekko!' says the man rapidly making his way over like he'd suddenly seen a long-lost pal or something. 'Thought I'd never find ya!'

'If you're from the papers, I got nothin' to say,' says Derek but feeling strangely intimidated by this powerful looking man.

'Wha' ya talkin' a'boot? Papers? Fuck off!' says Brian jovially enough. 'Do I look like a fuckin' gentleman o' tha press?'

'Who are ya then?'

'The name's Brian,' he says, grabbing his hand to give a full-on and crushing handshake. 'Pleased tae meet ya.'

'Tell me, do I look as if I got 'mug' tattooed on me forehead?' says Derek, releasing himself from the grip and cracking his fingers back into realignment.

'I'm wounded! I'm nae after anythin' if tha's wha' ya think. Quite the opposite in fact.'

'Oh yeah?'

'Straight up! I'm a bringer of glad tidings, my friend. I'm here because you seem tae 'ave some very important an' influential friends in this city,' Brian informs him as, cleverly, he starts to manoeuvre himself between Derek and the bar with the intention of edging him into further seclusion over by the darts board.

Noticing, Jimbo calls over. 'You alright there, mate?'

Derek nods to reassure him. 'I have?' he then asks, intrigued.

'Too fuckin' true, ya 'ave,' Brian continues without breaking stride. 'An' as a token of their respect an' admiration, they've asked me tae give ya a wee somethin',' he adds, reaching deep inside his black leather coat pocket and handing him a weighty and expensive looking box with the word 'Rolex' and the crown logo embossed upon it in impressive gold letters.

'What's this?'

'I'll tell ya wha' that is, Dekko, it's yours. Tha's wha' tha' is.'

Tempted, Derek goes to open it to have a look but resists. 'Nah. Nuthin's for nuthin,' he says, attempting to hand it back.

'Wha' d'ya mean, ya numpty? It's all yours! A gift! No strings attached!'

'Can't accept it. Sorry.'

'You will be. Six grands worth there, pal, buckshee!' says Brian, showing a touch of irritation.

'Six grand?' repeats Derek.

'You heard correct. Six thousand smackeroonies!'

'So, who are they then, these so-called friends o' mine?' he asks, still holding onto the box.

'Who are they? Movers an' shakers, the top fuckin' table, tha's who they are, Dekko. You obviously dinnae know how privileged you are.'

'What top table?'

'*The* top table! All you need to know is that they've heard of you, an' believe it or not, you know one o' them by default.'

'Whose fault?'

'Nobody's fault! You just know one of 'em,' Brian explains, rolling his eyes.

'I do?'

'Aye, ya certainly do. One Mistah Peter Green, yeah?' he says, now raising his eyebrows and looking for acknowledgement, 'aka, the infamous Pee-fuckin'-Gee!'

'Ah, I get it now,' says Derek, twigging. 'Clappie said he wanted to meet up, had something for me. Just take it back, yeah?'

'Forget tha' wee twat, he's out o' the picture. He had nuthin'. We're talkin' big time 'ere now, Dekko. Mon-u-fuckin'-mental!'

'We are?'

'Trust me, do I look like I'd lie tae ya? You're in the Premier League now an' they'd like tae meet up, get to know ya a wee bi' better, gi' ya a few pointers. Are ya wi' me?' says Brian and placing his hand firmly on Derek's shoulder.

'Why? Why would they do that?'

'Dekko, listen, if you wanna be where it's at in this city, make tha' money o' yours work for ya, then this is it, your golden opportunity. You dinnae wanna piss it all away in a place like this, now do ya?'

'I dunno. I quite like it 'ere.'

'You only get one bite o' this rosy red cherry, Dekko. Be warned. They'll nae ask ya again.'

Derek turns the box over in his hands. It feels like total quality to him, smooth and solid with the promise of even greater things inside.

'It's a fuckin' beauty, special edition,' Brian presses home, 'an' I know you ain't gonna be stupid enough tae give it back, now are ya?'

'So, if I was to agree then…'

'Is the right answer, Dekko!'

'Where an' when would I meet 'em?' he asks Derek now feeling strangely flattered.

'You leave tha' details tae me. I'll set it up. I've got your number.'

'You have?' questions Derek.

Brian dips his head. 'We look after our own,' he says, lowering his voice to emphasise the importance. 'As I said. Top table. Influential people. Now, you wanna drink afore I go?'

'I'll get you one, if ya like. Tab's open.'

'No, I'm offerin'. As I said, I dinnae want anythin' from ya. I'll stick one in,' says Brian, snapping his fingers to attract Jimbo's attention and slapping a five pound note down on the bar. 'Keep tha' change,' he says before turning back to Derek. 'Nice tae meet ya, Dekko. Stay lucky, eh?' he says, holding his thumb and not so little little finger up to his face. 'I'll call ya. We'll sort it. I'll pick you up in ma Beemer!'

Again, as he sees Derek now momentarily on his own, Detlef is about to make his move when, once again, someone else walks in, calling to him.

'Dekko!' shouts Phil. 'Mate!'

'"Ere he is! Rack 'em up, Jim!' says Derek, putting the box on the bar.

'Who was that fuckin' great big gorilla?' Phil asks immediately. 'An' what's that?' he adds, seeing the watch. 'Been wastin' yer money already, 'ave we? Flash bastard!'

'Nah, I've just been given it,' Derek admits.

'Wha' d'ya mean, ya just been given it?' says Phil. 'Pull the other one.'

Nosey as ever, Jimbo comes over as Derek eases open lid to reveal a very impressive timepiece nestled on a bed of shiny purple satin. 'Fuckin' 'ell,' he says, thrusting his jaw forward. 'Is it proper gold?'

'Heavy enough,' says Derek taking it out and sliding it onto his wrist.

'Given it? By who?' asks Phil again. 'That bloke that just left?'

'His name's Brian,' informs Derek, twiddling the knobs randomly and looking towards the clock on the wall. 'Six thousand pounds worth so he said.'

'Happens a lot does it? Some random person chuckin' six grand Rolexes about?' says Phil. 'Don't be an idiot, Dekko! What's the truth?'

'Some people want to meet up wi' me, that's all. Some movers n' shakers, so he said,' he says but not at all convincingly. 'Top table.'

'Top table? Movers an' shakers? You're bein' bloody set up, ya fuckin' prat! Open your eyes, man!'

'Bloody nice watch though, Phil,' comments Jimbo regardless. 'I wouldn't say no.'

'You need your bloody heads tested, both of ya!' repeats Phil in total disbelief. 'Probably a fake anyway.'

'Not a chance, look at it,' says Derek handing it to him. 'Quality that is.'

'But at what cost, Dekko?' continues Phil.

'He said it's for free.'

'No, you're not listenin' to me, mate…'

-

Outside, Brian is already making the call.

'Mission accomplished, PG. He's agreed to meet up.'

'Well done, Brian. I knew I could rely on you.'

'Slowly, slowly catch a monkey. You'll learn one day.'

'Trés drôle.'

'Oh, an' while I got ya, is there any danger o' an interim payment? A show o' good faith?'

'You'll be paid when you get him to us, Brian, not before.'

'Two grand!' Brian demands.

'One, and not a penny more.'

'So, when's it gonna be then? Tha' meetin'?'

'I'll call you back as soon as I arrange it with Sir Alun. Tomorrow sometime.'

'Then gae on wi' it. I dinnae want to be chargin' you interest.'

'Don't take the piss, Brian. Just pick up.'

-

With every fibre of his being now screaming out to go over to him, and with the pub steadily filling with even more people, Detlef understands there is going to be no ideal opportunity and, quite simply, he can wait no longer.

As Detlef stands to make his approach, Roxxii suddenly bursts into action with an ear shattering strum across the strings of her guitar.

'Hello, the Travellers!' she shouts out over the feedback. 'As many of you know, I'm Roxxii, an' I'm here to entertain you!' she starts with her regular opening line.

'What a racket!' calls out one.

'Get on with it!' yells out another.

'I'll get on with you in a minute,' she says, adjusting the levels on her amp. 'So, with no more beating about the bush, though none of you will be beating about my bush tonight!' she quips.

'You said that the last time!'

'She's not doin' Wutherin' Heights already, is she?' calls out another.

'No, I'm not doin' bloody Kate Bush already! Anyway, if you'll all shut up an' gi' me a chance, I've just found out we've got a very lucky man in our presence so I'm slippin' in a couple of ol' favourites especially for him. So, with no further ado, here's some Dire Straits for ya!' she says tapping her foot onto the loop box.

Now edging his way through the highly invigorated and jostling bar, closely followed by Maciej, Detlef finds himself standing directly behind his son. Nervously, he taps him on the shoulder, the touch alone seeming to send a bolt of electricity through his body. 'It's Derek, isn't it?' he starts off above the noise of the music.

'Bloody hell! Who's askin' now?' he answers, sounding exasperated and barely looking.

'My name is Detlef,' his father says.

'Det what? Can't it wait a bit? She's singin' this one for me,' says Derek with his eyes firmly fixed.

'I knew you and your mother many, many years ago,' Detlef persists, tripping over his words.

'Hah-hah! That's a new one. Nice try, mate. Just bugger off, yeah?'

'No, please. I don't expect you to remember, you were only a baby.'

'I can barely understand ya let alone hear ya, ya silly ol' sod. Where ya from?'

'Germany. I'm from Germany.'

'Fuck me! It gets even better!' says Derek, laughing. 'Nuthin' to do with me win on the lottery then?'

'That ain't workin', that's the way ya do it!' belts out Roxxii whilst winking in Derek's direction. *'Money for nuthin', get your chicks for free!'*

'What's up, Dekko?' Phil asks into his ear. 'He botherin' ya?'

'He reckons he knows me, that's all.'

'Oh yeah? Who is he?'

'Pass. Never seen him before in me life,' dismisses Derek.

'Tell him to fuck off then,' says Phil loudly enough for the old man to hear.

'You have it wrong, you don't understand,' pleads Detlef, imploring him.

Maciej can see Detlef's distress and puts an arm around his shoulders. 'Maybe you should not be so rude and listen,' he says, coming to his defence.

'And you are?' bristles Phil.

'I'm his friend.'

'I need to speak with you, Derek,' says Detlef, desperately trying again. 'It is important. Is there somewhere quiet?'

'No there fuckin' isn't! An' you don't call me Derek neither! Now piss off!'

'We gotta move these refrigerators, we gotta move these colour TV-ees!'

'Can you not see?' shouts out Maciej, about to spill the beans. 'Look at you both, look at your faces!'

'What d'ya mean?' says Derek now turning.

'I am your father!' Detlef bursts out. 'You are my son!'

Derek now squares up to him angrily. 'Don't you fuckin' dare!' he screams. 'My Dad died years ago! When I was a kid! Now get out o' my sight before I stick one on ya, ya money grabbin' bastard!'

'I'm not!'

'Right, that's enough! Get out o' here now, the pair o' ya!' Phil jumps in, pushing Detlef away.

'Do as he says, old man!' warns Derek, adrenalin now pumping through his body. 'Before I do summat I regret!'

'No, no! That's what you were told, we had no option, your mother and I.'

'That little faggot got his own jet airplane - that little faggot, he's a millionaire!'

'My mother? You dare mention my mother again and I really will go for ya, so 'elp me God I will!' shouts Derek, now incandescent with rage, the colour draining from his face, his hands clenching into fists. 'Fuck off!'

Swiftly, Maciej steps in between them. 'Come, Detlef. Let's go. Now.'

But Detlef isn't moving and resisting Phil as best he can.

'Everything alright over there?' calls Jimbo, alerted.

'No bother, Jim. These two are just on their way,' says Phil, now taking Detlef by the arm and turning him.

'Please, Derek. Please listen to me!' calls his father in a last-ditch effort as Phil now manhandles them both towards the door to the howls and jeers of approval from all in the pub.

Derek simply turns his back and picks up his pint, shaking. 'Un-fuckin'-believable!' he says.

'He's bangin' on the bongos like a chimpanzee!' sings Roxxii.

-

PG is just about to call Sir Alun when, surprisingly, he receives a call from the man himself.

'Peter, how are you?' he asks.

'Very good,' replies PG, genuinely surprised. 'You?'

'Yes, yes. Pleased to hear it. Now, this fellow that you mentioned. Did you get any further with him?'

'As it happens, Sir Alun, I have,' says PG, grinning like a Cheshire cat.

'Very good, my dear chap. I'm impressed. Let's arrange it then shall we? Do you have your diary in front of you?' he says, holding a letter of foreclosure from his bank in his hand.

-

'What the fuck was that all about, Dekko?' asks Jimbo when Roxxii finishes her number.

'That old twat was trying it on, big time, said he was Dekko's dad. Didn't he, mate?' says Phil, trying to laugh it off. 'The fuckin' cheek o' some people! They'll try anythin'.'

'He what? Beggars belief wha' people will do when they get the whiff o' a bit o' cash,' agrees Jimbo.

But Derek isn't going along with them, he's miles away and deep in thought.

'Don't let it get to ya,' insists Phil. 'Stuff like that is bound to 'appen!'

'Funny though,' says Jimbo, thinking aloud. 'If you stood the pair o' 'em side by side you could o' be forgiven, couldn't ya?'

162

With that, Derek bangs his pint down on the bar and, pushing people aside, dashes out of the door as quickly as he possibly can.

Outside, standing elevated by the entrance, he looks for them but can't see any sign. 'D'you see a couple o' blokes just head off?' he asks a group of people coming in.

'Just seen a taxi pull away, Dekko' says one.

'D'ya see what company it was?' he asks him urgently.

'No, mate, just an old Merc by the look of it.'

Derek then runs out through the car park and onto the road itself, looking frantically up and down the street.

'Hey, Dekko!' calls Phil from the steps. 'You'll get yourself run over like that, ya stupid twat! Come 'ere! Get inside!' he orders him.

-

PG is calling Brian yet again.

'All systems go. Arrange it for tomorrow,' he tells him.

'I cannae do that. I'll 'ave tae call him in tha mornin'. He'll be pissed in tha pub, an' I'm home wi' a drink in ma hand an' I'm nae going get pulled by the Polis for you nae nobody!'

'Can't you still call him?'

'PG, he's in tha fuckin' pub!' repeats Brian.

'Do it first thing then. Let me know.'

'I will.'

'And make sure he looks half decent, remember whom we are meeting here.'

'You wan' me to dress 'im as well now, do ya?'

'And get him to bring his cheque book.'

'You dinnae want much, do ya?'

'Just fucking do it, Brian.'

-

In the taxi, Maciej breaks their stunned silence. 'Detlef, you cannot leave it here,' he says. 'He knew. I could see it in his face.'

But Detlef is not really listening. 'My family warned me that this might happen. I am nothing but a selfish old man. It is time I went home and stopped making a fool of myself,' he says and on the verge of tears.

'No! You are no fool, Detlef! You must give one last try. He needs to understand. Every child deserves the truth, even if it is not so easy. Maybe you must go to see Ellen?' suggests Maciej, showing a level of maturity that belies his young years.

'But if I speak to her, I might only make matters worse.'

'Maybe, maybe not, but she is his mother ... and maybe she needs to know that you look for him too.'

On hearing this, Detlef can take no more and begins to cry. The shock and the emotion of it all is simply too much for him to bear. It gushes out of him like a torrent.

Chapter 17
Wednesday

As the first rays of daylight pierce a sliver of a gap between the heavy damask curtains, Detlef, still fully clothed and on top of the bed, opens his eyes.

He'd spent the night in such pitiable depths of self-recrimination and loathing that, yet again, he'd endured a terrible and fitful night's sleep, but this time so very much worse.

Now staring at the ceiling, gritty eyed and with those self-same and incessant thoughts continuing to plague him, it is nothing short of torture for him.

What had he been thinking with his disastrous approach to his son? In a busy bar of all places and surrounded by all those people! What sort of ridiculous fool does that? Derek had just thought he was some sort of conman, hadn't he? Of course, he had! And who could blame him? Turning up in a bar, out of the blue, to announce you are some man's father - and to one that had just won so much money! What an idiot! Unforgivable!

Besides, did it really matter that his son was so oblivious to the truth and that he believed his father to be long dead? No! It was his own selfish desire to make amends, nothing else. In any case, he'd seen with his very own eyes that Derek appeared to be happy, seemingly popular and amongst plenty of friends. What benefit was there to be had in digging up the past and exposing the story to which Ellen must have been somehow complicit herself? None whatsoever!

But worse than that, what if his son hadn't dismissed what he'd told him? Maciej had said on the journey home last night, hadn't he? He could see it in his eyes, he'd said. A seed of doubt might already have been planted, despite Derek's understandable and angry rejection at the very idea.

And, if so, what next? He could easily be responsible for causing untold harm and anger and rupturing Derek's relationship with his mother in the process - destroying it in fact! ... And there were grandchildren to consider! Heaven knows what impact it would have on them!

Then, as if all these gut-wrenching thoughts were not enough to deal with, he recalls the conversation he'd had with his wife soon after Maciej had dropped him back at the hotel. She'd been waiting desperately for his call and, of course, he'd tried to sound as relaxed and jovial as he could, asking after everyone, about her day, that he missed her, and that his search was going well, but he'd omitted to tell her the truth! Not that she was convinced. Not at all. She could tell. 'I am so worried about you, Detlef,' she'd said. 'Please come home!' she'd pleaded with him.

Even as he'd finished the call, unable to fully allay her fears, Detlef knew that this whole sad and sorry charade of mistakes, lies, and deceit could not carry on much longer. He needed to make some decisions – and fast.

-

Derek is beginning to rouse too, but he's strangely aware of a certain lack of space in his three-quarter sized bed with the duvet unusually tight over his shoulder and cool air drifting down his back. Alarmingly, he then feels the unaccustomed warmth of what seems to be another person's buttocks pressed firmly into his. *Shit!*

Slowly, he turns his head and can see what looks like the short and boyish hair of a fellow human being. *What the fuck?*

Horrified, he thrusts his hand down towards his groin only to discover that he is stark bollock naked. He never sleeps naked! He always keeps his pants on! *I don't bastard believe this!*

He buries his head into the pillow, pretending he is still in the Land of Nod and hoping against hope that this is all a very bad dream, but then his bedfellow begins to stir, entwining a leg around his, a toenail scratching at his calf. *Get the fuck off me!*

'Are you awake, Dekko?' whispers a deep and husky voice.

'Dave?' Derek asks bizarrely as the body turns, spooning into him and running a finger down his spine.

'Dave? Who the bloody hell's Dave?' asks the voice.

As Derek turns his head once again, he sees a pair of panda eyes looking at him across the pillow, and those of a woman at least. 'That would explain it then,' she says with a gentle chuckle.

'Explain what?'

'Don't worry. Your secret's safe with me.'

'What secret?'

'That you're gay,' she teases him.

'Gay? Course I'm not fuckin' gay!'

'It's alright. It doesn't matter. Nothin' to be ashamed of these days.'

'I'm not, I'm tellin' ya!'

'Who's this Dave then?'

'I don't fuckin' know. A mate.'

'D'you often sleep wi' your mates?'

'No! Don't be stupid. It's your voice.'

'Ah,' she says, getting it. 'That'll be the nodules.'

'Nodules?'

'Yeah, on me larynx. Terrible they are, first thing in the morning, after a gig.'

Derek turns onto his back as best he can, wedged against the wall. 'Look, sorry, love, but you'll 'ave to remind me,' he's forced to ask, 'what's your name again?'

'Bloody hell, Dekko! First you think I might be this Dave geezer!' she squeals. 'Now you don't know who I am at all! It's Roxxii! Don't you remember?'

'What? Roxxii?' he stutters and coughs. 'The singer?'

'Yeah! Roxxii the singer!'

'But where's all your hair gone?'

'Over there,' she says, pointing to what looks like some sort of long-haired cat lying dead on his chair. 'It's a wig. I got loads of 'em, every colour under the sun. It's why I keep mine short, see,' she explains, riffling what little hair she has.

Again, Derek clears his throat. 'So, how, how did you get here then?' he stutters.

'Christ, you don't remember much, do ya? I walked you home.'

'You did?'

'Yeah, you were a bit, how can I put this nicely? Unsteady on your feet.'

Derek winces as snippets of the night before start to reassemble themselves in his befuddled brain. 'So, did we, sort of, you know, do it?' he asks nervously but not really wanting to know the answer.

Roxxii holds a hand out in front of him, drooping her finger.

'Ah,' he says, unsure whether to be pleased or embarrassed. 'Sorry.'

'All men get it, once in a while, 'specially after a skinful like that!'

'You'd know all about that then?'

'I ain't no saint, Dekko, if that's what you mean! Besides, we both thought it was hilarious. I copped a right eyeful! The last turkey in the shop, remember?' she says, trying to make a joke out of it.

'Leave it out!'

'Gobble, gobble, gobble.'

'Stop!'

Roxxii wriggles seductively. 'We can always try again if ya like? Now you've sobered up, I'll even put me hair back on if it helps.'

It had been years, decades in fact, since he'd been to bed with anyone other than Marion and, for him, it still didn't feel right. He still felt like he was doing the dirty. 'It's not that I'm ungrateful,' he says by way of an escape, 'but another time maybe. Yeah?'

'Not what you said last night.'

'I said a lot o' things last night, I expect,' he says steeling himself for the worst.

'You sure did. All sorts,' she says, smiling again.

'Like what? Why am I suddenly worried?'

'Nuthin' horrible. You were charmin' in fact, very complimentary. Said I had fantastic voice for starters, that I could easily win that X factor show with a bit o' help.'

Derek tuts. 'What would I know? I know fuck all 'bout music.'

'You don't need to. You said you'd pay for me to be professionally recorded.'

'Did I?'

'You did.'

'How much is that then?'

'Well, it's not cheap.'

'We'll see, yeah?'

'You're not changin' your mind, are ya?'

'No, course not. Let us know,' he says, suddenly keen to get her out with something niggling him at the back of his mind.

'I can get some prices if ya like? See what we're talking about.'

'You do that. Look, I hate to say this Roxxi, but I'm full to burstin' 'ere an' I gotta get up, so, if ya don't mind?' he says.

'You'll have to climb over, I'm freezin'. I've seen it all before ya know.'

'So you said. But why don't you get dressed first, yeah? I'll close me eyes. Look,' he says, shutting them tight.

'You are funny, Dekko. Nice, but funny,' says Roxxii as she spins her legs out and, with her upper arms held tightly into her breasts, picks up her clothes that are strewn on the floor. 'Will you help me then?'

'Can't you dress yourself?'

'Not with my clothes, silly! With the singin',' she says as she fastens her bra over her stomach before spinning it around and threading it over her shoulders. 'If it's not too much?'

'If that's what I promised, I'll do it.'

'Oh, thank you! You're my very own Simon Cowell!'

'I bloody hope not, trousers up to his tits.'

Roxxii stands up, holding up her knickers, inspecting them before pulling them on. 'It'll certainly be a few thousand, what with studio time, an engineer, production, a couple of backing musicians maybe,' she begins to list out. 'But don't worry about that, I know one or two that will help me out. I'll try to keep the cost down.'

'Yeah, whatever, just let me know,' he says, his eyes still closed.

'You OK with that?'

'Yeah.'

'You're my knight in shinin' armour then, Dekko, that's what you are,' she says as she slips into her denim skirt. 'You can look now.'

'Thanks,' he says but not knowing entirely why.

As she sits back down on the bed to pull on her boots, she holds one up for him to see. 'Look. We match, you and me,' she says as a little reminder of how they'd met, like it might be a story they would tell together in the years to come.

'Oh yeah,' he acknowledges less than enthusiastically. 'Nice.'

'Are you trying to get rid o' me?'

'No, no! It's just me heads bangin' like a bad one, an' I've got things to do, tha's all.'

'I'll be in touch then?' she says as she finally goes to leave, leaning over to give him a kiss.

'You do that,' says Derek, turning his head away just a fraction.

-

Maciej cannot wait for Detlef to call and rings him himself. He'd been very worried about him all night.

'Ja?'

'Detlef, my friend, how are you today?' says Maciej trying to sound as upbeat as ever.

'Ah, Maciej, not so good, but thank you for asking. I was just about to call you.'

'Do you know what you will do now? Have you had time to think?'

'Yes, Maciej, I have. If you could collect me at one o'clock?'

'Where to? Not the airport?'

'No, I've decided, I need to go and see Ellen.'

-

Although Derek is relieved to hear the front door click shut as Roxxii finally leaves, there is still something else gnawing away at him and making him feel very uneasy, but, for the life of him, he can't quite fathom it out.

In his now eerily silent bedroom, he looks to the alarm clock on his bedside table. It's only just seven o'clock in the morning for chrissakes!

But then, behind it, he spots the Rolex box, now slightly crushed and battered. He picks it up and opens it, remembering who gave it to him.

Amazingly, the watch is still inside and outwardly intact, but it doesn't appear to be working. He holds it to his ear, shaking it, before, once again, winding it up, resetting the time and putting it on his wrist.

Then the penny drops!

That was it!

There was that old German geezer, wasn't there?

He'd said he was his dad, didn't he?

Ha!

The depths some people will go to when they smell money, eh?

The cheeky cunt!

But then, he recalls running out after him. He'd wanted to have it out with him, but as Phil and Jimbo had said, he was just some chancer pushing his luck, that was all.

His real dad, his namesake, had been a stevedore in the docks, a strapping man that had been killed on the quayside in a freak accident whilst unloading great ocean-going container ships from all around the world - tea, coffee, bananas, the lot. His grandfather had told him that, from as young as he could remember, sat on his knee, enveloped in pipe smoke, and hanging on to his every word.

As a boy, he'd been strangely proud of his father's seemingly heroic demise. It had been more than important to him and given him a certain status, an anchor so to speak, and something he'd dearly held onto as he grew up a fatherless child.

Nah! It was all bollocks. His father had died when he was just a toddler. Everybody knew that, everybody had said ... So what if the stupid old bloke looked a bit like him! That was nuthin' more than a coincidence. It could happen to anyone. Besides, other than the grainy and vague snapshot he keeps safe in his wallet, how could anyone be sure? And even if there is so much as a shred of truth in it, which there isn't, what must his family have been thinking? His lovely ol' mum? No, she'd never do such a thing! She'd never lie to him.

Derek then looks for his jacket and finds it laid strewn on the floor. He gets out his wallet and pulls out the photo to study it more closely. 'Nothing like 'im,' he concludes as he then hears his phone ring from somewhere under the rest of his clothes but unable to find it.

'G'mornin', Dekko, it's Brian,' he says. *'I thought you were never going to pick up!'*

'Oh, Brian, yeah. I was just thinking about you. D'you know what bloody time it is?'

'Yeah, it's tha early bird that gets the worm,' he jokes. *'You sound a wee bit rough, pal. Heavy night?*

'Could say that.'

'An' why not? I would if I was in your shoes! How's tha' lovely watch o' yours? It's a beauty, ain't it?'

'Yeah, lovely, thanks,' says Derek, checking the time on it but confused to see it now reads quarter to two.

'Good. Now look, I been busy on your behalf,' the Scot starts off. *'How are y' fixed today? Just a wee 'get to know ya' to set th' ball rollin'.'*

'What ball?'

'Th' meeting we were talkin' aboot?'

'Oh, yeah. Can't today, Brian. Sorry. Somethin' important's come up.'

'More important than this? I fuckin' doubt it!'

''Fraid so, it's me Mum. I got to go over an' see her again.'

'Wha time?'

'Dunno. This afternoon, I expect, after two.'

'There's still plenty o' time then.'

'No,' Derek puts his foot down, 'I'm not dashin' around like a blue arsed fly for you nor nobody.'

'You're puttin' me in a very difficult position 'ere, Dekko. Don't think these contacts o' mine are gonnae be best pleased.'

'I'm sorry about that, but tha's the way it is.'

'You still wannae do it, don't ya?'

'Yeah, yeah, o' course,' says Derek a little unconvincingly.

'Ya dinnae sound so sure?'

'I said I'll do it.'

'OK, let's fix it for definite then. How about we say I'll pick y' up from yours tomorra? Ten on tha dot?'

'You know where I live?'

'Nah, course not!' he lies, forcing a laugh. *'I was thinkin' from outside the pub.'*

'That'd be better.'

'Tomorrow it is then. Ten. Car park o' the Travellers. Yeah?'

'Yeah, OK then.'

'Oh, an' by the way, they've asked me to tell ya tae bring your cheque book wi' ya.'

'They 'ave?' asks Derek, dubiously. 'Why?'

'Just in case. We're talkin' investments 'ere, Dekko, big money opportunities. You dinnae wanna miss out, now di ya?'

'Er, no, s'pose not. I dunno where it is though.'

171

'Then ya'd better find it. It'll be in a drawer.'

'Probably.'

'An' put on some decent gear, an' all. No denims. You dinnae wanna look like the poor relation now you're as rich as fuckin' Croesus!'

'Creases?'

Brian laughs. *'Exactly! Get an iron oot, gi' em' tha once over!'*

'I haven't got an iron.'

'Ah, whatever,' Brian gives up. *'Just make sure you look clean an' tidy, yeah? Smart. An' look, nobody's gonnae be holdin' a gun to yer 'ead, so relax.'*

'OK.'

'Nice one. So where is she then? Your mother? She OK?'

'She's alright. Ashton Gate, a Nursing Home over there, but happy as Larry now I'm gonna get her out o' there.'

'Tha's the spirit, Dekko. Look after your family too. An' wi' a bit o' our help, you'll 'ave even more.'

'You reckon?'

'I do! Bu' tha' rings a bell,' Brian then says, feigning recognition. *'I knew someone in a home over tha' way once. Wha' was it called? Remind me again?'*

'New Horizons.'

'Tha's it! Memory like a fuckin' sieve, me. See ya tomorra. Drive safely, yeah?'

'I'll try,' says Derek.

-

Putting the phone down, Brian immediately calls PG.

'Tha's tha best I could dae,' he explains. 'We dinnae want to frighten him off, now do we?'

'How very irritating. We need to get on with it.'

''Kin' 'ell, PG! We're only talkin' twen'y-four fuckin' hours 'ere. Wha' does it fuckin' matter?'

'Language! I'll not let Sir Alun down. He's relying on me.'

'Bollocks tae 'im! He'll just 'ave tae wait. Anyway, I know where Dekko's off tae today. Sez he's gonna see his mum. I'll check it out, make sure he's tellin' me tha truth. OK?'

'OK, stay on the case,,' PG relinquishes. *'I'll go ahead and book a meeting room for tomorrow. Do you know Jurys Hotel on Prince Street?'*

'Yeah, o' course. As long as we don't end up in front o' one,' Brian jokes.

'Very amusing.'

'Please yerself.'

'Also, I'd like you to sit in, just in case we need to bring a little pressure to bear, if you get my drift?'

'So long as you're shellin' out for ma time, I could'nae gi' a shit.'

'And make sure he's got his cheque book on him.'

'Been there, done that.'

'And that he's dressed appropriately.'

'Tha' too.'

'I'll book it for eleven-thirty. I'm sure that will give you sufficient time.'

'Consider it done.'

'Tomorrow it is. Don't be late, Brian. I'm relying on you.'

Chapter 18

And so, it unfolds.

Detlef and Maciej are easily the first to arrive at the New Horizons Nursing Home in Ashton Gate, but, understandably, after the unceremonious rejection he'd suffered at the hands of his son still playing very heavily on his mind, Detlef fears yet another angry reaction and appears reluctant to get out of the taxi.

'You must do it,' Maciej urges him gently, sensing the old man's disquiet and unease.

Detlef doesn't answer, can't answer, but checks his reflection in the passenger side wing mirror, tapping his pockets for nothing in particular, like it was some sort of routine.

'I'll be here waiting for you,' the young man reassures him.

'I can't,' Detlef lets slip. 'I'm not so sure now.'

'You must,' repeats Maciej. 'It's why you're here. You need to put things straight. Go.'

That final word strikes a chord with him as, yet again, Detlef is reminded of how it had felt all those years ago on that first ever parachute drop and being terrified to leave the relative security of that rattling old aircraft. Now, as then, he knows he has little or no choice and steels himself. He's got to jump, so to speak, whether he likes it or not. *'Eintausendeins, eintausendzwei,'* he mouths to himself once again before pulling his jacket in tight and flinging open the door in one fell movement that momentarily belies his years.

'Good luck, my friend,' Maciej calls out after him, waving.

Detlef, not looking back but instinctively waving in return, desperately hopes for a soft and gentle landing.

-

Back at the Travellers, Phil and Dave are having a chat over a lunch time pint with Jimbo earwigging as and when time allows.

'And then,' says Phil, telling Dave the story, 'Dekko, as quick as ya like, runs out after 'im!'

'You're fuckin' jokin'!'

'I'm fuckin' not!'

'Why?'

'Christ knows. It was nuts.'

-

'I'm here to see Ellen Dando,' Detlef tells the young girl sat in a glass fronted office just inside the main entrance.

'Is she expecting you?' she asks.

'No, but I am an old family friend. I explained to one of your colleagues yesterday,' he says. 'Her name was Sheryl, I think. She said it would be alright'.

'Ah yes, Sheryl. She's not here at the moment, but OK. If I can just ask you to sign the visitor's book?'

Detlef takes the biro that is crudely sellotaped by a length of string to the spine and fills in his name and gives the Redland Hotel as his address.

'You'll find her in the Day Room,' informs the girl, releasing the security door. 'Straight in front of you at the end of the corridor, on the left. You can't miss it.'

-

'So, let me get this straight, yeah?' says Dave, lapping it all up. 'Some random ol' geezer, as cool as ya like, comes in an' says I'm yer dad? Just like that?'

'Yip.'

'Fuckin' quality! I've heard it all now,' he says. 'But wha' d'ya reckon? Any truth in it?'

'No, but wait a minute, I'm savin' the best 'til last,' says Phil, going in for the punchline.

'What?'

'Sittin' comfortably?'

'Get on with it!'

'He was a bloody Kraut!'

'You what?'

'A Kraut!'

'A German? What, like Seek Hile, ya mean?'

'Yeah!'

Dave lets out a huge guffaw, clutching at his side. 'W'ahh! Stop it! You're killin' me!' he yells.

'Don't mention ze war, eh?' adds Phil, laughing alongside, putting his index finger up to his nose and straightening a leg away from the barstool.

-

With the smell of braised meat and stewed vegetables still heavy in the air, Detlef makes his way down the corridor.

Fortunately, the doors to the day room are wide open, held in place by fire extinguishers, affording him an almost uninterrupted view inside.

The room is large too, overly so, and there is a sense of unenthusiastic activity from within with those sat around the central tables pawing over jigsaw puzzles or sticking things. Most, however, are collected at either end in front of one of the two television sets, each programmed onto different channels.

Nobody pays him any particular attention as he takes a tentative step or two inside.

It doesn't take him long to find her.

On the far side of the room, in a wheelchair, alone and gazing out of one of the large plate glass windows, he soon catches sight of her unmistakable profile, still clearly distinguishable to him after all these years. The shock of seeing her again shakes him, and, for a brief moment, he feels the need to hold onto the back of a chair for support and catch his breath.

-

'You say that, Phil,' cautions Jimbo, and not really sharing in their amusement, 'but stood side by side, they looked like two peas out a pod t'me.'

'Fuck me, Jim, you look like Les fuckin' Dawson but that don't make ya his fuckin' brother!' dismisses Phil and continuing to laugh.

'Reenie said she saw 'em in here on Monday,' Jimbo continues.

'Exactly! It gave 'em a bit o' time to plan it. They got whiff of a bit o' cash, heard some comment or other, and decided to chance their arm,' explains Phil. 'Bloody obvious, innit?'

'But what if Dekko's dad had still been alive?' persists Jimbo. 'Then the story would o' made no sense at all. There's more to this. You mark my words.'

'Stop it! They were just a couple of chancers givin' it a shot,' replies Phil, beginning to sound annoyed at all this conspiracy. 'End of.'

'And it could change everythin',' says Jimbo, still looking a bit twitchy.

'What d'ya mean, Jim?' asks Dave, now looking concerned himself. 'It could change everythink?'

'You know,' he says under his breath and leaning over. 'What he's promised us.'

'Nah,' says Phil, a note of uncertainty suddenly entering his voice too. 'Can't be true. Somebody would o' said.'

-

Nervously, gingerly, Detlef makes his way over but stops several feet short and pulls up a chair behind and to the side of her. Ellen is oblivious to his presence, her attention drawn to a dull and ragged butterfly on the windowsill given a new and fluttering lease of life in the overbearing heat of the place. For a few short moments, it gives him time to think how best to make his approach.

Sitting quietly, his hands held between his knees, he can see that the years have not been so kind to her at all as he recalls the young and beautiful woman that he'd last seen what was an eternity ago. Here, now, right in front of him, he beholds a particularly frail looking woman dressed in a tired cotton skirt and bobbled cardigan, her bandaged legs strangely inert and immobile, a hearing aid hooked loosely over one ear, a crocheted doll or some such rested on her lap.

But suddenly, from out of nowhere, she appears to smile as if a pleasant thought had come to head and she eases herself forward, accidentally dropping the doll to the floor.

Without even thinking, he stands and goes to pick it up, gently placing it back into her lap. 'Ellen,' he then whispers softly. 'Ellen, it is me, Detlef.'

'Detlef?' she says as if she were in a dream.

'Yes, Detlef,' he repeats.

Immediately, as if she were a ravenous Venus Fly Trap who'd just been triggered, her arms are around his head, pulling him hard down towards her, rocking him. 'Detlef, Detlef,' she cries softly into his neck. 'I'm so sorry. I'm so sorry.'

-

'So, where is he now then?' Jimbo continues to worry.

'Yeah. Not like him to be late on parade,' agrees Dave.

'Relax, the pair o' ya. That singer said she'd walk 'im 'ome safe last night,' informs Phil with a knowin' wink. 'Over 'im like a rash she was.'

'Yeah, I saw,' confirms Jimbo. 'Now there's a gold digger if ever I saw one. I tried to warn 'im.'

'There's your answer then!' howls Dave. 'You know what they say, pussy'll blow ya where dynamite won't! He's probably still back at 'ome givin' her one right now!'

Jimbo then walks out from behind the bar to peer over the net curtains. 'Her car's gone,' he observes. 'Went early this mornin'. A little Micra..'

-

Detlef manages to release himself from Ellen's surprisingly strong embrace and, with tears now blurring his vision, he speaks to her. 'No, it is I that am sorry, Ellen,' he says. 'Please don't blame yourself. It was all my fault, nobody else's.'

'There was never anyone else for me, you know,' she says, launching into the conversation she'd had with herself a million times over. 'Never, ever.'

Detlef stands back, strangely embarrassed, shocked even, and unsure how to respond. 'It has been very difficult for us both,' he says, regaining his composure.

'I've missed you every second of every day,' she continues, her hands now caressing his cheeks, her face alight and almost angelic as if all the years had suddenly just melted away.

'Ellen, not a single day has passed when I have not thought of you,' he says, truthfully.

'But how did you find me here?' she then asks, releasing him sufficiently such that he might sit down.

'I will explain,' he says, seeking out his handkerchief to stem the flow of tears now running freely down his face.

'I got all your letters in the end,' Ellen continues to gush.

'Yes, I know.'

'How?'

'I spoke to Joyce Farnell,' Detlef reveals.

'Joyce? How on earth did you find Joyce? She was the one with me on that first day in Weston. Remember?'

'Yes, I do. I went to your parent's old house.'

'You did?'

'Yes, the young woman there pointed me to where Joyce lives. She told me you were here, although she was a little worried to say.'

'Oh, thank heavens she did!' says Ellen before looking down at herself and to her wheelchair. 'But whatever must you think of me, Detlef, finding me like this?'

'It doesn't matter, *meine Geliebte*,' he says, dropping back into how he'd always addressed her. 'You and I, we are both getting older.'

'Meine Geliebte?' she repeats, her old eyes twinkling with delight as she remembers. 'I'd almost forgotten.'

-

'Give him a call,' suggests Jimbo to Phil. 'Find out.'

'Am I hell as like! He'll turn up. He might be with his son, or gone back over to see his mum, anythin'. I'm not his bloody keeper, Jim!'

-

'It was my father you see,' Ellen starts to explain. 'I didn't know your letters even existed until after he died. He wanted them destroyed but mother managed to hide them. She was so embarrassed when she told me, poor woman. She never knew what to do for the best. She was scared, I suppose. Like me.'

'And by then it was too late,' Detlef deduces.

'He was such a wicked man. I shall never forgive him. I tried writing back, let me see, it would have been nineteen eighty-three. Dresden, Hellerau,' she remembers very clearly. 'You wrote it on the back of the envelopes.'

'That's where my family were from. I had been living in Hannover for many years by then.'

'Hannover?'

'Yes. And when I received nothing in return, I thought that you wanted nothing more to do with me.'

'No! Nothing could be further from the truth. Do you want to see them?' she then asks eagerly. 'I still have them all.'

'Yes, I would, but maybe later. There is something I need to talk to you about.'

'It's Derek, isn't it? You want to find Derek,' she guesses correctly.

'Yes, I do.'

At that moment, Margaret casually walks over to them. She is quietly and professionally concerned and not a little inquisitive. 'Are you OK, Ellen?' she asks.

'Oh yes, Margaret, yes, perfectly,' she says sounding all chipper and unlike anything Margaret had heard in her before. 'This is Detlef, my Detlef.'

'How lovely, nice to meet you, Detlef. Ellen's mentioned you to me. Would you two like a cup of tea?' she asks.

'Ooh, that would lovely,' says Ellen, suddenly relishing the idea. 'Do you have any biscuits? Would you like a biscuit, Detlef?'

'I'll see what I can do, shall I?' says Margaret with a little laugh. 'You'll have to come here more often, Detlef. You've certainly put a smile on her face. Milk, sugar?'

-

'So, what you gonna do wi' yours then, Phil?' asks Dave. 'If Dekko don't change his mind that is.'

'None o' your bloody business!'

'Only askin'! I think I might bugger off, down to Spain or summat. Italy. Get some sunshine in and escape this miserable place.'

'Don't let us stop ya then,' says Jimbo, unable to resist.

'Gonna stay in the pub game, Jim?' Phil then asks him.

-

'She seems very nice,' says Detlef as Margaret walks away and making small talk together as if all the intervening years had suddenly gone and it had been only days since they had last met.

'Yes, she's lovely. She's my favourite,' says Ellen. 'I do hope she finds some biscuits to dunk,' she repeats, using her hand to demonstrate.

'Ah, yes,' says Detlef, smiling. 'Dunking biscuits. I remember it. So, Derek?'

'He's doing everso well, you know, my Derek. Sorry, our Derek,' she corrects herself. 'He's won the lottery!' she blurts out excitedly before her expression changes dramatically. 'But he doesn't know about you, Detlef,' she then confesses.

'I know, Ellen. I've seen him,' Detlef stops her.

'You've seen him?'

'Yes, I have,' admits Detlef now looking shamefaced himself.

'When?'

'Yesterday.'

'But he was only here yesterday.'

'It was last night, in a bar he uses.'

'In a pub? Did you tell him? What did he say?' asks Ellen very anxiously.

Detlef looks to the floor, shaking his head. 'I shouldn't have, Ellen,' he admits, 'not without finding you and seeking your permission. I'm so very sorry. I have been a very selfish and thoughtless man.'

'No, you have not! I have done this to both of you,' she says, continuing to blame herself for all the mistakes and lies of the past. 'It is all my fault!'

'But I fear that I have put you in a very difficult position, although I'm not so sure that he believed me. He thinks his father is dead, doesn't he?'

Ellen now begins weep. 'I had no choice. I was so young with nowhere to go, and like a fool I went along with it.'

'What's done is done, Ellen. None of us can change that,' says Detlef, reaching out and holding her hand. 'Derek was very angry,' he continues. 'He thinks, maybe, I was after his money. So, if you wish, we can pretend none of this has ever happened.'

'Oh, Detlef! He is your son! It has been far too long. He needs to know the truth. I should have told him years ago, when that bloody bastard of a grandfather of his died, so help me God for using such words!'

-

'I mean, I doubt you're gonna carry on runnin' this place?' Phil adds. 'You could get somewhere much better.'

'I like it, to be honest, Phil. We might even put an offer in to buy it, if the brewery'll listen?'

'Open your eyes, Jim. It's a shit 'ole,' says Dave.

'Oi! Don't start that again!' Phil warns him. 'We don't want a repeat performance, now do we?'

'What? I'm only sayin' how it is!' squeals Dave. 'Look at the state of it,' he adds, scuffing his foot on the tarry and threadbare carpet.

Margaret brings over two cups of tea but can see that Ellen's demeanour appears to have changed very noticeably. 'Oh dear, what's the matter?' she asks.

But before Ellen even has a chance to answer, the entire room is disrupted by someone yelling and shouting at the door. 'What the fuck's he doin' here?!' thunders Derek as he storms in, followed closely by Maciej who'd seen him arrive and had immediately feared for Detlef's safety.

'Derek! Please! Language!' Margaret tries to quieten him at once. 'I won't have this. There are others to think about here.'

'This is your father, Derek,' announces Ellen, her chin held firm and with as much dignity as she can muster. 'His name is Detlef.'

'You what?' Derek continues to shout as he looms over them.

'You were named after him,' the old lady carries on, her hands held firm on the armrest but, inevitably, beginning to crumble.

'No! My dad's dead! That's what you told me! That's what you fuckin' said!'

'Enough!' Margaret shouts over him.

'I'm so sorry, Derek, but it's the truth.'

'So, everything was a lie, was it? Is that what you're tellin' me? My life has been one big fuckin' lie?'

'Please, Derek, …' Detlef tries to interject.

'Don't you dare!' yells Derek, clenching his fist back at him. 'Don't you fuckin' dare!'

'Now, that really is enough, Derek!' demands Margaret and trying to take him by the arm. 'I'll have to ask you to leave if you carry on like this.'

'Don't bother yerself. I'm out o' 'ere!' he says before turning back to his mother. 'An' I never want to see *you* again!' he shouts at her before he turns to leave.

'Derek! Stop!' calls Detlef, attempting to follow. 'Derek, please wait!'

'No, sit down,' Margaret swiftly instructs him, fearing that any further confrontation could prove even more volatile and dangerous. 'This is not the place. I'm sorry.'

'But can someone stop him? Please!' Ellen calls out and on the verge of hysteria. 'Derek! Please listen to me! Derek!'

'I'm going after him! I must!' cries Detlef, now panic stricken himself. '*Was habe ich gemacht!* What have I done!'

'No,' repeats Margaret assertively. 'Stay here. I'll see what I can do,' she says before dashing out herself.

-

'If ya don't like it, David, you know what you can do,' says Jimbo.

'Why don't you try bein' nice for a change?' adds Phil.

'Jeez! Can't say nuthin' nowadays!' Dave protests just as a couple of blokes walk up quickly behind him, standing in over close - almost breathing distance.

'What's that then, Dave?' asks the one, a dark haired and swarthy looking type in a thigh length and expensive looking jacket, a heavy gold chain around his neck.

Dave looks up at him, momentarily shocked into silence.

'Unlike you to be lost for words,' says the man.

-

As Margaret runs out of the building, Derek is already in his car and beginning to pull away. Bravely, she steps in front of it, flagging him down and placing her hands on the bonnet. 'Get out of my way, ya stupid bint!' he shouts as he hits the breaks.

'Derek, would you talk to me?' she asks, walking around to the driver's side.

'Are you in on this, are ya?'

'I'm not 'in' on anything. I just work here,' she says.

'Then why are you bloody stoppin' me? It's nuthin' to do wi' you!'

'I like your Mum, Derek. She's a lovely lady. I don't like to see her upset.'

'Her upset? What about me?' he shouts and thumping the top of the steering wheel. 'She's just told me that old bloke in there is my fuckin' dad! I've never seen him before in my life!'

'I can't answer that, Derek, I don't know. But don't you think it might be a good idea for you to sit down quietly and talk with her?'

'Why the fuck should I? If she thinks I'm gonna help her out now, she can think again! She can rot in there for all I care! She'll get nuthin'!'

'You know you don't mean that. You're angry. I understand that, but she loves you. She talks about you all the time.'

'I was only a bloody kid! Who'd tell a bloody kid his dad was dead, eh? Who, I ask you?'

'I agree,' says Margaret, 'but there must have been a very good reason for it.'

-

'Alright then?' greets Dave like they were mates but patently ill at ease. 'Can I get ya both a drink?'

'Do ya wanna discuss this in 'ere or outside?' the man ignores the offer, speaking into Dave's ear.

Dave winces and appears reluctant to answer him.

'Come on! We ain't got all day!' the man continues. 'You know wha' it's about.'

'What's goin' on?' asks Jimbo. 'Not in my pub, ya don't,' he pre-empts.

'Who are these geezers, Dave?' Phil joins in.

'And you are?' asks the man, aggressively.

'Don't you threaten me, ya bastard,' Phil comes back at him, standing. 'You picked the wrong man!'

'It's alright, fellahs,' says Dave before pushing Phil back onto his stool and going join them. 'I don't want any trouble.'

-

'Ooh, I'm everso sorry, son, I made a mistake,' Derek is mimicking his mother's voice. 'He's still alive after all. Oh, and by the way, he's not who I said he was, he's a bloody German!'

'Talk to her, Derek. You must,' says Margaret.

'I fuckin' knew it, really,' he continues, thinking aloud. 'I always wondered why there wasn't anything of him about, no photos, nuthin', except for this poxy little thing!' he says, pulling out his wallet and showing her the photograph. 'She told me not to let anyone know she'd given it me, that it was our little secret. What sort of mother does that, eh?!'

'She wanted you to know then, didn't she? She wouldn't have given it to you otherwise.'

'Well, this is what I think of it now!' yells Derek, ripping the picture in half and throwing it past her and out of the window.

'Derek, you know you can't stay like this. She'll always be your Mum, whatever happens.'

Derek can no longer handle it, and, overcome with rage and confusion, he doesn't know whether to scream at the top of his voice or wail like a baby and holds his hands behind his head, face up to the roof of the car, blowing hard, hyperventilating.

'Look,' says Margaret, tapping him gently. 'Look.'

Derek opens his eyes to see Detlef, with Maciej just behind him, standing no more than a few yards from the front of the vehicle, his body trembling, his face pleading, his arms held open by his sides.

'Give him a chance, Derek,' suggests Margaret. 'You need to know the truth, whatever that might be.'

But then, suddenly, Detlef appears very pale and teeters. He is just about to fall when Maciej dashes forward and grabs him from behind to stop him hitting the ground. 'Come, Detlef,' he says. 'Let me take you home.'

'No, let's get him inside,' instructs Margaret urgently and going to help. 'Quickly.'

-

Up on the street, parked out of sight in his black BMW, Brian has been watching the whole sorry episode with intrigue and not a little concern. He's going to need to find out what's going on. He can't have this going tits up. Not now.

As he sees the nurse and the taxi driver help the old man into the building, he has every intention of tailing Derek to discover wherever he might go and starts his engine in anticipation.

But Derek's car doesn't move. Slowly, the door opens and Brian sees Derek's hand appear below it, picking up the torn pieces of photo strewn on the ground.

Chapter 19

Firmly supported by Maciej, Margaret leads Detlef into the treatment room. 'We should call the doctor,' she advises as she sits him on the examination couch and offers him a beaker of fresh water.

'I shall be fine,' Detlef declines but looking very pale and taking a necessary sip.

'Are you absolutely positive?' she worries. 'I think we should.'

'I'm sure,' he insists, 'but thank you.'

'OK,' she answers him uncertainly. 'It wouldn't hurt to check your blood pressure though, would it?'

To that, Detlef nods in agreement.

'Shall we get Ellen in here too?' Margaret then suggests as she helps him off with his jacket and goes to the cupboard to get the monitor. 'She'll be worried.'

'Of course. Yes.'

'Would you be so kind as to do the honours?' Margaret asks the young taxi driver.

'No problem,' he answers, hurrying back out to get her.

'Now, Detlef, lie back and relax,' Margaret continues as she rolls up his shirt sleeve and tightens the Velcro cuff around his upper arm.

'I wish that I could.'

'You must try. Close your eyes for a moment.'

-

Dave saunters back into the bar as if nothing had happened.

'So, what was that all about?' Phil asks him straight away.

Dave pulls up his stool, but a little awkwardly, a catch in his side. 'Nuthin',' he says, picking up his pint. 'I borrowed a bit o' kit off them and hadn't returned it yet,' he lies. 'Tha's all.'

'Oh yeah, what *kit*?' asks Phil suspiciously.

'Ladders, a bit o' scaffold, if ya must know,' he says, thinking quickly on his feet. 'I been paintin' some windows.'

'Is that it? Bit 'eavy 'anded for just that, weren't they?'

'There's scaffolders for ya,' Dave explains. 'Hard bastards in that game.'

'You must think I'm stupid!' says Phil.

'What?'

'Why couldn't they 'ave said in front of us?'

'Alright, alright! It got nicked an' I owe 'em for it,' Dave lies again, doubling down.

'Oh, right. How much?'

'What?'

'You heard. How much?'

'Five hundred. They're gettin' a bit 'eavy.'

Jimbo comes back over to join them. 'So, what was that all about?' he asks. 'I hope there ain't gonna be any nonsense?'

'Not you an' all!' Dave squeals. 'I've already just explained!'

-

No sooner is Margaret making a note of the readings when Maciej is wheeling Ellen in. Instinctively, she clasps her hand to her mouth as soon as she sees him. 'Whatever is the matter, Detlef?' she asks, her voice high pitched and shrill.

'I'm just very tired, that's all,' he tries to reassure her. 'I'm so very sorry to have started all of this. Will you ever forgive me?'

'Please, Detlef!' she exclaims emphatically, 'I've already said. This is not your fault. What happened?'

'It's nothing,' he says, still beside himself with guilt.

'Did you find Derek?' Ellen then asks. 'Did you speak to him?'

'He is in his car,' Maciej informs her.

'Sorry, but who are you?' Ellen asks him.

'Oh, I'm sorry,' says Detlef, berating himself even further. 'Ellen, Margaret, this is Maciej, my taxi driver. I don't know what I would have done without him,' he tells them.

Ellen gives him a smile. 'That's nice of you,' she says. 'Helping my Detlef. Thank you.'

'Pleased to meet you, Maciej,' adds Margaret before turning back to Detlef. 'So, look, your blood pressure is a little high. I do think it best that we call a doctor.'

'I shall be OK,' he refuses once again.

'Please do as she asks, Detlef,' pleads Ellen. 'I couldn't bear it if anything happened to you!'

'I know what's wrong,' he reveals. 'I'm on medication. Maybe I forgot this morning, that's all,' he tries to allay their fears.

'Do you have an illness? What's wrong with you?'

'It's nothing to worry about, Ellen. Old age, that's all.'

Ever considerate, Maciej then speaks. 'Shall I now wait outside again, Detlef?' he asks. 'You need some time alone, I think.'

'Thank you, but first, perhaps you could see if Derek is still there?' he requests. 'Please ask him to return.'

However, before Maciej even has time to reply, Derek's growling voice interrupts them all from just outside the door. 'Talkin' about me, are ya?' he can be heard to say.

'Oh, Derek, is that you?' his mother calls out.

He doesn't answer her but slowly steps into view.

'Come in, Derek,' urges Margaret. 'Take a seat,' she says pushing forward a plastic and utilitarian chair.

He refuses.

Detlef then elbows himself up the couch, eager to seize what is surely his final opportunity. 'Derek, *bitte,* please, can we talk, you and I?' he pleads.

'Not if you're gonna come out wi' all that German shite I'm not!' Derek snarls.

'Please be nice,' requests Margaret.

With considerable effort, Detlef now drops his legs over the side of the couch, unsure as to whether he has either the strength or the resilience to deal with such an obviously angry man. 'Please,' he repeats in English.

'You better get on with it then. I ain't got all day,' continues Derek in the same aggressive manner but, at least, allowing Maciej to pass.

'Please be patient, son,' says Ellen. 'He's had quite a turn you know.'

Again, Derek blanks her, speaking over her. 'So, what's your name again?' he asks, his face contorted with a look of distaste like he was being asked to sample an unsavoury foreign dish for the very first time. 'Det-lef or summat stupid, innit?'

'Yes, it is,' confirms his father. 'My name is Detlef.'

Again, Derek grimaces.

'Believe it or not,' Detlef continues, hoping to elaborate, 'you were named after me. It was the closest name in English your mother and I could think of at the time.'

'That's right,' agrees Ellen. 'From the very first moment we held you in our arms, we both said, didn't we, Detlef? This is our beautiful little Derek, we said.'

'Ooh, sing me lullabies too, did ya? How lovely for ya both!'

'Yes, it was lovely,' Detlef reiterates, firmly. 'You were a lovely child. But please, before we go any further, may I ask?' he says addressing the two women. 'Can Derek and I have some time alone together please? It is important.'

'No, fuck that fer a game o' soldiers!' Derek reacts immediately. 'I'm not bein' left alone in 'ere with 'im! He could tell me any ol' bollocks he wants!'

'Mind your language, son,' his mother now scolds him. 'Anyone would think I dragged you up, not brought you up. I'll not have it. Do you hear me?'

'Ah, shut up, you ol' bat!' Derek retaliates as he finally engages her. 'Do you honestly think I give a toss what comes out of your mouth anymore!'

'Now, that's enough!' demands Margaret again.

'Well wha' d'you expect? I've just discovered that she's lied to me all my life and now you want me to be all nicey-nicey? What planet are you all on, eh?'

'Please, Derek,' his father speaks to him once again. 'I can only begin to imagine what a shock this must be for you, but can we have ten minutes together? That's all I'm asking.'

'What part o' no don't you understand, old man?'

'You will, Derek! You will hear your father out!' his mother demands fiercely.

'Father? You call 'im my father!? Are you 'avin' a fuckin' laugh?'

'Language! Please!' Margaret tries yet again.

But Derek is not for stopping and carries on. 'What sort of fuckin' father ups sticks, never to be seen again, eh? Well, up until now that is - surprise, surprise!'

'I wanted to find you before it was too late, that is all,' says Detlef, fully understanding the insinuation.

'Yeah, sure ya did! Nuthin' to do wi' the fact I'm now worth millions?' he continues his spiteful tirade. 'Course not!'

'Of that I had no idea,' his father tries to put him straight. 'It is purely a coincidence, nothing more.'

'Coincidence? Ha! You must think I was born yesterday!'

'How could I have known, Derek? Ask yourself. I only flew here on Monday. I bought the tickets weeks ago.'

Derek ignores these unfortunate facts. 'But how can I even be sure?' he then questions his mother.

'Sure of what?' she asks, also knowing exactly what he means.

'Wha d'ya think? I dunno what you got up to, do I?'

'Tell me. Go on, tell me!' she pushes him, indignantly.

'That he's me dad, that's what!'

'Well!' she says, insulted, 'unless you were born by immaculate conception, my lad, he is!'

'It has to be said, you do look remarkably alike,' offers Margaret.

'Like Hell I do!' exclaims Derek, flexing his jaw and clenching his fists, despite the glaring and obvious similarity.

'Look at him! Can you not see?' Ellen continues ferociously. 'There was only ever one man for me!'

In the face of so much mounting evidence, Derek finally realises he can no longer deny what is so obviously the truth. His mother is totally adamant, he can see that, and he can also see that he and Detlef do look uncannily alike. However, unable to handle the wave of emotions that continues to envelop and destabilise him - confusion, anger, the outright sense of disbelief - it renders him temporarily speechless.

'Answer me,' demands his mum.

Derek pulls at his hair and starts to laugh as if he'd finally sussed it and that there some sort of game playing going on. 'This is a setup, innit? he shouts. 'Where's the cameras?'

'There are no cameras,' says Detlef, understanding. 'It is the truth.'

'Truth? You speak of truth wi' me very own mother inventin' some dead fuckin' dad in the hope it'd keep me happy! Don't take the piss!'

'Then you must find out why,' encourages Margaret softly. 'As difficult as it might be.'

'Why should I? She's a bitch!'

With that, Detlef, understanding only too well what the word means, can no longer hold back. 'Don't you dare call your mother that!' he says, raising his own voice. 'She is innocent in all of this! She had no choice! It was all my fault. Do you understand me? My fault!'

'I don't care who's bleedin' fault it was. The fact is, she's lied to me. End of. I can't take no more o' this shit!' shouts Derek as, once again, he turns to leave.

'Please don't hate me, son. Please don't go,' whimpers his mum, her strength all but gone and beginning to weep profusely again. 'It was not as you think. I was young and foolish.'

'Yeah, an' I was only a little kid for Chrissakes!' Derek yells back.

'Derek, please! Look at me,' implores Detlef, about to risk offering him an ultimatum. 'I'll leave here right now, if you wish, and you will never see me again.'

'Off ya toddle then! Go on! Go!'

'Or,' continues his father, 'you can hear what I have to say. The choice is yours.'

'What if I say no?'

'Then you will never understand.'

With all eyes now on Derek, something quite peculiar happens as he suddenly retreats into some kind of invisible bubble of his own making, standing motionless as if in some sort of trance. Detlef's words had resurrected a multitude of long forgotten memories previously held deep in the recesses of his brain - words that were almost identical to those uttered by his grandfather all those years ago when, sat on his knee, he'd told him what he 'needed to understand' too.

As a child, he would often lie awake in his bed at night peering at that one and only photograph, the very one now torn in two but safely pushed back into his wallet and wonder why his mother had always insisted that he keep it 'their little secret'.

He also recalls the sudden hushed voices and awkward silences that used to greet him when, innocently enough, he'd asked a question about his dad, only to be taken aside by his grandfather who'd either offer him the same old story, or, as he got a little older, give him a sharp slap around the backside for not shutting up about it.

No, the truth of the matter was that he'd always known that things were not quite as he'd been led to believe but had simply decided to take the path of least resistance and stop questioning it - bury it deep somewhere in his brain.

It didn't really make any sense to him back then, and it certainly doesn't make any more sense to him right now.

'Derek?' his mother calls to him, 'Derek? Are you with us?' she asks, bursting his bubble. 'Are you going to talk to your father? Yes or no?'

Chapter 20

For what seems like an eternity but, in truth, is little more than just a few short moments, father and son eye each other intensely - one, earnest and imploring, the other, bolshy and belligerent.

For his part, Detlef is acutely aware that this is the first time they have been alone together since Derek was but a tiny child and seeks to break their awkward and uneasy silence. 'Would you like to sit down?' he offers, gesturing towards the still unoccupied chair.

'Nah. I'll stand if it's all the same to you,' answers Derek, his thumbs thrust into his jean's pockets.

Detlef tries again. 'It may be more comfortable?'

'I said no!' Derek snaps back. 'Just say what you gotta say an' let's get it over and done with, yeah?'

With an involuntarily sigh, Detlef edges himself forward and with the words he'd rehearsed more times than he could possibly remember, he begins. 'I have waited years for this moment, Derek,' he says, his lower lip already beginning to thin and tighten. 'Not one single day has gone by that I have not thought of you.'

'Well, I ain't you!' Derek rebuffs him.

'Yes, yes. I understand that,' replies Detlef hesitatingly.

'How the fuck could I?' his son continues. 'I didn't even know you bloody well existed until five minutes ago! Sheesh!'

'I'm sorry, Derek. This must be very difficult for you. I'm so very sorry.'

'Difficult? Difficult?! You don't know the fuckin' meanin' o' the word! So, as I said, just get on with it. All I'm interested in is the facts, OK?'

Detlef drops his head, shaking it uncertainly. 'I had this all worked out,' he says. 'What I would say to you, but now I'm not even sure where to start.'

'Try the beginning,' says Derek, pitilessly. 'Why d'ya bloody leave?'

-

'Was just wonderin',' mutters Jimbo as he ambles back over to re-join Phil and Dave over on Crackers Corner. 'Last night ... that big Scots geezer ... Brian, whatever his name was.'

'Yeah, wha' about him?' asks Phil.

'What's he up to, d'ya reckon? That was a helluva lot o' watch to go givin' away for nuthin', tha's for sure.'

'Weren't it just,' answers Phil sarcastically. 'Definitely a fake.'

'I dunno so much, but whatever, why?'

'You heard what Dekko said as well as I did. Some twaddle about meetin' up wi' some movers an' shakers, or so he said. Gullible twat.'

'So, we need to keep an eye out, Phil. Steer 'im clear.'

'He won't do anythin',' he says, batting the comment away with the back of his hand. 'It's all talk.'

'You sure 'bout that?' chips in Dave.

'Yes, Dave! I mean, wha' would be the point? He's got more than enough money to last 'imself a bloody lifetime, and some! Why would he need more?'

Jimbo still isn't convinced. ''Ave a word though, Phil, will ya? Just in case,' he continues to worry. 'You know what I'm sayin'. You're his closest mate.'

'I did.'

'People like that will 'ang 'im out to dry.'

'Yeah, an' us with it,' groans Dave, his arms now folded on the bar, a cigarette smouldering between his fingers, his head only inches from a sodden towelling drip mat. 'Take Courage' it reads.

'Will you put a bleedin' sock in it, Dave!' Phil shouts him down again.

'Sorree fo' fuckin' breathin'!'

'An' even if Dekko did meet up with 'em, what they gonna do?' he adds. 'Frog march 'im down the bank wi' a shotgun to 'is 'ead?'

'Yeah! Maybe they might do just that!' exclaims Jimbo.

Phil picks up his pint and takes a steady mouthful. 'Alright. Alright,' he accepts, a tiny seed of doubt now planted in his own mind. 'If it keeps you couple o' wusses happy, 'I'll speak to 'im again,' he says. 'OK?'

-

'Before I begin, please let me say it was all meant to be so very different, son,' Detlef addresses him, foolishly and without thinking.

'Son?' barks Derek immediately. 'Son?! Don't you fuckin' dare! You've got no right! I'm not, never will be, your son, an' don't you fuckin' forget it!'

'But, Derek,' his father persists, swallowing hard and bracing himself for the inevitable backlash, 'you are.'

'That's enough!' Derek continues to shout. 'Bio-bloody-logically, whatever ya call it, tha's as maybe! But where I come from, it takes more than shootin' yer load up some bird to make you a fuckin' dad!' he adds, crudely and viciously.

Detlef doesn't fully understand at first but then gets the gist. 'That is your mother you are insulting once again!' he reacts. 'If I was a few years younger, I'd, I'd ...'

'You'd what? Gi' me a bloody good hidin'?' says Derek, smirking. 'Try it, ol' man. Go on, I dare ya,' he goads him, tapping his chin. 'Pity you weren't about when I was a nipper an' properly needed it!'

Detlef backs off, holding his hands up in submission. 'Please, Derek, this is getting us nowhere,' he says, fearing that it all might be slipping away once again.

'I should get one o' them bloody paternity test thingies,' says Derek, thinking aloud.

'If you wish,' accepts Detlef. 'I would have no problem with that.'

'We will then,' says Derek but with little or no conviction and only too aware that with the weight of evidence mounting, the answer would be a foregone conclusion.

'Can you not see that I am ashamed for what happened?' Detlef continues.

'No, I don't! I don't know you from fuckin' Adam!'

'Then why do you think I am here?'

'Mmm, let me guess?' Derek continues with his illogical accusation.

'I may be many things,' reacts Detlef, 'but I am not a, how do you say it? … *ein Betrüger.*'

'Don't you start wi' all that German bollocks again!'

'Derek! I don't want your money! I do not need any of your money!'

'Oh yeah? Got a nice stash o' your own, 'ave we?'

'I'm not a wealthy man, if that's what you mean? But how could I have known?' Detlef repeats. 'You can see my tickets if you wish. I have them right here,' he says, reaching into his inside jacket pocket and holding them out. 'I bought them weeks ago and only arrived on Monday.'

'You found me pretty damn quick then, considerin'! How'd that happen, eh?'

'That was luck, nothing else … an old friend of your mother's,' Detlef goes to explain.

'Who?'

'Joyce Farnell.'

Derek thinks for a moment before making the connection. 'What? The neighbour up the road from Nan and Gramps house?'

'Yes. That's where I went first, to your grandparent's old house. The young woman there suggested I went to see her.'

'Is she still alive?' asks Derek incredulously.

'Yes, she is,' replies Detlef, still holding out his tickets. 'Here. Take a look. Let me prove it to you.'

Derek waves them away. 'So why *are* you here then?' he demands.

Detlef pauses for a moment before answering. 'I need to make my peace with you, and your mother, before it is too late,' he says.

'Oh yeah? Plannin' on goin' somewhere, are ya?'

'I'm an old man, Derek. Time is not on my side.'

'Good! Do us all a bloody favour and die!'

Again, Detlef sighs heavily, shaky and upset. 'I understand that you are angry,' he says, his voice catching. 'But I need to apologise if nothing else.'

'Fine! Great! Apologies accepted!' says Derek like a truculent teenager and already turning towards the door once again. 'Can I go now?'

'No! Please! Not yet. There is more. Please. Listen.'

'Like what? I really don't think I can be arsed with this,' says Derek like it was all just a great inconvenience to him, nothing else.

'It was not as you might think. You need to know how and why.'

'Do I?'

'Yes, you do. It might help you make sense of it all. I need you to understand how difficult things were for your mother and I when you were born,' says Detlef.

'Oh 'ere we go!' Derek interrupts him again. 'Get the bloody violins out! So, things were a bit tough and you decided it was all a bit too much for ya. 'Bout the size of it?'

'No. That is not what happened at all. I made some mistakes, some big mistakes,' says Detlef, hinting at the events of the past.

'Too bloody true ya did!'

'I should have done things differently, for both of you, but things got very badly out of hand.'

'Oh yeah?' says Derek as if were of no interest to him, but, in truth, his curiosity growing by the second. 'Like how?'

'But are you prepared to listen? From the beginning?'

'I'm still 'ere, ain't I?'

'I came to England as a prisoner, Derek,' his father tells him. 'A prisoner of war.'

-

Reenie makes a surprise appearance behind the bar, a can of Pledge and duster in her hand.

'What you playin' at?' enquires Jimbo, helping himself to a bar snack from one of the cards pinned to the back wall. 'I hope you haven't left the telly on up there, wastin' electricity?'

'Eating the profits again, are we?' she says in retaliation.

'You what? Denyin' me a packet o' Cheesy fuckin' Cheddars now are ya, ya stingy cow?' he says, shoving a handful in his mouth.

'And look at the size of you, you greedy pig.'

'Do give it a rest,' Jimbo says. 'So, out with it, wha's the big idea?'

'Just doing a bit of cleaning,' she says innocently enough, squirting the hand pumps and giving them a cursory wipe.

'Couldn't it bloody wait? Can't you see we got punters in? You'll stink the place out.'

'Just had the Lottery people onto me,' she tells him. 'I've just been sorting out the presentation.'

'Oh yeah?' says Jimbo, his voice dropping ominously.

'They're bringin' proper photographers, an' the Press.'

'Are they now? But when?' he asks, emptying the last of the packet into his mouth.

'This coming Friday.'

Jimbo looks mortified, eyes agog. 'Friday! No way!' he says, sputtering bits of biscuit. 'Are you off your blinkin' trolley, woman? Tha's no time at all!'

'No, I'm not! We need this place looking spick an' span,' she retorts and giving the bar a liberal spraying. 'I've written you a list.'

'Oi! Tha's goin' in me beer!' complains one drinker.

'A list?' asks Jimbo. 'What sort of list?'

'A list of things that need doing.'

'Gi' me a break, woman! Haven't I got enough to bloody do?'

'It tastes disgustin'!' continues the drinker.

'Oh, shut up, it's only a bit o' polish!' Reenie admonishes him.

'I'm not drinkin' it! It might be poisonous!'

'Oh, give it 'ere!' growls Jimbo, pouring what little's left down the sink and pulling the man a generous amount in return. 'More money down the bloody drain!' he complains.

-

Despite himself, Derek is soon fascinated, enthralled even, to discover that his true father had not been some fictitious and dead Bristol stevedore after all. No, the man now sitting right in front of him had been a real live Nazi soldier, and still very much alive and kicking.

Somehow, he can't help but get a buzz out of it. It's exciting and reminds him of the Action Man figure he had as a boy, complete in a Stormtrooper uniform, and, like it or not, finds himself hanging onto Detlef's every word as he tells him further details about his past - his incarceration, his years on the farm - and, at last, Derek surreptitiously pulls up the chair, sitting on it back to front.

Then, careful not to disrespect the family, despite the cruel and wicked behaviour that had been shown towards him all those years ago, Detlef goes on to explain how he'd met his mother on the pier at Weston-Super-Mare in the summer of 1956, about their courtship and marriage thereafter.

'So, you got wed then?' says Derek, sounding surprised.

'Of course we did,' says Detlef almost indignantly.

'Tha's one thing I s'pose. At least I'm not a bleedin' bastard.'

Detlef doesn't understand this and looks at Derek, questioning.

'Born outside o' marriage.'

'No, you were not,' his father reaffirms.

'But she was already up the duff? Pregnant I mean?' Derek second guesses, having successfully worked out the timescale.

'Yes,' Detlef admits a little uncomfortably. 'She was.'

'Ah, I get it now! Shotgun weddin'!'

'Nothing could be further from the truth, Derek,' Detlef corrects him. 'I loved your mother. I would have married her in any case.'

'Would ya?'

'Yes. Most definitely.'

'So, where d'you live then? On the farm you mentioned? Wi' Nan and Gramps?'

'No, but here in Bristol. We found a place to rent.'

'Where?'

'Brislington.'

'Brislington?'

'Yes. All three of us.'

'What? Me too?'

Detlef nods. 'Yes, you too.'

'Bugger me! I never knew that!' says Derek, continuing to be amazed. 'I was only there a couple o' weeks back, tryin' to earn a bit o' money,' he recalls.

'And what I was trying to do too,' says Detlef as he is about to divulge the real reason for his departure. 'Trying to make some money.'

As Jimbo and Reenie continue to bicker, Phil has heard enough and interrupts them. 'Give it a rest, guys,' he requests. 'I'm trying to enjoy a quiet pint 'ere.'

'Yes, shut up, Jim,' says Reenie.

'No, you shut up!'

'Please, guys!' demands Phil. 'So, Reen, tell us, what's the deal wi' the Lottery people?' he then asks her and trying to be a go-between.

'Friday morning,' she says. 'Midday, with a photographer and a couple of people from the local press, maybe even one or two o' the big boys with a bit o' luck. I want this place to be all ship shape an' Bristol fashion.'

'Party time again, eh?'

'No! Not a drunken free-for-all if that's what you mean!'

'Good luck wi' that,' mumbles Jimbo.

'I heard that!' she says. 'I want it to be orderly, that's all! I want to put this place on the map!'

'What map? What for?' says Jimbo.

'Never you mind what for!'

'OK, OK,' he relinquishes and understanding he is on a hiding to nothing. 'I'll give it the once over in the morning. It'll look fine,' he offers, looking in vain to Phil and Dave for support.

'No, that will not be *fine*, as you put it!' Reenie dismisses his suggestion out of hand. 'I want it done properly … and there's outside to think about too!'

'Outside? Why, for cryin' out loud?'

'There's that broken table that needs getting rid of for starters, and there's cigarette ends all over the place. It looks a right mess,' says Reenie. 'And while I think of it, you can put the letter 'T' back up on the wall too. It's still in the cellar.'

'If you think I'm getting' up on a ladder in this weather, you got another think comin'!'

'I quite like the Ravellers,' remarks Dave. 'It's what we all call it now.'

'Who asked you?' Reenie slaps him down. 'I want all the brollies out as well.'

'Brollies?' says Jimbo, now sounding totally stressed and exasperated. 'Brollies!?'

'Yes please!' someone shouts out from down at the other end of the bar.

195

'Be with ya in a minute,' calls Jimbo before turning back to his wife. 'It's nearly bleedin' winter out there, Reen, or ain't you noticed? Who's gonna need brollies?'

'Just do as you're told. I'm not havin' this place lookin' like a tip, and I'm not going to miss out on a bit o' free advertising for you nor nobody.'

'Advertisin' what?'

'Things are about to start changing around here,' says Reenie with a look of devilment in her eye. 'You watch me.'

-

'We were desperate, Derek,' Detlef continues. 'I was desperate.'

'But there was the family to help you out, weren't there?' says Derek, not nearly understanding.

'That wasn't the case, I'm afraid.'

'How come?'

'Why do you think, Derek?'

'Search me. I dunno.'

'They didn't like me.'

'Why? What 'ad ya done? Well, other than get me mum up the duff that is.'

'It was my nationality.'

'What? Just because you're a kraut?' says Derek before correcting himself. 'Sorry, a German, I mean.'

'I can see you're not happy about it either,' says Detlef with a wry smile. 'I can tell when I speak all that *German shite*,' he gently mocks him.

'I never said that,' denies Derek, 'not really.'

-

'Changes? What changes?' asks Jimbo, already horrified at the thought.

'Wine for one thing,' says Reenie.

'Wine? Like wine out of a bottle, ya mean?'

'Yes, and food too. Nicer stuff. Nutritious. Chilli-con-carné, lasagne, pizza and salad, not just the Sunday roasts - and daily.'

'What? Ev'ry day?!' Jim near screeches.

'Yep, every day.'

'An' who's gonna do all that then, and run the bar? Bloody madness! You'd have to employ someone!'

'Salad? Who the fuck eats salad?' Dave joins in, laughing.

'Shut up, Dave,' Reenie admonishes him yet again.

'I'm quite happy with a pasty an' a pickled egg to be 'onest with ya.'

'See!' says Jimbo. 'All they want is ordinary grub, quick an' easy!'

'I don't think Dave is the arbiter of good taste, do you?'

'What? Bitter? I prefer lager,' Dave continues to laugh.

'Reen, we're just a basic boozer on an housin' estate offerin' a bit o' basic pub food,' her husband beseeches her. 'This ain't Clifton. We're not a bleedin' restaurant.'

'We'll see about that?' she says, ignoring this very obvious truth. 'I'm off to the wholesalers shortly to have a look.'

'What, now?'

'Yes, now!'

'Please, Reen!'

'Don't *please* me!'

-

'Money was very tight for us,' says Detlef slowly and deliberately. 'You must understand your mother and I had nothing, and, stupidly, I got involved with some bad people. Some very bad people indeed.'

'Oh yeah? Like who?' asks Derek disbelievingly.

'Derek, all you need to know is that I made a serious mistake and ended up in prison for the second time in my life.'

'Prison proper? For what?'

'That's not important.'

'Nah, nah, nah! That's nowhere near good enough! You can't not tell me now!'

Detlef lowers himself off the couch to stretch his legs, stalling. 'I am ashamed,' he says. 'Please understand this is very painful for me.'

'Don't care. You owe me!'

'I was involved in a robbery, Derek,' he tells him, hoping it might suffice.

'What sort o' robbery? Houses? Shops? What?'

Again, Detlef hesitates, still unwilling to answer.

'Come on!'

'Armed robbery,' says Detlef, quietly.

With that Derek's jaw appears to drop, literally. 'Whoa! Wha', wi' guns an' stuff?' he says in incredulous disbelief.

'Yes.'

'What? Where?'

Detlef now realises that he has no other option than to give his son full and proper explanation. 'It was a Post Office, near a lake. A place called West Harptree,' he tells him.

'What? Chew Valley lake, ya mean?'

'Yes, that was it. Chew Valley.'

'Mum took me there once when I was a kid!' Derek recalls as things now seem to drop into place. 'We took a bag o' bread to feed the ducks!'

'I was only the driver and lookout,' says Detlef, keen to minimise the part he had played.

'She walked me 'round this little village. I remember her being a bit upset. That must o' been why!'

'I had no idea one of the others had a pistol.'

'Did they use it?'

'Yes, they did.'

'Someone got shot?'

'Yes.'

'Killed?'

197

'She died, in hospital.'

'She? A woman you mean?'

'Yes. The postmistress.'

'Fuck me, Detlef!' says Derek, using his father's name for the very first time.

Detlef sits back down, holding his head in hands, covering his eyes.

'But not you,' Derek looks to clarify. 'You never shot no-one?'

'No! Of course not. Not then,' Detlef accidently let's slip.

'Wha' d'ya mean, not then?'

'That makes no difference to what happened between your mother and I,' Detlef tries to deflect him. 'It was long before I met her.'

'I'm not givin' up 'til you tell me!'

'War, Derek. Things happen,' says his father, dropping his hands and looking at him with a mixture of defiance and fear.

'So, you 'ave killed someone?' Derek pushes him very unsympathetically.

'Enough!' Detlef then reacts, sensing his immature relish at the idea. 'I will not talk of that, even for you.'

-

'Oi! Is there life on this planet?' shouts out yet another drinker, tapping and clinking his glass with his car keys. 'We're still waitin' over 'ere!'

'I'm comin', I'm comin'! I only got the one pair o' hands!' growls Jimbo, scowling at his wife. 'I'll stick a fuckin' broom up me arse an' all while I'm about it, shall I?'

'That's the first decent idea you've had all day,' she says with a laugh, leaving the polish and the duster on the bar and turning to walk back out. 'Now, chop, chop. There's a good boy. See you later.'

-

With Detlef's obvious refusal to talk of his active service years, Derek temporarily lets it drop. 'So, how much time d'you get then?' he asks instead.

'Six years.'

'Not too bad, considerin',' says Derek, glibly. 'So, I'd o' been how old?'

'You were two, just three maybe.'

'But I never remember seein' ya?'

'I never came back.'

'Why not?'

'It was made impossible for me.'

'You abandoned us, ya mean?'

At this, Detlef clutches at the edge of the couch, a single tear now rolling down his cheek.

'Please don't start cryin' on me,' says Derek, but a little more gently at least.

'I went home to Germany, yes,' Detlef then concedes.

'So, why didn't you take us with you?'

'That was not an option.'

'There's summat you're not telling me 'ere,' surmises Derek. 'What is it?'

Right at that crucial moment there is a gentle tap on the door and both men hear Margaret's voice call through to them. 'Sorry to interrupt,' she says, 'but Ellen wants to know if you two are alright in there?'

'Tell her we're fine. We'll be out in a minute,' Derek answers her. 'OK. I'll let her know.'

'So?' he then asks Detlef again, keen to continue. 'Out with it.'

'Derek, with me out of the way, you and your mother were allowed to remain within the family,' he answers him as honestly as he dare.

'Wha' d'ya mean? Allowed?'

'As I said, I was given no choice,' says Detlef now wincing slightly and holding his abdomen.

'You alright?' asks Derek with something like a look of concern.

'Yes. It's nothing,' says his father. 'But let's go and see your mother now, shall we?' he adds. 'She will be worrying.'

'But we ain't finished yet.'

'Later perhaps.'

'Wha' makes ya think there's goin' to be a later?' asks Derek churlishly but following it with a laugh.

'I think we now need to have a conversation between the three of us,' Detlef suggests. 'Don't you?'

'Alright,' accepts Derek. 'I still wanna know everything.'

But as Detlef stands, he nearly stumbles, holding at his side once again.

'Are you sure you're alright?' asks Derek, automatically reaching out to steady him.

'Yes, I shall be OK. It's just old age,' he repeats.

'As long as you're sure?'

'I am. But can I say one more thing to you before we go out?' asks Detlef.

'Go on then,' Derek invites him.

'Do not speak to your mother with disrespect ever again,' he gently reprimands him. 'She doesn't deserve it. Do I make myself clear?'

'Are you tryin' to tell me off again?' asks Derek, but this time with something of a boyish grin flashing across his face.

'Yes, I am,' says his father, allowing himself a little smile too. 'You owe her an apology.'

Chapter 21

Ellen is waiting patiently in the dayroom with an old pale green Clarks shoebox rested on her lap.

'Alright then, Mum?' says Derek as he ambles over towards her and by way of an indirect apology.

'Hello, son,' she coos, smiling and acknowledging it as such. 'You alright, you two?' she then asks.

'Yeah, OK, considerin',' concedes Derek.

'Ooh, that's what I like to hear,' she says. 'You can get to know each other a bit better now, can't you?'

'One step at a time, Ellen,' Detlef cautions.

'What you got there then?' Derek asks her, nodding at the box.

'Letters from your father there,' she says. 'Margaret just got them for me.'

This time, Derek doesn't react to her referring to him as such but still, he looks confused. 'I don't get it,' he says. 'You two must 'ave kept in contact then?'

'No, no, you don't understand,' his mother corrects him. 'I never knew of them until after your grandfather died. He wouldn't allow it, you see. He insisted Nan destroy them all.'

'Uh?'

'But thank heavens, she hid them instead.'

'What? Grampy?' says Derek in disbelief. 'Why would he wanna do a thing like that?'

'He could be a right tartar when he wanted to be, your grandfather,' Ellen tells her son. 'A horrible man on occasion, God rest his soul.'

'But I loved him, I did. He was a nice ol' bugger really, despite givin' me a good hidin' ev'ry now and then.'

'He loved you too, in the end,' she says, selecting the first letter that Detlef had written to her. 'Would you like to see this?' she asks him.

'What d'you mean? In the end?' says Derek.

'You're your father's son,' Ellen explains. 'It reminded him every time he looked at you.'

'Great! Thanks a bunch for that!' exclaims Derek. 'That's all I needed to bloody know!'

Quickly, Detlef interjects to prevent this new revelation turning things sour once again. 'Derek, you must realise, things were very different back then,' he says. 'As I said before, your grandfather never liked me because of my nationality. But he wasn't alone, believe me. We Germans, the ones that stayed on, were not so popular. People mistrusted us.'

'That's true, son,' corroborates his mother. 'The looks we used to get when people heard your dad's voice. Terrible they were.'

With both of his parents now staring back at him, Derek cannot help but feel a powerful stirring inside but, unable to make sense of this totally new emotion, but decides to diffuse it. 'An' still don't trust ya,' he says to his dad and with something of a laugh. 'Where's your towel, eh?'

'Oh, Derek!' admonishes his mother. 'Stop it!'

'What towel?' asks Detlef, confused.

Outside, Jimbo is already busy tidying up around the pub when Reenie walks up behind him, car keys in hand. 'Who's behind the bar?' she asks him accusingly.

'Who'd ya think?' he says, holding a rather tatty and faded Fosters umbrella and slotting it into one of the pub benches. 'I thought you wanted all this done?'

'I do,' she says and looking up to the letters pinned high on the front wall and tutting. 'But who's covering?'

'Phil!' Jimbo barks, 'at least while it's quiet. Be nice if you could stay around an' help out a bit, then I wouldn't have needed to ask him. There's bloody shed loads to do 'ere!'

'I told you what my plans are, Jim. I'm far too busy.'

Jimbo stands back to take a breather, hands on hips, his shirt out and agape, sweating profusely despite the chill weather. 'But is it that important you 'ave to do it all today?' he pleads with her.

'You should have kept on top of it then, shouldn't you? You seem to forget I've got to have everything sorted by this coming Thursday evening at the very latest.'

'I give up! Wha' the 'ells wrong with a bloody girt big plate o' sandwiches? Nobody'd complain!'

'I'll give you a girt big plate of sandwiches!'

'An' jus' like Christmas, it'll all be over in five minutes!'

'Just have it clean an' tidy by the time I get back,' Reenie instructs him. 'Do you hear me?'

'Yes, sir. No, sir. three bags full, sir,' growls Jimbo and scuffing a few cigarette butts away with his foot.

'I hope you're going to sweep those up' she says, getting into their car.

'No, sadly, your grandfather could never bring himself to forgive and forget,' continues Ellen. 'He hated Germans. He'd shoot the lot of them, he said.'

A wry smile flashes over Detlef's face. 'Those were his parting words the last time I saw him,' he tells her.

'When was that then, Detlef?' she queries him. 'He wouldn't even speak to you.'

'When I was released from the prison,' he reveals.

'He came to see you?'

'He didn't tell you, did he?' says Detlef, piecing more of the story together. 'I didn't want to tell you in my letters in case it made matters even worse. He came to meet me with his brother-in-law.'

'Uncle Gordon?'

'Yes, Gordon, that was it. They were waiting. They made very it clear as soon as I walked out of the gates.'

'What did they say?'

'It's not really what they said, Ellen.'

'They threatened you?'

Detlef doesn't answer her directly. 'They took me to what is now the airport. It was very different back then. Military. They put me on a flight to Lübeck on a transporter plane. I was handcuffed. I was given no choice.'

'Where's Lübeck,' asks Derek.

'In Germany,' answers Detlef.

'Handcuffed?'

'Yes, I was.'

'He worked up at Whitchurch, did Gordon,' remembers Ellen, her face now looking like thunder as it all begins to sink in for her too. 'Ground crew, he was.'

'That would help explain it,' says Detlef.

'So, you were planning to come back to us?' Ellen seeks to confirm.

'Of course, Ellen. It was always my intention, to come and get you both.'

'He wouldn't even come to our wedding, that bloody Gordon!' she continues. 'I never liked him! Surly man, miserable with it.'

'I'm so sorry, Ellen,' Detlef apologises yet again. 'It must have been so very difficult for you to be married to me.'

'Oh, Detlef! I wouldn't have had it any other way,' she insists. 'But you should have mentioned what they'd done to you in your letters. For years I've never been able to work it out, wondering.'

'They told me that if you ever found out they'd flown me out of the country, you and Derek would be put out onto the streets.'

'They what?!' says Derek, shocked by it. 'Never!'

'Maybe, maybe not,' adds Detlef, 'but it was a risk I was not prepared to take.'

'The bastards!' Ellen then yells, inadvertently scrunching the letter she held in her hand as the full depth of the collusion and deceit perpetrated by her family becomes ever more apparent. 'The bloody bastards!'

With that, Derek lets out a loud guffaw. He's truly amazed at his mother's animated reaction and hadn't seen her so energised in years.

'It's no laughing matter, Derek!' she tells him, trying to smooth out the envelope. 'How different our lives would have been had it not been for that hateful father of mine!'

'They also told me that you never wanted to see me again,' says Detlef, now deep in thought. 'I didn't know what to believe.'

'No, no! I never said that!'

'And that you'd applied for a divorce.'

At that, Ellen appears to flush with embarrassment before answering. 'Yes, I did,' she admits falteringly, 'but not until much later. They forced me do it, Detlef. Desertion they said.'

'I can see that.'

'*And* they forced me to change mine and Derek's name! Paid for it, they did. Deed poll.'

'What?! I had a different name an' all? asks Derek, now visibly reeling from the overload of information.

'You did.'

'What was it then?'

'Otto,' answers Detlef.

'Otter?'

'No! Otto, you twit,' says his mum. 'We're not animals!'

-

Dave is now well on the way to getting hammered. 'When do you reckon Dekko's gonna cough up then, Phil?' he slurs.

'Cough up? Wha' d'ya mean, cough up? He don't bleedin' owe it ya, ya twat,' Phil hisses at him whilst attempting to draw a couple of pints of lager, the nozzle spitting and sputtering froth and foam.

'You know what I mean.'

'He'll do it when he's good an' ready.'

'Which might be never.'

'Would you shut the fuck up an' keep quiet? Fuckin' lager lout!'

-

'I hope you don't mind, but I have something for you, Derek,' says Detlef as he reaches into his pocket and produces the tiny, knitted, babies bonnet. 'This was yours. I had it in my pocket when I was arrested and have always kept it.'

Ellen recognises it immediately. 'That was from the Ogden's,' she says, reaching out for it.

'Who are the bloody Ogden's?!' asks Derek, unable to keep up with it or take in much more.

'They were the farmers I told you about,' says Detlef.

'Loveliest of people,' says Ellen through her now silent and gentle tears. 'They came to our wedding you know. Miles they came. I still have that old orange sugar bowl, Detlef. Do you remember?'

'Have you? How could I forget?'

'We didn't get many wedding presents, did we?' she says.

'We didn't, did we?' acknowledges Detlef, taking her by the hand. 'But we had each other.'

'We did, Ellen. We did,' agrees Detlef as he then leans forward and kisses her lovingly on the forehead, cradling her face.

'Oi! You two, don't start all that carry on! I think I've bloody suffered enough,' says Derek.

Detlef smiles and steps back. 'I would have liked to have seen the Ogden's again,' he says wistfully, 'but it's far too late now of course. They would have died years ago.'

'There was your friend though, and their son,' Ellen reminds him.

'Yes, of course. Frankie. What was the son's name again? I forget.'

'Dick.'

'Yes, that was it. Dick.'

'We could've taken a trip down memory lane, couldn't we?' she says. 'Taken a drive over to Weston.'

Detlef pauses for a moment, thinking. 'Can you travel?' he asks, immediately taken by the idea. 'I have a few days left.'

'You try stopping me!' says Ellen, instantly overjoyed at the prospect.

'You'll need a bus with that wheelchair,' observes Derek.

'They have fold up ones here,' continues the old lady. 'I've seen them.'

'But will you need someone to help you?' asks Detlef, tactfully.

'Mmm, yes, I would,' says Ellen, sounding a little crestfallen.

'Maybe someone could assist?' suggests Detlef and looking at Margaret on the other side of the room.

'I could always ask her,' whispers Ellen, clapping her hands. 'I'm sure she would.'

'I can pay her,' says Detlef.

'No, I'll pay her,' says his son. 'I'd be 'appy to.'

-

'What I could do wi' a quarter of a mill' don't bear thinkin' about,' Dave continues to garble.

'But you been keepin' busy, ain't ya?' says Phil. 'Wha' wi' ya paintin' an' decoratin' an' that?'

'Yeah, but you know how it is.'

'No, tell me?' asks Phil.

'We're all fucked … well I am,' reveals Dave accidentally.

'So, that's what those two geezers were all about earlier!' susses Phil, dropping his head. 'Come on, tell me the truth.'

'I did!' Dave lies. 'I just owe 'em for that bit o' kit! Peanuts.'

'Yeah, right! You said somethin' different, summat about five hundred quid?'

'Piss off an' leave me alone!'

-

Ellen then plucks up the courage to pose the question that she simply had to ask but already knew the answer to. 'I see you married again, Detlef?' she says, having already spotted a wedding ring on his finger not long after he'd first walked in, but not the one that was theirs.

'Yes, I did,' he answers her almost apologetically. 'Her name is Gisella. We've been together for over forty years now.'

Ellen can be heard to emit a small whimper. 'I kept mine,' she then says, showing him her hand. 'Mum had put it in this box with all these letters,' adding, 'but I had to get a bit put in. It was too small by the time I got it back.'

Detlef simply doesn't know what to say to that and looks at the floor.

Seeing his obvious discomfort, Ellen quickly changes the subject. 'Did you have any more children?' she then asks him.

'Yes, Ellen, I did.'

'What! I've got brothers and sisters too!' cries Derek. 'Enough! Please, enough!'

'Just one. A girl,' says Detlef, smiling at the very thought of her. 'Her name is Renata. Would you like to see some photos perhaps?' he then asks. 'I have some here, and she has written a letter for you too, Derek. She asked me to give it to you should I find you.'

'And you have three grandchildren too, Detlef,' says Ellen, keen to tell him. 'Doesn't he, Derek? Three! I'd so love you to meet them all!'

'A letter? From my *sister*?' says Derek, his throat catching as he speaks the word.

'Such a shame they're getting divorced,' Ellen adds.

Chapter 22

Derek is driving back through the city on something akin to autopilot.

He's visibly shaking and one could easily be forgiven for thinking that he's simply suffering from a severe bout of the DT's and desperate for another drink, which, although true, is not nearly the half of it.

No, the truth is he simply can't believe what has happened to him in just a few short days and now, in the privacy and seclusion of his scruffy old car, it begins to engulf him like a tsunami.

With his chest lifting, shuddering, as he suppresses the urge to sob out loud at the realisation that not only does he now have more money than he knows how to shake a stick at but, to cap it all, and far more significantly, he's also got a real, live, talking, father... and a sister too.

A bloody sister!
Renata!
Bloody Renata!
What sort of fuckin' name is that, eh?

-

Not that far behind, Maciej is taking Detlef back to his hotel and, similarly, Detlef is in emotional turmoil too although, unlike his son, you would not notice it to look at him. He appears silent, expressionless.

Of course, he's happy at having succeeded in achieving what he'd set out to do and to find his long-lost son, but, disturbingly, the whole experience has also served to rekindle and intensify his already deep-rooted feelings of guilt and failure.

In particular, during those first few moments when Ellen had immediately told him that he'd been the only one for her and that there had been no other man in her life, it had shaken him profoundly.

Despite being forced into a divorce that she didn't want, she'd adhered to their marriage vows, hadn't she? She'd forsaken all others and, against all diminishing hope and expectation, had awaited his return.

The very thought of it disturbs him deeply.

-

Before he'd left the nursing home, Derek had begun to find all the revelations far too much and, fearful that he might 'let himself down' so to speak, he'd felt the need to escape, and fast.

The final straw had been when his father had given him a photograph of his sister as a keepsake together with the letter she had written for him, both of which are now rested next to him on the front passenger seat - her face smiling up at him, the letter as yet unopened.

So, after hastily exchanging phone numbers, quickly kissing his mum goodbye, and warmly shaking his dad by the hand and inviting them both to the presentation ceremony, (to which his mother had politely refused. 'It'll be too much trouble for you, son,' she'd said. 'You two spend some time together instead.') he'd made his excuses and left.

It was a close call too, as, no sooner had he stepped out of the building, he'd almost broken down right there at the entrance.

-

Moreover, as Detlef had discovered even more about the events of the past and the true depths to which Ellen's family had gone to break them apart and airbrush him from their lives, it not only invoked latent feelings of 'what if' in him but, also, outright anger too.

But how could he even think this way? That would be to deny his loving family waiting patiently for him back at home and his daughter's very existence, wouldn't it? It makes him feel as if he's committing some terrible act of treachery and being unfaithful all at the same time.

Then, as if things weren't complicated enough, there were his niggling worries and regrets about Derek himself.

As ashamed as he is to even think it, he is more than a little disappointed to discover that his son is not quite the upstanding and successful man he'd always hoped and envisioned him to be. Of course, he didn't really know what to expect, but he'd been saddened to find a rather coarse and foul-mouthed man, a heavy drinker and inveterate smoker in the unsurprising throes of a divorce. He cannot help but wonder how very different it all might have been had he been a constant figure in his life and a loving and caring father figure.

Added to all that, he worries for Derek's future, particularly with regard his recent great fortune and the pitfalls that it would almost certainly present. It is likely to be a disaster waiting to happen and, with so much money at his disposal, that he will be even more hellbent on drinking and smoking himself into an early grave.

As inappropriate and premature as it might be, and despite how any interference on his behalf might be misconstrued, he has a strong and innate desire to steer him in the right direction and to be that stabilising influence he'd always intended to be.

-

Next to her letter and the baby's knitted bonnet, Derek cannot stop himself from repeatedly glancing down to the photo on the passenger seat next to see his sister's face smiling back up at him.

Yeah, she was his sister alright.

It is as clear as day.

He could see it in the eyes, in the very shape of her face.

His attention is then drawn to the letter. He simply cannot wait any longer and snatches it up, ripping open the envelope atop the steering wheel. With tears immediately blurring his vision, he starts to read as best he can. *'Dear Derek, if you are reading this our father has been successful in his quest,'* it begins clearly enough, but then, more confusingly, it continues, *'in my craziest dream I never think this correspondence I will ever write. But here I struggle to find the words, sitting at my table in the rain and cloudy sky thinking it impossible like ice in the summertime, ...* 'Uh?'... *but with sunshine in my heart and pen held in joyful anticipation and bewilderment of the brother I never contemplated, or cast my eyes upon, even in the street, although I would not ever know it, I write this letter to you.'*

PAAA-ARP!

Terrified, the colour instantly draining from his face, Derek looks up to see a huge pantechnicon bearing down on him with smoke billowing from its tyres as it brakes hard, its horn blaring, its lights flashing.

Instinctively, miraculously, he swerves, violently snaking the car back into his own lane, clipping the kerb, and misses what surely would have been a devastating and almost certainly fatal collision only by inches.

Shaking even more dramatically than before, he pulls over and angrily berates himself. 'Don't kill yerself now, ya prat!' he shouts out loud, the letter still in hand, his knuckles white.

Then, as the adrenaline fuelled shock morphs into euphoric relief and near hysterical laughter, he recalls that it was only just recently that, kicked out, on his own, and penniless, he'd considered taking a trip down to the coast, driving off a cliff to end it all.

But now, nothing could be further from the truth.

Now, he just wants to live forever.

'It's only just fuckin' begun!' he shouts to himself.

For the very first time in his life, Derek has the burgeoning sense of his own identity, not some vague and sketchy idea that he'd been drip fed all these years. Wonderfully, it makes him feel more grounded somehow, more alive, and with a glorious and renewed sense of purpose.

Then, as he puts the car into first, the most ridiculous thought of all comes into his head.

He misses him already.

He misses his dad.

-

'Maciej?' Detlef then says, breaking their silence. 'I want to take Ellen to Weston-Super-Mare on Saturday. The nurse, Margaret, will be coming along to help. Can you do it?'

'Yes, of course! I love to go to the sea. It will be fun.'

'Ellen can use a fold-up wheelchair. They have them.'

'Easy-peasy.'

'And maybe to visit somewhere else on the way back. If we have time.'

'No problem. Where?'

'There is a small village in the countryside I would like to see. Norton St Philip.'

'I don't know it, but we can find it! You can have me for the whole day. If we get back late, it doesn't matter.'

'Thank you, Maciej,' says Detlef, but sounding rather breathless and holding his arm across himself.

'Hey, are you OK, my friend?'

'Old age,' he repeats his standard answer to it.

'Are you telling me the truth, Detlef?'

Still holding himself, he is reluctant to reply.

'Are you going to answer me?' Maciej persists.

'I am not so well, Maciej,' he admits.

'We need to get you to the doctor maybe? Like the nurse said?'

'No, that is not necessary.'

'Why not?'

'I know what it is.'

'You know?'

Yes. I have medication.'

'Can I ask?'

'I have leukaemia,' says Detlef without hesitation.

'Leukaemia? Like in cancer?' queries Maciej, looking very concerned.

'Yes, Maciej. Like in cancer.'

-

Just before he reaches home, Derek stops off at a branch of his bank. He needs some more funds and saunters over to the 'hole in the wall'.

Although he knows what he might expect to see, his eyes nearly pop out of his head when he actually sees the figures all lined up on the screen - £11,355,37.29. It's all in there, every last penny, less the £400 he'd already had - eleven million, three hundred and fifty-five thousand, thirty- seven pounds and ninety-nine pence, including the forty-two pence he already had in there.

-

'Are you a crazy man?' asks Maciej.

'What do you mean?'

'Coming here to the UK, looking for son when you are so ill. You should be at home, resting.'

'I could not do that, Maciej. It was now or never. But please, I do not want anyone else to know this. Do you understand?'

'Yes. OK, Detlef, but I think you go to the doctor.'

'Do you promise me?' says Detlef by way of a reply. 'No-one.'

-

Checking around and behind him for potential robbers and assailants, Derek taps the withdrawal button and selects 'Other Amount'. Tentatively, excitedly, he keys in the figure one followed by four zeros and presses enter. 'Ten grand,' he says. 'That should do it.'

But no, in an instant, it tells him he's only allowed two hundred. 'Nah, I need more than that,' he says before walking inside to join the end of a short queue leading to the two open cash desks.

Mercifully, it's not too long before he's called by a disembodied voice. *'Cashier number three, please',* it says before he steps forward, nonchalantly dropping his card into the hopper. 'I was wonderin' how much can I take out wi this?' he asks.

'Let's have a look for you, sir, shall we?' says the unsuspecting cashier.

-

At virtually the same time as Maciej is driving Detlef in through the gates of his hotel, Derek is arriving back onto his redbrick estate with various pockets now packed and bulging with wads of various large denomination bank notes.

Despite his urgent desire to get into the pub for a drink, his excitement at having so much cash on him for the first time in his life gives him an idea and, unable to stop himself, he makes his way to his old home and knocks on the door.

Cagily, Nigel opens it, at once looking terrified.

'Boo!' says Derek, grinning and raising his fist to make Nigel flinch.

'I don't want any trouble, Dekko. Please.'

'Stop frettin'!' Derek reassures him but puts his foot on the step such that his entrance will not be denied. 'I'm 'ere to see me kids, tha's all.'

Nigel moves aside, back to the wall, and lets him in. 'Jez and Julie are through there, watching the telly,' he says, pointing towards the sitting room.

'I know where it is, ya twat. I used to live 'ere once, remember?'

'Yeah, o' course. Sorry. I hear congratulations are in order.'

'Yeah, but you'll be gettin' get fuck all!' says Derek and taking great pleasure in saying so. 'I'm givin' Phil an' the lads thousands … they'll all be minted. Just think, eh? Could o' been you too.'

Nigel doesn't answer. 'I'll leave you to it, yeah?' is all he says.

'You do that,' insists Derek, but suddenly stopping dead in his tracks. 'Marion tells me my lot 'ave cost you a lot of money,' he says.

'I wouldn't say that,' answers Nigel. 'It's not a problem ….'

Derek cuts him short. 'I won't see out o' pocket,' he says snidely, chucking a bundle of notes onto the lower steps of the staircase. 'Tha' should cover it, an' some.'

-

Detlef is calling his wife.

'I've found him, my love,' he says.

'Oh, Detlef! That is wonderful news! How is he? What is he like? You must tell me!'

'I've found Ellen too,' he then reveals.

The line falls silent for a second before Gisella responds.

'How is she?' she asks.

'Not so good,' Detlef tells her. 'She is in a wheelchair and living in a nursing home.'

'I'm sorry to hear that, Detlef. Will you see her again?'

'I don't think so,' says Detlef, uneasy about telling her the truth.

'But if you do,' replies Gisella rather intuitively, *'please send her my best wishes.'*

-

Derek sticks his head in around the sitting room like it's an everyday occurrence. 'Alright then, kids?' he says.

'Dad? What are you doing here?' asks Julie, looking up and looking a little uncomfortable.

'Just thought I'd just drop by an' say 'ello. That's OK innit? Say hello?'

'Does Mum know you were coming around?'

'No.'

'She doesn't like it, Dad.'

'Tough. Don't care. How are you both then?'

'Yeah, alright,' answers Julie.

'Jez?'

'Yeah, alright,' he repeats.

'Not been charged yet then?'

'No.'

'Fair enough, no news is good news, yeah?'

''S'pose.'

'Where's Janice?' their Dad asks. 'I ain't bloody seen her since I 'ad me big win!'

'At work,' Julie explains. 'She does long hours.'

'Oh yeah, forgot.'

Then, unsure as to whether to even ask their father to sit down, all three watch the television for just a few short seconds.

'Good programme?' Derek asks.

'Yeah,' says Julie.

'What's it called?'

'Blue Planet.'

'What's it about?'

'The Earth, animals and stuff. Interesting. He's in Africa now.'

'Who is?'

'David Attenborough.'

'Ah, yeah. Him. I'll take ya there one day if ya like?'

'That'll be nice,' says Julie. 'I'd like that.'

'We'll do it then. Now, listen, I'm being presented wi' me cheque on Friday mornin', twelve o'clock, down the pub. It would be great if you could all be there.'

'We got school, Dad,' Julie points out.

'Call a sickie or summat! It's not every day, is it?'

'I'll have to ask Mum.'

'Oh, tell 'er she can come an' all if she likes. There'll be a glass o' wine or two. That'll get her there.'

'She doesn't touch it anymore, Dad.'

'Tha' right?'

'Yeah.'

'OK. But I don't want you-know-who there,' says Derek, alluding to Nigel.

'He wouldn't anyway.'

'Good. Oh, an' before I go, I just thought you might like this,' he says, pulling out three one thousand-pound bundles of fity-pound notes with a yellow paper band around each. 'Bit o' pocket money for ya. One o' them is for Janice, mind. You take it, Julie. Make sure she gets it, yeah? That little bugger'll only nick it!'

'Wow! Thanks, Dad!' they both say.

'Friday, yeah?' he repeats as he turns to leave. 'I'd like all me family there if you might be so kind?' he says. 'Alright?'

-

All are present and correct over on Crackers Corner as Derek finally walks his way in but not performing one of his bows, not even a little one.

He knows the boys are going to rip into him something chronic as and when he tells them that he's half German, but, quite honestly, he couldn't give a stuff. In fact, he quite relishes the idea.

'Speak o' the devil,' says Jimbo.

'How's life at the top then, me ol' mucker?' greets Dave.

'You wouldn't believe it if I told ya,' Derek answers him.

'So, what you been up to?' asks Phil. 'An' before I forget, you an' me need to 'ave a chat about these 'movers and shakers' you been bangin' on about.'

'Forget 'em. It's just a chat.'

'It'll be a big mistake.'

'Will it?'

'Yeah!'

'Wish I hadn't mentioned 'em to ya now.'

'How's the watch?' asks Jimbo.

'Good,' Derek lies.

'Where is it?'

'Left it at home. Don't want it gettin' robbed.'

'So, who are they?' Phil persists.

'Who?' says Derek, being evasive.

'You know who I bloody mean!'

'Businesspeople, that's all. Investors. People that might help me not piss it all up against a wall, tha's all.'

'Sound like a bunch o' sharks to me!'

'Stop frettin', I ain't gonna do nuthin' stupid. Anyway, more importantly, how much is that tab o' mine, Jimbo?' he asks him.

Jimbo picks up the notebook from beside the till. 'Are you ready for this?' he says.

'Yep, fire away,' says Derek.

'It's just shy of nineteen hundred quid, Dekko,' says Jimbo fanning the pages. ''Ere, you can take a look if ya like.'

'Don't worry. I believe ya,' he says as he pulls out another huge roll of banknotes that he'd stashed down the front of his jeans and begins to count it out onto the bar.

Naturally, within seconds, the entire pub is alerted. It's like they could smell it and start to nudge each other as they watch in amazement at the sight of so much money.

'There. Couple o' grand. That do ya?' says Derek, snapping the last note tight between the fingers of each hand before placing it onto the pile.

'Thanks, Dekko,' says Jimbo, picking it up like it wasn't really his. 'Can't tell ya what a relief this is.'

'I was never gonna let ya down, you know it.'

'I'm not sayin' you were! Let me put it somewhere safe, yeah? Be back wi' ya in a mo.'

'Don't be too long,' Derek tells him. 'We need some drinks 'ere,' he says with another sweep of his arm implying the whole pub yet again. However, this time, his generous offer is greeted with a distinct lack of enthusiasm, even a groan or two, like they expected it or weren't really that bothered.

'Can we 'ave some o' that money instead?' says one.

'Yeah, I've had a belly full o' free beer,' adds another.

'No, you fuckin' can't,' says Derek. 'I got summat to celebrate.'

'What now?' asks Phil with a hint of dread.

'You'll never believe it if I told ya.'

'Try me.'

'I got a Dad.'

'What, that old geezer, ya mean?' asks Dave. 'He's definitely for real?'

'Yeah, he is,' confirms Derek. 'An' a sister,' he adds, his bottom lip already going.

Chapter 23
Thursday

Yet again, Derek is woken by the sound of someone banging and yelling at his door, and, yet again, he feels as rough as. The previous evening's celebrations had gone on well into the night - and some.

'You in there, Dekko?' shouts the echoey and disembodied voice.

It had started off as quite a cathartic experience for him, telling his mates all about his dad and sister. Emotional. But then, when the tears had all but dried and the booze had inevitably taken over, it had turned into a drunken free-for-all, as ever.

'You were s'posed tae be a' tha pub waitin'!'

'You what?' he calls back drowsily, unable to place the tell-tale accent through the incessant pounding in his head like he was at a Heavy Metal gig complete with a pumped-up crowd baying for more. 'Who the fuck is it?'

'Who tha fuck d'ya think it is? Please dinnae tell me you're no' ready yet!'

'Sorry?'

'I, we, cannae keep these people waitin'!'

'Wha' people? Who are ya?'

'Jeezus-aitch-fuckin'-Christ, Dekko!'

'Jesus? Am I dead or summat?'

'You fuckin' well will be! It's Brian! We go' a meetin' in town!' he yells, his nose pressed hard into the frame. 'D'ya no remember?!'

As the penny drops, Derek jerks his head off the pillow. 'You're gonna 'ave to give us a couple o' minutes 'ere, Bri,' he says. 'D'you wanna come in for a minute? Make a cuppa?'

'No, I dinnae wanna come in an' make a fuckin' cuppa! I'm nae your mother! Jus' ge' up, ya lazy bastard!'

'I am, I am!' insists Derek, noisily bashing the wooden headboard against the wall for effect. 'Listen! I'm gettin' dressed right now!'

'An' pu' summat decent on, yeah? Clean an' tidy. Dinnae fo'get who we're seein'!'

Reaming the crystalline crud from his eyes, Derek peers down beside the bed and, despite the request, hastily pulls on yesterday's crumpled and acrid smelling clothes before crashing into the bathroom to brush his teeth and splash his face.

'Lateness is no' a word in my vocabulary,' Brian continues to boom.

'I'm bein' as quick as I can!' Derek sputters, blindly feeling for his coarse and gritty towel and vigorously rubbing his face.

'I'll be in me motor, a bla' Bee'mah, right outside. You go' two minutes, no' a second longer. Tha' mee-tah's tickin'! D'ya hear me?'

'I hear ya,' calls Derek, picking up a can of air freshener he'd inherited when he'd first moved into the place and spraying himself liberally before hurrying into the kitchen to pull on his boots and grab his jacket.

Sure enough, no sooner is Brian at the bottom of the stairwell, pressing the fob and flashing his car into life and pulling out his phone, when Derek appears behind him, panting and wheezing at the exertion. 'Don't suppose you got some parrots-eat-'em-all, 'ave ya?' he asks. 'Me 'ead's givin' me some serious gip 'ere.'

Brian turns and gives him the once over. 'Are you takin' tha pish, pal?' he says.

'An aspirin then?'

'No, I dinnae 'ave a fuckin' aspirin! Could you no' 'ave made bit more o' an effort? Look at tha state o' ya!'

'Wha's wrong wi' me? I look alright,' insists Derek, holding onto the concrete pillar to lift his feet one by one and quickly buff his boots on the backs of his jeans.

'Your jacket's ripped tae fuck for starters,' growls Brian, looking at the collar. ''An 'ave ya no' go' a razor?'

Derek fingers his chin. 'Designer stubble,' he says, managing a grin. 'George Michael gets away wi' it.'

'You're no George fuckin' Michael, ya scruffy baw'bag! .... An', phwoaar, wha's tha' disgustin' stench?'

'Says Pine Forest on the tin,' says Derek, lifting his arm. 'Nice, innit?'

Brian grimaces as much in submission as disgust, wafting his hand in front of his nose like he was batting away an angry wasp. 'I gi' up. You'll 'ave tae do. We're late enough as it is. 'Ave ya a' least remembered your cheque book like I asked ya?'

Derek slaps his forehead with the palm of his hand, immediately regretting it.

Suppressing the urge to lash out, Brian begins to speak very, very, softly. 'Now, be a good boy an' go back up an' get it, yeah?' he says. 'Ya might need it.'

'Wha' for? I got plenty o' cash on me,' replies Derek, tapping at his bulging wallet and showing him the still very significant wads of money crammed into almost every pocket.

'You wannae watch ya dinnae get fuckin' robbed, ya numpty! Jus' do as I ask, eh?'

'Why? Wha's the problem?'

Gently, Brian now reaches out and takes Derek's lapel between thumb and forefinger, flicking away some invisible speck of dirt. 'Wha's tha problem? I'll tell ya wha' the problem is, shall I?' he speaks into his ear. 'You've been given a once in a lifetime chance to mix wi' tha big boys 'ere. No' only tha', if you're good an' behave yerself, you mi' even be offered a place a' tha top table an' make all tha' money o' yours work for ya ...'

'Yeah, maybe,' says Derek whilst trying to ease himself away, 'bu' I'm not makin' no promises ...'

'... an' ya dinnae wanna look like the poor fuckin' relation any more than you do,' continues Brian, his voice dropping in barely concealed threat. 'D'ya get it, do ya?.'

'I'll get it then, shall I?'

'You get it then,' repeats the Scot, folding down Derek's collar and clapping him twice on either side of his face - a double hit - slap, slap. 'Like fuckin' pronto, Tonto. Yeah?'

As Derek disappears back upstairs, Brian pulls out his phone to make the call. 'Be there in twenty, PG,' he says with an uncharacteristic note of uncertainty in his voice.

'You're cutting it very fine, Brian!'

'Don't you fuckin' start! You go' nae idea!'

'Is he presentable at least?'

'We're on our way.'

'Just bloody step on it! Sir Alun will be here shortly!'

With Derek at last in the car, chequebook curled up in his hand, Brian speeds off, racing up through the gears and seriously putting the BMW through its paces.

'She's got a bit of oomph ain't she?' says Derek, laughing nervously and bracing his knees against the walls of the footwell for support, his neck pushed hard into the headrest as Brian continues to floor it. 'I might 'ave to get one o' these meself! Whoah!'

'Two-poin'-eight litres o' pure fuckin' muscle,' says Brian, grinning. 'So, wha' time d'ya make it?' he then asks, alluding to the Rolex and looking to settle things down and make small talk.

'Dunno,' answers Derek, his hands now clenched to either side of the seat.

'Where's tha watch?'

'By me bed.'

'By your bed? Why? You forget tha' too?'

'I was gonna tell you about it. Sheesh!'

'Wha'?'

'It's eff-u-c-kayed.'

'Wha' d'ya mean? You broke it already?'

'No!'

'Wha' then?'

'It's all over the shop,' says Derek, his head now being thrown from side to side as Brian begins to weave in and out of rows of poorly and double-parked cars. 'It don't keep the right time.'

'Nae bother, I'll ge' ya another,' says Brian before swiftly moving on. 'So, tell me, how was ya mother yesterday?'

'You've got more?'

'I said I'll sort it. So, how is she? All tickety-boo, I hope?'

'Yeah. She's fine. Is it a fake?'

'Wha'?'

'The watch.'

'No, it is nae a fuckin' fake, Dekko!' Brian lies, dropping the car from fifth to second in one manoeuvre and hanging a hard left such that Derek now almost falls into him. 'I said, I'll gi' ya another. Dinnae fret! Tell me about your ol mum. Bet she's happy? Her son bein' a millionaire!'

'Why are you so interested in her?'

'I'm only askin'! Showin' a bit o' friendly concern!'

'Try not to kill us both though, yeah?'

'Ah, stop ya haverin', ya English featherweight! Well?'

'Yeah, she was, in the end.'

'Wha' d'ya mean, in the end?'

'Oh, you know, I found out some things, family stuff.'

'Oh aye, like what?' asks Brian, probing.

'Turns out I got a father.'

'A father?' repeats Brian, putting two and two together as to what he'd seen. 'An' ya did'nae know aboot 'im?'

'No. I thought he was dead … when I was a kid … but he wasn't … he isn't … it's hard to explain.'

'Try me.'

'He just turned up out o' the blue.'

'Fuckin' good timin',' says Brian sarcastically. 'Sure 'e's no' some sort o' con merchant?

'Nah, just a coincidence.'

'No such thing as a coincidence, Dekko. You wannae watch yerself. He's after summat.'

'Yeah, that's what I thought first of all, but, as it turns out, he had no idea, couldn't o' done. He's my dad alright. It all fits. We even look alike 'parently.'

'You reckon?'

'I got a sister too.'

'A sister?'

'I know. I can't believe it meself.'

'So, who is he, this father o' yours?' Brian continues to question.

'His name's Detlef.'

Brian takes his eye off the road to look at him for a second. 'Weird name,' he says.

'Watch out! There's a man an' 'is dog crossin' the road!' alerts Derek, pointing.

'Dinnae tell me he's a foreigner?' says Brian, blasting his horn to force the man to yank his dog back onto the pavement before speeding the wrong way down a one-way street.

'German,' says Derek, shaken.

'How's that then?'

'The war. POW.

'Fair enough. Make fuckin' good motors, the krauts,' Brian exclaims. 'Fuckin' stoatahs!'

As the unlikely looking pair finally park up and are entering the smart lobby-cum-meeting area of Jurys Hotel in the heart of the city, there's a discernible sense of movement from the various groups of smartly dressed business types and tourists with Derek in particular being viewed with barely concealed distaste and suspicion. 'Posh in 'ere, innit?' he says over loudly, admiring the spacious and modern layout as laptops are being edged a little bit closer and handbags pushed a little further back into the low-level and sumptuous brown leather loungers.

'Aye, lovely,' Brian replies unenthusiastically whilst sending PG a speedy text. '*Here*' is all it reads. *'So is SA! I'm coming up'* comes the instantaneous reply.

'Sorry, but you're gonna hate this,' Derek then tells him, sheepishly.

The Scot looks at him uncertainly. 'Fuck me. Wha' now?' he asks.

'I gotta go for a… you know…,' he says, standing up on the balls of his feet and cupping his own backside.

'Fuckin' 'ell, Dekko, can ya no' hold it in? PG's on his way.'

'No, I can't! I'm touchin' cloth 'ere. It was all a bit of a rush this mornin'.'

'If ya must, bu' make it snappy, eh?' says Brian urgently.

'I'll make ya a crocodile sandwich if ya like,' quips Derek before hurrying off to the gents.

At that very moment, missing him only by seconds, a fraught looking PG emerges from the lift. 'Where is he then?' he demands.

Without a word, Brian gestures towards the toilets. PG shudders. 'Go in and hurry him along, I cannot keep Sir Alun waiting any longer,' he insists.

'Will I fuck! You go!'

'Language, Brian!' PG hushes him. 'Don't draw attention.'

'I'd o' preferred it if ya'd asked me tae shoot tha fuckah,' Brian now whispers, his hand involuntarily forming the shape of a pistol. 'An' be warned, he looks like he's spent tha night in a friggin' shop doorway. I tried. Believe me, I fuckin' tried.'

'You seem to be losing your touch,' PG reprimands him. 'I might be demanding a discount for poor quality service,' he says.

'You fuckin' try it an' I'll 'ave 'im outa tha' door before you can say William fuckin' Wallace,' growls Brian under his breath as the pair of them wait stiffly for Derek to re-emerge, which he does, eventually, flicking his hands and drying them under his armpits.

Suppressing the urge to return to Sir Alun and call the whole thing off, PG greets him like the quintessential smiling assassin. 'You must be Derek,' he says, immediately steering him towards the lifts but without making physical contact. 'Remind me, have we met before?'

'Not to speak to,' answers Derek, 'but I've seen you about. Who hasn't? You're famous.'

PG avoids the last comment. 'Yes, I think I've seen you too,' he says. 'Now, come. There's a couple of people I'd very much like you to meet.'

Exiting the lift on the lower ground floor and walking along the corridor to a row of meeting rooms on their right, PG stops outside one named The Colston Suite. Pausing briefly, he lets himself in first. 'Gentlemen, this is Derek Dando I've been telling you both about,' he says, his jaw stretching taut in nervous anticipation of Sir Alun's likely reaction.

But he needn't have worried. Sir Alun doesn't bat an eyelid. 'Derek! Sir Alun Tate,' he says, standing to greet him and taking him firmly by the hand. 'I can call you Derek, can't I?'

'You're a Sir?' says Derek, suitably impressed. 'Like a proper Sir?'

'Yes.'

'Nice one, never met a Sir before, but I prefer Dekko if it's all the same to you, Alun.'

'*Sir* Alun,' Sir Alun quickly corrects him, 'and this is Piers,' he adds, introducing a slight and bespectacled man dressed in a sharply cut pin stripe suit and tie. 'My FD.'

'Your hefty?' asks Derek, almost laughing at the idea. 'Is he good at karate or summat?'

'No. *Eff, dee*,' Sir Alun finds himself explaining. 'Financial Director.'

'Ah, sorry,' says Derek. 'Only I thought, he don't look like 'e could knock the skin off a rice puddin'. No offence, mate, yeah?'

'None taken,' says Piers, smiling and playing along.

'So, shall we make ourselves comfortable, gentlemen?' Sir Alun then suggests.

The windowless room is arranged in typical business-like fashion with a pair of facing sofas separated by a coffee table at one end, where the men now go to seat themselves, (apart from Brian who continues to stand at a distance but in attendance) and a small conference table at the other with pads and logo'd pens at the ready. Right next to it, there's a flip chart displaying an artist's architectural drawing of a large waterfront development with the words, 'Tate Holdings' written clearly upon it.

'Tea, coffee?' Sir Alun asks, pointing towards another table along the back wall where all the refreshments are neatly laid out. 'A biscuit or two perhaps?'

'Don't suppose there's a beer, is there?' asks Derek. 'Bit of a night last night, ya see,' he explains. 'Hair o' the dog an' all that.'

'I don't think that would be very sensible, Dekko,' says PG, still looking very ill at ease.

'Nonsense!' Sir Alun overrides him. 'I'm sure that could be arranged. Perhaps your man could oblige, PG? Put it on the tab,' he insists. 'Celebrating were you, Dekko? I know I would be if I were in your shoes!'

PG repeats the request to Brian. 'Would you be so kind as to ring down to reception and have them send up one or two bottles?' he asks him.

'I'd prefer a proper pint,' requests Derek.

'A man after my own heart,' Sir Alun agrees with him effusively. 'Jolly good. I enjoy a real ale myself.'

'Why duncha join me then? We could make it a party.'

'Bit early for me, Dekko!' says Sir Alun to an obsequious ripple of strained and awkward laughter. 'I think I'd better stick to tea for the time being. Would you then be so kind as do the honours, Brian?' he then asks. 'White for me.'

Inaudibly, Brian mutters under his breath. 'I'm no' a fuckin' skivvie,' he says but doing as he's told all the same.

'Now then, Dekko,' continues Sir Alun, his arms spread wide on the back of the sofa. 'Peter's told me of your tremendous piece of good fortune.'

'Who's Peter?'

'Peter.'

'Peter who?'

'Peter,' repeats Sir Alun, nodding in his direction.

'Oh, you mean PG!' gathers Derek.

'I do?'

'Er, yes, Sir Alun, my initials you see,' PG explains, now wishing that the ground would open and swallow him whole. 'PG, Peter Green.'

'I always thought it was from the tea leaves,' says Derek with a wink and lifting a boot for them all to see. 'Remember them chimps?'

'Sugar, Sir Alun?' Brian calls over.

'No,' he answers rather tetchily, his seemingly relaxed façade beginning to crack a little. 'Just bring it over here so we can simply help ourselves. So, where were we? Ah yes, … great and exciting days for you, Dekko.'

'Yeah, you could say that.'

'May I be so bold as to ask you how much you actually won?'

'Sure, it ain't any secret. Not far off eleven an' a 'alf million.'

'A very tidy sum indeed! I'm impressed! Which brings me to the reason we've asked you here today.'

'Yeah, I was wonderin',' says Derek, now sounding a little cagey.

'Please don't be suspicious, dear chap. We simply thought that you might benefit from some collective advice and direction here. There are a few of us involved altogether, all very successful businessmen, and when we heard of your great news, and you being a citizen of this wonderful city of ours, we wondered whether we might be of assistance to you? And you to it, perhaps?'

'Fire away then. I'm all ears.'

'Good. Now, such a huge amount of money would be difficult enough for any man to handle,' Sir Alun begins to explain, 'but by investing and consolidating such enormous wealth you would not only protect it but turn a very handsome profit too.'

'To be honest, I dunno wha' you're talkin' about. I just got it all in me bank,' says Derek with one eye already on the door and anticipating his beer.

'Dead money, Dekko. The interest rate is beyond pitiful.'

'Yeah, I get that, but the lottery people told me to take me time an' weigh up me options before I do anythin' rash.'

'And very good advice that is too,' concurs Sir Alun, 'but, believe you me, if you don't make suitable provision and consider your position very early on, it's also possible to lose money very quickly too.'

With that, Derek laughs. 'Tell me about it! I spent a shed load down the pub for starters! An' I've promised a few o' me mates silly money! I'm a prat really.'

Sir Alun forces his own laugh. 'You certainly want to be careful then. You don't want to fritter it all away,' he warns before sitting further back. 'Dekko, tell me, other than these friends you have just mentioned, have you considered what your major purchases will be? Who will be your likely beneficiaries?'

'Well, I need a nicer place to live, an' I've definitely gotta get meself a new motor, but it'll be me kids mostly,' answers Derek. 'But anyway, I got millions. Plenty to see us out I would o' thought.'

'But you'll still want to invest it wisely for them, won't you? You don't want them wasting it either. Can I ask, how old are they?'

'Got me there,' says Derek, genuinely unknowing. 'Two's still at school, tha's Jules an' Jez, then there's Janice who works in Marks up at Cribbs Causeway, bu' not for much longer with a bit o' luck.'

'I think it would be a mistake to give them too much, Dekko. They need to understand the value of money. You should insist they still work or study and earn it.'

Derek chortles. 'You obviously don't know about me son, he's a right little bugger,' he says. 'But me youngest, Jules, she will,' he adds. 'She wants to be a doctor.'

'A doctor? Wonderful. Just goes to show!'

'Yeah, we ain't all stupid.'

'No, no, Dekko! I'm not suggesting that at all!' Sir Alun backtracks. 'What I'm saying is you'll want to invest in their future, ensure they reach their potential, and that they're comfortable for the rest of their lives, even, if I dare say it, when you are no longer around.'

'Give it a bloody rest, Alun. I ain't bloody dead yet.'

'*Sir* Alun,' he corrects him yet again. 'But you know what I mean, I'm sure. And then there's your wife to consider? You are married I take it?'

'Well, no, not really, but she's gettin' fuck all if you'll pardon my French?'

'Ah, I see. But you are not divorced as yet?'

'No.'

With that, Sir Alun adopts a particularly grave looking expression. 'Then you need to be very careful indeed,' he says. 'Trust me, I know this from bitter personal experience.'

'So, you been through the hoop then?'

'I wouldn't go so far as to say that, but I strongly suggest you tie as much of your money up as quickly as you can before she's able to get her hands on it.'

'Over my dead body!' says Derek. 'I don't want her to get an effin' bean!'

'And that's how we can help you, Dekko, advise you,' says Sir Alun reassuringly. 'Now, I don't know how much you know about investments, stocks and shares, and the like?'

'Not much. Bugger all if I'm 'onest,' says Derek showing a little more interest.

'Don't worry. Most don't. But let me tell you one thing, there is nothing so secure as property. It outperforms virtually everything else in the long term - gold, oil, you name it, it beats them all hands down.'

'Safe as houses, eh?' says Derek, smiling at his own wit.

'No flies on you!' Sir Alun congratulates him. 'Then you'll have seen that property gets more and more expensive year on year.'

'Yeah! Did you see how much they wanted for that bloody poxy little garage in London somewhere? Tens of thousands it was! Stupid money!'

'Precisely! And, as you are cash rich and certainly not in need of any loans or mortgages, you can capitalise on this booming market with consummate ease.'

'Con-soo-ma-what?'

'Easily, Dekko. Very easily.'

'Ah, right. Mind you, *Sir* Alun,' Derek says, stressing his title, 'Me, I've only ever rented.'

'Again, dead money, I'm afraid. A fool's game.'

'I know it, but if that's all you can afford….'

'But you can afford it, Dekko!' says Sir Alun looking for acknowledgement. 'That's the point. You are now in the realms of the super wealthy!'

'Yeah, s'pose I am. Is that beer on its way up yet?'

'I'm sure it'll be here very shortly,' says Sir Alun before continuing. 'You can now afford pretty much anything you want. It's why I've brought Piers along with me, to explain how you might benefit from a very exciting new development in the Cumberland Basin that our small but select consortium are currently developing.'

'Cumberland Basin? I know the area. Rough as fuck when I was a kid,' says Derek.

'But now very much on the up and up, let me tell you.'

'Tha' right?'

'Yes. People are lining up to live there now. It's become very desirable.'

'Who'd o' thought it, eh?' says Derek with a tut but lighting up immediately as he hears a tap at the door.

'I think that might be your beer, Dekko,' says Sir Alun. 'So, without further ado, let's cut to the chase. If we all now go over to the conference table, Piers will explain further,' he adds, handing over. 'Piers?'

'And there you have it,' says Piers, finishing his presentation to reveal the last sheet on the flip chart, a picture of a golden sunrise over the port area of the city, the sky bespeckled with colourful air balloons. 'Mathew Wharf,' it says. 'The Prestigious Heart of Maritime Bristol'

For a moment, they all wait in silence whilst Derek takes another large mouthful of beer. 'Very nice,' he says at last, smacking his lips, 'but can I ask?'

'Fire away,' says Sir Alun.

'It's all very swish, but how does it affect me?'

'Right. Let me tell you,' says Sir Alun, going in for the kill. 'We are looking for further interested parties to profit from and help us realise this once in a lifetime investment opportunity.'

'What, an' you're askin' me?' says Derek almost in disbelief.

'Why not? As Piers has just explained, the rewards for getting involved are, to put it mildly, very significant, and you have the money in abundance. Even as a short-term investor, you could double your money very quickly.'

'Dunno about that. Sounds too good to be true.'

'The figures speak for themselves, Dekko.'

PG then chips in. 'And just so you know, Dekko, I'm in on this too. I'm in the process of liquidising some cash, selling one or two of my other properties in order to buy in,' he says. 'It's a golden opportunity and I, for one, am not going to miss out.'

Derek thinks for a minute. 'Could I buy one o' them penthouses then?' he asks. 'You know, like the picture of the one with the hot tub on the balcony?'

'Of course, you could, and at a very good price, for those in at the off,' says Sir Alun, hiding his insincerity. 'But at this stage, we are looking for investors, not buyers. That will come later and when the huge rewards roll in for all of us.'

'So how long are you lookin' at?'

'Planning permission was granted over two years ago, Dekko, and building is already well under way with the first units going up for sale in the New Year, so just a few months at the most.'

'So how come you need money now?' asks Derek astutely, 'if it's nearly finished?'

'Good question, and I'll give you an honest answer. Like all projects, we are running close to budget and, as such, are prepared to release more equity to give ourselves a more comfortable buffer zone. It is common practice, believe me. Moreover, we are not prepared to compromise on quality. What's the phrase? Don't spoil the ship for a ha'peth o' tar?'

Derek takes another glug of beer. 'But I don't know nothin' about investin', let alone property, Sir Alun. So, sorry, I'm gonna have to bow out,' he says.

At that point, Piers coughs discretely. 'Gentlemen, if I might interject,' he says, 'but there is something I should have mentioned in my presentation that even you might be unaware of, Sir Alun. We have already had a lot of interest, particularly for the penthouse suites and we have already started to allocate them.'

'I had no idea,' says Sir Alun, feigning ignorance. 'That's excellent news.'

'Yes, I was only talking to a very wealthy buyer this week. A footballer, I believe. He put his name against one and has now paid his deposit.'

'Excellent.'

'Which footballer?' Derek asks, biting immediately. 'Is he a Rovers player?'

'Yes, Rovers,' confirms Piers, adding, 'certainly not City.'

'No!' agrees Derek. 'Couldn't 'ave that! Who was it then? Wha's 'is name?'

'I couldn't possibly tell you that, Dekko. That is confidential, but, safe to say, I understand he is a leading goal scorer,' reveals Piers with a knowing wink.

'Who could that be then?' Derek begins to wonder excitedly.

Piers then addresses Sir Alun. 'I would have to check,' he says, 'but, as things stand, I believe there is now only one penthouse left unreserved.'

'Which one?'

'The one at the very top.'

'Oh, I had my eye on that,' lies Sir Alun.

'I might 'ave to fight you for it then,' says Derek, laughing

'I'm afraid it's first come, first served,' says Piers. 'That's our policy.'

'An' there's pubs underneath, you say?'

'Yes, and very many more in the area.'

'An' underground parking?' Derek continues to confirm, effectively selling himself.

'Two spaces for each of the penthouses.'

'Only I quite fancy the idea of a drop 'ead Aston. Don't wan' it gettin' slashed, now do I?'

'No, certainly not. Beautiful car,' says Sir Alun playing him along.

'Or maybe a Beemer like Brian's there. Shit off a shovel that thing!'

'Another lovely car that you would want kept secure and not left out on the street overnight.'

'But where would me mates park when they visit?' Derek then asks.

'There are plenty of municipal car parks in the area, and as a resident, I believe you can rent allocated spaces,' says Piers. 'I can look into it if you like?'

'OK. That'd be good.'

'Are you interested then?'

'Might be. I could 'ave me ol' mum to stay over too,' muses Derek. 'It's got lifts innit?'

'Of course. In the case of the penthouses, straight to your own door.'

'Wow! That'd be good. Like summat off o' James Bond. So how much are they? What are we talkin' about 'ere, Sir Alun?'

'Remind me, Piers,' he says, uncertain as to where his financial director is going with this.

'There are five penthouses in total, costing between one and a quarter and one and a half million pounds each,' informs Piers, as straight faced as you like, 'and, as I said, the only one left available is the most expensive. It's the biggest, you see, with far and away the best views. Stunning in fact.'

'One an' a half million? For a bloody flat?' says Derek, aghast. 'It ain't even got a garden.'

Even Sir Alun is momentarily taken aback by the figure but, poker faced, goes along with it. 'They are the best that money can buy in Bristol, Dekko,' he says. 'But if you don't think you can afford it, I will take it.'

'I could afford em 'all if I wanted,' says Derek feeling strangely insulted and doing a quick calculation in his head. 'It's just a lot of money for somewhere to live, tha's all I'm sayin'. Is tha' the best you can do?'

Again, Piers interjects. 'Well, we are not in the habit of discounting, but as you are a cash buyer with no lead time to consider, and as a show of good faith, we could reduce it by, say, two hundred and fifty thousand if you are prepared to commit today,' he says.

'That sounds very generous, Piers. Are you sure?' says Sir Alun.

'Yes, we can do that. But at this late stage, we would need a minimum of a seven hundred and fifty thousand pounds as a deposit with the balance of five hundred thousand to be paid on handover,' he says, as cool as you like.

'What? You want the money like right now?' asks Derek.

'I think so, Dekko, considering the very generous discount we're offering?' insists Sir Alun. 'And just think of your potential new neighbours?'

'Yeah! Tha's true. I could sort out a season ticket, couldn't I?'

'You could. Drinks after the match with the players too I daresay. What fun you'll have!'

'An' I could always sell it, couldn't I?'

'You could, and make a very decent profit into the bargain,' confirms Piers. 'It's a classic win-win situation for you.'

'I was always told money makes money,' says Derek.

'Gentlemen, I think we have a very shrewd operator in our midst,' Sir Alun praises him again. 'So, do we have a deal?' he asks, offering his hand.

'I'll need a receipt,' says Derek, taking yet another slurp of his beer and putting it down on the table like he'd just answered a question as a starter for ten on University Challenge.

'Piers can organise that for you.'

'Anyone got a pen then?' Derek asks, taking his dog-eared chequebook from his pocket along and inadvertently pulling a very large wad of banknotes out with it in the process.

'Why on earth are you carrying so much cash, Dekko?' Sir Alun asks him. 'You must have thousands there.'

'No real reason, Sir Alun,' he says. 'Never been able too before, tha's all.'

Piers hands him a fountain pen, taking off the lid.

'Tate Holdings,' says Sir Alun.

'Tate ...Hol..d...ings,' repeats Derek, speaking as he writes.

'Seven hundred and fifty thousand pounds,' Sir Alun continues.

'How many noughts is that?' asks Derek.

'Four.'

'Oh yeah.'

'And your signature?'

'Sorry. Been a while since I done this,' says Derek, tearing it out.

'Congratulations, Dekko! You are the proud owner of one of Bristol's most desirable and fashionable properties,' says Sir Alun, wafting the ink dry. 'And while Piers is preparing your receipt, may I say it has been an absolute pleasure meeting you and doing business with you.'

'Brian, perhaps you'd like to give Dekko a ride home? I'll be in touch with you later,' says a now relieved and smiling PG.

'Hey, I got another pint to finish yet!' complains Derek. 'Nobody goin' to join me? Celebrate an' that?'

'Another time, Dekko,' says Sir Alun. 'There's no peace for the wicked I'm afraid. I'll get nothing done if I have a drink now. But you can invite me to your housewarming if you like? I would be honoured.'

'Yeah! I'll get some bottles o' bubbly in, eh? A man o' your tastes. My Marion used to love that Lambrusco.'

'I don't know that I've ever tried it,' says Sir Alun. 'Is it nice?'

'No idea, but she swore by it. Sweet as, she said.'

'Right then, Dekko?' Brian chivvies him along. 'Why don't ya take your beer down to the bar and I'll join ya if ya like?'

'Yeah, OK then, Brian,' agree Derek. 'Cheers then, fellahs. See you all soon.'

'Yes, cheerio, Dekko,' says a smiling Sir Alun. 'Have a safe journey home.'

As the door closes, Sir Alun, Piers, and PG wait for a few moments in stunned yet hilarious silence until they are sure the coast is clear.

'Unbelievable!' says Sir Alun. 'Like taking candy from a baby! I've got to hand it to you, Piers, bloody well done! Your story about the footballer was a master stroke!' he adds, handing the cheque to him. 'One and a half million as an opening gambit! I'd have settled for two thirds of that, you scoundrel!'

'Basic intuition,' says Piers with a swagger of the head.

'I never doubted it for one second,' says PG, now looking very pleased with himself.

'You could have fooled me, the look on your face when he first walked in!' says Sir Alun, laughing. 'But what a sad excuse?' he continues. 'Certainly, we won't be actually allowing him to move anywhere near it of course, this isn't a bloody Social Housing project!

Can you look into it, Piers? How we extricate ourselves from any purchase without losing the money. There must be a clause?'

'Don't worry. There was nothing specific in the receipt I gave him. It will be quite simple. I'll also get this express cleared,' he says putting the cheque away in his attaché case and locking it, 'should he decide to change his mind.'

'Yes, you do that,' says Sir Alun before turning to PG, 'which reminds me, dear chap, when we are likely to see your contribution? Soon I hope?'

'Sir Alun,' says PG like he was being insulted, 'I think you'll find I will have deposited five hundred thousand into the holding account by end of play tomorrow.'

'Excellent news, Peter, or is it PG?' he teases.

'Tres drôle,' he replies. 'And don't let me forget, I have that oil painting you were interested in in my car. The Dufy. You can take it home if you wish, see if you like it? It's only small.'

'With a big price tag, I presume? I shall hang it on my wall and have a think.'

Down in the bar, Derek is already ordering himself a third drink having emptied the second before the lift had reached the ground floor.

'You've just bought yerself one hell o' a gaff, Dekko,' Brian congratulates him.

'Yeah, ain't I just. An' I beat Sir Alun to it!

'Ya did.'

'Always fancied livin' down by the docks to tell ya the truth.'

'You'll 'ave a view and a half, that's for sure, watchin' all the boats comin' and goin'.'

'I hope I don't lose contact wi' me mates though,' Derek worries for a moment.

'Nae bother, Dekko! Your real pals will stick by ya, and as for the others, the hangers on? Fuck 'em.'

'True. Can you drop us off at the pub after?' asks Derek.

'Yeah, o' course, tha's wha' I'm here for. An' your bairns. They'll love it. Plenty tae do in the city. Cinemas, places tae eat, tha lot.'

'They will. You can join me if ya like, at the Traveller's.'

'Sure. That'll be pleasant,' Brian lies.

'Don't suppose you got a pen on ya, 'ave ya?' Derek then asks.

'No, but they'll 'ave one behind the bar. Why?'

'Summat I gotta do.'

'Wha'?'

'Got to write out a few more cheques.'

'Who to?'

'Me mates.'

'How much?'

'Quarter of a mill' each,' Derek reveals.

'Fuck me, Dekko! How many of 'em?

'Three altogether.'

'Do you no' think you're bein' a wee bit over generous?'

'I just spent as much on a deposit for a fuckin' flat, Brian!' says Derek. 'Besides, I'm gonna need some people to play with, ain't I? It'll be no good there all on me own.'

'I'll play wi' ya, Dekko,' says Brian with a smile of intent. 'If ya like?'

Chapter 24

It's well into the afternoon by the time Derek and Brian get back to the Traveller's and it's as dull as ditch water in there.

The punters, such as there are, are all perched around one end of the bar studying form in the racing sections of their newspapers, or watching it unfold live on the muted television screen above their heads.

Derek's appearance arouses a soupçon of extra interest of course, but once again, rather outweighed by a larger dollop of begrudging ambiguity despite his continuing and generous largesse. Somehow, they now preferred it when he was piss-poor with hardly a pot to piss in. He was less of a disruption back then, less of a daily reminder of their own mundane and often desperate existence now riding on the two-forty-five from Haydock Park.

But Jimbo's no fool, he knows which side his bread's about to be buttered. 'Here's my bestest customer,' he announces as soon as soon as he catches sight of him, although a little perturbed to see Brian in tow.

'Tel'meh, Jim,' garbles one squint-eyed old sot, already seven sheets to the wind, 'wha' d'e 'ave fer 'is dinnah, eh?'

'Wha' you prattlin' on about now, ya daft ol' fool?' Jimbo brushes his comment aside.

'Just thought ya mi' know,' the old boy replies, '… seein' as you're so far up 'is fuckin' arse.'

Pointing his finger in silent reprimand, Jimbo begins to pull Derek's pint. 'Wha's yours then, Brian?' he asks.

'Bottle o' Newky Brown.'

'You wanna glass?'

'Nah, I'll 'ave i' by tha neck.'

'Thought ya might,' mutters Jimbo as he turns to retrieve a bottle from one of the two coolers installed under the till. 'So, what's new then, Dekko? How'd your meetin' go?' he asks, knocking off the top and clinking it into the empties bin.

Derek doesn't answer. 'What's that ol' fellah on about just then?' he asks instead.

'Nuthin'. Ignore 'im. How was your meetin'?'

'I don't want people getting' pissed off.'

'Ignore him. How did it go?' Jimbo repeats.

'How d'you know I been to a meetin'?'

'Last night?' prompts Jimbo. 'Although to be fair, even pissed you weren't givin' much away.'

'Course. Yeah,' answers Derek. 'Don't remember too much about it to be honest wi' ya.'

'Why am I not surprised? The amount you're chuckin' down your neck, you're startin' to seriously addle your brain, mate.'

'Probably,' Derek admits, 'for the time bein' at least.'

Jimbo laughs, but insincerely. 'You wanna ease off a bit,' he warns.

'I will,' concedes Derek, 'but not just yet, eh? Too much fun.'

'An' been on it again already, I see,' adds Jimbo, spotting the tell-tale signs - the slight wobble of the head, the teetering back onto his heels, the sticky toffee voice.

'Hey, Jim, enough yeah?' Derek then reacts. 'None o' your bleedin' business what I do.'

'I'm not lookin' for an argument,' says Jimbo, raising his hands and backing off. 'Your body.'

'I get it in the neck enough bad enough wi' my little Julie.'

'Well, you wanna listen to her then.'

'She wants to be a doctor, ya know.'

'I know. You told us 'bout that too.'

'Did I?'

'Yeah, you did,' says Jimbo, tutting in disbelief. 'So, come on then, give us all the gory details. This meetin o' yours?'

'I will, bu' after you've seen wha' tha' ungrateful lot want first,' says Derek. 'I'm not 'avin' anyone sayin' I'm a stingy fuckah!' he adds loud enough for them all to hear.

'Don't worry yerself, Dekko. They don't, not really, just the odd one or two who don't know a good thing when they see it,' says Jimbo, directing his comment towards the old sot who is already edging his near empty glass forward an inch or two. 'Besides, you got your big day comin' up tomorrow,' he adds as he begins to pour pints for each and every one of them without even asking. 'I'll tell ya, fellah, Reenie's really gone to town for ya. Never seen so much bloody food,' he calls back over his shoulder. 'Talk about feedin' the five fuckin' thousand!'

'Appreciated,' says Derek. 'Ask her how much I owe her.'

'Mates rates,' says Jimbo. 'We ain't rippin' ya.'

'Nice. Cheers,' thanks Derek. 'I'm lookin' forward to it,' he adds. 'I'll 'ave most o' me family here wi' me too wi' a bit o' luck … except me mum o' course. She wouldn't be able to 'andle it she said, not in a wheelchair.'

'Tha's a shame. Haven't seen her in years. Alright is she?'

'Yeah. Sound. Me dad's taking her over to Weston on Saturday.'

'Tha's nice for her.'

'Did I tell ya he was comin'? Me dad?'

'Yeah, ya did! About a hundred bleedin' times!' says Jimbo, now laughing out loud. 'Your brain must be like a pickled fuckin' walnut!'

Derek wibbles his lips with his forefinger, crosses his eyes.

'An' talkin' o' pickled nuts,' says Jimbo with a knowing wink, 'how was it wi' Roxxii the other night?'

'Very funny.'

'Only askin'.'

'Fuck off!'

'Alright, alright! Keep yer 'air on!'

'That's wha' I said to 'er.'

'What?'

'Nuthin'.'

'It's like talkin' in fuckin' riddles wi' you,' says Jimbo, laughing again. 'So, for the last time of askin', what 'appened at this meetin'? Who was there?'

'You'd never believe it if I told ya,' says Derek, now warming to the idea of telling him his news.

'Try me. Elvis? Mr Blobby? Mother fuckin' Theresa?'

'I quite liked Elvis - huh-huh-huh - not tha' fuckin' Noel Edmunds though.'

'Just get on wi' it, yeah?' says Jimbo.

'OK, OK,' says Derek, taking a big mouthful before he begins to list them out. 'So, there was Brian 'ere o' course, he took me over, … PG, …'

'Knew it!' exclaims Jimbo, curling his lip. 'I mean PG, Brian, not you - before you try chewin' me face off.'

Brian at last takes his bottle from the bar, twisting the neck in the crook of his arm, wiping it clean. 'As if,' he says with a grin. 'You go' me fo' tha wrong man.'

'Bu' the main bloke was this right posh geezer, weren't he Brian?' Derek continues.

Brian nods in agreement. 'Aye, minted,' he confirms.

'Alun Tate his name. *Sir* Alun Tate,' says Derek.

'Wha'? Like as in like a Knight o' the Realm ya mean?' asks Jimbo incredulously.

'Don't look so fuckin' surprised! I'm movin' in elevated circles nowadays, me ol' mucker!'

'Are ya now?' says Jimbo, suspicious.

'Yeah, I am! Proper toff he was, very la-di-dah.'

'Plum in his mouth?'

'Could say that. An' there was this other geezer there too, Piers or summat or other his name was, his FD.'

'Oh yeah?'

'Tha' stands for Financial Director.'

'I know.'

'I didn't. He looked like Himmler in his glasses. Anyway, gave me this very interestin' presentation, they did, even got me a couple o' pints.'

'I'm sure they did.'

'Pitched a couple of ideas too.'

'Wha' d'ya mean, pitched a couple of ideas?' asks Jimbo, now preparing himself for the crux of it all. 'Wha' 'ave ya gone an' done now?'

Derek pauses for a moment before throwing his head back and holding his hands to his mouth like a loudhailer - *Ta-ta-ta-ta-ta, ta-dah!* he goes, blowing a fanfare through his fists.

Unable to ignore his noisy antics, and with the feeling that they should at least acknowledge the drinks now sat in front of them, one or two of the other punters look over and raise their glasses. 'Cheers,

Dekko,' says one. 'Yeah, yer good health,' adds another. 'Got somethin'
else to celebrate, 'ave we?'

'Too bloody true, I 'ave!' Derek announces.

'Why don't I like the sound o' this?' says Jimbo.

'Are you ready?'

'Probably not.'

'I just bought ...,' Derek shouts out, '... wait for it ...'

'What?'

'A fuck-off apartment!'

'A flat you mean?'

'No-o! Flat, my arse! A bloody great big bastard penthouse!'

'A penthouse?' repeats Jimbo calmly enough, but, like a duck on
water, his legs going twenty to the dozen underneath. 'Where?'

'Down in the docks. Cumberland Basin.'

'Cumberland Basin?'

'Will you stop copyin' everythin' I say? But yeah! Cumberland
Basin!'

'Wha' d'you wanna go there for?'

'It's bloody top notch, tha's why, Jim! Up an' comin'! You wait
'til you see it! Views overlookin' the river, hot tub on the balcony,
underground parkin' for when I get meself a flash new motor, trees -
lots o' trees - boats, an' bars a-fuckin'-go-go! The full kit an' kaboodle!
Be like bein' on a luxury 'oliday everyday o' me life livin' there!'

'Sounds great,' says Jimbo but sounding less than enthusiastic.

'Not to mention one o' the Rovers players has just bought one
too!'

'Who?'

'They couldn't tell me. All very hush hush ya see. Leadin' goal
scorer, 'parently.'

'Do they 'ave one?'

'Shut up! Bu' wha's wrong wi' ya? Ain't ya pleased for me?'

'Yeah, o' course I am, but ...'

'Bu' what?'

'Well, uppin' sticks an' that. Here's where all your friends and
family are, Dekko. Ain't we good enough for you no more?'

'Don't be stupid! Course y'are! I'm not suddenly turnin' into
some toffee-nosed twat, ya twat!'

'So why then?'

'Bloody 'ell, Jim! It's not like it's the other end o' the world! I'll
still be in Bris'ol. You an' the lads can visit any time ya like, stay over!
We'll 'ave a ball! Besides, it's not even built yet.'

'Wha' d'ya mean, it's not built yet?' exclaims Jimbo
incredulously.

'Will you stop repeatin' me!'

'Sorry.'

'Cos it's a new development, tha's why!' Derek explains to him
like he was talking to a child. 'Brand spankin' new! Yeah?'

'Well, yeah, I s'pose,' Jimbo doubtfully accepts.

'An' as they said, if I got in quick, an' wi' property bein' the way it is, together wi' the huge discount I negotiated, even if I decided to sell it, I could make a serious killin'. Tens of thousands - prob'ly more!'

'So, how much was it then?'

With that, Brian interjects. 'I dinnae think that's any o' your business,' he says.

'Don't matter, Bri, Jimbo's a mate. I don't care,' Derek overrides him.

'Well?' persists Jimbo.

'One an' a quarter if ya must know,' Derek reveals, eager, in fact, to tell him in truth.

'One an' a quarter million? For a bloody flat?'

'A penthouse!'

'Still, that's a shed load o' money, Dekko.'

'But two hundred and fifty thousand less than what they were originally askin' for it!' Derek tries to justify. 'D'ya see where I'm comin' from now?'

'I think they did more like.'

'Oi! I'm not a bleedin' idiot! I only gave 'em a deposit!'

'Tha's summat at least. Five percent? Ten?'

'What's that when it's at 'ome?' asks Derek, unable to do the calculation.

'Ten percent is one hundred and twenty-five thousand, Dekko,' Jimbo answers him.

'Well, nah, I gave 'em a bit more than that,' he admits a tad sheepishly.

'What then?'

'Seven-fifty if ya must know.'

'Three quarters of a million pounds? As a deposit?'

'Yeah. Why not? I can afford it.'

'On a place that ain't even built yet! Are you off your bleedin' rocker?'

Again, Brian steps in but even more forcibly. 'As he just told ya, landlord,' he says firmly, 'Dekko's got his sel' a deal an' a half.'

'Tha's as maybe,' says Jimbo, 'but …'

'… an' an investment for tha future open only tae the very privileged few.'

'But…'

'Bu' nuthin'!' Brian now stops him dead in his tracks, dropping his head and staring him down. 'Turns out, Dekko's a very shrewd operator.'

'Shrewd? Now I've heard it all!'

'Oi, Jimbo, ya cheeky cunt!' complains Derek. 'Besides, it's only money!'

'Only money? 'Ave ya heard yerself, Dekko?' comments Jimbo, rather unwisely.

'Wha' ya talkin' about?'

'It was only less than a week ago that you had fuck all,' Jimbo reminds him, '…. an' I mean fuck all! You didn't even 'ave the pound coin to *pay* for your fuckin' lottery ticket!'

Derek falls silent for a few seconds. 'I think you might be forgettin' summat, don't you?' he says pointedly.

Understanding exactly what Derek means, Jimbo realises his mistake and backs off fast. 'I'm only tryin' to look out for ya best interests, Dekko,' he says, his tone instantly changed from the righteous and indignant to the regretful and whimpering.

'Well don't. I don't need your help. I can look after meself, make me own decisions. Geddit?' says Derek and just as his phone goes off in his pocket. 'Sorry, Brian, but I gotta take this, could be important,' he says whilst ignoring Jimbo and walking to the other side of the pool table.

'Yeah?' he answers.

'Mr Dando?'

'Yeah, speakin'.'

'It's Bill Jefferson here, solicitor.'

'Ah, OK, thought you might be the Lottery people.'

'The who?'

'Nuthin'.'

'Right, with regard Jez. I've just left a message with your wife to call me.'

'Ex-wife,' Derek corrects him.

'Apologies, ex-wife. Look, I'm afraid to tell you the police are going to charge him with causing death by dangerous driving and theft of a motor vehicle.'

'But he says he wasn't drivin'!'

'His fingerprints were on the steering wheel.'

'Shit!'

'Indeed. We've got a date for his court appearance. Ten o'clock next Tuesday at Bristol Magistrate's.'

'Are they going to lock him up?'

'It's a possibility, Mr Dando, if it goes to Crown Court. Let's see what we can do, shall we?'

'I'll make sure he's there.'

'Do you know where the court is?'

'Do bears shit in the woods?'

'I'll take that as a yes then.'

'Yeah. Sorry.'

'But look, we'll need to go through a couple of things beforehand. Any chance you and your son could come into the office?'

'When?'

'Very soon. How would first thing tomorrow morning suit?'

Derek takes the phone away from his ear, thinking. 'No can do,' he says. 'I got this presentation ceremony.'

'Mmm, awkward. Late afternoon then?'

'Could be a bit messy.'

'Mr Dando, I can't stress enough how important this is, and I can't do Monday, I'm in court all day. I'll have to get hold of your son's mother instead.'

'Oh no you won't! I'll do it,' Derek insists. 'Don't you work Saturday mornin's?' he chances.

'No, not as a rule,' says Jefferson rather sharply. *'I have a life too.'*

'I'd make it worth your while.'

'Please! I'm not interested in anything like that, but, OK, on this occasion, I'm prepared to see you on Saturday morning if that's the best you can do. Shall we say eight-thirty? It should only take us half an hour.'

'Can't we do it over the phone?'

'No, we can't! There's paperwork to be completed. I shall need your signature. Your son is a minor.'

'Only it's a bit early.'

'Look, I'm trying to do you a favour here, Mr Dando. I don't think you appreciate how serious this is.'

'Er, right, OK then. If we must.'

'Yes, we must! Eight-thirty. Please don't be late.'

'We'll be there. Bye, oh, and, er, thanks.'

-

Over in Redland, Detlef is sat on edge on the edge of his bed. After yesterday's tumultuous and stressful sequence of events, he'd wisely decided to spend the day taking it easy and to call his wife and daughter. He needed it. They needed it. But now, restless and unwilling to remain in his room any longer, he rings Maciej.

'Sorry I did not call you earlier, but are you available?' he asks,

'Of course! I'm always available for you, my friend,' answers Maciej, upbeat as ever. *'But how are you feeling?*

'Better.'

'Are you sure?'

'Yes, I'm sure, Maciej. Thank you for asking.'

'Then where do you want to go?'

'I was thinking that I might like to see Derek this evening. Surprise him. Do you think he might be in the pub?'

'Sure! We can try. What time?'

'Can you pick me up at six?'

'On the dot, Detlef,' Maciej assures him. *'Not a second later!'*

-

'Issues?' pries Brian as Derek rejoins him.

'Nah, nuthin'. My boy, he 'ad an accident, a car accident,' says Derek by way of a short explanation. 'Gotta go to court.'

'Serious?'

'Some young kiddie got hurt,' Derek conceals.

'Och. Tragic. Sorry to 'ear it. Bad?'

'Bad enough.'

'Who's tha brief?'

'Bill Jefferson, down in the precinct. That was 'im just then.'

'Dinnae know 'im. Small fry. But you know wha' they say, Dekko, it's not wha' ya know, it's who ya know, if ya get ma drift?' advises Brian, tapping his nose.

'I s'pose. Never thought.'

'I mean, money's nae problem for you anymore. Things can be, how can I pu' this? ... Arranged.'

'Ha! You talkin' about a bribe?'

'No-oo! As if,' Brian jests with him. 'We'll talk, eh? On the QT.'

Right at that very moment and before Derek has chance to further reply, Clappie makes an unexpected appearance in the doorway, but stopping dead in his tracks as soon as he sees Brian's ominous presence dominating the bar.

'Alright then, Clappie,' greets Jimbo, blowing any chances of him making a rapid and discrete U-turn.

Hearing his name, Derek turns. 'Hey, Clappie! Fancy seein' you 'ere! What ya 'avin'?' he asks immediately, pleased, as ever, to have another drinking companion.

'Don't mind if I do, Dekko,' he says before walking over, albeit a tad reluctantly.

'Wha' you doin' 'ere?' growls Brian, suspicious and sneering.

'Last time I looked, this was a public house,' Clappie replies in some show of timid defiance. 'Just thought I'd drop in on the off chance, say hello. Tha's all.'

'I'm glad ya did! What's it to be?' reiterates Derek.

'I'll 'ave a pint o' what you're on if tha's alright? Hope a bit o' your luck might rub off,' he says.

Curtly, Derek turns to Jimbo. 'You heard the man,' he says Derek, the landlord obediently doing as he's told. 'Yeah, it's good that you turned up, mate,' he carries on. 'I got the lottery people comin' 'ere tomorra if you fancy poppin' down? Twelve-ish it starts. Plenty o' grub, booze on tap, an' it'll not cost ya a fuckin' penny!'

'Count me in on that,' says Clappie, relaxing a little. 'Always up for a freebie, me.'

'You'd do well tae remember tha' nuthin's for free,' says Brian.

'What is your problem?' Clappie asks the now particularly ferocious looking Scot. 'Wha' 'ave I ever done to you, eh? Nuthin', tha's what!'

'Give it a rest, guys,' Derek insists. 'Let's just 'ave a bit o' fun, eh? Relax.'

'Dinnae flatter yersel',' Brian continues, nevertheless. 'I've nae problem wi' a wee pipsqueak like you at all,' he adds, pinching his fingers together as if he was squishing a gnat and putting his still nearly full bottle back down heavily onto the bar. 'Anyway,' he then announces. 'I go' to go.'

'But we only just got here!' complains Derek. 'You ain't finished your beer yet!'

'Sorry, bu' I cannae stay 'ere an' ge' pissed all afternoon, Dekko. I go' things tae dae, people to see. Twelve ya say? Tomorrah?'

'Yeah.'

'An' remember, if ya wannae discuss wha' we jus' mentioned, call me. Stay lucky,' reminds Brian before putting two fingers up to his eyes then pointing them directly at Clappie. 'An' you too.'

'I don't think he likes you very much,' jokes Derek as they watch him leave and the door close shut behind him.

'The feelin's mutual, my baba. Nasty bit o' work. I can enjoy me pint in peace now.'

'Nah, 'e's alright,' dismisses Derek. 'His bark's worse than his bite.'

'Don't you believe it. He's PG's gorilla. Top banana.'

-

Already sat outside in his car, Brian is on the phone to PG.

'Question,' he says quite aggressively.

'What?'

'I've no' long left Dekko in the boozer an' tha' twat Clappie's just walked in.'

'And?'

'You dinnae know nuthin' aboot it then?'

'No, Brian, I don't. Why should I?'

'Are you sure? Bit o' a coincidence. Wha' does he know?'

'Nothing. Is it a problem?'

'No' as yet, bu' 'is mate, the landlord, was givin' Dekko a hard time over his wee purchase today.'

'So what? Nothing he can do about it.'

'I dinnae want this goin' tits up, PG,' warns Brian. 'I wan' my cut!'

'Do stop fretting. We're on the case. The cheque will be cleared soon enough. You'll get your payment.'

'Good. Oh, an' jus' so ya know, I dinnae 'ave a chance to tell ya, his father has jus' turned up out tha' blue too.'

'Why are you telling me all this nonsense? What's your point?'

'Wha's 'is game, tha's all ... an' he's a Kraut.'

'What's that got to do with it?'

'Jus' lettin' ya know.'

'Fine. Just keep tabs on him, Derek I mean. Keep in close. We might not be finished with him just as yet.'

'I'm one step ahead o' ya on tha'. I'll be joinin' 'im tomorra for 'is cheque ceremony tomorrah. The lottery people will be here.'

'Really? He didn't say. Where? In the pub?'

'Where else?'

'Mmm, interesting. I might put in a little appearance myself. What time?'

'Midday.'

'Will Clappie be there?'

'Aye, seems like it. I just heard Dekko invite 'im.'

'*Good. Strength in numbers, Brian. Just make sure you get there early. I don't want to find myself on my own amongst that rabble. Understood?*'

'OK. Oh, another thing…'

'*What?*'

'Tha' watch o' his.'

'*The Rolex?*'

'Aye. It's fucked.'

'*Then bring another. You have enough. I'll give it to him. It'll be a nice touch.*'

-

'PG was right pissed off wi' me cos' o' you, Dekko,' Clappie is saying, having a gentle dig.

'I 'ad a lot goin' on, Clappie,' he apologises. 'Sorry.'

'Tha's why e' got tha' Scottish goon involved. Thought I was goin' to lose me job.'

''Ere, let me make it up to ya,' says Derek, pulling out four or five fifty-pound notes from his top pocket and thrusting them into Clappie's grateful hands, 'this do ya?'

'You sure?'

'Course I'm sure.'

'You're a bloody diamond, my baba! Tha's wha' you are, a bloody diamond!'

'No probs.'

'So, 'ave you seen 'im yet?' asks Clappie, relieved to be putting some money into his wallet. 'PG, I mean.'

'This mornin'.'

'Bugger! I was still hopin' to persuade ya. Get back in the good books. So, wha' 'appened?'

'Cut a long story short, I bought meself place down by the river.'

'What? Not tha' thing in Cumberland Basin he's involved in wi' that Sir Alun nob?' he seeks to confirm.

Derek laughs. 'Yeah, tha's 'im. I met 'im.'

'An' you bought one, ya say?'

'I 'ave,' says Derek proudly. 'Stonkin' it is, in the pictures.'

Clappie goes quiet, averting his gaze.

'Wha's the matter?' asks Derek.

'Nuthin',' says Clappie, quietly. 'I'm sayin' nuthin'.'

'At that point, Jimbo sheepishly sidles up. 'Sorry 'bout that, Dekko,' he offers an apology. 'I didn't mean to upset ya nor nuthin', mate. You know me. Just concerned, tha's all.'

'Hey-up. Am I interruptin' some sort o' lover's tiff 'ere?' asks Clappie. 'I'll leave ya to it, if ya like,' he suggests, keen to change the conversation.

'No! You stay right where you are!' Derek insists.

'Problem?' asks Jimbo.

'Dunno. Clappie knows summat, but he's not tellin',' says Derek but somehow not wanting to know.

241

'Oh, yeah?' says Jimbo, already second guessing. 'What?'

'Spit it out,' demands Derek, 'or I'll ''ave tha' money back!'

'I can't.'

'You bloody well will!'

'Gi' me a break, Dekko,' says Clappie, his face contorting. 'They'd 'ave me head on a spike.'

'If ya know somethin', Clappie, you gotta tell,' says Jimbo, all conciliatory, diplomatically.

'I just 'eard there'd been some hiccups,' offers Clappie, 'tha's all.'

'Hiccups? Wha' the fuck's that supposed to mean?' asks Derek with the feeling that, once again, his stomach is about to fall out of his arse. 'They gave me a receipt an' everythin',' he defends himself, pulling out the already crumpled envelope as proof.

'Please don't bite me 'ead off, Dekko,' chances Jimbo, 'bu' d'you mind if I take a look?'

'Oh, alright,' acquiesces Derek, thrusting it into Jimbo's hand. 'See?'

He opens it up and offers the A4 sheet up to the light cast out from behind the optics. 'But it's just a handwritten note, Dekko,' he observes rather cautiously.

'So what? It's on a proper letterhead!'

'Looks like a photocopy to me, mate. An' where's the address? It's just a PO Box number.'

'But it's signed!'

'Who by?'

'That Piers bloke,' says Derek, adamantly. 'He bloody signed it!'

'Can you read it?' says Jimbo, handing it back to show him. 'I can't. It's just a bit o' scribble. He didn't even print his name.'

Derek, now even more ashen faced than before and with the feeling of nausea in the pit of his stomach now reaching epic proportions, falls silent and eyes Clappie as if he were somehow to blame.

'Don't bloody look at me!' he squeals. 'Not my fault!'

'I'm sorry to 'ave to say this, Dekko,' persists Jimbo and seriously pushing his luck, 'but d'you think you might just be a little bit out of your depth 'ere?'

Clappie fingers his chin nervously, sighing in resignation at what he is about to say. 'There's jus' some rumours,' he reveals.

'What rumours?' asks Jimbo.

'I just 'eard that Tate's been around the block a few times, tha's all.'

'Wha's that supposed to mean?' asks Derek.

'Oh, you know …. company name changes, trades not bein' paid, stuff like that.'

'Bloody 'ell, Dekko! You gotta stop that cheque, mate!' says Jimbo more assertively. 'You'll lose the lot.'

Derek glares at him but says nothing.

Having started, Clappie now seems keen to divulge more. 'It's Sir Alun said this, Sir Alun did that,' he moans like he'd had enough of it himself. 'PG's gonna get burnt big time too if he don't watch out. He's right up to his neck in it from what I can make out.'

'So, who is he then, this Sir Alun character?' enquires Jimbo, intrigued.

'Dunno really. I've never actually met 'im, but I do know that he lives in some monster gaff just outside o' Bath.'

'That don't mean jack shit, some big house, does it?' says Jimbo.

'No, it don't. You're right,' agrees Clappie. 'Mortgaged up to the eyeballs if truth be known.'

'I bloody doubt it,' says Derek in some desperate and futile attempt to turn a blind eye to the terrible and emerging truth. 'You could tell. The way he was dressed. His shoes. Everythin'. He's rollin' in it.'

'An' 'ere's an example,' continues Clappie, 'only just recently, through PG, a couple o' mates o' mine did a bit o' gutterin' work for 'im, lead work. It took them forever to get their money, and not all of it either. A right arrogant twat, they said.'

Derek continues to bury his head. 'He was alright wi' me,' he says. 'Very nice.'

'Didn't even offer 'em a cup o' tea!' adds Clappie, incredulously. 'He's lucky they didn't bloody strip the bloody roof rather than fix it!'

With that, Jimbo leans forward and places both hands on the bar to gain Derek's attention. 'So, are you gonna stop that cheque then?' he repeats. 'Shout me down if ya like, tell me to fuck off, bu' I only got your best interests at heart.'

'Dunno, I'll 'ave to 'ave a think,' he says, cupping his pint glass in both hands.

'Wha's there to think about? You're bein' scammed, Dekko.'

'I'd listen if I was you,' offers Clappie. 'But remember, I said fuck all.'

'Let's 'ave another drink,' says Derek. 'As I said, I need to think.

Chapter 25

With the pub filling steadily as people knock off work and slip in for a quick pint or more, the rest of the afternoon whips by in no time at all, and, as was ever going to be the case, Derek is thoroughly rat-arsed by the time Detlef and Maciej make their surprise appearance - roaring drunk in fact.

'Someone to see you, Dekko,' Jimbo alerts him, shaking his head at the sad inevitability of it all.

'Fuckin' 'ell! Wha' you doin' 'ere, Pops?!' Derek shouts as he stumbles over to welcome him, throwing his arms around his neck and almost, but not quite, kissing him on the cheek. 'Brilliant to see ya! Fuckin' brilliant! You should o' told me!'

For just a few short seconds, Detlef is pleasantly surprised and taken aback to be greeted in such a way until it becomes obvious that his son's behaviour is almost entirely due to alcohol. 'How are you, Derek?' he asks in return but failing to disguise a look of disappointment on his face.

'Fan-bloody-tastic!' yells Derek. 'You?'

'Yes, I'm OK. You don't mind if Maciej joins us, do you?' Detlef asks.

'Not at all! Any friend of yours!' says Derek, reaching around to shake his hand but over vigorously. 'So, what are the two of ya 'avin' then, eh?' he asks insistently. 'You got some fuckin' catchin' up to do, I can tell ya!'

'I can see,' says Detlef, forcing a smile.

'Well, you gotta give it some wallop, ain'tcha?' Derek carries on before throwing his arm around Detlef's neck once again and into something akin to a headlock. 'Life's too bleedin' short, innit? Ha-har!'

'What do you recommend?' asks Detlef, coughing and struggling to ease himself free.

'A proper English pint, tha's what!' says Derek. 'You wait 'til you taste it. Nectar o' the bloody Gods it is! Better than tha' German lager shite! It'll put hairs on yer chest!'

'I know it, Derek,' Detlef reminds him. 'I lived here for many years. Do you not remember?'

'Oh yeah. Sorry. Forgot. And wha' about your mate, ol' *Mitchee Mutchee* there? Wha's 'e want?'

'Just a coke for me, thanks,' Maciej answers for himself.

'A coke? That's not a fuckin' drink!' rages Derek, aghast. 'Don't be a tosser, 'ave summat decent! Anythin' ya like!'

'He's asked for a coke, Derek,' repeats Detlef firmly. 'He is driving.'

'Ha! No bugger bothers wi' that 'round 'ere! Vodka then. Can't smell it. You ask my mate! He'll be 'ere in a minute! Just take it steady!'

'I don't think that's a good idea, Derek. And, please, his name is Maciej.'

'Whichever, whatever. Oi, Jim! Drinks! Over 'ere! Now!' Derek then shouts. 'I wanna introduce you to me dad!'

Again, under the circumstances, Detlef doesn't quite know how to feel being called that. Certainly, over the years, he'd thought how wonderful it would be to be referred to as a father by his very own son, but here, now, it feels somehow tainted and insincere with Derek appearing even more drunk and unrestrained by the second.

'Be right with ya, Dekko,' Jimbo calls back, busy down at the other end.

'This is Clappie by the way,' Derek then says, pointing to him slumped on his stool, his back to the bar, an inane grin fixed upon his face. 'Good man he is, one o' the best.'

Detlef nods and smiles politely as Clappie manages to open one eye and lift his hand in acknowledgment.

'Just a bit of a lightweight, tha's all. Can't 'andle it,' says Derek, laughing and teetering. 'So, wha'choo been up to today?'

'Nothing much, Derek. I stayed in the hotel,' informs his father. 'I needed to rest.'

'Yeah, I bet. How are ya? Better I hope?' but adding before Detlef has a chance to answer, 'where's tha' then? Where ya stayin?'

'Redland. That's right, Maciej, isn't it,?' says Detlef, including him.

'Yes, Redland Park Hotel,' he says. 'It's a lovely old building, like castle.'

'Castle, eh? Nice,' says Derek. 'I jus' bought meself a penthouse down in the docks, modern as fuck it is! One an' a quarter million it cost me! Can you believe tha'? One an' a quarter million fuckin' pounds! Who'd o' thought it, eh?'

'That's a lot of money,' says Maciej, cautiously impressed.

'Innit just? Bu', mind you, I mi' 'ave to send it back. Dodgy 'parently,' Derek then spews out without making any sense at all. 'Not built neither,' he adds with a belch. 'Bastards. Tha' footballer's gonna be well pissed off!'

At that moment Jimbo comes over. 'Detlef isn't it?' he says, rolling his eyes sympathetically and offering his hand. 'I'm Jimbo, the landlord and a pal o' Dekko's. So, he's tellin' you both about this place he's bought, is he?'

'Don't start again, Jim. Let's get the drinks in first. Me dad'll 'ave a proper pint an' tha' little streak o' piss jus' wants a Coke,' says Derek in his attempt to be humorous but failing miserably. 'Oh, and stick another in for me, an' one for Clappie over there. In fact, get the whole pub another! I'm celebratin'!'

'Clappie's had enough, Dekko,' says Jimbo. 'An' why don't you ease up? Just for a bit, yeah? Wi' ya dad 'ere, an' that.'

'Fuck off, Jim! Remember who's payin' for all this!'

'Derek, please,' his father then says. 'Perhaps it would be better if we meet up over a coffee? I'll come back tomorrow, for your ceremony.'

'Why? Wha' 'ave I said? You've only just got 'ere! Please don't go! There's some more of me mates I want to introduce you to,' says Derek scanning the bar for a friendly face and, thankfully, seeing Phil walk in as if on cue.

As Derek goes to greet him, Jimbo quickly beckons Detlef in closer. 'Don't leave just yet,' he pleads. 'We need to have a word with him. He might listen to you?'

'I doubt he is in the mood to listen to anybody,' says Detlef.

'I think he would you. He ain't stopped talkin' about ya.'

'That is something, I suppose.'

'Sick o' hearin' about ya to be honest,' says Jimbo with a warm and friendly smile.

'He drinks far too much,' says Detlef. 'He needs help.'

'Yeah, we know that, but that ain't it. I think he might be in a spot o' bother. Danger even.'

'Dad, this is Phil!' Derek shouts as they come back over and stopping Detlef's and Jimbo's conversation. 'Me best mate!'

'Er, no hard feelin's from the other night, eh?' Phil says, offering his hand. 'Dekko's put us in the picture. Detlef innit?'

'Yes. Hello, Phil. Don't worry, I understand. You thought you were defending your friend.'

'Well, yeah, 'bout the size of it, what with him comin' up on the lottery an' you just turnin' up like that. Just seemed a bit of a coincidence.'

'Yeah! Wha' a laugh! Thought he was a right fuckin' gold-digger!' says Derek as he urgently grabs at the bar for support. 'Oops-a-daisy! Wha' ya 'avin', Phil?'

'Bloody 'ell, Dekko! You're seriously bolloxed already!' he says. 'Can you do 'im a coffee, Jim?' he asks.

'Coffee! Fuck off! Talk about fuckin' party poopers! Let's 'ave a giggle!' wails Derek.

'Sit 'im down, Phil,' orders Jimbo. 'There's summat important we gotta talk about now you're all here. Are you gonna tell 'em, Dekko, or am I?' he asks.

'Not again, Jim! Leave it, will ya? I'll do it, alright! I'll stop it!'

'Stop what?' asks Phil. 'Drinkin'?'

'Nah!' shouts Derek, 'I'll tell you all.'

'And about Jez too,' suggests Jimbo. 'I think your dad might like to know. It's his grandson after all.'

'Derek?' asks Detlef.

'I will, Pops, but first, as Phil's now 'ere, I got summat for ya! Dave can ''ave his later,' garbles Derek as he pulls out three cheques together with notes of various denominations that fall and scatter onto the floor.

'What the bloody hell you up to, Dekko?' asks Phil, second guessing. 'There's money goin' everywhere!'

His hands weaving all over the place, he gives both Phil and Jimbo a two hundred-and fifty-thousand-pound cheque each. 'I've filled 'em all out, all you gotta do is put in yer name in,' he slurs. 'You can 'ave one an all if ya want, Pops,' adds Derek, 'more if ya like!'

As the two recipients fall silent, poleaxed and not knowing what to say, Clappie is miraculously alerted from his stupor. 'I'll 'ave one too, if ya like,' he says, dribbling.

Chapter 26
Friday

It's the morning of the show. It's all happening.

Reenie's been in the kitchen since silly o'clock preparing a huge chilli-con-carne, now simmering in an industrial sized saucepan on the cooker.

She'd not long taken final delivery from an outside caterer too - well, a couple of local women who work out of their own homes for a bit of extra cash that is. Still, she'd insisted on nothing but the very best from them, and she'd got it. She was as happy as she can be.

Wrapped in cling-film, and on virtually every available surface, there are several large stainless steel trays of crustless triangular cut sandwiches, quiches, vol-au-vents, barbecue and coriander flavour chicken strips, rollmops, buffet pork pies, mini scotch eggs, sausage rolls a-go-go, tubs of coleslaw, potato salad, green salad, and cherry tomatoes (all of which were destined to go to waste of course), olives (those too), bread sticks, two dozen French baguettes, a full round of Brie and one of Camembert, a wedge of holey Emmental, a serious block of Cheddar, a small Stilton (she can't stand the stuff, just for show, she'd said) together with jars of pickled onions, enough grapes to sink a battleship (she'd only wanted 2lbs, not 2kgs) - oh, and two bloody great big trifles in deep glass bowls which she'd also made herself.

All that is left for her to do is to cook off the rice, put the peanuts, crisps, and Bombay mix into bowls, cut the carrots and celery for the party dips, pull off the cellophane, fold a large pack of red paper napkins into pirate-hats, and, finally, put it all out. Hey-presto! Job done!

Simultaneously, through in the bar and under orders as ever, poor Jimbo is huffing and puffing at the unnecessary effort of it all despite being a quarter of a million pounds better off. He's struggling with the large and cumbersome piece of framed chipboard that fits neatly over the pool table and which serves as an additional and makeshift buffet table for the occasional birthday, the odd wedding or wake.

'Have you got the tablecloth for this bloody thing?' he calls out as he whips away his fingers to allow the board to drop heavily into place - *th'wump!*

'Don't you worry yourself about that!' she shouts back. 'I haven't heard the sound of that vacuum cleaner yet!'

'I'm doin' it in a minute, woman! I'm bloody doin' it!' he yells as, quickly, he hits the button on the old Henry with his foot, sparking it noisily into life and silencing his wife at least.

-

Just a mile or so down the road and nursing a sharp and stabbing headache made even worse by his two yapping hounds still desperately awaiting their early morning walk, Clappie is wrestling with the onerous decision of whether or not to phone PG to tell him what he'd heard said in the pub last night.

He liked Dekko, liked him a lot, and didn't really want to upset or betray him, but there was his own livelihood to consider and, nice a bloke as he was, Dekko isn't about to start paying his bills for the foreseeable future, is he? No. There was no huge cheque for him last night.

So, in the desperate hope of getting back in with PG, together with the slim possibility that there might be a little something in it for him too, Clappie picks up the receiver.

-

In the dining room of the Redland Park Hotel, Detlef is sitting down to a very modest breakfast - a slice of thinly buttered toast and a coffee. Having had three and a half pints of beer the previous evening, and more alcohol he'd had in years, it's all he can stomach or manage.

Stirring his cup, he's again deep in thought and beginning to feel ever more homesick. His trip to find his son seems to have lasted far more than just a few short days and, not only is he missing his family tremendously, but he's also becoming exhausted by it all and continues to be unsettled by the unrelenting emotions of guilt and betrayal together with concern for his son and his family.

Even after the lengthy calls he'd made to Gisella and Renata the day before, he'd still failed to tell them the whole truth. Not only was he unable or unwilling to divulge the true nature of Derek's character, or the impact the events were having on his own health and wellbeing, but also that he'd planned to take Ellen out on their day trip together. It made him feel very uneasy indeed and not something he felt he could easily discuss at opposite ends of a telephone line without being completely misunderstood.

He had, however, informed them both that he was going over to see Derek again, to which they'd both asked that he pass on their best wishes (which, under the circumstances of Derek's severe drunkenness, he'd omitted to do) and had also forewarned his wife that he might not be back until a little later and so not to wait up for his regular night-time call. But she was having none of it. 'I cannot rest until I know you are back safely,' she'd insisted. 'Please ring me when you return to the hotel.'

So, when at last he did finally get back, well after eleven o'clock (made even later by the fact that they'd had to bundle Derek into the back of Maciej's taxi to take him home, such was the state he was in) Gisella could easily detect that he had been drinking and she'd remonstrated with him for taking such an unnecessary risk. *'Ich kann es kaum erwarten, dass du nach Hause kommst,'* she'd said, turning the conversation around to speak of his imminent return.

'I cannot wait to come home too,' he'd replied to her in English before quickly correcting himself.

'Ha!' she'd laughed, but not entirely in jest. 'Are you becoming an Englishman already?'

'… an' that's what I heard,' says Clappie in conclusion. 'Straight up, PG. Honest.'

'*Are you absolutely sure? Not one of your silly wind-ups?*' he questions, sat in his office and playing with a desk toy, a Newton's cradle - *tick-tack-tick-tack.*

'Yeah! No! I wouldn't be tellin' ya otherwise, would I?'

'*You still sound a little slurred to me.*'

'Not denyin' I'd had a few, but, jeez, I know what was said! He's gonna stop the cheque!'

The line goes silent for a few seconds.

'Are you still there?' asks Clappie as his dogs start baying for his attention once again.

'*Yes, of course I'm still here! Can you not shut those blasted animals up? I need to think!*' he snaps, uncharacteristically raising his voice.

Clappie puts down the receiver and takes them in his sitting room, shutting the door. On returning to the phone, he can clearly hear PG ranting to himself.

'*Why do I get involved with these blasted people? Fucking lowlife!*' he's saying.

'Unlike you to use that sort o' language,' says Clappie. 'You alright?'

'*Shut up! What time was it when you heard all this?*'

'I dunno. Early evening, I s'pose.'

'*Are you positive? Was it after the banks close do you remember? Four-thirty.*'

'Good-god, yeah! It was well after his old man turned up, so about six-thirty, sevenish I'd say. They were all talkin' about it - him, his dad, Jimbo behind the bar, his mate Phil, all of 'em.'

'*Interesting,*' says PG, his tone changing into one of a plan being hatched.

'What is?'

'*His father you say?*'

'Yeah, or tha's wha' he says he is.'

'*He's that elderly German that's suddenly appeared on the scene, isn't he?*'

'How d'you know that?'

'*Never you mind. What's his name?*'

'Dunno, begins with a D, I think.'

'*I shall have to find out. Derek has children too, doesn't he?*'

'Whoah, PG! I ain't getting' into anythin' 'eavy like that.'

'*Just relax. I'm not an idiot.*'

'I'm not sayin' you are.'

'*Better not be either. Are you heading there for the presentation this morning?*'

'Said I'd drop in, help him celebrate. That's alright, innit? Brian's goin' too I think.'

'I know.'

'Not much escapes your notice, does it?'

'No, it doesn't, and you'd do well to remember it. So, midday, yes?'

'Yeah, that's what he said. Kicks off about twelve.'

'Good. I might need you both.'

'You comin' an' all then?' asks Clappie in disbelief.

'Yes.'

'It's gonna be alright, isn't it?'

'Of course! Now, go and drink some coffee and clear your head.'

'OK, OK, I will, but before you go, … I hate to ask, … is there any chance of a little summat for all o' this, PG? A little thank you? I do try me best for ya, you know that.'

'You've heard the phrase 'shoot the messenger', Clappie, haven't you?'

'Well, yeah. Everyone 'as, ain't they?'

'Then you can thank me for not doing just that … or having your limbs rearranged. I'll see you at midday. Don't let me down, and don't be late,' says PG before ending the call and swiping the toy off the desk, crashing it to the floor, breaking it.

-

With a couple of hours to wait before Maciej picks him up, Detlef returns to his room to take some further and much needed rest.

Trying to relax on the bed, he does at least recall that last night had not been entirely unpleasant for him, far from it. There were elements that he'd quite enjoyed with Derek's friends all being very supportive and amiable towards him. Sure, there were some jibes at his nationality, but for the best part it had all been good natured and jovial. Strangely, it had taken him back to those Friday evenings so very long ago when, in the company of the other farm hands after a long and hard week's work they'd enjoyed a beer in the Fleur-de-Lis, Norton St Philip or cider in Tucker's Grave and when they'd began to show him more respect and refer to him by name, not 'that bloody Kraut' or 'Bosch Boy.'

However, it is not long before Detlef is worrying once again about Derek's extremely excessive drinking, and, in addition, there is his lottery win too. He can easily foresee the pitfalls and potential danger that such a huge and life changing sum would likely present, particularly to someone pursuing a solitary male existence and exhibiting such reckless and rudderless behaviour, made infinitely worse by his addiction. It concerns him greatly to see his son so obviously drinking himself to death.

In the quiet stillness of his room, he knows he must try to talk to him, in sobriety, and attempt to steer him towards a more wholesome and worthwhile lifestyle, and all before his return home on Sunday! Moreover, as he had discovered last night, it is not only his son's life he needs to consider, but that of his three grandchildren too, and those he is shortly about to meet. In particular, he is concerned for the young boy

Jez and the trouble he had found himself in. It is all worrying him very deeply indeed.

-

Woken by a bout of coughing and still fully clothed, Derek opens his eyes and can immediately see the receipt from Tate Holdings lodged up and facing him on his bedside table with the words 'Stop the bloody cheque!!!!!' scrawled right across it.

At that very moment, his phone rings. It's Phil.

'You stopped it yet?' he asks immediately and without any preamble.

'I ain't awake yet,' groans Derek.

'You ain't got long. Twenty-four hours! You gotta get on with it!'

'I know, I know.'

'So, how you feelin'?'

'Been better.'

'I'm not fuckin' surprised, Dekko. You were a right arse 'ole last night in front 'o your dad.'

'Was I?'

'Yeah, you were, called us all cunts, 'im too, when we wouldn't let you 'ave another drink.'

'Did I?' says Derek, cringing.

'Yeah, you went ballistic before we managed to bundle you home.'

'So, was it you that got me back 'ome?'

'Yeah, in that little Polish lad's taxi. Your dad too.'

'Me dad too?'

'Yeah.'

'Fuck.'

'It was a right fuckin' palaver tryin' to get you up your stairs.'

'Fuck.'

'You gotta sort your drinkin', Dekko. It's gettin' seriously out o' hand. He's worried about ya, your ol' man.'

'Is he?'

'Yeah. He reckons you'll end up killin' yerself.'

'He ain't the only one.'

'Wha'd'ya mean by that?'

'Julie.'

'Oh yeah. You said. Well, you'd better start listenin' then.'

'He still comin'? Me dad?'

'Think so, tha's what he said.'

'I'll stop it then, shall I?'

'Yeah, you do that, an' the cheque.'

'Don't you want it then? Yours?'

'Very funny, you know wha' I mean. I left the receipt there for ya, by your light. 'Ave ya seen it?'

'Yeah, I got it 'ere in me hand.'

Well do it then, yeah?'

'OK. I will.'

'Oh, an' Dekko.'

'What?'

'Thanks, mate.'

'Shut up before I change me mind,' says Derek, walking to the kitchen to find the telephone directory.

-

Working on the premise that the cheque has already been stopped, PG knows he's got to act fast. He needs answers, solutions, and, hopefully, vitally, before Sir Alun gets wind of it. Moreover, he simply can't have his own carefully laid out plans be destroyed like this or, indeed, jeopardise his own very significant investment in the harbourside development.

It seems to him, as he starts to get himself ready and at the bathroom sink, gently lathering his face, razor in hand, that if one final act of gentle persuasion will not win the day, then perhaps some slightly more heavy-handed tactics might be called for. The stick needs to be enacted, he considers, the carrot put away.

As he stretches his skin taught with his fingertips, he considers who might be his best point of leverage and easiest potential target.

-

It seems like an eternity before the bank finally answers.

After giving his details and passing security, Derek is surprised to find his call is swiftly redirected to another department. He'd made a mistake he tells them. No problem, they reassure him. Even though a request for 'express clearing' had already been placed, he was in time.

He was OK, they inform him.

He was in the clear.

Although relieved to be off the hook, Derek can simply bear it no longer. 'Stuff this for a game o' bleedin' soldiers,' he says, pulling on his clothes and grabbing his jacket and it's not long before he's waving frantically above the net curtains and knocking at the pub door yet again.

'Bloody hell, mate, we ain't nearly ready for ya yet,' says Jimbo as he slides the bolts and unlocks the latch.

'Gonna let us in then?'

'O' course! Don't worry. I can't thank you enough.'

'Wha' for?'

'The bloody money, wha' d'ya think?'

'Oh yeah. You're welcome. Forget it. Just give us a bloody pint,' he pleads.

'Funny last night, seein' your old man takin' you off 'ome to bed,' says Jimbo, pulling the beer through into a large plastic jug. 'You never 'ad that before, did ya? A dad lookin' out for ya like that?' he adds.

'No.'

'He's a good bloke, Dekko, your dad. Solid. I know it's a bit late in the day, but you're a lucky man.'

Derek turns away and picks up the cue ball from the pool table, dropping it into a pocket. He's welling up, hiding it, but not knowing entirely why.

'Hey, Reenie!' Jimbo calls out. 'Look who's just turned up! Come through an' 'ave a look what she's done for ya, Dekko,' he insists. 'I think you'll be impressed.'

Chapter 27

With Jimbo now busy with the Brasso and Derek already well into his fourth pint of the morning, both turn as they hear voices and movement from outside.

The first to enter is a smartly dressed young woman in a suited jacket and skirt, her bum holding the door, in her arms a methuselah of champagne. 'Hi guys!' she says, bubbling with well-trained excitement. 'I'm Beckah … from the lottery!'

'And I'm Patrick,' announces the second with a courteous wave - an older chap with a serious looking camera slung heavily around his neck, a telescopic tripod held firmly in one hand. 'And this is Tobes,' he adds as a young lad follows in behind them carrying a large piece of stiff white card and trying very hard not to bend or catch the corners.

Beckah eases the heavy bottle onto the bar and immediately spots Derek sat at the far end. 'Ah, Dekko, brilliant!' she says. 'You're already here. I was told you prefer to be called that rather than Derek? Is that right?'

'Yeah, bu' how d'you know it was me?' he asks, genuinely surprised. 'I've never seen ya before in my life, 'ave I?'

'I can always spot a winner,' she says cheekily.

'How?' he says, doubtfully.

'Well, only sometimes,' she then admits, laughing. 'I was in the offices when you came in to pick up your cheque. I saw you. We all did. You and your friends are famous!'

'Ah, yeah, OK … next,' dismisses Derek as Jimbo, flushing pink, randomly wipes a few nozzles with his duster. 'Tha' what I think it is?' he then asks, gesturing towards the card held by the young lad.

'Might be,' she says, continuing to tease, 'but you're not allowed to look at it yet. It'll ruin the surprise.'

It's Derek's turn to laugh. 'Hate to tell ya, girl, but l already got it in me bank,' he informs her.

'I know you have,' she says as Toby carefully sets it down, dutifully making sure that it faces the wall. 'But you wait 'til you see it, your name on it, all those numbers. Brings it to life somehow. I've seen people go all silly.'

Derek waves the comment away. 'So, is it mine to keep then? Afterwards?' he asks.

'Sure is.'

'I'll stick it on the wall next to me Rovers poster, shall I?'

'I would. Definitely. Get it framed. Lots do.'

Alerted by the voices in the bar, Reenie makes her appearance, a large bowl of wobbling trifle held tight to her chest. 'Hi, you're here already,' she says, carefully putting the dessert down on the nearest table and wiping her hands on her apron. 'I'm Irene,' she introduces herself. 'Landlady and licensee.'

'Yes, Irene, we spoke to you on the phone, I believe,' says Beckah. 'Dekko gave us your number.'

'That's right, we did, and I'd like to take this opportunity to welcome you to the Traveller's Rest, an honest to goodness public house in this wonderful city of Bristol of ours,' she says like she was pitching for England's Best Kept Pub or something.

'What a welcome! That's so nice of you. I do love a proper boozer.'

Reenie flinches. 'I hope we're a little bit more than that?' she says a tad indignantly.

'Yeah, of course. Sorry. I didn't mean anything by it. I just love my pubs. Proper pubs. Like this one,' backtracks Beckah before quickly returning her attention. 'Now, Dekko,' she says, 'we just need to discuss a couple of details before we get started. You OK with that?'

But Reenie isn't finished yet, she'd been rehearsing. 'As you can see,' she continues with a sweep of her arm like she was now presenting the prizes on a TV game show. 'I've laid on some very tasty homemade food for everyone.'

'I can see. You've been very busy. Thank you everso much. So, Dekko, ...'

'Yes, and I'm pleased to announce we're in the process of redesigning our menu to cater for the more discerning diner.'

With that, Jimbo, now cringing with embarrassment, ducks his head under the bar on the pretext of rearranging the glasses. '*The more discerning diner,*' he silently mimics her. '*You don't want chips wi' that, you wanna a bit o' bloody lettuce!*'

'Good idea,' Beckah placates her. 'We all have to reinvent ourselves nowadays, don't we? Take on board new ideas?'

'Exactly! You hear that, Jim?' says Reenie. 'Where are you? Where've you gone?'

'Here, love,' he says, reappearing like some dishevelled old glove puppet.

'Did you hear? Beckah agrees with me.'

'Does she, my petal? Tha's lovely.'

'And I've got some super cheeses too,' Reenie carries on. 'Big ones. Would you like a little taster now?'

'Bit early for me, Irene, cheese,' Beckah answers uncertainly. 'I've not long had breakfast.'

'It'll only take me a minute. I'll get a knife.'

'No, honestly. Later maybe?' Beckah stops her as politely as she can.

'Perhaps some of our chilli con carne then? I've got some freshly boiled rice, ... or d'you want a crusty French stick?'

'Please, Reen!' implores Jimbo. 'As the girl said, a bit later, yeah? They got more important things to discuss right now.'

'I was only offerin'! Thought they might like a bit o' somethin' before they got started.'

'No, no, that's very kind of you, and we will, but not just yet,' says Beckah apologetically. 'It's really appreciated. Honestly. More often than not, we have to make do with a shop bought sandwich.'

'Just help yourself when you're ready, love,' offers Jimbo.

'It's Jim, isn't it?' Beckah asks him as Reenie huffily returns to the kitchen. 'Thank you, Irene,' she calls after her.

'Don't worry. She'll be alright,' reassures Jimbo, offering his hand. 'But, yeah. Tha's me, chief bottle washer an' head-sweeper-upper - at your service.'

'I know the feeling,' says Beckah, pulling a bit of a face. 'Look, I don't suppose you've got somewhere cold for that bottle, have you?' she says, pointing at the champagne. 'Only I don't want it going off like a rocket.'

'Yeah, sure. I'll find a space in the chillers out the back,' he says, lifting it up. 'Phew! Whopper innit?'

'Isn't it just! Weighs a ton. My arms were killing me. Oh, and we've got some flutes in the car, just in case you need them. Not that I'm saying you do,' she adds now being over cautious.

'Yeah, yeah,' accepts Jimbo, 'that'll be good. We don't 'ave that many wine glasses.'

'Yes, we do!' they all hear Reenie's voice call from out the back. 'I bought some!'

Jimbo tries to laugh it off. 'Ignore her,' he mouths whilst drawing his finger across his neck.

'So? Puttin' on a marchin' band for me an' all, are we?' Derek pipes up, joking.

'No, there's no band, Dekko,' says Beckah now looking totally ill at ease and confused.

'Flutes?' he repeats, helping her along.

'Ha! Sorry! Being a bit slow this morning!'

'Shame though,' adds Derek. 'I enjoy a bit o' woodwind.'

'You should have said,' says Beckah. 'I'm sure we could have done something.'

'But don't you worry, mate,' says Jimbo with a wink. 'I got a bit of a surprise for ya later, on the music front.'

Derek guesses straight away. 'Oh no! Not Roxxii?' he says.

'But I thought you liked her!'

'I do, singin', but not … you know … that. She'll be over me like a bloody rash again.'

'There's gratitude for ya!' says Jimbo but laughing. 'Wish I hadn't bothered.'

'I'm gonna need another bloody pint now!' exclaims Derek like it was the furthest thing from his mind. 'So, what you all 'avin'?' he asks them all. 'Join me why don't ya?'

As was ever going to be the case, it's not long before the Traveller's Rest is almost full to bursting with very many more than its usual Friday lunchtime trade. Loads more, in fact.

For starters, there's a sizeable contingent from what can only be described as the 'Professional Funeral Goers Brigade' who'd got wind of the free-for-all event and, incongruous in their overly smart clothes and buffed up shoes, hover impatiently over by the heaving tables of covered food.

Roxxii, too, had added to the numbers considerably when she'd arrived in fifteen-seater minibus filled with family and friends, all dressed similarly in cowboy hats and bootlace ties. Cheered on by them, she'd covered Derek in lipstick wet kisses as soon as she'd walked in, telling him that she had the details of a recording studio that she'd like him to take a look at. 'You can come and sit in if ya want, you lovely man, you,' she'd offered, all smiles and pussy-cat pouts. 'After all, it's you that'll be payin' for it!'

It's also apparent that Reenie had not been slow in spreading the news either, as, also over by the buffet, but sneakily slipping out the odd sandwich or two from underneath the clingfilm, a few members of the local press await the main event in typical hangdog fashion, their camera cases tucked in close by their feet, notepads peeping dog-eared from out of their waxed jacket pockets.

But the real buzz of activity is over on Crackers Corner of course, where Derek, together with Phil and his wife Betsy and Clappie in shameless attendance, is happily holding court. He has a new and eager audience and they're lapping it all up, but not before he'd ensures they all have a drink in their hands. 'Look lively, Jimbo!' he calls again and again. 'People are dyin' over 'ere!'

It's then that Phil notices Marion arrive with the three children. 'Hey, Dekko, your family's 'ere,' he tells him with a nudge and interrupting him full flow as he spouts off about the relative advantages of holidaying in an all-inclusive hotel on the Costa del Sol over a self-catering private villa, even if it does have its own private pool. 'I mean, who wants to be fuckin' cookin', eh?' he's asking. 'Waste o' drinkin' time, innit?'

'Oh, an' look out, your dad an' his driver 'ave just walked in too,' Phil adds. 'Best o' luck.'

Eagerly, as Derek goes over to greet them, he can see that Detlef and Maciej are standing directly behind Marion and the kids but, not knowing each other from Adam, are totally unaware of each other's presence. 'You made it then?' he shouts above all the heads and pushing his way through.

With little more than a discrete but knowing nod towards Detlef, like he might just be someone he happened to know, Derek approaches his children first. 'Hello, you lot!' he starts off. 'Marion. Now, before I get you all summat to drink, there's someone I'd like you all t'meet,' he says like it was an everyday occurrence.

Detlef now realises what is obviously about to happen and who are standing directly in front of him - his very own flesh and blood. Swallowing hard and feeling wholly unprepared, he surreptitiously sweeps his hand over his thinning hair and smooths himself down.

'Jules, Jez, Janice,' Derek addresses each of his three children in turn, 'this,' he says as he moves around to put his hand on his father's shoulder, 'this,' he repeats, pausing for dramatic effect, 'this is your granddad.' Just like that he says it. No preamble, no explanation, just straight out with it. *Wallop!*

To be fair, Detlef hadn't been sure what to expect upon meeting his grandchildren for the very first time either, but, certainly, he hadn't considered it would be anything like this, so abrupt, so unceremonious, and being jostled back and forth by the boisterous and noisy pub crowd. He smiles at them, lifting his hand in greeting. 'Hello,' he says.

As they all return his gaze with incredulous ones of their own, he can easily see the family resemblance in each of them. But it is Janice, in particular, that catches his attention. Despite her look of open-mouthed astonishment, it is the very shape of her face, her misleadingly doleful eyes, and even the way she stands with one leg turned in and an arm held loosely across her abdomen like she might be perpetually bored that reminds him so much of his daughter back at home.

'Is this another one of your silly jokes, Derek?' asks Marion almost aggressively.

'Nope.'

'But I thought ...'

'Then you thought wrong then, didn't ya?' says Derek, grinning. 'I'd like you all to meet me dad,' he reaffirms.

'They didn't know I would be here, Derek?' Detlef questions him.

'Nope, I wanted it to be a surprise,' he says before leaning in towards him. 'Sorry 'bout last night by the way,' he whispers.

But before any of them has even a chance to let it remotely sink in or to ask a question, Patrick the photographer's voice booms out from over by the bar. 'Ladies and gentlemen, can I have your attention please?' he shouts, clapping his hands. 'In just a few short moments, weather permitting, we shall be going outside to present Dekko with his cheque and take a few photos (to which there is a typical ripple of cheers and jeers) and Dekko has expressed his wish to get as many of you in the shots as well. So, for those that would like to join us, or just watch if you've got something to hide and don't want your boss or the other half to see you in the pub on a Friday morning (greeted with yet more groans and laughter) please feel free to make your way outside and join us.'

As the crowd then begin to stir, Jez speaks. 'But he's dead, ain't he, your dad, Dad?' he asks, confused. 'Tha's what you told us.'

'I had it wrong, son.'

'Are you being serious?' asks Julie, repeating her mother's suspicion.

'Serious as I'll ever be, love,' he says. 'This is your gran'dad alright. Look at us,' he says, putting his face parallel alongside his father's. 'Peas out a bleedin' pod. See?'

Now unsure whether to hug them, shake hands, or simply await their reaction, Detlef makes an almost indiscernible movement forward. 'My name is Detlef,' he says but almost drowned out as the exiting crowd gain momentum on either side of them. 'And you must be

Marion, the proud mother,' he continues, politely addressing her first and offering her his hand.

'Hi,' she reciprocates and instantly recalling a visit she'd made to see Ellen only just a few months back when the old lady had said she'd nearly ending up living on a farm shortly after she got married and something about a German farmhand there. At the time, Marion had simply put it down to a bit of confusion, or the onset of dementia. 'Were you and Ellen … together?' she seeks to clarify.

'Yes, we were married,' Detlef confirms.

'You were married?! So, who was the bloke that worked in the docks, Dekko?'

'Don't you get it, Marion?' says Derek, sounding exasperated. 'He was a lie! He never existed!'

'I don't believe it. What? Your own family told you that?'

'Yeah! My bloody family!' says Derek, getting out the now sellotaped together photo from his wallet. 'This is Detlef here. Me mum gave it to me years ago. Told me to keep quiet about it, although I didn't understand why.'

Marion takes it to have a look then passes it to Detlef.

'But what sort o' name is that?' Jez then asks, finding it all very amusing. 'Detlef or whatever. An' why does he talk all funny?'

'Because he's a German, son,' explains his dad and sounding strangely proud of it.

'German?' repeats Janice.

'Yeah. Problem?'

'No! Not at all!'

'What? German, like Audi TT's ya mean?' says Jez.

'Yes,' Detlef confirms, smiling to himself. 'German like Audi TT's.'

'Wow! Say something then! Go on!'

Detlef hands the photo back to Derek before obliging. *'Mein Name ist Detlef und du musst Jez sein. Wie geht es dir, mein Enkel?*

'Did he just say my name?' Jez hoots. 'I heard it! Will you write somethin' on my arm?' he then requests, lifting the plaster cast.

'If you would like?' says Detlef, looking for approval from the rest of the family before reaching into his jacket for a pen. 'How did you break it?'

'Don't ask,' says Derek. 'But can you do it later, Pops, yeah? We gotta move.'

Marion, still in a state of shock, speaks again. 'I must admit,' she says, 'it's true. You do look alike, the pair of ya. That photo, looks just like Dekko as a younger man.'

'Yeah! I was just thinkin' that. Bloody identical in fact!' exclaims Janice before throwing caution to the wind and planting a kiss on Detlef's cheek. 'Welcome to the family, ya poor ol' sod, you!' she says. 'You'll probably end up regrettin' it soon enough though!'

Detlef, thoroughly taken aback by this unexpected show of affection and obvious sign of acceptance, is unsure how to react.

'I've never had a Grampy,' says Julie, sweetly, reaching forward to touch him on the arm and giving him a gentle kiss too.

Derek, now surrounded by almost his entire family and standing in his beloved pub, a tsunami of high-spirited and raucous people now trying to sweep them out the door, feels happier and more content than he could possibly ever have imagined in his entire life. It was like he'd won the jackpot all over again, but, somehow, this time, it felt even more important - more special. 'Well, you've got one now, Jules,' he tells her, beaming from ear to ear, 'an' 'ere he is!'

Just in sight of the pub, PG's dark maroon Jaguar pulls up nose to tail behind Brian's beefy black BMW.

As Brian gets out to approach, PG presses the button and lowers the kerbside passenger window. 'Have you seen Clappie yet?' he asks as he watches the photographer spread the legs of his tripod and people beginning to spill out.

'He'll be amongst tha' lot somewhere, gettin' pissed up,' says Brian, his forearm on the roof, his face all but filling the gap above the window. 'So, wha' d'ya wannae do?'

'Watch. Wait. Jump in.'

'I'll jump in alright!' says Brian and with the suggestion of a head-butt. 'I wan' ma cut!'

'I meant get in the car, you fool!' PG reprimands him. 'Have you remembered the watch?' he then asks.

'Aye, it's in ma motor.'

'Well go and get it and brin g it back here.'

'Now, can everyone clear the steps?' calls Patrick, loudly and clearly. 'We just want some photos of Dekko and his family on their own first of all,' he instructs the crowd.

As people obediently move themselves out of shot, Julie and Jez line up on one side of their dad with Janice holding onto Detlef's arm on the other. But Marion holds back, uncertain as to what to do, uncertain as to whether she is family. She looks to her ex for an answer. 'Dekko?' she asks him, her eyes wide and demanding an answer.

'Just shut up an' get in,' he tells her.

Sat in its cradle attached to the console, PG's phone begins to ring.

'Tha' who I think it is?' asks Brian seeing the name come up.

'Yes. Keep quiet,' he warns him before picking up. 'PG speaking,' he answers.

'Sir Alun,' says Sir Alun, the anger already palpable in his voice.

'Ah, Sir Alun, I was about to call you.'

'Were you?'

'Yes.'

'What about?'

'The paintings,' PG lies. 'I was wondering …'

'I'm not interested in the bloody paintings, Peter! I'm interested in the money!'

'What money?'

'Don't take the piss! You know exactly what I'm talking about!'

'I'm sorry?'

'That cheque. It's been stopped.'

'Stopped?'

'Yes, stopped! What's happened?'

'Are you serious?'

'Of course, I'm fucking serious! This morning. Piers called the bank.'

PG falls silent for a moment. 'The bastard!' he then says. 'I'll go and see him, sort it out. Don't worry.'

'You'd bloody better! When?'

'Very shortly, Sir Alun,' says PG. 'I'll get onto it right now.'

'Have you got it, Beckah?' asks Patrick as the boys from the local press take up their positions behind him.

Carefully, Toby hands over the oversize cheque for her to present.

'Here you are, Dekko,' she says, turning it around to finally let him to have a look. 'What do you think of that then, eh?'

Slowly, Derek reads it. *Derek Dando,* it says - *Eleven million, three hundred and fifty-five thousand pounds,* all written large and as clear as day, and, sure enough, it does have an unexpected and powerful effect on him as, spontaneously and from somewhere deep inside, he lets out a great roar - a giant guffaw of relief and joy that finally obliterates any lingering sense of 'pinch me and wake me up' disbelief that he still might have harboured.

He takes it from her, snatches it almost, and holds it aloft for everyone else to see, the sounds of groans, cheers, and the whirr of reflex cameras filling the air.

'So, wha's the plan then?' asks Brian as they watch the events unfold.

'I need to get him on his own,' says PG.

'Then wha'?'

'A quiet word in the first instance.'

'If you dinnae mind me sayin', you dinnae sound so sure.'

'Shut up! Just do as I say. I want you to act as if everything is in order and we are just here to wish him well. Just watch my back. I want Clappie in there too.'

'I can see 'im now. Look. says Brian, pointing. 'See tha top of e's peanut heed?'

'Yes. Good.'

'Bu' why don't we jus' pu' tha frighteners on him,' Brian repeats. 'I mean, it's not as if he's gettin' nuthin' fer 'is money, is it? Tell 'im he's go' a contract, tha' you'll sue 'im, tha' we can make 'is life very uncomfortable if he dinnae play ball.'

'It's about expediency, Brian. I want a quick solution, like today, not some drawn out court case. I'll tell you as and when to play rough, do you hear me?'

'OK. Your call. An' just so's ya know, the ol' fellah standin' next to 'im is tha' German I was tellin' you about, the one tha' sez he's 'is father.'

'I'd guessed as much but thank you.'

'Great, I think we've got that,' Patrick calls out loud once again. 'Now, Dekko, if you and your family can move forward a touch such that as many people as possible can get behind you and up onto the steps, we'll get that champagne out.'

'Thought you'd never ask,' Derek shouts back eagerly and loving every moment.

As the crowd now move in behind them, with Phil, Betsy, together with Clappie squeezing in alongside, Toby, who'd already removed the foil and eased out the twist on the wire cage, hands him the bottle.

'Ah, champagne,' observes PG. 'Time to make an entrance, methinks,' he says as, purposefully and simultaneously, both he and Brian open the doors and step out.

Of course, Derek simply cannot resist shaking the bottle as vigorously as he can and like he'd seen done so many times on the winner's rostrum of a Formula One race on the telly. Needless to say, the cork does go off like a bloody rocket, flying high up into the sky.

To more great cheers, and with the bubbly spuming out and wasting itself on the pitted and crumbling tarmac, all eyes attempt to follow its trajectory before it bounces harmlessly at PG's feet who is crossing the road. He bends to pick it up and inspects it, smells it, and nods approvingly. 'Nice bottle, Derek,' he says, 'very nice indeed. Do you mind if we come and join you?'

Without waiting for an answer, Brian clears a path for PG to stand directly behind such that his face is framed between that of Derek and his father's. 'You need to take a knife and cut a coin into this,' suggests PG and passing the cork over.

'Nah, you're OK. You keep it,' says Derek.

'But it's meant to be good luck. I'm sure I've got some money on me somewhere,' PG continues and rummaging in his pockets.

'No. Honestly. You have it.'

'Here, I've found it. A fifty pence piece,' says PG like he hasn't heard and now offering him both the cork and the coin. 'That should do it.'

'OK. I'll do it later, yeah?' Derek agrees and putting them in his pocket.

'You do that. So, I was wondering, might have a friendly little chat when you've finished here? Discuss a few things?'

'But I got all me family 'ere, PG,' says Derek, beginning to squirm. 'Could be difficult.'

'Only five minutes. Somewhere private. Oh, by the way, I've got another watch for you. I shall have to have words with the jewellers about the other one. Brian, can I have it?'

'Nah, leave it. They're a bit heavy on me wrist to be honest,' Derek tries to refuse again.

'That's not nice, Derek. It's a gift.'

'Look. I'm sorry, PG,' he says and knowing the pretence is up, 'but I just changed me mind, alright?'

'What's that?' PG feigns ignorance.

'You know, the penthouse. It ain't really me, now is it? Somewhere posh like that?' he offers by way of an explanation.

'Ah, that explains it. I wondered why Sir Alun was getting a tad nervous when I just spoke to him.'

'Is he?' asks Derek guiltily.

'Yes. And we don't want to upset him, now do we? Not wise, upsetting someone like Sir Alun. Very unwise indeed. Now, this little chat?'

Detlef, listening intently and fully understanding what this is all about, speaks up. 'He says he doesn't want to talk to you.'

'And you are?' PG enquires with a sneer.

'His father.'

'Ah yes, a little bird has told me about you. Strange you should turn up right now, isn't it?'

'What are you saying?'

'I think that's entirely obvious. Don't you? It's amazing what'll crawl out of the woodwork at the smell of all Derek's money.'

'Now that's enough, PG,' Derek rebukes him. 'That's not true an' I don't want any trouble.'

But PG leans in even closer, his mouth only inches from Derek's ear. 'Tell me, have you had a paternity test done yet? I would if I was you,' he whispers but loud enough for Detlef to hear.

With that, the old man suddenly looks very pale, his body rigid. 'Leave my son alone, please,' he warns him.

'I shall do as I please,' PG informs him.

'Leave us alone,' Detlef warns him once again.

PG scoffs. 'I don't think I'll be taking any orders off an old kraut like you,' he says.

Big mistake.

With the words barely left PG's lips, Detlef turns and with the force, speed, and agility that belies his age, double punches PG hard to the face, and then, for good measure, delivers a sharp uppercut into his rib cage, immediately folding his body in two.

Th'wack, th'wack, wumph!

PG crumples to the floor like the proverbial sack of potatoes.

Again, the cameras burst into action.

They catch it all, every last moment.

Chapter 28

As they all excitedly shuffle their way back up the steps, Jez, despite one arm being in plaster, is clacking the fingers of both hands hip-hop gangsta style. 'Wha' was tha' all about?' he's whooping. 'Wicked!'

Clicking his fingers reprimanding dad style, Derek attempts to silence him. 'Alright, you,' he insists, a minor graze to the side of his face, a tiny droplet of blood already congealing on his cheek. 'That's enough, d'ya hear me? Enough.'

All the same, Jez could be forgiven his excitement. The atmosphere is buzzing with chat and laughter and copycat jabs. They all relish a bit of fisticuffs - love it they do.

You see, pretty much everyone that knew PG, or had just heard the tales, understood that one day, he'd probably had it coming to him. But who, in their right bloody mind, would have thought it would have been Dekko's Dad, an old German bloke that most didn't even know existed until just a few short minutes ago, would be the one to give PG what for?

None of them. Not a single one.

'Paff, paff! Bloody nice combo, ol' fellah!' congratulates one of those now boisterously crowding the bar and demanding yet more free drink.

'Yeah, jus' like Boom-Boom Minter,' offers another much older man, grinning and remembering.

Others, however, are not quite so gushing in their praise. 'Braver man than me,' says a third but gleefully eyeing him like he was already a dead man walking.

It was madness. Glorious, but madness all the same.

Now, albeit safely ensconced on Crackers Corner together with his newly acquired family member and friends, Detlef is looking anxious and not a little embarrassed. He's trembling too - not with fear you understand, no, but with an adrenalin rush he'd long since forgotten. 'I'm so sorry, Derek,' he's repeating. 'What was I thinking? I should not have hit him. I've ruined your big day.'

'Well, wouldn't go so far as to say that, Pops,' reassures his son, tapping the now rather battered and soiled presentation cheque wedged between him and the bar with his foot. 'Although your timin' might o' been a bit better. I'll gi' ya that.'

'Are you alright?' Janice then asks her grandfather. 'You look a bit shaky. Do you need to sit down?'

'Thank you. You are very thoughtful, Janice,' Detlef accepts as she pulls him up a barstool.

'Can I call you Grampy?' she then asks.

Detlef looks a little confused at that, unsure of the word.

'Like grandad, only shorter,' explains Detlef.

'Of course,' says Detlef, thrilled at the idea.

265

'Bloody good job I stopped that Brian geezer in his tracks though!' interjects a pumped up and exhilarated sounding Phil, keen to remind them of the huge part he'd played in preventing more serious injury. 'He took some stoppin', I can tell ya. Like a bloody gert big ox, he was!'

'Yeah, ain't he just! Cheers, Phil,' Derek thanks him, wiping his forehead to emphasise what a close-run thing it might have been.

'The ol' forearm lock, see,' Phil goes on to explain, his chest ballooning as he clasps his fist to his elbow to show them all the grip. 'Learnt it in the merchant navy. One manoeuvre … 'round the back o' the neck … twist … on the deck … goodnight Eileen!'

'Ha! I owe ya one,' Derek thanks him once again.

'You can always call us quits if ya like?' jests Phil with an exaggerated wink.

'What? Two-hundred and fifty big ones for a two an' a half minute tussle?' exclaims Derek, now laughing out loud. 'Bloody expensive minder ain't ya, mate?'

With the mention of such a huge sum of money, Marion stiffens and snatches a poorly disguised look of expectation at her ex. *Where was hers, she thinks? After all, she's still the mother of his three children, isn't she? She deserves something … at the very least.*

'But you could kill someone like that,' Julie then tells her father's friend.

'Are you talkin' to me, love?' Phil asks, turning.

'Yes, I am. Twisting his neck like that. It's very dangerous. You could easily have fractured a vertebra. C1 to C7 they're called.'

Vacantly, Phil looks at her. He hasn't got a clue. None of them have. 'Are they now?' he says but still none the wiser.

'She wants to be a doctor,' Derek explains. 'Head's always in a book.'

'I heard. I'm impressed,' acknowledges Phil, 'though I dunno where you get your brains from. It certainly ain't from your ol' dad. He's as thick as …..'

'Oi!' Derek stops him in his tracks.

'Two short planks!'

'Tha's more like it!'

'But don't you fret,' Phil continues to address the young girl. 'He got up good as gold when I finally let 'im go.'

'But that doesn't necessarily mean anything, not with neck injuries,' she continues to berate him.

'Leave it, Jules, eh?' pleads her father. 'He was fine. Didn't you hear 'im *givin' it all o' that* when he an' PG scarpered?' he adds, yapping his fingers like a cornered rockpool crab.

'Then you watch he don't come back through that door with a baseball bat or something,' Marion cautions them. 'People like that don't just forget, ya know. He's the sort that might even have a gun!'

'A gun? Don't be bloody silly, woman!' dismisses Derek, hooting. 'This ain't Miami-bleedin'-Vice!'

'I'm so sorry,' repeats Detlef. 'I should *never* have hit him.'

Nursing his ribs and with the obvious beginnings of a black and swollen eye, PG flicks the indicator on his Jag and urgently waves Brian into a bus stop lay-by.

It had been years, decades in fact since he'd found himself subjected to actual physical violence and this called for some very stern retaliatory measures indeed. Ground rules needed to be re-established before his reputation was damaged beyond all recognition.

With Brian now sat alongside him, he snarls. 'What is the point of you?' he asks, peering into his rear view mirror and tweaking his nose to check that it's not broken. 'Look at the state of me!'

'I'm nae fuckin' Superman, PG!' growls Brian defensively, his own pride severely dented. 'Tha' bastard 'ad me from behind. Could o' broken ma fuckin' neck!'

'Pity he didn't.'

'Fuck off!'

'They need teaching a lesson they'll never forget,' continues PG. 'They'll pay for this, and some. And I want that money back!'

'Oh yeah? So how d'ya propose doin' that?'

'No, it's what *you're* going to do about it, Brian.'

Brian looks at him in disbelief. ''Ave I go' fuckin' mug written all over ma face? Di' ya nae see all the fuckin' cameras?'

'So?'

'So, if anyone so much as touches a hair on their heeds, tha law wou' be all over me like a fuckin' rash. I'd be in tha frame - literally!'

'Now you listen to me, and you listen very carefully. If you and I are to continue our relationship, and a very lucrative one it is for you too, you'll do as you're told! I will have my pound of flesh. I will have my retribution.'

'An' wha's tha gonna achieve? How is tha' goin' tae ge' ya tha money back?'

'Coercion, Brian,' says PG darkly. 'There are children too, are there not? I saw them. I will not, cannot, let Sir Alun down.'

Brian doesn't even consider it. 'Nah, fuck tha' fer a game o' soldiers. Sorry, bu' you're on yer own wi' this one, PG,' he replies, his hand already on the door lever and about to get out. 'I mi' be many things, bu' I'll nae touch kids.'

'I'm only talking about putting the frighteners on them, a threat, nothing terminal, you fool!'

'Too fuckin' late, pal. It's all got outa hand. I'm no spendin' time in tha slammah again for you nae no one,' rejects Brian. 'You'll 'ave ti find someone else tae dae ya dirty work.'

'You seem to forget something, Brian. You'll get nothing if you do not see this through,' PG warns him.

'Call it ma partin' gift,' says Brian, opening the door. 'I'm finished wi' it.'

'You stay right where you are!' PG shouts, grabbing at him. 'I'll pay you extra! Name your price!'

Brian simply shrugs him off. 'I said no! An' while I'm at it, give 'im this pile o' shite yersel'!' he says, chucking the now misshapen and slightly crushed Rolex box onto the dashboard and exiting the vehicle.

Now in a state of near apoplexy, PG launches himself across to the passenger seat and scrambles to open the window. 'You get back here, you Scottish cunt!' he rages after him, launching the watch back out into the road and after him. 'You're nothing without me! Do you hear? Nothing!'

But Brian simply ignores him, gets into his car, calming flicks the ignition, and drives past without so much as a second glance, crushing the Rolex under the wheels as he does.

-

'Don't you worry, Gramps!' Janice continues to comfort him. 'Happens all the time 'round 'ere! Fights an' that.'

'Speak for yourself,' complains her mother.

'It'll be all over tonight's Evenin' Post, I know that much,' worries Jimbo, joining in. 'Photos, headlines, the lot. You mark my words.'

'So what?' poo-poos Derek, glugging happily at his beer.

'I'll leave you to deal wi' the police, shall I?'

'Bloody relax, will ya, Jim! It'll put this place on the bloody map! Tha's what Reenie wanted, innit? Queuing halfway round the block they'll be! I can see the 'eadlines now,' says Derek, picturing them. 'Riot at the 'Ravellers, it'll say. PG gets a pummellin'! Ha!'

'Larrupin' on tha Lotto!' adds Phil and laughing at his own suggestion.

'It's not funny, you two. Them bloody Lottery people disappeared pretty quick too,' Jimbo continues to fret. 'Christ knows what they're gonna make of it all? Reenie's gonna go apeshit.'

'Oh, am I now?' she says from right behind him but sounding surprisingly calm and unruffled. 'Wasn't quite what I was hopin' for, but the way I see it, any publicity is better than no publicity.'

'See! Told ya!' says Derek triumphantly. 'My thoughts exactly, Reen!'

'Precisely, Derek,' she says, 'and with that in mind, I've just had a word with the reporters over there,' she continues. 'They said they'd give me a good write up, a free advertorial, as long as they can have a chat with you and your dad. Would that be alright? They want your side o' the story, Detlef.'

'I would prefer not,' he replies immediately, shaking his head.

'Wouldn't hurt, would it, Pops?' asks Derek, still enjoying the thought of a few more moments of fame.

'No,' Detlef repeats firmly. 'I don't want to be in the newspapers. I'm sorry.'

-

Wincing with the pain in his side, the harsh reality truly begins to dawn on PG. What is he now to do? What will he tell Sir Alun?

In his desperation, he picks up his phone and begins to dial.

-

'An' while I'm thinkin' about it, Dekko,' says Phil, 'wha' was tha' prat Clappie playin' at? I swear I saw 'im take a swing at ya!'

'He did!' confirms Derek but still laughing about it. 'It was 'im that caught me on the side of the face, the two-faced C-U-next-Tuesday.'

'He didn't?' says Jimbo, astonished. 'What? After all them beers you bought 'im?'

'Yeah! An' I bunged 'im some foldin', feelin' sorry for 'im!'

'Once a PG boy, always a PG boy, I s'pose,' observes Jimbo.

'We'll 'ave to 'ave a word with 'im,' says Phil, quietly looking forward to the prospect. 'Explain a thing or two.'

'But it was strange,' adds Derek. 'It was sort of half-hearted, like he didn't mean it.'

'Don't matter. We'll still 'ave 'im.'

'Just leave it alone now, lads,' pleads Jimbo. 'Please.'

'Yes, leave it,' agrees Marion, uninterested in all their continued fighting talk. 'Detlef,' she then pries. 'Can I ask? What actually made you lash out like that? Must have been something pretty bad?'

'Mar!' Derek tries to silence her.

'I'm only asking!'

'Well don't!'

'It's alright, Derek,' says his father. 'It is a fair question.'

'Called him a Kraut, didn't he,' Derek answers for him but mouthing the word into the back of his hand so as not to cause further offence.

'No, no. That was not it, Derek,' Detlef corrects him. 'I was used to that, years ago.'

'Huh? So what was it then?'

'He was threatening you, Derek - how do you say it? He was trying to bully you. I will not have anyone talk to my family like that. It is unacceptable.'

With that, Derek reels back in amazement. His dad had been defending *him*! Standing *his* quarter! He'd never had that experience before - ever! It made him feel, well ... bloody marvellous. Complete somehow. Like it was the missing piece of the jigsaw.

'And you must have heard what he was implying,' adds Detlef.

'What?'

'That I am not your father and that I'm only after your money.'

Derek stands back for a second, looking intently into his father's eyes. 'Well, more fool 'im, cos you are an' you ain't!' he exalts. 'Now, what's everyone want to drink?! We got things to celebrate an' I'm bloody gaspin'!'

-

'Ah, Clappie, at last,' says PG, smoothly and calmly and as if nothing of any consequence had happened. 'Why weren't you picking up? Not in hiding, I hope?'

-

Derek and his family are, at last, in the queue to the buffet tables, paper plates in hand. 'Comes to summat when you 'ave to wait to get fed at yer own do, innit?' he groans light-heartedly but, already obviously quite drunk, not really having an appetite for anything other than more booze.

'Hey, Dekko!' he then hears someone call out to him, overly loud. 'My main man!'

It's Dave.

Turning, Derek can immediately see that all is not quite right with him. He looks particularly scruffy and dishevelled, and, worryingly, as he nears, Derek notices what look like sores or burns to his lips. Quickly, he steers him away from his family and over into the corner towards the Gents.

'Everything alright?' asks Phil, noticing.

'Yeah, no problem,' Derek waves him away. 'Be wi' ya in a minute.'

'So, how ya doin', you ol' moneybags, you?' asks Dave, friendly but aggressively agitated at the same time - his eyes manic, his breathing, short and laboured.

'Yeah, I'm good, which is more than I can say 'bout you by the looks o' things. You're totally out of it,' says Derek and already sensing that the shit is about to hit the fan.

'Ha, ha, ha! Yeah, 'spect yer right. Been partyin', ain't I? Big stylee! No sleep 'til Brooklyn!'

'You sure?' Phil calls over again.

'Yeah,' confirms Derek.

'Look, that money?' asks Dave, urgently. 'Can I 'ave it? Like soon … now … I need it.'

'What's the rush?' says Derek, second guessing.

'Don't play silly buggers wi' me, mate. You promised.'

'Let me 'ave a look at your fingers.'

'You what? Why?' wails Dave, feigning incredulity.

'Come on, let's 'ave a look.'

Reluctantly, Dave flicks his hands out, but only briefly.

Quickly, Derek grabs hold of one and turns it over to reveal his tell-tale scorched fingertips. 'You effin' idiot!' he says. 'Get out o' 'ere before Jimbo cops eyes on ya!'

'Who cares? Stuff 'im!'

'He'll stuff you if you don't watch out,' warns Derek.

'I don't give a fuck! Not now. Not when you gi' me what you said. It'll be easy street all tha way.'

'Come back when you've cleaned yourself up, yeah?' Derek suggests as gently as he can. 'We'll see then, shall we?'

'Fuck off, Dekko! You're not goin' back on your word, are ya? I need tha' money!'

'An' I know a crack 'ead when I see one, Dave,' he says under his breath. 'An', to be honest, I don't want you round me kids like that neither. OK?'

Phil can stand back no longer and walks over. 'Wha's the problem?' he asks.

'This little prat. Can you give us a hand? Let's get 'im gone,' says Derek taking Dave by the sleeve.

As Phil grabs him too Dave screams out. 'Get your hands off me!' he yells, twisting and turning.

Hearing, Jimbo calls out from behind the bar. 'Hey, what's goin' on over there?' he demands.

'Nuthin', Jimbo,' Derek quickly replies. 'Dave 'ere, he's just goin'.'

'Am I fuck. I just got 'ere. I want my money! Two hundred and fifty thousand, you said!'

'Shut the fuck up! You want the whole pub to know?' says Phil angrily.

'What of it? I'll make even more. I'll have doubled it this time next week,' he hisses and giving Derek a glimpse of a half a dozen wraps of crack in his inside pocket. 'I got connections, ya wankah! I gave ya tha chance!'

Angrily, Derek pulls the last of the three cheques out of his jacket pocket. 'If you think you're getting' this after showin' me that shit,' he says, ripping it in half and half and half again, 'you got another think comin'! Now fuck off! I'm not bein' 'eld responsible!'

'You bastard!' cries Dave as he drops to the floor to retrieve the pieces. 'You fuckin' bastard!'

'What's going on, Dekko?' Jimbo asks again as he now lifts the hatch and hurries over.

'You don't wanna know, Jim.'

'Is he on drugs? Are you on drugs, Dave?'

'Too fuckin' right I am!' he shouts as he attempts to reassemble the pieces. 'Top notch, class A fuckin' drugs, if ya must know!'

'He's off his 'ead! I'm callin' the police,' says Jimbo.

'No! Leave it, Jim!' Derek insists.

'First a fight, now this! I'm not 'avin' it!'

'Hold yer 'orses, mate!' says Phil. 'Dekko's right. You'll only make matters worse, for you as well as 'im.'

'Just get 'im out o' my sight then,' he demands. 'You're banned, Dave!'

'Like I give a fuck, Jim! D'you think I'll miss this fuckin' shit hole?'

'That's it! Permanent! Where's my phone?'

'No, stop, Jim!' Derek insists again. 'They'll only bang 'im up. We can't do that. Let's just get 'im up and out o' 'ere, like pronto. Phil?'

'Alright, if we must,' Phil agrees and bending down to lift him up, 'but he'll need some help, Dekko, some proper help.'

'I need tha' money you'd promised me, Dekko!' Dave continues to scream and trying to fight them off. 'Tha's what I fuckin' need. You promised me!'

'Sorry, Dave,' repeats Derek as he and Phil, their arms held wide, begin to herd him outside like he was a mad and rabid dog. 'You'll get no money from me. Not like this.'

'I fuckin' will!'

'You fuckin' won't! We'll talk tomorra.'

'You might as well 'ave signed me death warrant, ya bastard!' Dave accuses him.

'I might o' saved you ya bloody life!' counters Derek. 'Now as I said, let's get you gone. You need to get your head down.'

'Fat chance o' that,' scoffs Phil.

-

'Have you got that?'' PG is telling Clappie. 'I want you to get back there now.'

'I can't,' he says.

'Tell him!'

'I took a swing at 'im for you. They'll beat me to a pulp!'

'You do it now, or it might not just be your head on the block.'

'Wha' d'ya mean?

'Woof, woof,' says PG. 'Do I make myself loud and clear?'

Chapter 29

Over at the New Horizons Nursing Home, Ellen is eating her lunch from a rather unappetising and meagre looking plate.

'Are you sure you can manage, my love?' asks Margaret as she watches the old lady struggle to feed herself. 'Would you like me to cut it up a bit for you?'

'I can do it,' Ellen answers quietly, 'but thank you.'

'Are you OK?' asks the carer, concerned and pulling up a chair.

Ellen swallows hard on a piece of undercooked carrot, dipping her head and patting her chest. 'Oh, I don't know,' she says, looking a little vague and distant.

'Tell me. What is it?'

'Bit nervous, I suppose.'

'Nervous? What on Earth for?' asks Margaret knowingly but her voice rising as if to suggest there is absolutely no need to be. 'You'll have a smashing time.'

'I hardly slept a wink last night.'

'Just excited, I s'pect? Like being a kid at Christmas all over again.'

'Yes, I suppose. At least my Derek seemed to get on with his father in the end,' the old lady voices the other reason for her concern.

'It was touch and go for a while,' agrees Margaret, smiling, 'but yes, Ellen, I think you can safely say that he did. They did.'

'I do hope so,' she says, adding, 'but it's just Detlef and me tomorrow though.'

'And me don't forget!' reminds Margaret pretending to be insulted. 'I'm coming too! We can't have Detlef taking you into the Ladies, now can we?'

'No, certainly not!' says Ellen, her face appearing to flush at the very idea.

'But don't fret, I shan't be playing gooseberry,' Margaret teases her. 'I'm sure I can go and entertain myself somewhere or another - in the penny arcades or something.'

Ellen sits back, reminiscing, and smiling at last. 'I used to love those as a girl,' she says. 'All that noise, all those lights.'

'Me too. Still do,' says Margaret, adding, 'but you never win anything, do you?'

'Never,' agrees Ellen with something of a chuckle. 'And then there was the carousel too,' she adds, her mind being cast back. 'A big one.'

'In Weston? Was there really?'

'Oh yes. Famous it was. Right on the front. I went on it with my friend Joyce.'

Margaret pulls a face. 'Rather you than me,' she says with an exaggerated shudder. 'I'd have been terrified.'

'Why?'

'All them teeth, and their tails always missing! They used to give me terrible nightmares,' says Margaret but light-heartedly, 'and that organ music!'

'I could hear it in the distance,' remembers Ellen, 'and the Punch and Judy.'

'Don't get me started on that either! All that hitting and the crocodile!'

'Sausages!' says Ellen, managing to crack a joke and prodding hers on her plate.

'Ha! Yes! Sausages! That's more like it, Ellen! That's what I like to see!'

-

At last all sat down at a table with his family, together with Phil and Betsy in silent attendance, and with his plate stacked high with way more food than he is ever likely to eat, Derek breaks their temporary silence as they all begin to tuck in. 'So, you're takin' me mum out tomorrow then, Pops?' he says more by way of an announcement than a question. 'Off to the seaside for the day, yeah?'

'Yes, we are,' confirms Detlef, taking an inquisitive bite from an egg and cress sandwich.

'What? You're taking Nan out, Gramps?' enthuses Janice and getting used to addressing him that way. Enjoying it, in fact.

'That's nice,' agrees Marion. 'She'll love that, she will. Whereabouts you going?'

'Weston-Super-Mare,' Detlef tells them.

'Oh, lovely! Bit o' sea air. It'll do her the power o' good.'

'But how are you getting there? She'll be needing a wheelchair,' worries Janice.

'Maciej can take it in his taxi,' answers Detlef. 'It will fold up in the...,' he hesitates, unable to remember the word.

'Boot?' Marion finishes his sentence for him.

'Yes. Boot. Thank you.'

With that, Derek looks left and right. 'Where's he gone, Pops, your driver?' he demands to know. 'He was only 'ere just a minute ago.'

'Outside, waiting,' Detlef informs him. 'He thought he should leave us.'

'No, no! I'm not 'avin' that! Sat out there all on his tod!' objects his son, pulling the pastry off a sausage roll and popping it into his mouth. 'He's been good to you, an' now takin' me mum out too,' he sputters. 'Bloody good workers, some o' them Poles.'

'Yes. He's been very helpful. Very kind,' says Detlef. 'I don't know what I would have done without him.'

'Then go and get him, somebody,' insists Derek, belching into the back of his hand. 'Tell him to get 'imself back inside an' get 'imself a drink an' a bite to eat an' join us.'

'I'll go,' offers Julie.

'OK,' her mother allows her. 'But be quick, you hear?'

-

'So, how long ago was that then, if you don't mind me asking?' enquires Margaret.

'Forty-eight years ago, this June just gone, the sixteenth,' answers Ellen as quick as you like. 'It was when Detlef and me first met.'

'Oh, wow! I didn't realise, Ellen. That'll make tomorrow even more special then, won't it?'

'Yes. We were on the Grand Pier,' she reveals. 'It was just before we left to get back on the train. Joyce and I were taking a last look out along the beach.'

'How romantic! I can picture it all now, the sun on your face, sea breeze in your hair - just like in the films.'

'Don't know about that!' says Ellen, blushing again. 'But it was everso sunny. Boiling, in fact. My legs turned to jelly as soon as I set eyes on him.'

'I bet they did! He's still a very handsome man, let me tell you.'

'He is, isn't he?'

'I think so.'

Ellen then looks down at her legs. 'But what I'd give for these damn things to work properly, Lord strike me down for using such language!'

'We'll manage,' Margaret reassures her, 'but I think you might have to be a bit lucky on the weather front this time around, the forecast isn't looking that great.'

'Don't suppose it is,' replies Ellen, peering out and into the unwelcoming greyness outside.

'But you've got a good coat, haven't you?'

'Yes. Hanging up on the back of my door. The one with the detachable hood.'

'I know the one. You'll need it,' says Margaret, adding, 'still, it'll bring back some wonderful memories, won't it? A nice day out together?'

Ellen nods, pulling her hankie from her cardigan sleeve to wipe her eyes and mouth.

'Now, Detlef said he'll be here just after eleven with that nice young Polish taxi driver,' continues Margaret, 'so we'll make sure you're all spruced up and ready to go. Yeah?'

'Yes, that would be lovely. Nice young man. Polite,' agrees Ellen. 'I hope he drives safely though. Not like a mad thing.'

'He will. Look, would you like me to bring in my rollers and a bit of make-up?' she then suggests. 'Bit of lippy? We want you looking your best, don't we?

'Would you mind?' asks the old lady, her almost non-existent eyebrows lifting pitifully at the very thought.

'Not at all. What about a dress too? Or a skirt and a top? I could wash and iron something for you if you like? I've got a tumble dryer at home.'

'Would you? Would you really?'

'I wouldn't ask otherwise, you silly billy you. Just tell me and I'll get it.'

Ellen thinks for a moment. 'There's a nice blue dress hanging in my wardrobe,' she suggests, 'long it is, with pansies on it, a bit of lace around the neck and cuffs.'

'Sounds pretty.'

'My Janice bought it for me. I've hardly worn it yet.'

'Did she? How lovely. Even better.'

'Laura Ashley or something or other, so she said.'

'Ooh, very posh! I'll take it home tonight. Make sure. We'll have you looking like a million dollars!'

Ellen then places her knife and fork alongside each other as if she'd finished. 'He remarried, you know,' she blurts out, inspecting the back of her frail and liver-spotted hands and turning her wedding ring.

'I know, Ellen,' coos Margaret sympathetically. 'Still, you two will have a wonderful time. Now, a little bit more, please,' she insists, spinning her hands in front of her mouth. 'You're going to need to keep your strength up. It'll be a long day.'

'I shall be leaving here soon, you know,' the old lady then announces.

'I expect you will,' acknowledges Margaret, pulling a sad face, 'what with your son's big win an' all that.'

'Yes, he's promised to buy me a little ground floor flat with a garden.'

'That's wonderful, Ellen. I'm so pleased for you. You deserve it.'

'And carers.'

'Perfect.'

'But I shall miss you.'

'Aww, I'll miss you too.'

'Will you come and visit?'

'Of course, I will, my love!' insists the carer. 'You try stopping me!'

-

'We went there once, didn't we mum?' asks Janice. 'To Weston.'

'Yeah, well, Brean Sands, just up the road,' Marion replies less than enthusiastically. 'A right scruffy little caravan. You could barely swing a cat.'

'It was alright!' complains Derek. 'Cosy it was! Besides, I got it through a mate of a mate o' mine. It was all we could afford at the time. Not now though, eh?'

'Tiny it was, dirty too,' continues Marion, 'with only two small beds and that smelly calor gas stuff for cooking, even the lighting!'

'An' don't forget the Elsan toilet in the cupboard!' Derek reminds her, laughing. 'Desperate, you said! Remember?'

'How was I s'posed to know there were no chemicals in it?'

'Wha' a bloody stench! Ha!'

'Shut up, Derek!' Marion reprimands him. 'Please, not in front of your dad.'

276

But Derek isn't stopping. 'It was like a battle of the pongs, what wi' Jez's nappies stinkin' the place as well!' he continues to joke.

'Sorry, Detlef,' Marion apologises. 'What must you think of us?'

The old man simply shrugs, smiling. 'It's OK,' he says. 'It is nice to listen.'

'Was I there too then?' asks Jez.

'You were,' answers his mum.

'You bought me a dot-to-dot book,' Janice then recalls, 'and some felt tips.'

'Didn't have much choice, did we?' Marion continues to grumble. 'Had to keep you occupied somehow. It chucked it down best parts o' the week,'

'But it didn't matter, Mum,' says Janice. 'As Dad said, it was cosy, all of us together. Best holiday we ever had.'

'Only one you mean.'

'Wha' d'ya mean? I took you all to Porthcawl too!' says Derek.

'How old was I then?' Jez interrupts again.

'Hardly a holiday!' says Marion, not letting it go. 'I told you the car wasn't up to it. We had to come home early. D'you remember that?'

'I said, how old was I?' repeats Jez more loudly and seemingly keen to stop his parents bickering.

'In Brean? You'd been about eighteen months,' his mum tells him. 'You took your first steps there.'

'Did I?' questions Jez, leaning forward and eager to know more. 'What? In the caravan?'

'You did,' confirms his dad. 'Right little tearaway. Couldn't stop ya once you'd started.'

'Not that you saw him do it,' says Marion, still unable to bite her lip. 'You were in the pub half the time.'

'Mu-um!' Janice then tries to stop her too.

'Yeah, leave it out, Mar,' requests Derek. 'Let's not ruin it. This is nice.'

Marion takes a sip from her lager and lime then huffily folds her arms across her chest, saying nothing and looking put out.

'I do remember bein' on a beach or summat,' continues Jez.

'Yeah. That was it!' Janice remembers too. 'Huge it was. People were flyin' kites everywhere.'

'An' it's where your mum fell pregnant with our Julie,' says Derek, grinning lasciviously and just as she walks back in with Maciej.

'Too much information, Dad!' squeals Janice in mock horror. 'Poor Julie!'

'What have I done now?' she asks.

-

Despite Derek's insistence, Dave does not go home and 'get his head down'. No, of course he doesn't.

With his mind racing and the promise of so much money all but gone - *the fucking bastard* - he knows he now has a monster of a problem on his hands and urgently needs to buy himself some time or things could turn very ugly indeed.

So, tucked up tight against the wall and with his shoulders hunched, he hurries back towards the crack den whilst trying desperately to construct his excuses. *Derek was too pissed celebratin', he'll tell them. He's promised to sort it in a couple of days, he'll say. Relax, there's no problem! You'll get your fuckin' money!*

Simultaneously, a similarly nervous and agitated looking Clappie is heading in the opposite direction and back towards the pub and they almost, but not quite, bump into each other.

'Alright, Dave,' says Clappie in recognition.

'Yeah, alright,' grunts Dave in return.

'Off somewhere?'

'Not particularly,' lies Dave before chancing his arm. 'Wanna buy bit o' gear?' he offers.

'You what?'

'S'good stuff.'

'Piss off, Dave. I'm not into that shit.'

'Alright, alright! Only offered! No need to be rude. So, where you off to? The pub?'

'Might be, might not. How come you ain't there? You an' Dekko are old mates, ain't ya?'

'I thought.'

'Wha's 'appened? Summat serious?' asks Clappie sensing a possible opportunity.

'Nuthin'.'

'What?'

'Nuthin'!'

'What?!'

'Let me down, ain't he?'

-

'It's where we met, Ellen and I,' Detlef then tells them all. 'On the pier. It was in the summer of 1956. I bought her a candy floss.'

'No expense spared then?' says Derek, continuing to joke.

'Did you live in Weston then, Gramps?' continues Janice whilst admonishing her dad with a shake of the head.

'No, I was just visiting for the day too,' he answers.

'Bristol?'

Detlef smiles. 'Not at first,' he answers her again. 'I lived near a small village, over near Bath.'

'Whereabouts?' asks Marion, emerging from her self-imposed silence. 'I used to have a friend in Bath.'

'Norton St Philip.'

Marion taps her lips, pretend thinking. 'No, never heard of it,' she says. 'So, what were you doing there?'

'Working on a farm. I was a labourer.'

'You don't look like a farmer.'

'I was sent there during the war,' announces Detlef.

'You were in a war?' asks Jez excitedly.

'Yes, I was. The Second World War, Jez. Maybe I will tell you about it one day. But not now. It is a long story.'

'If you don't mind me asking, were you a POW?' Marion guesses correctly and beginning to piece it all together.

'Yes, Marion, I was,' Detlef admits.

'A what?' asks Jez.

'A prisoner of war,' answers his grandfather.

'A prisoner of war?' repeats Jez excitedly and clacking his fingers again. 'Wicked!'

'Wha' did I tell you earlier? Enough!' reprimands his father, again.

'It's OK, Derek,' says Detlef. 'I understand the boys interest.'

'It's all beginning to make sense now,' Marion thinks out loud.

'Wha' d'ya mean?' asks her ex. 'All makes sense now?'

'Your mum. She mentioned something not so long back,' she reveals, 'although I couldn't make head nor tail of it at the time.'

'Like what?'

Marion pauses for a moment. 'She just said she might have gone to live on a farm and that there was a German farmhand there,' she says.

'Why didn't you tell me for chrissakes?'

'Didn't seem important,' admits Marion. 'Besides, you an' I had already split.'

'So, you still go over to see her?' asks Derek.

'Of course! I still love her, ya know.'

Before Derek has chance to respond, he hears his phone go off in his pocket, a text message. 'Who the bloody 'ells this?' he says, irritated at being interrupted but pulling it out and reading all the same. 'I don't bloody believe it! It's bleedin' Clappie! He wants a word. He's outside!'

'The cheeky bastard!' says Phil, immediately standing. 'I'll sort 'im out if ya like, mate?

'Would ya, Phil? I could well do without any more nonsense today to be honest wi' ya,' says Derek.

'Not a problem, Dekko. Leave it with me,' insists Phil, already making for the door. 'I'll send 'im on his way wi' a flea in his ear.'

'You go careful, Phil,' worries his wife.

'Yes,' agrees Detlef. 'I have caused enough trouble.'

'Would you like me to come too?' Maciej then offers.

'Nah, you're alright,' dismisses Phil. 'It's only tha' streak o' piss Clappie we're talkin' about.'

'Just to keep an eye out for ya, Phil,' insists Derek. 'Would you mind, Maciej?' he asks.

Chapter 30

Pumped up and ready to go, Phil appears at the top of the steps with Maciej close in behind. 'Wha' d'ya want, ya fuckin' rat-faced little weasel, ya?' he snarls as Clappie hovers small and seemingly insignificant below them. 'I w'wuz jus' lookin' t'talk to Dekko,' he stutters, nervously thrusting his hands into his pockets.

'Tough shit. You got me instead.'

'I'm not lookin' for n'no trouble, Phil. PG just wanted me to pass on a message, tha's all.'

'Wha' message?' Phil demands whilst almost imperceptibly edging forward like a predator about to strike.

'I can't. He told me not to tell no-one else.'

'Oh, did he now?'

'Well, y'yeah, he did.'

'Then you leave me wi' no choice,' says Phil as, with surprising agility, he launches himself down the steps to grab Clappie by the scruff of the neck with one hand and slap him hard across the side of the head with the other - *th'wack!* 'Tha's for takin' a pop at my mate, ya two-faced little bastard!' he shouts. 'Now, tell me, wha' is it you gotta say?'

With his ear ringing loudly, his cheek already beginning to glow beetroot red, Clappie tightens his lips and scrunches his face - refusing to answer.

'Spit it out, or you'll get another!' Phil warns him, now clenching his fist and ramming it hard up into his chin.

'Bu' he'll kill me, Phil!' Clappie pleads. 'He'll kill me!'

'Not before I fuckin' do, he won't,' Phil growls, reaching down and grabbing him by the balls. 'If ya wanna keep yer family jewels in one piece, you'll tell me - now, spit it out!'

Clappie creases up in agony. 'Arrgh! Please, mate, stop!' he begs him.

'I ain't your fuckin' mate neither! Now, tell me!'

As Phil squeezes ever harder, Clappie, gasping and breathless, finally cracks. 'He said, he said ...'

'Said what?'

'He said to tell him to watch out for his family!'

'He said what?' asks Phil incredulously.

'His three kids.'

'Are you fuckin' serious?! His nippers?'

'He gave me no choice,' Clappie continues to sputter. 'He said he'd shoot me dogs an' all if I didn't do as he said!'

'Fuck your fuckin' dogs! We're talkin' about kids 'ere!'

'Leave 'im alone!' a disembodied voice then calls out.

Turning, Phil sees Dave emerging low from behind a car and lets out a great roar of laughter. 'I might o' fuckin' guessed!' he hoots. 'Two for the price o' one! We got Druggie Dave as well! You two in cahoots or summat?'

'I said, leave 'im alone!' he repeats.

'Look, Dave, it's none o' your business,' Phil advises him sternly. 'Now, as we told ya before, be a good boy an' fuck off … or you'll be next.'

'No! I want wha' was promised me!' Dave shouts back defiantly and, out of sight, dips down to reach into his sock.

'Tha's all PG wants too, Phil,' says Clappie rather foolishly.

'Oh, does he now?'

'Yeah, he said if Dekko sticks to the deal, then that'll be an end to it.'

Incensed by the threat and the suggestion, Phil is about to deliver a headbutt when Maciej, still at the top of the steps, shouts out in warning. 'Watch out, Phil. Dave has knife!'

Catching the glint of a blade, Phil instantly throws Clappie aside, sprawling him onto the broken and frost damaged asphalt, grazing his hands. 'Put tha' away, Dave!' he shouts in warning, approaching him with arms held wide. 'Pu' that a-fuckin'-way I said!'

Inside, Derek is chatting away happily. 'Speakin' o' 'olidays,' he's saying. 'I can take you all somewhere amazin' now, can't I? How d'you fancy goin' skiing? Switzerland or somewhere. I still got that poster on me wall back home. Always fancied the idea.'

'You? Skiing? Don't make me laugh,' says Marion. 'You'd end up killin' yourself.'

'Somewhere hot an' sunny then … on an 'airy-plane?'

'Ye-eah!' reacts Jez, shrieking. 'That'd be brilliant, Dad! Awesome!'

'Spain, then?' he suggests. 'A great big villa with a pool. Or even Greece? I 'eard it's quite nice.'

'Ooh, yes please!' enthuses the youngest of his two daughters. 'We did Greece at school. The Gods. Zeus. Aphrodite. They had loads of Gods.'

'Afro who?' asks her dad.

'But what about Ibiza?' interjects Janice, thoroughly animated by the idea but hoping to go somewhere more exciting. 'We can go clubbin'. I've always wanted to go there!'

Unexpectedly, her dad thinks for a moment before nodding his approval and grinning. 'Don't see why not?' he says, throwing same lame looking dance moves with his arms. 'I like a bit o' *oomsch-ka, oomsch-ka* meself.'

'You'd look ridiculous, Derek,' chastises her ex but laughing along all the same. 'Besides, d'you think it'd be appropriate?' she then questions with obvious reference to herself.

'Why? You wanna come an' all?' he asks, smirking. 'Frightened you'll miss out?'

Wide-eyed and mad looking, Dave lunges towards him and, instinctively, Phil drops to the floor, scissor-kicking his legs from out beneath him. 'Nobody pulls a fuckin' knife on me, ya bastard!' he yells before leaping on top of him, a forearm pressed to his throat whilst furiously grabbing at the flailing hand holding the weapon. 'No-one, d'ya hear!'

For the second time today, Marion folds her arms tight across her bosom. 'Up to you,' she says peevishly.

'Wha' d'ya mean, up to me?' asks Derek, enjoying every moment.

'I just don't think it'd be a good idea,' she says. 'I've got Nigel to think about now. It'd be unfair on him.'

'Well, he ain't bloody comin', tha's for sure!'

'Who even said I'm coming?' Marion reacts.

'Your loss, a free luxury holiday.'

'Oh, go on, Mum!' urges Julie.

'Yeah. Please, Mum!' pleads Jez. 'It'd be amazin'!'

'I'll take ya dancin',' offers Janice. 'Just you an' me, yeah?'

Marion unfolds her arms and picks up her drink. 'Oh, I dunno,' wavering, she says.

'Wouldn't hurt, would it? All the family together one last time?' pursues Derek. 'No silly nonsense. Separate rooms an' all that.'

'No! There certainly won't be!'

'So, wha's it to be? Yes or no?'

'I'll have to have a think,' concedes Marion. 'Maybe.'

With the knife still in Dave's hand, Phil turns it back and, in the struggle, the runs the blade firmly across Dave's leg, cutting his trackie bottoms, immediately drawing blood.

'Arggh!' he screams. 'You've fuckin' stabbed me, ya cunt!'

Swiftly, Maciej jumps in, also trying to grab at the knife. 'Give it to me,' he yells, 'before someone gets hurt big time!'

'Take it, take it! I'm fuckin' bleedin to death here,' cries Dave as he looks down to see the light grey cotton fabric darkening swiftly.

Derek turns his attention to his father. 'So, d'you fancy the idea, Pops?' he asks. 'All your lot too? I'm payin'. Flights, food, accommodation, the whole shebang! We can all get to know each other then, can't we?'

Detlef appears to nod keenly. 'I shall ask them, Derek,' he says.

'I can get to meet me sister then, can't I?'

'I hope it's all alright outside,' interjects Betsy, thinking aloud.

'Ah, don't fret, love,' Derek reassures her. 'Your ol' man can 'andle the likes o' Clappie any day o' the week ... so, 'ave you all got some cozzies then, bit o' suntan lotion?'

Nevertheless, Betsy stands to go outside. 'I'm going to check,' she says.

Ashen faced at the sight of blood, Dave whimpers. 'I'm dyin',' he groans. 'I'm dyin'.'

'Bullshit!' says Phil but looking worried. 'It's barely a scratch. I hardly touched ya.'

'We need to make sure, Phil,' advises Maciej. 'We need to take him inside.'

'I'll leave you all to it then,' says Clappie seizing the opportunity to make his escape.

'You stay right where you are!' Phil yells at him as Dave then passes out. 'I ain't finished wi' you yet! Now, come an' help us get this stupid bastard inside.'

''Ave you seen the state of my hands? Cut to ribbons!'

'Jus' pick 'im up!' orders Phil.

'Can we go soon, Dad?' asks Jez eagerly. 'Can we?'

'Well, we'll 'ave to see,' says his dad alluding to his impending court case.

Now horribly reminded, Jez's demeanour changes in an instant, his head dropping, his shoulders sagging. In the excitement of the moment, he'd clean forgotten.

'Court appearance?' asks Detlef with immediate concern. 'What court appearance?'

'Yeah, we gotta be up mega-early tomorrow mornin' cos o' this silly little bugger an' go see tha' ol' duffer Jefferson,' says Derek without fully explaining.

'Who's Jefferson?'

'His solicitor,' Marion informs him. 'Jez had a very bad car accident, Detlef,'

'What on Earth's happened, Phil?' gasps Betsy as she meets them struggling up the steps with Dave being supported either side by Maciej and Clappie, her husband holding him by his feet.

'Nuthin',' he answers her. 'Just a scratch. Mind out the way, yeah?'

'Is that how you broke your arm, Jez?' his grandfather asks him.

'Yeah,' Derek answers for him, 'but tha' ain't the worst of it, one of 'is mates got killed in the process!'

Detlef looks momentarily shocked. 'I'm very sorry to hear that,' he then says.

'Tha's wha' ya get for nickin' cars, innit?' continues Derek.

'I wasn't the one who was drivin'!' Jez again protests his innocence, upset clearly returning to his voice.

'I can see that, Jez,' soothes his grandfather, recognising the obvious and honest reaction in the boy.

'Driver or not, he might end up in the nick - you know, young offenders prison I mean,' explains Derek.

'I know what the word means, Derek,' his father reminds him.

'Would you come with me?' Jez asks his grandfather whilst scowling at his father. 'You're the only one here that seems to believe me.'

'What time do you need to be there, Jez?' asks Detlef without a moment's pause.

'I believe you!' protests his mum.

'And me,' adds Julie.

'Well, Jez?' his grandfather asks him again.

'Early!' says Derek, continuing to speak over him. 'Half-past-bloody-eight!'

'Let the boy answer, Derek. How long is the meeting?'

'Dunno,' says Jez. 'Not long, don't think.'

'Just some paperwork,' says Derek, but suitably chastened. 'Half an hour tops.'

'Would it be OK if I come along too?'?' Detlef asks.

'Yeah, sure. Fine by me,' answers Derek but with his attention drawn to the commotion over by the door.

'Christ almighty! What now?!' shouts Jimbo from behind the bar, slapping his forehead in disbelief as he sees the group stumble in with Dave's limp and lifeless body swinging in between them.

'Got any plasters, Jim?' Phil calls back. 'We got a live man not walkin' 'ere!'

Quickly joined by Derek, Jimbo hurriedly lifts the hatch to usher them all through and into the kitchen where Reenie is busy tidying.

'Has he OD'd?' asks Derek not having seen the blood on his leg.

'What's he doing here? I thought you'd just banned him?' Reenie asks her husband indignantly.

'I did!'

'Then why's he back?

'How do I bloody know?'

'I do,' says Derek as Dave drops his feet and Maciej and Clappie turn him to sit him in a chair. 'Whoah! Is that blood?'

'He pulled a knife on me,' Phil tries to explain his innocence. 'I was just tryin' to get it off 'im, tha's all.'

'Fuckin' 'ell, Phil!'

'I only had him by the wrist, Dekko! I didn't actually go to stab 'im! It just happened!'

'Somebody's going to have to take a look,' says Reenie. 'I'll get a cloth. I'm not having him bleed all over my floor!'

'I'm not doin' it!' cries Jimbo. 'Just chuck some water on his face, that'll bring 'im 'round.'

'Come, I will do it,' says Maciej and carefully easing the tracksuit bottoms down to reveal a bloody but straight two inch gash to his thigh. 'I don't think it has cut artery, but we must keep his leg up and apply pressure,' he correctly observes.

'Can't we just bandage him up?' suggests Jimbo ridiculously but pulling up another chair for his leg.

'No, we need to call an ambulance,' insists Maciej as he takes the cloth from Reenie and presses it firmly onto the wound.

'So, what 'appened?' asks Derek as Reenie goes to make the call.

'Speak to Clappie,' says Phil. 'Tell Dekko wha' ya told me, ya little shit!'

'It was PG,' he starts off hesitantly.

'Yeah? Go on,' says Derek, intrigued.

'He's threatenin' your kids, Dekko,' blurts out Phil before Clappie can say another word. 'Unless you give 'im that money back.'

Derek looks stunned. 'Is this true, Clappie?' he asks.

'Yeah, it is,' he admits.

'D'ya see now, Dekko?' says Phil, feeling exonerated.

'Threatenin' my kids?' Derek repeats.

'Where does PG live, Clappie?' Phil then asks.

'I can't tell you that, Phil,' he says and looking even more nervous.

'You can! Now, where?'

'A big h'house over in R'redland,' answers Clappie, stuttering once again.

'Right, can I borrow you, Maciej?' continues Phil.

'Phil, no!' stops Derek, immediately understanding his friend's intention. 'I don't want you getting' involved!'

'But this has got to stop, Dekko. Like now!' insists Phil. 'It's the least I can do for ya.'

'You're not goin' to nuthin' stupid, are ya?'

'Nah! I'll just explain a few things, tha's all. You stay here with yer dad an' that an' I'll be back before ya know it.'

'Make sure you do.'

'An' you, Clappie,' Phil then turns his attention, 'you're comin' wi' me too!'

'No, I'm not!'

'Yes, you are! No ifs, no buts! Now fuckin' move it!'

Chapter 31

Dave, his leg still propped up on the chair, finally comes to and opens his eyes.

'Back in the land o' the livin' then?' observes Derek in a tone offering little or no sympathy but, still, holding a bloodied J-cloth to Dave's exposed and naked thigh.

'What ya doin'?' he groans. 'Wha's 'appened to me fuckin' leg?'

'You tell me,' says Derek.

Confused, Dave thinks for a moment. 'It was Phil!' he then recalls. 'He stabbed me, the cunt!'

'Oi! I'll not have that sort of language in my kitchen!' Reenie reprimands him, flicking a tea towel in his direction and angry at the incursion. 'Don't care how hurt you are!'

'He'll fuckin' pay for this,' Dave threatens, ignoring her.

'Are you listening to me?'

'Big fuckin' time!'

'I'll be glad to see the back of you once an' for all! You were always nothing but trouble, all the years we've ever known you!'

'Ooh, thanks for nuthin',' Dave finally acknowledges her, 'sat 'ere bleedin' to death.'

'You're your own worst enemy, that's your problem!'

Derek then takes up the cudgel. 'So, wha' d'ya mean, he'll pay for this?' he asks, pressing the wound a little harder.

'Bloody ouch, Dekko! Careful!'

''Ere, you hold it then!' he says, taking his hand away.

'Report 'im to the police, tha's what! Sue 'im for criminal injuries!' shouts Dave, lifting the cloth to inspect the wound. 'Jeezus-aitch-fuckin'-Christ!'

'You? Go to the police? Don't make me laugh,' says Derek. 'You'd be the one gettin' banged up, not 'im!'

'You seen this?' asks Dave, still looking at the cut.

'Yeah, nasty, but you attacked Phil! It was *your* knife!'

'Tha's as maybe, bu' I didn't do this to me fuckin' self, now did I?'

'You won't 'ave a leg to stand on,' says Derek, unintentionally cracking a pun.

'Tha's it, go on, 'ave a laugh at my expense why don't ya?' whimpers Dave, gingerly replacing the cloth.

'Who's laughin'? I'm not!' says Derek, 'but I'll tell ya what,' he starts to suggest, 'if you're prepared to tell the medics that it was an accident an' you tripped an' fell, I might save you the bother.'

With that, Dave lifts his head with interest. 'Wha' d'ya mean, save me the bother?'

'Let's call it a bit o' compensation, shall we?'

'O-kay,' Dave drawls, the pound signs popping up inside his head, 'then I want all tha' you promised me.'

'Not a cat's in Hell's chance!' Derek rejects immediately. 'I've already told ya!'

'Then the police it is.'

'Go on then,' Derek calls his bluff, offering him his own phone. 'Do it. I'm sure the police would love to hear about what you got in your pocket.'

'Shut up, Dekko, yeah?' says Dave, gesturing towards Reenie. 'Didn't take you for a fuckin' grass!'

Reenie forces a laugh. 'You must think we're all stupid. Where's that flamin' ambulance got to?' she asks.

'Ambulance? I don't want no fuckin' ambulance!'

'You do, and you'll flippin' well get in it too!' she insists. 'I'll not be held responsible. And let me tell you, David, when you've gone, you'll never step back in this pub as long as my name's over the door, and there's an end to it!'

-

'Wha' d'you plan to do, Phil?' asks Clappie, fidgeting nervously in the back seat of the taxi, inspecting his grazed hands, teasing out a bit of grit. 'I can't 'ave PG knowin' it was me that showed you where he lives. He'll 'ave me guts for garters!'

'Tha's the least o' your worries,' says Phil. 'But, fine, you keep out o' sight. Just give us directions and call him, make sure he's at home.'

'How can I do that, Phil?!' Clappie squeals. 'I ain't got his home phone number. He'd never give it out, only his mobile. He'll suss me out straight away!'

'Jus' do wha' I say, ya little shit - or else.'

-

Dave shakes his head, looking morose, defeated, and physically wounded - literally. Not only is he kicked out of his local boozer for good this time, but, far more importantly, it's the final realisation at having had such a large fortune snatched from his grasp, and all through his own stupidity. It is almost too much to bear. 'So, how much were you thinkin'?' he asks self pityingly.

'Ten,' says Derek, firmly.

'Ten grand? Is that all? That ain't gonna do for 'alf of it, Dekko.' 'Ten.'

Dave pauses for a moment, roughly calculating his debt. 'It's gotta be at least thirty, Dekko, mate,' he pleads.

'Fifteen.'

'Twenty-five.'

'Twenty.'

'I need twenty-five, Dekko,' Dave implores him. 'I'm up to me fuckin' neck in it,' he admits. 'I'm beggin' ya.'

Derek looks him squarely in the eye. 'OK,' he agrees, 'but that'll be yer lot. Not a penny more. Wipe out what you owe. I'll do you a cheque. Sort yourself out, yeah?'

'Can't ya do cash?'

'No, I can't do bloody cash! It's a cheque or nuthin'. Express clear it if ya must. You got a pen, Reen?'

'Don't think I have, Dekko,' she answers, tapping her apron pockets and looking around. 'No, but Jimbo'll have one. I'll go and ask.'

'No, I'll go,' says Derek, turning to leave. 'Oh, an' one more thing, Dave,' he adds.

'What?'

'How can I put this nicely?'

'What?!'

'I don't want you anywhere near my friends an' family no more,' Derek delivers the final bombshell.

'You what?' Dave squeals and looking genuinely upset. 'Why?'

'Because.'

'But you an' me, we go back bloody years!'

'It's the drugs, Dave! It's always the drugs wi' you. I don't wan' it anywhere near my kids anymore. You've become a fuckin' liability.'

'Bu' you used to use 'em!'

'Tha's as maybe, but years ago, an' nuthin' like the crap you stick in your body nowadays!'

'Fuckin' 'ell, Dekko!'

'When you get clean perhaps?' Derek offers an element of potential reconciliation.

But Dave isn't listening or hasn't heard. 'I never took you for a two-faced cunt an' all!' he shouts.

'I'll not tell you again!' Reenie shouts back, stepping forward and cracking the tea-towel hard at Dave's shoulder, making contact. 'Where's that bloody ambulance? I've had enough!'

-

'I'm waitin', Clappie,' says Phil.

'Gimme a minute! I'm thinkin'!'

'Jus' tell him you've delivered his message. Report back. Ask.'

An equally concerned Maciej now looks to Phil. 'But please, tell me you will not do something bad,' he says. 'I love it here. I have life. House. I don't want to get into trouble.'

'Relax, Maciej,' Phil tries to reassure him as Clappie scrolls through his contacts. 'I'm just gonna return the compliment, tha's all. Explain a thing or two. It'll be nuthin' to do wi' you.'

'It's ringing!' hushes Clappie. 'Shut up, yeah?'

-

The paramedics are coming in through the pub door.

'Out the back,' Jimbo instructs them, quickly showing them through just as Derek is coming in. 'Got a pen?' he asks.

'A what?' says Jimbo looking and sounding particularly flustered.

'A pen. You got one? S'not difficult.'

'Over by the till! In the pot. I'm getting' too old for all this shit!'

'It's only a pen, Jimbo. Keep your 'air on!'

'I'm sorry. It's not you, Dekko. It's just …'

Derek stops him. 'S'alright, mate. I understand,' he says.

'Fuck me! I'm comin'! I'm comin'!' Jimbo then shouts as yet another crew of drinkers are raucously demanding more booze. 'Sorry, Dekko.'

'It'll all calm down in a minute,' he suggests without any good reason. Can't Reenie take over for a bit?'

Jimbo looks at him in incredulous disbelief. 'See them pigs out there?' he says, looking out and above the net curtains. 'Flyin', they are! Fuckin' flyin'!'

-

'But what will you do, Phil?' Maciej persists in hushed tones. 'You might make things worse.'

'Not bothered,' he answers but not nearly so quietly. 'His sort don't phase me. Never 'ave, never will.'

'I done it, PG,' Clappie is saying but waving his hands frantically to silence the voices in the front.

'But, please, no fighting,' Maciej requests again.

Phil laughs, flexing his fingers, cracking his knuckles.

'Yeah, seriously worried he is,' Clappie continues but now huddling himself into the corner and trying to cover his head and the phone with his arm. 'I've given him your number,' he lies.

'You got anythin' 'eavy in the boot, Maciej?' Phil then asks. 'A spanner or summat? A big screwdriver?'

'Course I'm on my own, PG!' says Clappie unconvincingly. 'It's only the radio.'

'No!' rejects Maciej. 'You cannot have them!'

'No! I'm just in me motor. I'll turn it down.'

'Don't be a spoilsport,' continues Phil, drumming the dashboard in excitement. 'I just got a little idea, tha's all.'

'It's a play. It's not only you tha' likes a bit o' Radio 4,' says Clappie, thinking fast.

Phil then turns around. 'Well, where is he? At 'ome?' he mouths at least, but aggressively.

Again, Clappie shoos him away. 'Dekko said he'll call ya. Go an' watch the telly, PG. Stick up yer feet,' he chances.

Phil continues to glare at him, threatening him with his fist.

'No! I'm not tryin' to tell you what to do, PG!' Clappie apologises and somehow realising that the game is up. 'Jus' wanted to make sure you're home safely, tha's all!'

-

'You must be Dave,' says the first paramedic as he enters the kitchen and sees him on the chair.

'Yeah, tha's me. How d'ya guess?' he says sarcastically and lifting the cloth to show them. 'You might as well finish me off now an' 'ave done with it.'

The paramedic kneels to inspect his leg. 'Let's not get silly about it, but this is a nasty cut,' he observes. 'You'll need some stitches. How did it happen?'

'Tripped an' fell, didn't I,' says Dave, at least sticking to the story.

'Must have been something very sharp.'

'Cake,' he explains. 'I was jus' cuttin' meself a bit.'

'O-kay,' says the paramedic doubtfully and noticing the burns to Dave's mouth, his fingers. 'Did you have it on your lap?'

'What?'

'The cake.'

'No! I ain't that stupid! As I said, I tripped an' fell. I just 'ad the knife in me hand. Just a bit pissed, tha's all.'

'Only alcohol?'

'Yeah! Course, *only* alcohol!'

'Mmm, did you lose much blood?'

'Here's his trousers,' says Reenie, offering them for inspection. 'A bit, but not that much.'

'Where's the knife?' the paramedic continues.

'Over there,' Reenie lies, pointing to a suitable looking one over by the sink. 'Just washed it up.'

'Was it clean? Before the accident I mean?'

'Had a bit o' cake on it,' says Dave.

'Dirty then?'

'Not really, just a bit o' jam sponge.'

'Right,' says the now rather bemused and suspicious looking paramedic, 'then you might need a tetanus too.'

'I don't want no bleedin' injections!'

'Let's just get you into a wheelchair and over to A&E, shall we? They'll advise you there.'

'I don't want no ambulance either!'

'You'll do as you're told,' warns Derek as he re-enters the kitchen, tapping his jacket pocket. 'I'll see you get this later,' he says, 'when you're fully mended.'

-

'So, is he there?' Phil asks.

'Think so,' says Clappie, now shaking in fear. 'He knows, ya know. I could tell.'

Phil shrugs as if it is of no consequence. 'Does anyone live with him? Wife? Kids?'

'PG? No! He's a confirmed bachelor!'

'Gay then.'

'Nah! Dunno. Never thought,' says Clappie, thinking. 'He's got a housekeeper though.'

'A woman?'

'Yeah, think so. He's mentioned her.'

'Good. Dogs?'

'No! He hates them, the bastard!'

'There you go then. You won't mind if I give 'im one for you, now will ya?'

'Don't you dare mention my name!' wails Clappie.

'Why? What ya gonna do?' asks Phil, a manic and evil looking grin on his face.

-

With Dave loaded onto the stretcher and safely into the back of the ambulance, Derek at last returns to his family.

'What's going on, Dekko?' asks Marion, very concerned.

'Nuthin',' he answers. 'Just Dave bein' Dave,' he offers glibly.

'I don't want my children exposed to all this mayhem.'

'Neither do I,' says Derek. 'Jus' said as much.'

'Especially little Julie here,' his ex continues. 'I think we should go.'

'Maybe it would be a good idea, Derek,' says Detlef, agreeing with her. 'I will stay.'

'No, please! Don't go yet,' he pleads, desperate to keep his family all together and sat around him. 'It's all over. He's gone. You won't see 'im again.'

'You sure?'

'Yeah, I'm sure,' says Derek, assertively.

'So, no more shenanigans?'

'No, no more shenanigans! Now, about this holiday,' he tries to steer it back.

-

As the taxi drives slowly down PG's leafy avenue, Clappie, his head barely visible above the bottom of the window, speaks up. 'Over there,' he says. 'Next on the right.'

Phil looks intently as they pass. 'Bloody nice gaff considerin' he ain't much more than a glorified tea leaf,' he snarls. 'Are those his two motors outside?'

Clappie peers up just enough to see both the Jaguar and the Range Rover parked on the drive. 'Yeah, tha's them,' he confirms.

'Good, he's in then,' says Phil pointing to a parking space on the opposite side of the tree lined street. 'You pull up over there, Maciej,' he instructs him. 'This won't take long.'

'Please go careful,' pleads the young driver. 'Nothing stupid.'

'Don't fret. Now, your boot? Is it open?'

'I said no, Phil. Please.'

'It's either his cars or him,' says Phil like it was the best two options. 'Just keep your engine running, yeah?'

-

'I'll get some brochures, shall I?' continues Derek, addressing his children and trying to rekindle the previous excitement.

'But how did that man cut his leg, Dad?' asks Julie.

'Just bein' silly, love,' he answers her. 'He's just a bit of a wank … a twit,' he quickly corrects himself.

'Dad! Will he be OK?'

'Yeah, 'course. He's off to hospital now. They'll look after him there.'

'I'm going to be a doctor,' she says.

'I know. You told me,' says Derek, reaching out to touch her. 'I'm proud o' my littl' girl. I'll help ya. I'll help all o' ya,' he promises. 'Whatever ya want.'

'Pity you didn't say that years back,' says Marion.

'But I hadn't won the lottery then, Mar,' he tries to defend himself.

'Doesn't matter, Derek,' she says. 'Money ain't everythin', ya know. You don't need money to help. You don't need money to be happy.'

-

Phil finds a brace tucked down by the side of the spare wheel. He picks it up, feeling its weight and, approvingly, raps it two or three times into the palm of his left hand. 'This'll do nicely,' he says before marching into the drive and towards the first of the vehicles - the Jag.

'What's he up to?' asks Clappie, now lying flat on the back seat and completely out of sight. 'Wha's he doin'?'

'That lovely Jaguar,' says Maciej in sad astonishment as he watches Phil smash a wing mirror clean off with a single swipe and stove the driver's door in with his foot.

In an instant, PG appears at the top of his steps. 'What are you playing at!' he yells. 'Get off my property immediately!'

Phil turns to confront him, grinning.

'I'll call the police!'

'No, you won't,' says Phil, laughing dismissively. 'They'll be all over you like a fuckin' rash. You got a lot o' skeletons, mate!'

'Leave my vehicles alone!'

'Not 'til I've finished,' continues Phil, turning his attention to the Range Rover, clattering the brace onto the bonnet before 'spider-webbing' the windscreen with a resounding crack.

'Stop! Why are you doing this?'

''Ave a guess!'

'Is a chap called Clappie with you?'

'Who? Dunno wha' you're talkin' about. Never heard of 'im.'

'So, who's behind this?'

'Me,' says Phil, matter of fact. 'All my own idea,' as he starts to attack the headlights on both vehicles - *smash!*

'Stop!'

'No, I won't stop! This is what you get' -*bash!*- 'when you' - *crash!*- 'threaten' -*wallop!*- 'my mate!'

'Stop I say!'

'Why? Do you want some?'

Horrified, PG, incandescent with rage but feeling entirely powerless to do anything about it hurries back inside, locking the doors, sliding the bolts.

Immediately, Phil races up after him and into the portico. 'Let this be a lesson to ya, PG!' he yells in through the door before taking a swing at the lion's head door knocker, knocking the brass ring clean off and sending it flying through the air. 'Now, fuckin' back off, ya cunt, or it'll be your head next time! D'you hear me?'

Behind the door, trembling with rage, PG doesn't answer.

'I said, d'ya hear me?' Phil shouts again, larruping the door once more for good measure to leave a deep splintered indentation in the woodwork, before walking calmly down the steps to return to the waiting taxi.

Detlef and Maciej are easily the first to arrive outside Jefferson's offices, soon to be followed by Jez.

Predictably, Derek is nowhere to be seen and already ten minutes late.

-

Ellen had had a broken and fitful night's sleep. She'd been awake since the early hours, waiting and wondering and cradling her doll for all it's worth.

At long last, she hears a gentle tap followed by Margaret's welcome and gentle tones. 'Good morning, Ellen,' she hears her say. 'Can I come in?'

'You don't need to ask.'

'Did you sleep OK?' asks Margaret as her head appears around the door.

'Oh, you know.'

'All the excitement, I expect. Never mind.'

'Bit nervous really.'

'That's understandable. Let's glam you up a bit, shall we? Make you look a million dollars.'

-

'Pick up the bloody phone, Brian,' PG is saying, his own held in his hand.

-

'He is here,' says Maciej, pointing, as he spots Derek appear from around the corner, half walking, half jogging.

'Where you been, Dad?' yells Jez fretfully. 'We been here ages!'

'I'm 'ere now, ain't I?' his father calls back, out of breath and looking dishevelled as ever. 'Chillax, will ya?'

'I thought you'd forgotten!'

'Course I hadn't forgotten!' (although he very nearly had and, in his inevitable inebriation, had failed to set his alarm)

'How are you, Derek?' his father asks him pointedly.

'Fine, Pops,' he answers but without a word of apology. 'Great day yesterday, weren't it? Feel a bit withered 'round the gills now, mind you,' he adds, trying to laugh it off.

'I'm not surprised,' says Detlef, understanding the gist, the reprimand clear in his voice.

'Tellin' me off again, are ya?'

'Why don't you stay out the pub for a few days now, Dad?' his son then implores him. 'You look a right state.'

'You sound like your sister!'

'Then maybe you should listen,' says Detlef.

'Alright, alright. Give it a rest. I might surprise you all an' go on the wagon,' hints Derek as they begin to ascend the stairs before adding in a hushed voice, 'but don't tell this bastard I won the lottery, yeah? I don't want 'im chargin' me an arm an' a leg. OK?'

'It's PG,' says PG.

'*I can see that,*' says Brian. '*I thought I'd told you to fuck off,*' he growls and ending the conversation before it had even begun.

Margaret is now doing Ellen's hair, having already dressed her in the freshly washed and ironed Laura Ashley frock. 'Smells lovely,' the old lady's saying, smoothing the fabric on her knee, 'and so soft. What *do* you use?'

'Just a bit of fabric conditioner,' replies Margaret, taking a hairpin from her teeth, 'Nothing expensive. Freesias, I think.'

'Doesn't matter what it cost,' says Ellen, immensely grateful for all the help and attention. 'I always loved freesias. I'd often buy a bunch.'

'Lovely, aren't they? They do a nice lavender one too,' Margaret tells her. 'I always make sure I've got one or the other. You've got to smell nice, haven't you?'

Ellen doesn't answer, aware that it had been years since she'd given it that much consideration.

'Tell you what, I've got some perfume in my bag,' Margaret continues. 'Light it is. Subtle. Would you like a splash behind your ears when we've done?'

'Ooh, can I?'

'Of course, you can. Now, how do you want it? Curled up or curled under?'

'Please, take a seat,' says Jefferson, scowling at the clock on the wall. 'We did say eight-thirty sharp, Mr Dando,' he complains rather tetchily.

'Yeah, sorry 'bout that, only we been celebratin'. Sortin' out a family 'oliday,' Derek offers in explanation. 'Well, if this silly little bugger don't get himself banged up that is,' he adds.

'That's why we're here and what I'm trying to prevent,' says the solicitor.

'Wha's his chances, d'ya reckon?'

'That's for the court to decide. But let's remain positive, shall we?' says Jefferson. 'So, who do we have here?' he then asks, looking at Detlef.

'This is me dad,' answers Derek, 'Jez's gran'dad.'

Still standing, Detlef offers his hand, forced to introduce himself properly. 'My name is Detlef Otto,' he says. 'I'm very sorry we are late,' he apologises more earnestly.

The solicitor's eyes widen everso slightly. 'Thank you. Much appreciated,' he says. 'I'm Jefferson, Bob Jefferson. Pleased to meet you.'

Detlef moves around such that he and Detlef are seated either side of the now hunched and nervous young lad and places a reassuring hand on his shoulder.

'Your surname's Otto, you say?' Jefferson repeats.

'Yes.'

'An unusual name. Do I detect an accent?'

'Yes, I'm over from Germany visiting my family.'

'I see, so, moving on,' says Jefferson, pushing back his glasses with his finger, 'we need to go through some paperwork before Jez's court appearance on the …,' he riffles through the folder on his desk, '… yes, here it is, on the thirteenth. Next Tuesday. Ten o'clock.'

'That's a bit bloody ominous,' says Derek. 'The thirteenth. Can't we change it?'

'I don't think we need worry about superstitions like that, do you?' Jefferson brushes the comment aside. 'Now, as Jez is a minor, I shall need a couple of signatures from you, Mr Dando.'

'Sure. No problem. Got a pen? I always seem to be lookin' for pens nowadays.'

Jefferson hands Derek a biro and slides the paperwork over to him. 'I've marked where you need to sign with a cross,' he tells him.

'Where?'

'At the bottom … and over the page,' says the solicitor but looking hard at Detlef as he does so. 'Please forgive me, Mr Otto,' he then says, unable to stop himself, 'an impertinent question perhaps, but did you once live in Bristol?'

'Yes, I did,' says Detlef looking a little perplexed.

'In the late 1950's perchance?'

'Yes. Why do you ask?'

'Oh, nothing. Sorry. Forget I mentioned it,' says the solicitor, feeling very unprofessional as the words left his mouth and aware that Derek's hand is still hovering uncertainly.

'No. Please tell me,' Detlef insists.

'I think I remember your name, that's all.'

'Next to this X?' asks Derek.

'Yes, that's it,' says Jefferson, lifting himself from his seat to point, 'and similarly on the next page.'

'Ah, yeah. Got it. Ta.'

'I have no secrets,' Detlef pursues.

Jefferson sits back, spreading his hands, fingertips together. 'It was the first court case I ever attended, Mr Otto. I was just a rookie at the time. Bristol Crown Court. I remember it quite vividly, that's all.'

'When was that then?' asks Derek, listening intently whilst signing his second signature with an even more elaborate flourish than the first.

'Let me think?' says the solicitor, trying to remember. 'It would have been in the February of 1959. Would that tie in, Mr Otto?'

Detlef nods almost indiscernibly, swallowing.

'There was a man on trial there with your name, and not one I'm likely to forget. Please forgive me if I've mistaken you for someone else.'

'No, that was me,' Detlef acknowledges.

'You were the young driver. Is that correct?'

Detlef dips his head again. 'Yes,' he says.

'You were genuinely unaware, weren't you?' Jefferson seeks to confirm.

'What's that, Gran'dad?' Jez interjects. 'Driving what?'

'Please, forgive me, Mr Otto,' repeats Jefferson, berating himself. 'I'm being completely inappropriate. We must push on.'

'No. Please continue,' says Detlef, but visibly overcome by this astonishing coincidence.

'I think I've said enough, but fair to say we all considered you very unfortunate to receive such a sentence. A slight miscarriage of justice, you might say?'

'What's that gran'dad?' asks Jez. 'What's he talkin' about?'

'I will tell you later, Jez.'

'Anyway, I'm pleased to see you alive and well after all these years,' offers Jefferson before quickly steering the conversation back around. 'So, Jez,' he continues, 'some things you will need to know…'

-

'All done, Ellen,' says Margaret. 'Let me find you a mirror so you can tell me what you think before I give it a quick spray.'

'Oh, I'm sure it will be perfect,' says Ellen, lifting her hand and patting the underside of her hair with the lightest of touches.

'I just want to be sure you're happy. We want to look your best, don't we?'

'You can't make a silk purse out of a sow's ear!' says the old lady, chuckling.

'Nonsense! You look beautiful!'

'Stop it,' says Ellen, instinctively reaching for her doll. 'You'll make me go all shy.'

'Do you want to take that with you today?' enquires Margaret. 'Your dolly?'

Ellen holds it up, looking at it, thinking. 'I think I'll leave it here,' she says.

'Probably a good idea,' reinforces Margaret. 'You don't want to go losing it, do you?'

'No. Never.'

'Good. Now, you've got some nice warm boots, haven't you? It'll be a little cold and blowy on the promenade.'

'In the bottom of my wardrobe,' Ellen informs her, adding 'if they'll go over these damn bandages o' mine, please forgive me.'

-

'That was easy enough,' says Derek as they walk out and into the precinct. 'But fancy that, Pops, him remembering you from all those years ago? Weird or what!'

'Yes. It is a small world,' agrees Detlef but still appearing a little shocked and disturbed by it all.

'I never thought to ask … how old are you exactly?'

'I shall be seventy-eight in a couple of months, Derek.'

'You're not! Seventy-eight? Bloody 'ell! You're doin' alright on it, ain't ya?'

'So, are you going to tell me what's goin' on?' asks Jez again. 'How did he know you, gran'dad?'

'It is a long story, Jez,' Detlef answers him, 'and I will tell you one day. But, just so that you understand, I too was a very foolish young man many years ago and ended up going to prison for it.'

'You went to prison?' says Jez in astonishment. 'Did ya? Did ya really?'

'Yes, I did.'

'What was it like?'

Detlef doesn't answer his question directly. 'Let my mistake be a lesson to you, but I'm sure it won't come to that for you,' the old man tries to reassure him.

'So do bloody I!' agrees Derek. 'We won't be able to all skip of to Tenerife or whatever together, will we?'

'Tenerife? Janice wants to go to Ibiza, Dad.'

'Don' care, as long as it's hot an' sunny. That's what we want, Pops, innit?'

With that, Detlef places his hand on Derek's sleeve. 'There is something I must tell you, son,' he then says. 'But not right now. I really must get back to Maciej. I can't be late for your mother.'

'What? You can't say that and not say!' says Derek, high pitched.

'I will see you tomorrow, before my flight home,' Detlef reassures him.

'Tomorrow? You're leaving tomorrow?'

'I did tell you last night.'

'Oh, I don't remember!' says Derek, chastising himself. 'But you can't! What time?'

'I need to be at the airport by midday. The flight is at two.'

'I wish I was comin' to Weston wi' ya now you said that!' says Derek looking truly taken aback.

'I will call you later, Derek,' says Detlef. 'We can have some time together tomorrow morning. Just you and me. We can say our goodbyes then. Yes?'

'But you don't know where I live! Quick! Let me show you so you can find me!'

'I haven't got time,' says Detlef, worrying. 'Maciej will find you easily enough if you give me the address.'

'It's not far. Just around the back. It'll only take a couple o' ticks,' insists his son, pulling him by the sleeve in return.

'When am I goin' to see you again gran'dad?' Jez questions Jez anxiously. 'Can't you stay around for Tuesday? I'd like you there too.'

'I'm sorry, Jez. I can't. But I will phone you, always. Your sisters too. Your father will explain everything when I've gone.'

'Explain what?!' protests Derek again. 'You're really startin' to worry me now! Just let me just show you where I live. Yeah?'

Detlef looks at his watch.

'Please, Dad! It'll only take a couple o' minutes! I'd like it.'

Chapter 33

With Derek having insisted on showing Detlef whereabouts he lived and encountering much heavier Saturday morning traffic than Maciej could possibly have anticipated, they are running much later than the old man would have liked and making the journey to pick up Ellen not without its anxieties - but that wasn't the half of it. No way near.

Shifting uneasily and unable to sit comfortably, Detlef finds himself torn, caught between a rock and a hard place, struggling both physically and emotionally.

Not only is he disturbed by the extraordinary and disquieting coincidence that had just occurred at the solicitor's office and the very painful memories it had invoked - the shattering realisation of the irreconcilable damage done to his young family at the time, the agonising sense of isolation after his arrest, the loss, the shame, the yearning - but, simultaneously, he is still plagued with feelings of disloyalty and abandonment towards his poor wife back at home.

Then, and if that wasn't enough, it had pained him tremendously to have to say goodbye to Jez and he dearly wishes he could stay for longer and offer the young boy some much needed help and support - but he can't. In fact, the inherent and powerful feelings of attachment he'd developed towards all three grandchildren, and so soon, is heart wrenching for him and he can't help but wonder when, if ever, he will get to see them again. Understandably, undeniably, and yet again, it all starts to make him feel more than a little unwell.

'Don't worry, my friend,' Maciej tries to reassure him, clearly sensing the old man's silent distress and unease. 'Everything will be OK. We will be there shortly.'

-

Very unusually for him, if ever in fact, Derek had walked his son back home such was the boy's obvious distress. 'Don't fret, eh? You'll get to see your gran'dad again on holiday I expect,' his dad had said to him before swiftly changing the subject to tell him about all the things he was going to do with his money - the lovely bungalow he was planning to buy for Gran and the sudden idea of buying a proper grandstand season ticket for the Rovers such that the pair of them could go and watch them together. 'Hey, there's a thought!' he'd added excitedly. 'When I get meself a new place too, you can come an' stay over after the game. I'll 'ave plenty o' space! We'll 'ave great fun, you an' me!'

Jez was so appreciative of their chat and the rare moment spent together that he'd given his dad a fleeting but purposeful hug before turning on his heels and heading quickly indoors.

Clearly touched by this surprising and welcome show of affection himself and now standing alone outside his old family home, Derek finds himself in a quandary, uncertain as to what to do next. Instinctively, he checks the time to see whether the doors might as yet be open. Not that he would be refused entry of course, he knows that, but, somehow, he finds himself feeling less than enthusiastic about spending the whole day on the razz yet again.

Besides, as all his children are now telling him, he's got to take his foot off the pedal and dry out a bit – and, deep down, he knows it.

'Bloody kids, eh?' he says, pinching his nose, stifling a sniff. 'Who'd 'ave 'em, eh?'

-

Mercifully, when the taxi does eventually pull into the New Horizons car park, late but not overly so, Detlef is at least relieved to see Ellen ready and waiting by the main entrance with Margaret standing by in close attendance - both warmly dressed, both waving energetically, and both obviously very excited and keen to go.

'She insisted on waiting outside, Detlef!' Margaret tells him, half by way of an apology, half in jest as he gets out to greet them. 'Couldn't stop her, I couldn't. She's like a mad thing today, she is!'

Although still not feeling 100%, Detlef can't help but raise a smile. 'Let's have a lovely day, Ellen,' he says to her as he leans forward to give her a peck on her cheek. 'You look lovely too,' he compliments her.

Ellen shudders with girlish delight and anticipation. 'Get away with you!' she bats him away, colouring up. 'You always were a bit of a charmer.'

'Isn't he just!' says Margaret, smiling, and releasing the brake to wheel Ellen down the ramp and alongside the taxi where the old lady manages to stand sufficiently to slide her bottom onto the rear seat. 'You see, told you I could do it!' she says triumphantly as Maciej folds the wheelchair adeptly and stows into the capacious boot of his Mercedes.

-

Derek, still dithering, miles away, is startled to hear the familiar sound of his old front door shuddering open as it always did. It's Marion. 'Alright then, Dekko?' she calls to him.

'Oh, you. Yeah. Hi,' he says, rudely snapped back into the here and now.

'You OK? You look like a little boy lost,' she asks.

'Me? Nah! Just thinkin'.'

'What about?'

'Nuthin'.'

'Up to you. How did it go with ol' Jefferson then? All good?'

'Yeah. Just a couple of signatures, tha's all.'

'Okey-dokey. Anyways, just wanted to say thanks for walking Jez back home. He's more worried than he lets on - well, we all are, aren't we?'

'He'll be alright,' Derek tries to dismiss like it was a given.

'Fingers crossed. I could see he appreciated it. Nice o' you.'

'S'alright, I am 'is dad!'

'Yeah, and long may it last,' says Marion, unable to stop herself.

'Wha's tha' supposed to mean?'

'Forget it. How's yours?' she deflects.

'My what?'

'Your dad.'

'Wha's this? Twenty fuckin' questions or summat?'

'Flippin' 'eck, Dekko! I'm only askin' about your dad. He's a nice man. A gent.'

Derek raises his eyebrows, signalling a half-hearted apology. 'Yeah. It's good to 'ave 'im about, all things considered,' he concedes.

'I like him.'

'Nuthin' to dislike, well, other than he's a bloody German,' he tries to make light of it but sounding ridiculously proud at the same time.

'Strange to think you didn't even know he existed this time last week,' Marion muses.

'Yeah, innit just.'

'All this time not knowin' - almost beggars' belief.'

'Don't you start!'

'What 'ave I said now?'

'He IS my dad!'

'I know he's your bloody dad, you idiot!' exclaims Marion. 'Just look at the pair o' ya! You'd have to be blind!'

'Well then. OK. I'm sorry.'

'An' so should you be! I just thought he looked a bit tired,' she adds.

'Did he? Didn't notice,' Derek says, preferring not to think about it but remembering what Detlef had said, or not said, to him less than an hour ago.

'Is he alright?'

'How do I know? Think so.'

'Look, it's cold standing here. Got time for a cuppa?'

'What?' says Derek, sneering and exaggeratedly peering over her shoulder. 'Tha' bastard Nigel out or summat is he?'

'Stop it, Dekko. No need for all that nonsense again.'

'Well, wha' d'you expect?'

'He won't be back 'til later,' Marion tells him.

Derek considers it, but for no more than a fraction of a second. 'Nah,' he rejects, 'I'm a bit busy.'

'Oh yeah? You don't look that busy. What you up to?'

'Will you stop stickin' your nose in! I can do what I like now.'

Marion ignores him. 'I've just put the kettle on,' she tries again.

'Clever you.'

'Not thirsty then?'

'Prob'ly,' says Derek, his thoughts now certainly directed elsewhere.

Marion laughs - a forced laugh. 'Might o' guessed,' she says.

'Why d'you always think it's about the bloody pub?' Derek reads her.

'Cos it is, Dekko. Always was.'

'We must o' lived on different planets, you an' me,' he says in oblivious denial. 'I worked too, ya know.'

Marion holds up her hands. 'I'm not here to fight,' she says, lowering her voice and trying to eliminate the sound of exasperation, 'the offers there if you want. It's your shout.'

Derek pulls a face.

'Save yourself some money.'

Derek now rolls his eyes and laughs. 'Like I give a toss anymore,' he says. 'An' yes, it is my shout, an' don't you forget it.'

'I heard,' she says under her breath.

'Speak up. Heard what?'

'That you been paying for everyone's drinks since your win,' she says but kicking herself as she does. 'That's what.'

'Tha's wha' this is really all about, innit?' he says. 'The bloody money.'

'No, despite what you might think, it's not!'

'Not somehow!'

'You've always been a fool wi' your finances, Dekko, and you bloody well know it!'

'Tha' right?'

'Yes, it is! And as I told you yesterday, money don't buy you happiness.'

'It bloody well helps, I can tell ya that!'

'That's as maybe, but you're just the same ol' Dekko underneath.'

'What's THAT supposed to mean?'

'You know.'

'No, I don't. Tell me!'

'Take a look at yourself,' she answers him. 'You'll end up drinking it all, or givin' it all away, one or the other.'

With that, Derek's heard enough. 'I'm off,' he says. 'Nice chattin' to ya.'

'Wait a minute!' Marion stops him. 'There's something else.'

'What now?!'

'Just wanted to say how nice it was yesterday, all together,' she comes at him, leftfield.

'You what? Wha's that to do wi' the price of eggs?'

'Well, after things settled down they were,' she then qualifies.

'You just tell me I'm a useless pile o' shit, then you tell me this? What you playin' at?'

'I've given it some thought, that's all.'

Derek raises his eyebrows, questioning.

'I've decided to come,' Marion announces.

'Come where?'

'Bloody hell, Derek! On holiday! You, me, an' the kids! D'you not remember a thing?!'

-

'Right! Off we jolly go!' says Maciej, jumping back into the driver's seat and setting up his SatNav. 'Buckle up! Today, I think we go on magical mystery tour!'

'Just like one of your favourite Beatles songs, Detlef,' says Ellen, her memory being triggered.

He looks at her, astonished that she should know it.

'You told me about it in one of your last ever letters,' she reminds him. 'Remember?'

'I don't, Ellen. I'm sorry.'

'I went out and bought it soon after,' she says. 'Played it to death, I did.'

Involuntarily, Detlef lips tighten. The seemingly constant reminders of times past and times lost becoming almost too much to bear.

'Are you alright?' Ellen asks him, noticing.

'Yes,' he reassures her. 'My memory is not so sharp nowadays.'

'You saw them play too, didn't you?' she adds.

'You saw the Beatles, Detlef?' says Maciej, seriously impressed.

'Yes, I did. In Hamburg,' he tells them.

'Wow! Lucky man!'

'When was that then?' asks Margaret, equally impressed. 'It was the early 60's when they were in Germany, wasn't it?'

'Yes, it was, let me think …,' Detlef casts his mind back. '1962,' he recalls.

'Not long after then,' Ellen pieces it together, her face dropping a little at the thought.

'I worked there for a while, in Hamburg,' Detlef tells them. 'There was still much to be done.'

'I bet there was,' says Margaret knowingly. 'Here in Bristol too. My aunts and uncles still talk about it even to this day.'

-

With the DT's now coming fully home to roost, and despite all of his best intentions, Derek's resolve is already beginning to crumble.

Cursing himself, he inspects his hands before shaking them vigorously in an unsuccessful attempt at a 'reset'.

He can't help it.

It's as if he's being pulled by an all-powerful electromagnet.

-

But Ellen doesn't want to dwell. 'Couldn't stand that Mick Jagger though,' she says, puckering her lips and clapping her hands in front of her face and making them all laugh, 'all that strutting about in them jeans of his!'

'Ellen!' Margaret reprimands her jokingly.

'We-ell,' she says, drawing the word out, 'it's not as if he had that much to show off.'

Still laughing, Margaret reaches back to touch the old lady on her knee. 'You OK before we set off? All nice an' comfortable back there, the pair of you?'

'Very comfy, thank you.'

'That's what I like to hear.'

'Shall we get going then?' the old lady suggests like she was fed up of waiting.

-

'After a top up already, are we?' says a smiling but resigned looking Jimbo as he ushers Derek in.

'Yeah, bu' just the one,' he says. 'Don't gi' me anymore.'

Jimbo giving him an old fashioned look. 'When 'ave you only had just the one, Dekko?' he says. 'I got no chance.'

'Straight up!' Derek insists. 'I gotta start lookin' after meself a bit better. I'm under orders.'

Jimbo now nods in genuine approval. 'OK, mate. Nice one. Pleased to 'ear it,' he says. 'So, how d'it all go this mornin'?'

'Yeah, fine, but you'll never guess.'

'What?'

'Ol' Jefferson knew my dad. Remembered him he did. I couldn't believe it!'

'No-o! Really?'

'Really!'

'How?'

'In court, before me dad was imprisoned.'

'Imprisoned? Your dad was imprisoned?'

'Didn't I tell ya?'

'No! I think I might o' remembered that, Dekko,' says Jimbo, reaching for a glass and drawing off the remains of last night's beer from the lines.

'I don't 'ave to tell you everythin'.'

Jimbo holds up the half-filled glass, inspecting the clarity. 'Prison, eh?' he says, giving it a swirl. 'Who'd o' thought it?'

-

'What the bloody hell is going on, Peter?' Sir Alun is demanding over the phone.

'I'm still onto it, Sir Alun,' PG tries to reassure him. 'I can only but apologise ....'

'Apologise? Are you taking the p, i, double s?'

'No! Not at all,' PG sputters.

'We need to meet up. This is getting quite serious now.'

'I can't. I'm temporarily without transport.'

'In God's name why? Had them impounded? Missed the finance payments?'

PG laughs. 'No. I'm having some work done,' he lies.

'A lame excuse,' Sir Alun cuts him short. *'Now look, Peter, I've, we've, committed to the next stage of the development because of that money and the contractors are insisting on payment upfront. Without it, we are up shit creek without a bloody paddle! Do you understand?'*

'I understand very well, Sir Alun, and I will resolve it,' says PG but in truth not knowing what to do at all.

Derek watches as Jimbo finally squeezes the head onto his beer. 'Yeah. Armed robbery, back in the late 50's,' he reveals.

'Tha's a bit serious, innit? He don't look the type.'

'He was only the driver, mind you.'

'Still, bit of a dark horse,' says Jimbo, handing him his drink.

Derek takes it, eagerly supping best part of it in one go. 'Where I can lay me hands on a decent motor, Jim?' he then asks, cuffing his lips.

'I would never have suggested the idea had I have known it might backfire like this,' PG continues to apologise.

'Too late for that! So, tell me, what <u>are</u> you going to do, Peter?' demands Sir Alun.

'I have someone on it as we speak,' he lies.

'Good. We need to schmooze this Dekko character, and fast, get him back on board,' demands Sir Alun before taking a more conciliatory tone. *'Look, tell me, PG, as a plan B, do you have any additional funds you can lay your hands on in the interim?'* he asks. *'You know you'll be paid back as soon as cash flow allows.'*

'I don't know about that, Sir Alun,' PG stutters. 'As you very well know, I'm already heavily committed.'

'So am I! What about all those works of art, those wonderful masterpieces you're always telling me about? Can't you sell one or two of them?'

'I have already,' again PG lies. 'The only pieces I have left are only of moderate value.'

'Secure a loan then,' Sir Alun suggests.

PG coughs. 'On what?'

'Your house, of course! Mine's mortgaged up to the hilt until this all comes to fruition. It's no time for getting cold feet. What is it that they say? He who dares, wins? We'll soon be making millions.'

PG hesitates, desperately hard trying to weigh up his options. 'So, how much are we looking for?' he asks, albeit reluctantly.

'Seventy-five thousand.'

'Seventy-five thousand!'

'As a minimum.'

'That's a lot of money to conjure out of thin air, Sir Alun.'

'Then you'd better hope you and your man come up trumps or we both risk losing the fucking lot!'

PG falls silent, shocked to hear Sir Alun use such language.

'Come, come, Peter,' he urges and readopting a gentler approach. *'It's chicken feed in the scheme of things. You know it. I know it. Can you not do it?'*

'Yes, of course I can do it!' PG reacts and taking the ascendancy for the first time in their relationship. 'But I shall need some assurances, further equity.'

'You know how to kick a man when he's down,' says Sir Alun, jocular and sarcastic all at the same time. *'But let me think … how about an additional one-point-five percent?'*

'Two,' insists PG, 'and in writing.'

'Of course, in writing! What do you take me for, Peter? A common criminal?'

-

'First thing I'd o' done if I was in your shoes, get meself a car,' says Jimbo, animated by the idea himself.

'But I'd like summat, you know, a bit more spacious, not a tiny sports number. Get the family in.'

'But you'll need to watch it 'round here though,' cautions Jimbo. 'The kids'll ''ave the wheels off an' up on bricks before ya know it.'

'Be alright. I'll get meself one o' the garages.'

'You'll be lucky – full o' shit most of 'em.'

'I was thinkin' one o' them new Rover 75's.'

Jimbo lets out an exaggerated groan. 'Nah! You can get yourself summat much better than that!'

'Bu' I've always 'ad Rovers.'

'Rust buckets!'

'Like what then?'

'Anythin'! You name it, you can 'ave it!' You could 'ave a fuckin' McClaren if ya wanted!'

'A what?'

'Million pound super car, Derek, but no room to swing a cat mind you.'

'Bollocks to them then, I do quite like those Lexus thingies.'

'Bit old man.'

'I don't really care, Jim. Fact is, I need something like now - today,' he announces.

Jimbo looks at him in disbelief and astonishment. 'That's pushin' it a bit, me ol' mate. Why?'

'Might be goin' somewhere.'

'Oh yeah? Where?' says Jimbo, second guessing.

'Never you mind. Got any ideas?'

Jimbo thinks for a moment. 'Well, I know Perkins 'ave got some high end motors. You know, just up off the ring road.'

'Yeah! Course! Hadn't thought o' them.'

'Tell ya what,' says Jimbo, thinking, 'they had an old Roller out front the other day. Saw it when I was passin'.'

'Did they now?' asks Derek, immediately taken with the idea. 'A Roller?'

'Yeah, an old Silver Shadow by the looks of it. Goldy coloured.'

'Gold?'

'Yeah.'

'Is it still there?'

'Dunno. Maybe.'

'Can you take me up there, Jim, like pronto?'

'Sorry, Dekko, I've got to open up soon,' answers Jimbo before immediately thinking again. 'Look, if we get it insured,' he then suggests, 'you can always borrow mine if you're pushed.'

Derek pulls a face.

'Tha's a no then?'

'So, can you take me, yay or nay?'

Jimbo puffs hard, looking at his watch. 'I'll have to ask Reenie,' he says.

'How much was it?' Derek asks. 'Can you remember?'

'Does it matter? Three, three an' a half I seem to remember.'

'I'll 'ave to be payin' cash to take it away. We'll need to go to the bank first.'

'Fuck me! You don't want much, do ya?'

Derek laughs, necking the last of his pint. 'Tell ya what, pour us another,' he says sliding his glass over the bar, 'you sort it out with Reenie, I'll give 'em a ring, then we'll get goin', yeah?'

'That didn't last long,' says Jimbo as he calls gently out the back and up the stairs. 'Reen, love,' he says. 'We need your help.'

Chapter 34

Despite the chill and dreary weather, it's a pleasant enough journey as the taxi finally escapes the confines of the city and drives out swiftly along the A370 towards Weston-Super-Mare.

Their conversation, too, is pleasant, excited even, as they point out an ancient old church here, a quintessential chocolate box cottage nestled amongst the naked trees over there, a bevy of bright cock pheasants dangerously conspicuous in the bleak and wintery fields.

It had literally been years since Ellen had ventured out into the open countryside and she is enthralled by it all. 'Good job I brought my coat,' she's saying, but, in truth, not in the least bit concerned. 'Look at them poor birds. Frozen they must be.'

-

'Only two owners from new,' the salesman is telling them but, tight in his three piece suit and short back and sides, viewing Derek's dishevelled and scruffy appearance with thinly disguised distaste and suspicion. 'Full service history,' he continues, flat and toneless and little more than feeling obliged to go through the motions, 'and a genuine sixty-four thousand miles on the clock.'

'Smashin' motor, Jim, duncha think?' says Derek luxuriating in the driver's seat, hands held firmly on the steering wheel and admiring the complicated array of dials, switches, and levers. 'It's like sittin' in a bastard Jumbo Jet in 'ere, it is!'

'Too bloody true!' agrees his friend, equally impressed and sat alongside him. 'These seats are better than me soddin' armchairs back at 'ome. Plush as.'

In the back of his mind, Derek is amazed that he should even be sat in one, let alone easily able to buy it. 'First time I ever been in a Roller to be 'onest,' he admits.

'British engineerin' at its best,' continues Jimbo, 'an' that smell. Can ya smell it? Go on, 'ave a whiff.'

Derek inhales deeply. 'Yeah!' he acknowledges. 'S'like bloody perfume, it is - but for blokes!'

'Proper leather, see,' Jimbo explains unnecessarily, 'an' all this wood. Tons of it.'

'Walnut, innit?' enthuses Derek, guessing correctly and vigorously rubbing the fascia with his forefinger.

Instantly, the salesman coughs in reprimand, now convinced he has little more than a couple of fantasists on his hands. 'Right then, gentlemen,' he says, clapping his hands as if to signify the end of their little moment of make-believe, 'seen enough, have we?'

'Might 'ave, might not,' answers Derek, resting his arm out of the open window like he already owned it.

'Only I'm a bit busy.'

'So am I!' Derek replies, irritated at the attitude but still intent on buying it. 'Ain't my money good enough for ya or summat?'

The salesman looks a little awkward, suddenly unsure whether he might, possibly, have misjudged him.

'So, wha's your best?' Derek then demands.

'It's on the windscreen, sir. Three, nine, nine, five.'

'I'm sure he could do a bit better than that, Dekko,' Jimbo chips in.

'I've got a nice Ford Granada if price is an issue,' the salesman tries the humiliation tactic.

'Do I look like I want a fuckin' Ford Granada?' Derek rebukes him. 'I want this, an' I wan' it right now!'

With that the salesman appears entirely backfooted. 'What? Right *right* now, you mean?' he sputters.

'He gets it, Jim!' exclaims Derek. 'He must be a bleedin' genius!'

'Better get 'is skates on then, hadn't he?' says Jimbo, enjoying Derek's game.

'That might be a bit difficult,' says the salesman, hesitating.

'Why?' questions Derek.

'It's Saturday.'

'So?'

'Our mechanics will need to do its final checks and the workshop's closed,' the salesman explains.

'Has it been serviced?' asks Jimbo.

'Well, … yes. The basics.'

'Tax disc?'

The salesman leans in to look at it. 'Eight, nine months' worth,' he says.

'Then you can do your checks later then, can't ya?' Derek tells him.

'But I'm sure you understand we can't let it go without full and final payment, sir. Will you be needing finance for example?'

Derek then grins broadly. It's the moment he's been waiting for. 'Does it look like I need fuckin' finance?' he says, reaching into his bulging pockets to pull out two huge rolls of £50 banknotes held together with elastic bands.

With that, Jimbo guffaws, loudly, lapping it up. 'Think he'd better start sharpenin' his pencil, Dekko,' he says, 'an' a bit bleedin' sharpish!'

-

'Tell me, did you have anything to do with the visitor I had yesterday?' PG is asking Clappie on the phone in a voice that sounds like he might be auditioning for the part of Shere Khan in a remake of The Jungle Book.

'What visitors?' Clappie replies, desperately feigning innocence.

'He, or they, arrived just before you called me and told me to relax and put up my feet. Interesting coincidence, don't you think?'

'Dunno what you're talkin' about, PG.'

'And, strangely enough, I still haven't heard from Derek, Dekko, or whatever you call him. You did pass on my message, I presume?'

'Course I did! I told ya.'

'Then you need to find him, jog his memory, and report back to me as soon as you have.'

'Why? What ya gonna do?' Clappie worries.

'Never you mind. Just do it.'

'I've got no idea where he is, an' he ain't gonna pick up his phone to me now, is he?'

'Go to that disgusting pub again! Find out!'

'Jeezus, PG!'

'And I'll thank you for not taking the Lord's name in vain either or you might be needing him yourself,' says PG before adding, 'and you'll not get another penny from me until you do.'

'Jeezus, PG!'

'Are you not listening to me?'

'Yeah, sorry, bu' I've got me dogs to feed an' everythin'.'

'Then you'd better get on with it, hadn't you?'

-

As the taxi closes in on the coast, talk soon turns to what they'd like to do today, where they'd like to go, what they'd like to see.

'At some point, I'd like to buy us all a meal,' Detlef suggests to them.

'Oh, that'll be nice,' twitters Ellen. 'I've got quite an appetite all of a sudden.'

'That's good to hear,' says Margaret, 'but there's no need as far as I'm concerned, Detlef,' she then adds. 'I brought myself a sandwich and a banana. Plenty enough for me.'

'No, please,' Detlef insists. 'I want to thank you both, you and Maciej, and I have an idea.'

'Oh, what's that?' asks Ellen, even more intrigued.

'You will have to wait and see,' he says.

-

With the deal done, the rolls of banknotes taken and locked away in the safe, the salesman hands Derek the keys and his portion of the logbook. 'Sorry if there was any misunderstanding earlier, sir,' he fawns.

'Forget it. You're 'appy, I'm 'appy, everybody's 'appy,' Derek accepts.

'But, please, forgive me,' the salesman continues, his curiosity getting the better of him, 'only you're not that big Lottery winner I heard about, are you?'

'You cheeky cunt!' Jimbo reacts. 'Nuthin' to do wi' you where he got 'is money!'

But Derek laughs. 'You got me for the wrong bloke, mate,' he denies. 'Me granny died. Left me a few quid,' he jokes.

'Only we've got a lovely E-type coming in next week,' pursues the salesman and not entirely believing him. 'Five-point-three litre V12.'

''Ave ya? A V12?' says Derek, immediately impressed but not really having any idea.

'Red.'

'Red?'

'Yes. Comes in Monday.'

'Monday?'

'Immaculate condition. Concourse.'

'Bloody 'ell! I could get into this classic car buying malarkey summat rotten!' says Derek, already taken with the idea. 'How much?'

Jimbo immediately intervenes, moving in between him and the salesman and turning his back. 'Leave it for the time bein', Dekko,' he advises his friend. 'Get used to this one first, yeah? There'll be plenty of others.'

'Not like this one there won't be, but OK,' responds the salesman, almost but not quite taking the hint. 'Nice doing business with you, Mr Dando,' he says. 'The Shadow's a beauty. Enjoy her.'

'Don't you worry 'bout that,' says Derek, flipping the leather and enamelled metal Rolls-Royce key fob around on his middle finger. 'I will.'

'And remember, bring her in so we can give her the final once over, yes?'

'I won't forget.'

'Next week perhaps? You can always cast your eye over the Jag then, can't you?'

'Oi, mate,' growls Jimbo, 'You got yer money. Just piss off, yeah?'

-

'It's PG, Brian,' says PG

'Fuck off, PG!' says Brian, slamming down the phone.

-

'I was just thinking,' says Margaret looking over into the back seat, 'we could leave you two alone for a short while if you like? The pair of you don't want to be stuck with us following you around the whole day, now do you?'

'Oh, can we?' asks Ellen, immediately taken with the idea but with Detlef looking more than a little unsure.

'Don't worry,' says Margaret, reading him. 'I'll make sure Ellen's all OK. You do have a phone, don't you?'

Detlef nods.

'That's alright then. Will you be alright pushing her wheelchair? It's quite easy.'

Again, Detlef nods.

'Are you OK with that, Maciej,' Margaret then asks him.

'Yeah, for sure!' he agrees enthusiastically. 'We can go for walk on the beach.'

'Yes, find some shells maybe.'

'But no swim!' he jokes. 'Looks chilly-bloody-willy.'

-

PG calls again. 'Brian! Hear me out!' he shouts before he has a chance to hang up again.

'I thought I told ya to fuck off. I'm nae interested. Dinnae call me again.'

'Name your price!'

PG hears Brian laugh. *'You could'nae afford me,'* he says.

'Oh, I can. Try me.'

'I'll no be threatenin' wee bairns, PG.'

'No one is asking you to threaten children, Brian. On the contrary. Someone needs to be taught a lesson. You've met him before.'

'Who?'

'That friend of Derek's outside the pub, remember?'

'Oh, him.'

'Yes, him. Let's call it a bit of retribution and be well paid to do it too. Interested now?

'Mi' be. Wha' ya offerin'?'

'And I want Derek too.'

'Wha? Beaten up?'

'No, Brian,' says PG like he was trying to explain to a child. 'Found and delivered safely back to me.'

-

'Right,' says Jimbo, 'you off then, mate?'

'Yeah, reckon I am,' says Derek, looking at the Rolls-Royce but, somehow, now feeling like a bit of fraud and a man above his station.

'Get in it then! I wanna see ya pull away.'

'I will if you gimme a minute!'

'You alright? Wha's wrong?' asks Jimbo, sensing Derek's reluctance.

'Nuthin's wrong,' says Derek, tapping the roof. 'Why should it be?'

'No, you got no reason at all. Just take it steady, yeah?' his friend advises. 'It's a big ol' block.'

Derek opens the satisfyingly heavy door and, once again, stares into the opulent interior. 'Who'd o' thought it, eh?' he says, the reality of his wealth suddenly manifest and like it was about to represent leaving a great big chunk of his old life behind. 'Little ol' me buying summat like this?'

'Just drive the damn thing, Dekko,' Jimbo instructs him, but nicely. 'Go where you gotta go, mate. It's only a lump o' metal.'

'Thanks for all your help an' that, Jim,' Derek then offers, his voice catching. ''Preciated.'

'Shut up, ya twat! It's me that needs to thank you. Reen an' I are forever in your debt.'

'Never thought I'd hear you say that neither,' says Derek with a smile.

'Say hi for me, yeah?'

Derek at last eases himself in, searching for the ignition. 'I will,' he answers, pulling the seat belt across his shoulder, 'like finding a couple o' needles in bloody haystack, mind you.'

'Just give it your best shot. Now, go on. Fuck off.'

Chapter 35
Weston-Super-Mare

Even on such an overcast day, and as if by some quirk of nature, the interior of the taxi is instantaneously lit more brightly as they turn onto Marine Parade at the far end of the sea front.

'Ooh,' reacts Ellen, shielding her eyes, 'bit blinding, isn't it?'

'You alright, my love?' asks Margaret, turning to check. 'It's off the water.'

'I know, but I'm not complaining,' the old lady warbles happily. 'It's just lovely to be here. I'd just forgotten how bright it was.'

'Should o' brought you a pair o' sunglasses. Never thought.'

'What? Me? In sunglasses?' says Ellen, tittering at the idea. 'Too old for all that now.'

'Wow! What's that thing?' interjects Maciej, excitedly pointing to the pier as it slowly emerges through the mist and projecting itself far out into the Bristol Channel. 'It's like something from Star Wars of the Worlds!'

'The Grand Pier,' Detlef quietly informs him from the back seat, having already been looking out for it, the tiniest hint of a catch in his throat.

'How did they even build them all the way out there?' comments Margaret. 'That's what I'd like to know.'

'And why?' asks the young taxi driver, still enthralled by it. 'We have some in Poland too I think, but I've never seen it before. Do you know it, Detlef?' he then asks.

'Yes, Maciej, I do - we both do,' he answers as Ellen takes the opportunity to slide her hand across the seat towards his, something she'd been aching to do all journey.

'Don't tell me, you two met there?' guesses Maciej, snatching a glance.

'We did. He was sat on the benches down the middle,' says Ellen for the benefit of all. 'You were wearing sunglasses that day, weren't you, Detlef?'

'Yes,' he recalls. 'I was watching you.'

'Just like a film star, he was,' Ellen continues to reminisce. 'Such a beautiful young man.'

With that, Detlef cringes in embarrassment, but nicely, gently squeezing her hand in return. 'You looked beautiful too, *meine Geliebte*,' he says.

Again, Ellen shudders in delight to hear it. 'My friend Joyce and me, we were looking out along the beach before we left,' she reminisces, thoroughly animated, 'and the people! The children! Thousands there were!'

'I remember it well.'

'And the carousel! Do you remember that too, Detlef? The organ music?'

'I do.'

'Is it still there, I wonder?'

'Don't think so, Ellen,' says Margaret. 'Not when I was last here it wasn't. A shame really.'

'Yes, it is a shame. I'd love another go,' says Ellen, her infirmity temporarily forgotten.

-

'So, what you gonna do wi' yours then, Jimbo?' Phil is asking him.

'Oh, I dunno, mate,' he replies uncertainly. 'We've cleared the debts, put some away for a rainy day, maybe take a bit of a break if we can.'

'You look like you could do wi' a break. You look fuckin' knackered.'

'Thanks.'

'You're welcome.'

'Fancy covering for us for a week?' asks Jimbo without any expectation.

'Yeah, I can do that if you're payin',' says Phil, jokily. 'You plan on stayin' here then, in the pub game?'

'Yeah, reckon. It's a lot better now, not bein' shit scared o' the post anymore.'

'I'll gi' ya that. Helps big time.'

'So, wha' about you?' Jimbo asks. 'Or 'ave you already spent it all already?'

'Spent it, my arse! I ain't that stupid! We're wipin' the mortgage for starters, waitin' on a settlement figure.'

'I would. Sensible.'

'Mind you,' Phil adds with a grimace, 'don't suppose it'll go that far. Betsy's already got it all planned out - a new kitchen, sort the garden out, decorate, new beds for the kids. List is bloody endless.'

Jimbo tuts, laughing in collusion. 'Tell me about it,' he says.

'Bu' I'm still gettin' meself a nice bloody motor, don't care wha' she says!' insists Phil, vigorously taking a slurp of beer as if to emphasise it. 'Bollocks to 'er!'

'You should be so lucky. First Dekko, now you. Not allowed nuthin', me.'

'Aww, ya poor ol' sod! Me 'eart bleeds for ya!'

'So, what ya thinkin'?'

'Not an' old Roller, tha's for certain! Wha's he like, eh? An ol' bloody Roller! Silly twat!'

'They got an E-type comin' in up at Perkins, V12,' muses Jimbo. 'I'd love one o' them, I would.'

'Well, buy it! Dekko gave *you* the money, not her.'

'What, an' park it here outside the pub?' says Jimbo. 'Nah. I've learnt to take the path o' least resistance. Not worth it.'

'Your life,' says Phil, matter of fact. 'I bought meself an Autotrader, lookin' at Imprezas.'

'A Subaru, ya mean?'

'Yeah, Subaru. Fast as fuck! Four point eight, nought to sixty! Whoo-fuckin'-oosh!'

Jimbo looks at Phil almost pityingly. 'You mind you don't go killin' yerself,' he warns. 'You're bloody mad enough as it is, you boy-bleedin'-racer you.'

-

'Fancy a ride?' suggests Derek, standing at the door of his old house but looking up to the front bedroom window.

'A what?' asks Marion, poking her head out and peering in amazement at the immaculate and glinting two-tone Rolls-Royce parked at the kerbside.

'A ride.'

'Is that yours?'

'Yeah. Just bought it. Well, wha' d'ya reckon?'

'You can take me 'round the block if ya like, I s'pose,' she says. 'Never been in one before.'

'Neither 'ad I 'til now. Smooth as. But I'm off to Weston, like now,' he tells her.

'Weston? You're kiddin' me. That's bloody miles away!'

'Not really, only an hour or so.'

'Oh, I dunno, Derek. Is this such a good idea?' says Marion, looking and sounding a tad confused and flustered.

'Wha' d'ya mean?'

'You know exactly what I mean.'

'S'up to you. Just thought you might like a day out, tha's all. We're all goin' on 'oliday together, ain't we?' Derek offers an explanation.

Marion shrugs. 'Tha's what I said,' she accepts. 'S'pect so.'

'So, wha's the difference?'

'Nigel.'

'Ah, fuck 'im. None of his business.'

'I'd 'ave to tell 'im.'

'Do as ya like.'

'Off to see your mum and Detlef?' Marion then surmises.

'My *dad* ya mean,' Derek corrects her. 'Yeah, I am.'

'Course. Sorry. Your dad. Where you meetin' them?'

'Not sure. Somewhere. I'll find 'em.'

'You don't know?'

'Nope.'

'It's not a small place, Dekko, Weston.'

'So? I'll gi' it me best shot.'

'Be like findin' a needle in a haystack.'

'Alright! Alright! I'll find 'em, I said. Well? You comin' or not?'

Marion leans back in, thinking to herself. 'I'd have to be back before they come home from school,' she says.

'Speak up. Can't hear ya.'

'I said I'd have to be back for Jules and Jez,' she repeats, popping her head back out.

'They got keys, ain't they?'

'Well, yeah.'

'So, what's the problem? They're big enough. Leave 'em a note.'

Marion thinks for a moment. 'Oh, I don't know,' she worries once again.

'I ain't got all day, girl. It's make your mind up time,' Derek hurries her. 'Nice if ya did,' he adds as an afterthought [i].

Marion holds her hand to her neck, unsure whether to be flattered or not. 'Would it?' she questions. 'Would it really?'

'Jeezus, woman! Wouldn't be bloody askin' ya otherwise, would I?'

'You'd have to give me five minutes. Can't go lookin' like this.'

His memory jogged, Derek suppresses a groan. 'Chuck summat on quick then,' he says instead. 'You'll be fine.'

-

'Not you again, Clappie,' sneers Jimbo as he sees him hovering nervously at the door, 'Wha' is it you want this time?'

Clappie doesn't answer, already looking like a lamb to the slaughter and rooted to the spot.

'Come 'ere, ya little tosser,' Phil orders him, turning on his stool, beckoning. 'I got a question.'

Clappie starts to stutter again. 'You're n'not gonna hit me again, are ya?' he says.

'No! I'm not goin' to bloody hit you again! I wanna know wha' your boss 'ad to say about the little bit o' bodywork I did for 'im yesterday?' says Phil with an exaggerated and wicked laugh.

Clappie edges closer, but very warily. 'Seriously angry, he is,' he says. 'Never heard 'im like it.'

'Why? I thought I did a nice job. No pleasin' some people, is there?'

'He knows it was me that showed you where he lived. I'm in serious deep shit.'

'Tha's what 'appens when you mix wi' such low life.'

'You don't know 'im like I do, Phil,' says Clappie as he finally stands alongside. 'He won't let it rest there, not never.'

Again, Phil laughs, but not nearly so certainly. 'His type don't frighten me, let me tell ya!' he insists.

'I'm sure he don't,' Clappie tries to placate, 'but you wanna watch your step all the same. He can be a right nasty sod when he wants to be.'

'Do I look bothered?' says Phil, waving the comment away. 'So, why *are* you here?' he repeats. 'Or can I guess?'

'He's still askin' me to find 'im,' Clappie admits.

'Well, as you can see, he ain't 'ere,' Jimbo joins in. 'So, about turn,' he instructs, spinning his finger towards the exit, 'an' off ya toddle.'

'Gimme a break, lads,' Clappie pleads. 'It's bad enough wi' me dogs howlin' back home wi' hardly any food. I don't know wha' to do for the best. PG jus' wants a chat, tha's all. See if he can improve on the deal, I s'pect.'

'Yeah, course he does!' says Phil.

'Is Dekko at home d'ya think?' chances Clappie very foolishly.

Before Phil has time to react, one of the old pissheads along the bar pipes up. 'Nah, bought 'imself a Roller, the lucky bastard,' he blurts out. 'Alright for some, innit? Lucky cunt.'

'Oi you, enough!' Jimbo tries to shut him up.

'Wha's the problem? I mi' be fuckin' stupid, bu' I ain't fuckin' deaf! I 'eard ya talkin' about it! Pissed off to Weston for the day, he has,' the old soak garbles on like he hasn't heard at all, 'get 'imself a stick o' rock, no doubt.'

'I said zip it!' snarls Jimbo, reaching to snatch his drink away but beaten as the old boy proves that his reflexes are in full working order when it comes to such things.

Clappie then turns to leave, but Phil stops him, grabbing him by the sleeve.

'You jus' told me to go, so I'm goin'!' he wails. 'Make your mind up!'

'Well, I'm tellin' ya to stay now!'

'Why? Wha' am I goin' to do, eh? I got no motor an' no money even if I wanted to chase off after 'im! I'm potless! Not a bean,' says Clappie, pulling his pockets out like a hang dog's ears. 'Look!'

'Good. You leave Dekko well alone. Now, sit down 'ere where I can keep an eye on ya,' Phil demands, patting the stool next to him. 'I'll get you a bloody beer if you're that broke,' he says.

'Would ya, Phil?' asks Clappie, looking completely taken aback. 'Would ya really?'

'Just told ya, ain't I? Least I can do for nearly ripping your balls off, I s'pose. You alright wi' that, Jimbo?'

'I ain't got a problem wi' that,' he accepts. 'Pint is it?'

'If ya don't mind?'

'I got some old meat in the fridge too if ya wan' it, Clappie?' Jimbo then offers as he picks up a glass. 'Can't see your dogs goin' 'ungry. It ain't their fault, all this shit.'

'Wow! Cheers, guys. I don't deserve all this,' he says, the relief at being able to feed his dogs clear on his face.

'No, you're right,' says Phil. 'You fuckin' don't.'

-

'That was quick,' says Derek as Marion slides herself in over the smooth leather seats, nicely dressed and smelling of perfume. 'Turned over a new leaf, 'ave we?'

'Darned sight better than that other dirty old wreck o' yours,' she says, ignoring him, stretching her legs, flapping her elbows. 'Plenty o' space.'

'Don't you start gettin' any funny ideas, girl,' says Derek lasciviously.

Marion turns sharply, pulling a face. 'I'll get back out right now if you're gonna carry on like that,' she says.

Still smirking, Derek draws his finger across his neck.

'Let's just get goin' or we'll never get back,' she instructs him.

'Your wish is my command, milady,' he replies, trying, but failing, to sound like Parker off the Thunderbirds.

-

'D'you need the loo yet, Ellen, or are you OK?' Margaret discretely asks her after they park across from the Grand Atlantic Hotel and are out on the pavement, wheelchair set up. 'I'm sure they'd let you go in there if you want.'

'No, I'm fine for the moment, thank you,' she answers.

'That's where I'd like to take us all for something to eat,' Detlef then announces.

'Oh, that's really not necessary, Detlef,' repeats Margaret. 'You two go alone.'

'As a token of my gratitude to you all,' he insists. 'Do you remember, Ellen? I promised you I'd take you there one day, but I never did.'

'Oh, yes! I do!' says Ellen, immediately transported. 'How lovely of you to remember, Detlef.'

'Yes, I do remember, Ellen, and lots more besides,' he says.

-

'Here ya go,' says Jimbo, handing Clappie a carrier bag full of meat scraps and other leftovers.

Clappie takes it, untying it and opening it to take a look. 'Ah, cheers, mate!' he says. 'They'll love all this, they will - but can I go an' feed 'em now?' he requests. 'They'll be howlin'.'

'As long as you don't do anythin' stupid,' Phil allows him. 'I want you back 'ere in 'alf an hour. D'you hear me? Not a minute more, or I'll be after ya!'

-

'Still got your appetite then, Ellen?' Margaret enquires of her.

'I could certainly eat something,' she warbles. 'Quite hungry in fact.'

'Excellent.'

'In an hour?' Detlef suggests. 'I shall need to book it. Margaret? Maciej?' he seeks to confirm.

'Yeah, fine by me,' agrees Maciej. 'Very kind of you.'

'Thank you, Detlef,' Margaret accepts Detlef's generous offer before turning back to Ellen. 'You can always have my banana if you like,' she says. 'Keep you going?'

-

As Clappie descends the steps of the pub, bag of meat in hand, he can't help but notice what looks like the tail end of a Rolls-Royce heading out, shortly to be followed by a black BMW slowly cruising by and slowing down, a fearsome face clearly seen eyeing the pub even through the dark tinted windows.

Chapter 36

'Detlef, just a thought,' says Margaret as he rejoins them, having booked a table for lunch at the Grand Atlantic Hotel, 'but would you two like to wander off by yourselves for a short while?' she tentatively suggests.

'Oh! That would be lovely,' reacts Ellen, immediately taken with the idea.

'I'm sure you'll both be alright,' continues Margaret, 'and you don't want Maciej and me tagging along *all* the time, now do you?'

'Will you be OK with the wheelchair, Detlef?' Maciej asks, voicing a little concern.

'Yes, of course,' he answers, but, in truth, still not feeling quite 100%.

'Please say, Detlef,' Margaret seeks to confirm.

He nods. 'I will manage,' he asserts, masking himself..

'So, what time are we eating?'

'In an hour.'

'We'll meet back here by the taxi then, shall we? All go in together,' says Margaret. 'You have Maciej's phone number, don't you? Just in case.'

Again, Detlef nods.

'Plenty of charge?'

'Yes,' both men answer together.

-

Clappie appears in the pub doorway yet again, this time holding his stomach, wincing.

'Thought you'd gone to feed those hounds o' yours?' says Jimbo, surprised to see him back so soon.

'I th'think I've gone an' done s'summat stupid,' replies Clappie, reverting back into stutter mode.

'You what, ya say?' Phil demands, immediately alarmed by it..

'It was tha' B'Brian,' Clappie tries to make his excuses. 'He forced me. He's told me to tell ya.'

'Tell me what? Wha' ya done now, ya stupid little wanker?'

'PG's cars.'

'Wha' about 'em?'

'He said someone's gonna pay for the damage, big time.'

'He can fuck off!'

'Pay *very* heavily, he said.'

'Where is he? Is he still out there?' says Phil, slamming down his pint, ready to fire off once more.

'No. He's gone.'

'Gone where?'

Clappie falls silent.

'Where's he gone, Clappie?' Phil shouts. 'Fuckin' tell me! Where!'

'He's gone after Dekko,' he reveals, expecting to be assaulted once again. 'Off to Weston.'

'You told 'im?' says Phil, angry, incredulous, and urgently tapping his pockets for his keys. 'You little piece o' shit! I could rip your fuckin' head off!'

'Leave him alone!' says Jimbo before calling out the back and up the stairs. 'Reenie!' he yells, 'I need you to cover! I'm goin' out! Like now!'

-

As Margaret and Maciej wander off towards the town centre, Detlef cautiously pushes Ellen over the road and in the direction of the pier. 'Shall we?' he asks her.

'Oh, yes please, Detlef,' she trills. 'Feels like only yesterday, doesn't it?'

-

Randomly flicking a switch here and pushing a button there, Derek is slowly getting used to his luxurious new vehicle. 'Wha's this one do, d'ya reckon?' he says, twiddling with it.

'You mind you don't make us crash,' Marion warns him. 'Keep your eye on the bloody road!'

Derek ignores her, caressing the leather steering wheel, running his hands around it. 'D'you know what?' he asks.

'No. What?'

'I'm looking forward to seeing him again.'

Marion looks at her ex knowingly. 'Must have been quite a shock for you,' she acknowledges.

'Yip. Was.'

'Nice man.'

'Yeah.'

'Lovely.'

'Alright!'

'You OK?'

'Shut up, Mar,' says Derek, but with no aggressive intent and before finding yet another dial to play with. 'I'm fine. Yeah?'

-

'Are you onto them yet?' PG is demanding to know over the phone.

Brian sighs, already sounding irritated. *'Might o' guessed.'*

'Well?'

'Wha' d'ya think?'

'I don't know. Tell me!'

'I'm on tha case. I'm trackin' 'em down now.'

'What? Derek and the thug that trashed my cars?'

'You're nae an idiot.'

'Shut up. So, where are you?'

'Fuck me, PG! You dinnae wanna know much!'

'Remember who's paying.'

'Jeez! I'm on ma way to Weston-Super-Mud if ya mus' know.'

PG can't help but groan in distaste. 'Weston-Super-Mare?' he says. 'Terrible place. Why on earth would you want to go there?'

'Because I fancy a stick o' rock, ya pea brain fuckin' numpty, ya! Why d'ya think? An' I shall bi claimin' mi mileage too!'

'OK, no need for all that,' says PG, backing off.

'I'll deliver ya their heads on a plate soon enough, 'ave nae fear 'bout tha'.'

'I'd prefer Derek's still attached to his shoulders if you don't mind. I want him delivered.'

Brian manages a laugh. *'If you insist. It'll be ma pleasure,'* he growls before ending the call.

-

'We'll need to go careful,' worries Jimbo as Phil speeds off. 'We don't want this all goin' tits up.'

'I didn't ask you to come.'

'I know that, but that Brian's not one to be messed with. Tha's all I'm sayin'.'

'Oi! Who was it that decked him just the other day?' Phil reminds him. 'Besides, Dekko's our bloody mate, Jim! An' we owe 'im! Both of us.'

'I know that! It's why I'm 'ere.'

'We gotta finish this fuckin' PG nonsense once an' for all!'

'We warned Dekko not to get involved,' recalls Jimbo.

'We did, but tha's all by the by now.'

'But shouldn't we be callin' the police first?'

'The police?' exclaims Phil, laughing. 'What ya gonna tell 'em? Tha' we're all goin' over to Weston for the day an' things might get a bit feisty? Might be a bit of a punch up?'

'He could be armed.'

'Armed, my arse! This ain't Miami-fuckin'-Vice, ya knob 'ead! You been watchin' too much telly.'

'Chance 'ould be fine thing,' says Jimbo. 'All I ever seem to do nowadays is work.'

'Well, let's sort this an' you can put your feet up for a bit, can't ya?' says Phil. 'Pay for some bar staff. We could do with a pretty young barmaid rather than your ugly mug all the time!

'S'pose. Thanks.'

'Is the right answer. Now, let's get there.'

-

Now out beyond the western fringes of the city and, with a clear road in front of them, Derek pushes his foot more firmly onto the accelerator, smiling broadly as he feels the automatic transmission drop a gear and the solid thrust of the engine cut in. 'Flippin' lovely, innit?' he says gleefully. 'Smooth as a baby's arse.'

'Yeah, very nice, but, please, you take it steady!' Marion warns him again.

'Relax, will ya! This thing's built like a bloody shit brick house!'

Still, Marion double checks her safety belt, jiggling the buckle. 'You'll never change, you idiot,' she says, 'always were a bloody madcap.'

'Wha' d'ya mean?' he squeals like he truly has no idea.

'Was just the same when we used to go out on your bike,' she reminds him. 'The times we nearly come off that thing wi' me on the back - sozzled.'

'You? Sozzled?' he teases her.

'Shut up! You know what I mean! You! It was always you that pushed your luck.'

'Well, I'm sober as a judge now,' says Derek, pressing his foot even more firmly to the floor, the 'flying lady' on the bonnet noticeably lifting a fraction, 'so, 'old on to ya 'orses, love! We're off!'

-

'Ooh, it's changed quite a lot, hasn't it?' says Ellen as they arrive at the entrance to the pier, a little disappointed to see how different it looks. More modern.

'Yes,' agrees Detlef but, still, his mind immediately cast back with a mixture of fond and not so fond memories.

'They call it progress, don't they?'

'Yes, I think they do,' he agrees with a melancholy smile.

'Anyway, never mind, we're here now. Would you buy me a candy floss, Detlef?' Ellen asks, a twinkle in her eye and reaching inside her bag. 'I've got some money in my purse.'

'Put your money away,' he says.

'No. My turn,' she tells him, fishing out a five pound note. 'Only a small one, mind. We can share it if you like? I shan't want much.'

-

'Fancy a bag o' sweets?' asks Derek as he unexpectedly turns sharply into a filling station and pulling up. 'Still like Revels?' he remembers. 'I'm a bit peckish, an' I need some baccy.'

'I'd prefer some fruit pastilles,' says Marion, 'or marshmallows if they ain't got any.'

'Whatever ya like. You can 'ave all three if ya like. You can 'ave some money too, if ya want?' offers Derek as he opens the door to hear and see a black BMW flash past at breakneck speed. 'Shit. He's in a bit o' a hurry,' he laughs. 'Some mad bastards about, ain't there?'

'What you sayin', Dekko?' asks Marion, her mouth agape.

'Well,' he says, drawling, 'I've come to think life's too short for grudges.'

'What do you mean?'

'An' as you say, there's the kids to think of,' Derek continues. 'You know I'm not tight. Not really. 'Half a million do ya?' he then throws in.

Marion covers her mouth with her hand.

'But I don't want that Nigel gettin' his hands on any, understood?' says Derek as he steps out. 'In fact, I'd prefer it if wasn't there at all,' he calls back. 'Marshmallows you say?'

'Or fruit pastilles,' Marion manages to answer, shellshocked.

Chapter 37

Unknowingly, Brian parks up not more than five or six cars away from Maciej's taxi on Marine Parade.

Looking intently into his wing mirror, he waits for a small family group to pass by before stepping out to retrieve a sports holdall from the boot. Unzipping it, he pushes aside various tools to uncover a knuckle duster, slipping it into his pocket, before searching out his kebbie stick - thigh length, weighty, bulbous - and deftly slides it into his loose fitting trousers, looping the leather strap onto a hook attached to his belt for that very purpose.

Not that far away, the Rolls-Royce is attracting a considerable amount of attention as it is forced to crawl through the central streets of Weston, slowed to a snail's pace not only by the other traffic but also by pedestrians milling about on either side, in front and behind.

'Everyone's gawpin' at us, Dekko!' Marion squeals, unnerved by it all.

'Yeah, good, innit?' he says, lapping it up. 'S'like bein' famous.'

'Feels like I'm on show. I don't like it.'

'I do,' disagrees Derek, offering one blatantly inquisitive couple something akin to a royal wave. 'Now, I'm sure there's a multi-storey car park somewhere hereabouts,' he thinks out loud.

'Unlike you to pay for parkin',' comments Marion, 'even now.'

Derek taps at his bulging wallet. 'Not bothered no more,' he says. 'Besides, I don't want this beauty bein' towed away, or some oiks tryin' to snap me flyin' lady off. Look at her. Beautiful.'

'Don't care, so long as you hurry up. Everyone's starin'! Look at 'em all!'

'I'm goin' as fast as I can, woman! Wha' d'you want me to do? Mow 'em all down?'

Marion shrugs, returning to their earlier conversation. 'So, you're gonna give me half a million quid then, are ya?'

'Yeah. Tha's what I said? Ain't it good enough?' he confirms, but sarcastically.

'No, plenty,' she accepts before adding, 'but why don't I believe you?'

'Are you blind in them ears of yours?'

'What's that supposed to flippin' well mean?'

'I'll write you a cheque when I've got a bloody moment! That's what! You'll get it. Today!'

Marion pauses for a second or two before responding. 'And so you should,' she says, unable to stop herself, 'after all I've done for you.'

'Here we go a bloody 'gain. Are you never 'appy?'

'I'd need at least that to put up with all this bloody nonsense,' she then exclaims, distracted by even more staring onlookers. 'Who do they think they are? Nosey blighters!'

'Marion. Relax, will ya?' insists Derek, now sounding a little exasperated himself. 'You'll get your money an' they're not doin' us no harm,' he repeats.

'We'll see.'

''Ave you never had a good ol' look in a posh car? See who it might be?'

Still, she shields her face. 'So, where d'you think you might find your mum and dad?' she then asks, changing the subject. 'It ain't gonna be easy.'

'Winter Gardens?' suggests Derek. 'Good o' place as any to start.'

'I dunno. I'd say along the prom first, on the pier.'

'Nah, be too cold for me mum on a day like this. She'd be freezin'.'

'Well, that's where she and Detlef met. She told us the other night,' reminds Marion before shouting at yet another onlooker peering in far too close. 'It's only a flippin' car!' she shouts. 'Go away!'

'Did she?'

'Yeah, she did. But your decision. That's where I'd go first anyway. Oh, piss off!'

'There!' shouts Derek, pointing at an illuminated P for parking sign. 'An' there's spaces!'

'At last! I can't wait to get out o' this bloody thing. It's like bein' in a damned goldfish bowl!'

'No pleasin' some people, is there?' says Derek, unable to stop himself grinning. (She's never going to change, he thinks. It's the way things always were - bickering, but, somehow, he likes it. Misses it in fact.)

With that, Marion turns herself in the seat, her bottom sliding easily on the smooth leather seats and faces him. 'I wouldn't go so far as to say that,' she says, gently tapping him on the knee and with a look as if she were transported back to less troubled and happier times. 'You're a silly ol' sod underneath it all, aren't you?'

'You reckon?' he teases her back in return. 'Don't you believe it. Things 'ave changed.'

-

Ellen pulls off a piece of the candyfloss from out of its polythene bag, tasting it. 'Ooh,' she reacts as the sticky sweetness hits her tongue. 'I'd forgotten how sugary it is. Blue too! Don't they do pink anymore?'

Detlef shrugs, smiling. 'They had green ones,' he says with a light-hearted but exaggerated grimace.

'And no stick. What *is* the world coming to?' she says, tittering. 'Would you like to try a bit?'

Despite his diabetes, Detlef pinches off a tiny piece. 'In for a penny, in for a pound,' he says, digging up an old phrase from long, long ago, and popping it into his mouth. Melodramatically, he shudders, but laughing too, searching for his handkerchief.

Ellen quickly reaches into her sleeve and offers him hers. 'Spit it on the ground,' she tells him. 'No-one will see.'

'We were much younger then,' Detlef says, accepting it and wiping his mouth. 'I don't eat sweet things any longer.'

'Don't you?'

'No.'

'Me neither, not really,' she agrees, a touch wistfully. 'Where did it all go, Detlef?' she then adds.

'I don't know,' he says. 'It's all gone so quickly.'

Ellen nods in agreement, squeezing her handkerchief before poking it back up into her sleeve.

'Shall we walk up to where we first met?' Detlef then suggests,

'I'd like that,' she says, perking up at the thought. 'I'd like that very much.'

'I'm sure we can remember,' he says,. 'It was up there on the left, wasn't it?' he adds, gesturing further up the pier.

'It was,' Ellen confirms. 'Looking out to Brean Down. I was there with Joyce. It was a Saturday. Saturday the 7th of July, we were waiting to go to the station,' she recounts, 'half past four and noisy. Do you remember how noisy it was? I do.'

-

Phil and Jimbo leave the car tucked up on a side street, half on the road, half on the pavement.

'You'll get it towed away,' warns Jimbo.

'So what?' says Phil. 'We ain't got time.'

'Your lookout, mate.'

'I'll buy meself another. Let's get down to the pier and work our way back,' Phil instructs. 'Just keep your eyes peeled, yeah? They're 'ere somewhere or another.'

-

Brian is briskly making his way along the esplanade and up towards the Trocadero, his hand in his pocket, holding the top of the kebbie stick and moving it in synchronicity with his pace. Disconcertingly for some, he's looking at every passing person, even glancing down onto the near empty beach with its very occasional and solitary dog walker, just on the off chance.

-

Detlef and Ellen cannot help but fall silent as they look out across the Bristol Channel and at the exact same point they'd been some forty-eight years previously.

Eventually, Detlef breaks their silence. 'I don't know what to say, Ellen,' he says in hushed tones like he might be in a church.

'Me neither,' she replies. 'It was always about the bloody money, wasn't it?' she identifies.

'*Ja, sehr schwierig,*' says Detlef before apologising and correcting himself. 'Yes, it was. It was always very difficult.'

'Please, don't apologise. I remember when I first heard your accent, standing right here. But you didn't say anything first of all, you were miming like that Mark Marco or whatever his name was. But I liked it. I was a bit mesmerised.'

Detlef smiles. 'I'm surprised you could understand me,' he says.

'Oh, I understood you alright,' says Ellen with a momentary flashback to the cheekiness of her youth.

Detlef bends down to cradle her head, kissing her softly on the cheek. 'I couldn't keep my eyes off you either,' he says.

On hearing that, the old lady looks up into his face, her chest giving way to a huge shudder like she was about to burst into tears. 'I wish I could have done more to keep you out of trouble,' she says, stopping herself.

'No,' says Detlef, already shamefaced. 'It was not your fault. You had a baby to look after. Do not blame yourself. It was my stupidity, no-one else's.'

Again, Ellen shudders, but this time as a result of a sudden and chilly gust of wind. 'Can we go now, Detlef?' she asks him. 'Only it's getting a bit blowy.'

'Would you like to go to the hotel?' he suggests. 'We are a little early, but if you are cold?'

'I think I would,' Ellen agrees happily. 'We could have a lovely hot cup of tea together, couldn't we? In the Grand Atlantic like you said. Very posh.'

'I'll phone Maciej when we get there,' says Detlef, 'to let them know.'

'There's no rush,' the old lady replies. 'They'll get there when they're ready.

-

'D'you think they might have gone to a pub or somethin'?' says Derek as they exit the car park. 'Grab a bite to eat?'

'No! I don't think they've gone to a pub or something,' repeats Marion, immediately recognising his ruse.

'One quick pint wouldn't hurt, would it?' he says. 'Got to keep our strength up.'

'No, Derek! Let's get down to the pier like we said.'

'Wouldn't touch the sides.'

Marion grabs him by the hand. 'Come on!' she demands. 'Now's not the time! We're here to find your mum an' dad, not get fuckin' sloshed!'

'Spoilsport.'

'Come on!'

-

'Ellen?' asks Detlef, bending down to speak into her ear as they stand at the pedestrian crossing adjacent to the pier entrance.

'Yes?'

'Later, if you are not too tired, I'd like to see the Ogden's farm on the way back. Would you mind?'

'No, of course not, Detlef. You asked me before. I never ever saw it. Never went there. I'd like to.'

'You met them at our wedding, didn't you?'

'I did. I've still got the orange sugar bowl they gave us.'

'Yes, I remember. You told me.'

'Did I? Although I don't know where the spoon got to,' the old lady continues. 'Lost it ages ago. Shame. I hate losing things.'

'Never mind. But thank you. I'd just like to have one last look,' says Detlef as the green man on the sign flashes and beeps to signal it is safe to cross. 'Let's get that cup of tea.'

-

Continually looking left and right, Brian sweeps up into the pier, heading towards the far end.

Literally, moments later, Phil and Jimbo are doing much the same thing. 'One quick whizz up an' down 'ere,' says Phil, 'then we'll head back into town. Yeah?'

'Worth a bash, I s'pose,' agrees Jimbo but already wheezing heavily at the exertion of it all. 'Can I have a minute? I'm knackered already.'

'You need to get in the gym, Jim, ya overweight lard bucket, ya,' Phil teases him. 'But, No. Ya can't. We gotta keep goin'.'

'But…'

'But nuthin'! We need to find Dekko, like now. Mark my words, that Scottish thug'll be closin' in, an' fast.'

-

Back in Bristol, phone in hand and sat in his Chesterfield chair, PG is unable to relax. Unusually for him at this time of the day, he'd even poured himself a drink but had barely touched it. He stands up and begins pacing up and down. He's angry - very - and desperate for news.

Less than a half hour since, he'd fielded yet another call from Sir Alun Tate. It was unusual, the third of the morning, and he'd sounded particularly irate and threatening to issue further shares, diluting PG's in the process or even eliminate him from Tate Holdings and the dock development altogether unless the promised £75,000 was forthcoming, and fast.

Breach of contract, he'd said. It was madness. There was no contract. It was a verbal agreement.

-

There are no other people at the end of the pier when Phil and Jimbo see Brian and he sees them, not another living soul. Momentarily, they are rooted to the spot, weighing each other up.

'Wha' are you two fuckers doin' 'ere?' the Scot then shouts at them, laughing and as if relishing the prospect.

'Lookin' for you,' retorts Phil, growling in kind.

Surreptitiously, and concealed in his pocket, Brian slips the knuckleduster onto the fingers of his right hand before releasing the kebbie stick with his left and sweeping it out like a sword.

'Watch out, Phil!' yells Jimbo immediately. 'He's got a gert big lump o' wood!'

Innately, Phil reacts, dropping low like he was in a scrum and charges at him like a raging bull. Despite taking a heavy blow to his forearm and a slight glancing blow to the side of his head from the knuckleduster, his momentum forces Brian back, knocking him off balance.

Horrified, terrified too, Jimbo hesitates at first as the two men begin to wrestle but, overriding his fears, rushes in to help, his bulk thrusting Brian even further backwards, crashing him into the railings.

'Tha's it, ya English cowards! Two o' yoos onto one as ever!' he roars, lashing out and flailing at them with his stick and his fist but, at such close quarters, to far less effect.

Swiftly, Phil then reaches for his lower leg, lifting him and arching his body half way over the balustrade. 'Come on, Jim!' he yells. 'Push the bastard over!'

'Be the last thing ya ever fuckin' did!' warns Brian, thrashing about, twisting and turning.

'Too late, mate,' says Phil as, in a concerted effort, both he and Jimbo flip him over the top, dropping him some 40ft into the cold and murky waters of the Bristol Channel. *Ker-splosh!*

Immediately, they peer over the side to see what looks like an arm holding a kebbie stick above the surface as if it might be Excalibur. 'Fuck me, Phil!' panics Jimbo. 'We've drowned 'im! We gotta call someone!. Police, coastguard, anyone! Someone!'

'What for, Jim?' he answers him, staring him down, expressionless, and seemingly unconcerned. 'I didn't see anybody. Just looked like a bit o' driftwood t'me.'

'But …'

'But nuthin'. Don't tell another fuckin' soul! An' I mean no-one!'

PG can wait no longer. He needs answers, like now, and makes the call to Brian.

'The number you are calling is currently unavailable. Please try again later,' comes the instant reply.

'Where the hell are you, you bastard?' PG spits. 'At the bottom of the bloody ocean or something?!'

Chapter 38

Both Derek and Marion are incredulous to see Phil and Jimbo hurrying down the pier just as they are about to head up it - thoroughly gobsmacked in fact. 'What the fuck you two doin' 'ere?' Derek shouts to them, his arms held wide in astonishment.

'Hey! Dekko! Marion!' Phil shouts back before turning towards Jimbo like a ventriloquist. 'Say nuthin, you hear me? Nuthin!' he hisses.

'Well?' Derek repeats as he nears them.

'You two back together again or summat?' Phil deflects.

'Are we fuck!'

'Only askin'.'

'Well, don't. So?'

'Jimbo tells me you bought yourself a fuck off Roller,' Phil deflects again but noticeably holding at his forearm, wincing. 'You'll 'ave to gimme a ride.'

Derek ignores the reference to his car and looks at him disbelievingly, pointing at his forehead. ''Ave I got the word stupid cunt tattooed up 'ere?' he demands. 'Come on, wha's goin' on?'

'Chill out, mate! Nuthin's goin' on!'

'Are you followin' me about?'

'Fuck me, no! Thought we might gi' you a hand finding your mum an' Detlef, tha's all. After all you done for us.'

'Me dad, ya mean.'

'Yeah, sorry. Your dad.'

'An' what you done to your arm? You look like you're in bleedin' agony.'

Gingerly, Phil holds it out, looking at it as if surprised. 'What, this? I dunno. Just a bit o' cramp, I expect,' he says. 'Damp air. I get it every now an' then.'

Derek then notices Jimbo's gaunt and ashen face. 'An' you, you look like you seen a fuckin' ghost! This is weird. Wha's wrong wi' the pair o' ya?'

Jimbo stares down to the wooden slats of the pier floor, forcing Phil to quickly continue the conversation. 'You ain't found 'em yet then, I take it?' he says.

'Does it fuckin' look like it? Is he alright?'

'What?'

'Him.'

Phil shrugs as if he hadn't noticed. 'Well, no point wastin' your time up there, we've checked,' he continues, gesturing behind him. 'Been right up to the far end and back.'

'Tha' right?' says Derek but still not at all convinced.

'We know how important it is to ya, Dekko - findin' 'em,' emphasises Phil. 'We were sayin', weren't we, Jim?' he says, prodding him.

Jimbo nods, but almost indiscernibly.

''An 'specially before your dad goes back.'

'Don't remind me.'

'Tomorrow innit?'

'I said don't remind me,' repeats Derek but now looking even more intently at Jimbo.

'He's worried about the pub,' says Phil. 'You know what he's like.'

'Reenie in charge, is she?' Derek hazards a guess.

'Yeah. Who else?'

'Ah. Explains it. That it, Jim?' Derek seeks to confirm. 'Reenie?'

'Yeah. Reenie,' he answers.

'Fuck me! He speaks!' says Derek before continuing. 'Look, don't s'pose you two fancy a quick snifter somewhere or other, do ya?' he chances. 'Could murder one, me. Wring its bloody neck.'

'No, Dekko!' Marion interjects, stopping him once again. 'Let's find them first. What would your dad think if you turned up stinkin' o' booze again? And your mum.'

'Alright, alright! It's like bein' married all over a-bloody-gain!' he complains.

'She's right, Dekko,' Phil backs Marion up. 'Later maybe? Back at the ranch? You can tell us all about it then.'

'What? You off already?'

'Nah, not yet. We'll carry on lookin', but we can't be long. We gotta be headin' back for poor ol Jimbo 'ere. Stop 'im frettin'.'

'Yeah. I s'pose,' Derek reluctantly acknowledges.

'We'll call ya if we find 'em. Yeah? You ready, Jimbo?'

Once again, he doesn't answer, looking distant - miles away.

'Jimbo! You comin' I said?'

'What is wrong with 'im?' asks Derek again. 'Is he on drugs or summat?'

-

'Shall we sit by the window?' suggests Detlef as he pushes Ellen into the near empty but warm bar area of the Grand Atlantic Hotel, its tired interior looking dated but still reflecting elements of its glorious heyday.

'Yes, that would be lovely,' says Ellen. 'I love a good view. Makes a change looking out of my window, day in, day out.'

'Tea?' he then asks, understanding he must go to the bar to order.

'Yes please! Can you ask if they have any biscuits?'

'Yes, of course.'

'Just one though. I don't want to ruin my appetite.'

-

'Wha' was tha' all about?' Derek is saying as they walk up towards the Winter Gardens. 'Jimbo never normally leaves the pub, other than when he joined us to pick up me cheque. D'you see his face?'

'I don't know him as well as you, but he looked like he was going to be sick to me.'

Derek manages a laugh. 'Perhaps he'd had a dodgy pot o' cockles?'

Marion laughs too. 'I love a cockle, me.'

'Oi you, ya dirty cow!'

'Just having a bit o' fun, that's all.'

'Are ya?'

'Yeah. I am, Dekko. I am. Like old times.'

-

'I think it's bleedin' broken,' says Phil as they make their way back into the shopping area of the town. 'S'no good, you're gonna 'ave to take me to A&E.'

'Aren't we gonna look for Derek's parents like you just said?' says Jimbo, still not connecting.

'You don't seem to understand, Jim. I said I think it's fuckin' broken! It's killin' me!'

'But I'm not insured!'

'So fuckin' what? I can't drive like this. Besides, we've done what we came here to do. Protect our mate.'

'I never came here to drown no-one, Phil.'

'Shut the fuck up, Jim! Zip it! Shit 'appens. OK?'

'What if they find the body? What then?'

'Nobody saw us. We were the only ones there. He'll be bobbin' his way down to Ilfracombe by now. No-one needs know. Just keep your fuckin' trap shut, yeah?'

'But wha' if there were cameras?' Jimbo cautions.

Phil hadn't considered that and looks momentarily gaunt himself. 'Let's just hope there wasn't,' he says. 'Come on, let's go. I'm sure I saw the sign for the hospital on the way in.'

-

'We should be making our way back,' says Margaret. 'They'll be there soon.'

'Yeah, OK,' agrees Maciej but spotting Phil and Jimbo on the other side of the street as he does. 'Wow! There's Dekko's friends, I think,' he says.

'Where?'

'There,' he says, pointing. 'Hey, guys,' he calls out.

'I don't know them.'

'I do. Hi! How ya doin'?'

'Who's that?' Phil asks Jimbo.

'It's that little taxi driver. Polish lad. Watch out, he's comin' over.'

'Well, act bloody normal this time. Understand?'

-

'Please tell me you have some news, Peter,' Sir Alun Tate is saying over the phone, but in a particularly quiet yet urgent tone of voice.

PG can no longer keep up the pretence. *'No, I can't get hold of him,'* he says. *'I'm drawing a blank. I'm as frustrated as you.'*

'Shit. Listen. I've just spoken to Piers, he will be calling you.'

'What about?'

'I can't say right now. I've got to go.'

'What about?' repeats PG.

'Just make sure you keep your phone on,' says Sir Alun, ending the call.

-

'We're here with Detlef and Ellen, Derek's mum,' explains Maciej. 'This is Margaret. She's Ellen's nurse.'

'Ah, right. Nice to meet ya, love. Where are they then?' asks Phil.

'Here, in Weston. They are walking together.'

'Dekko's here too,' reveals Jimbo. 'He's looking for them.'

'Is he?' asks Margaret. 'Is he OK?'

'Sober you mean?' says Jimbo, getting her meaning.

'No,' she answers defensively. 'Just wondered.'

'Don't worry,' says Phil. 'He's sound as a pound. He just wanted to be with them before his dad goes back. He's here with his missus tryin' to find them.'

'We are going back to see them at the big hotel right now, get something to eat,' explains Maciej.

'The Grand Atlantic?'

'Yes,' confirms Margaret.

'Shall we call them, Phil, tell them?' says Jimbo.

'Yeah. Can you do it? Pass it over to me?' he says, realising he cannot hold his phone and dial.

'Perhaps I should call Ellen and Detlef too,' says Margaret, introducing a note of caution. 'It might be a bit of a shock,'

'I think they would like the surprise,' suggests Maciej, excited by the idea. 'I think they will like it.'

'Do you think so?' worries Margaret.

'Yeah! Why not? We all like surprises.'

Jimbo then hands Phil the phone. 'It's ringin',' he says.

As Phil mistakenly tries to take it with his injured arm, he screws his face up in pain.

'Are you alright?' asks Margaret.

'It's his arm,' Jimbo blurts out. 'He slipped and fell on the pier,' he explains.

'Hey, Dekko! Great news, mate! We found 'em!' Phil shouts down the phone whilst eyeballing Jimbo in reprimand.

-

'Peter, it's Piers,' says Piers, monotone and monosyllabic.

'Yes, I guessed. Sir Alun just told me you would be calling,' says PG, short and abrupt. *'What's this all this clandestine nonsense about?'*

'Not to put too fine a point on it, we're in a spot of bother.'

'I've got no more money if that's what you're asking!'

'No, it's not that,' Pierce corrects him. 'It's not about the money, per say.'

'What then? Spit it out.'

'It's about Tate Holdings. We need to get our stories straight.'

-

'I can't fuckin' believe you just told that Maciej kiddie an' the nurse tha' I tripped an' fell, Jimbo,' says Phil as they are now hurrying back towards his car. 'I told Dekko it was the fuckin' cramp.'

'How you gonna use that as an excuse with your arm in plaster, eh?' reacts Jimbo. 'This is a right fuckin' mess! Perhaps we should just tell the truth, that it was an accident, that he attacked us with his stick thing?'

'Are you mad?' says Phil. 'It was two on one, we chucked him over the edge …. Just get me to the hospital, yeah? Jeezus!'

-

As yet unseen, Derek quietly approaches his mum and dad still sat in one of the large windows of the hotel. 'Surprise, surprise!' he says, covering his mother's eyes from behind.

'Oh! Who's that? she shrieks, almost jumping out of her skin.

'S'alright, Mum. It's only me. How ya doin'?' says Derek, laughing. 'Dad. OK?' he adds.

You could have given me a heart attack then!' Ellen complains.

'What are you doing here, Derek?' Detlef asks, shocked himself.

'Just fancied seein' ya. That's allowed, innit?'

'Hello again, Detlef. Ellen - Mum,' Marion then greets them, correcting herself to call her ex mother-in-law the way she once did. 'Sorry to surprise you like that.'

Ellen turns in her wheelchair to see her. 'Oh, how lovely to see the pair of you!' she says, clearly animated. 'Are you back together?'

Derek pulls a face. 'Not you as well,' he says.

'How are you, Marion?' Ellen asks. 'It's been ages.'

'Yes. Sorry. You know, up and down.'

'Come here and sit next to me.'

'Do you want to join us for something to eat?' Detlef suggests.

'Yeah, sure. Be nice,' answers Derek, 'but I don't suppose the bar's open just yet, is it?' he adds. 'The lights are on.'

Chapter 39

Phil, bent over and cradling his arm, is sat in the waiting room of the Weston General Hospital with Jimbo standing alongside. There are no spare chairs available.

Even for a Saturday, it's already very busy with the full gamut of the sick and the injured crowding the area - a loud and still laughing young football player, his leg stuck out, and another hobbling in fresh off the pitch - elderly people, one nursing what appears to be kitchen utensil or secateur related gardening accident, bloodied - the dishevelled and ubiquitous drunk, teetering, and ranting angrily at the ever patient security guard - a distressed middle aged woman, crying, but being comforted by a family member or friend, her hand heavily wrapped in a damp towel to cool what is likely to be a very nasty scald - and all interspersed with the usual plethora of other tight lipped or whimpering sorts showing no sign of physical damage or impairment, but simply looking worse for wear and a little sorry for themselves.

'Hope I don't have to wait too long, Jim,' groans Phil, now sweating profusely. 'This is startin' to crease me up summat chronic.'

-

'Looks nice,' says Derek as the waitress brings the last of their food to the table.

'Oh, yes. Lovely, isn't it,' agrees Ellen. 'I've got quite an appetite all of a sudden. Thank you, Detlef.'

'Don't worry, I can get this,' offers Derek.

'No, Derek. It is my treat,' Detlef stops him.

'A puddin' too if ya like!'

'But thank you.'

'I'll bring your cutlery,' says the waitress. 'Sauces? Salt and pepper's on the table.'

'You can bring me another pint, if ya like' says Derek, jocular but insistent all at the same time. 'Same again, please,' he says, draining his glass and cuffing his lips.

'Go steady, Dekko,' advises Marion, pleading almost. 'There's the drive back don't forget.'

'Relax. Just one more ain't gonna hurt. We're eatin' ain't we?'

'I'd listen to her if I was you, Derek,' warns his father. 'Now you're here, I was hoping you might be able to join us to Norton St Philip to see where I used to live.'

'Were ya?' asks Derek, taken with the idea. 'I've heard of it. Where is it?'

'Towards Bath.'

'Yeah, that's it!' remembers Derek. 'There's a cider pub nearby, Tucker's Grave or summat or other.'

'Yes, I know it,' recalls Detlef. 'There and the Fleur de Lis.'

'During the war?'

'After the war,' Detlef corrects him.

'We went there once, Mar,' says Derek excitedly. 'D'you remember? On me bike?'

'How can I ever forget! That scrumpy cider was lethal,' she says, laugh in embarrassment.'

'Yeah! You ended up in a ditch! You were bolloxed!'

'Please, Dekko. What will everyone think!'

'You mentioned it,' says Derek, standing up.

'Where are you going? We're about to start eating,' complains Marion.

'I'll only be a couple o' ticks,' he says. 'You lot can go ahead.'

-

PG is beside himself in anguish. He's dialling one of his legal beagles, a woman that had rescued him from countless scrapes over the years and one that specialised in criminal defence and prosecution. He'd first met her in his early twenties when she'd represented him as the Duty Solicitor at the old magistrate's court on Bridewell Street, now long closed. On and off, he'd paid her very well indeed since then and she was virtually at his beck and call.

'Yes, Peter,' she says, *'to what do I owe the pleasure?'*

-

Derek finds the waitress just as she's about to return to the bar. 'Can you cancel that, love?' he asks.

'You don't want it?'

'No.'

'Anything else?'

'Don't think so.'

'Oh, OK.'

'No, wait a minute,' says Derek, pausing. 'I'll 'ave a squash.'

'Half or a pint?'

'A pint.'

'Orange or blackcurrant?'

'Didn't know it was so complicated.'

The waitress shrugs.

'Orange, with a tiny dribble of blackcurrant,' he answers with a smirk.

'Really?'

'Really.'

'OK. Customer's always right. I'll bring it over.'

'Nice o' ya. Ta. Thanks'

-

Phil is at last in a curtained examination room, a nurse inspecting his arm. 'How did you say you did it again?' she's asking.

'I said. Slipped. Fell,' he says, grimacing even under her gentle touch.

'Only there's a lot of bruising,' she observes. 'A distinct line.'

'That'll be the kerb,' Phil offers an explanation.

'Ah, you didn't say that.'

'Didn't I? I am now,' he says.

337

'So, that's the long and short of it,' says PG, having explained.

'Why on Earth did you get involved? I thought you were smarter than that?' she says, matter of fact but not a little astonished.

'He's a Knight of the Realm, Jennifer! He's had his shoulders touched with a sword held by none other than the Queen herself! Why should I distrust him?'

'But it never occurred to you that there might be other nefarious intentions?

PG doesn't answer.

'Right, let's not make a drama out of a crisis,' says Jennifer. 'I shall need to see the paperwork, the contract.'

'There's not that much to see. There were only three transactions.'

'So, how much in total.'

Again, PG doesn't answer.

'Your place or mine?' asks Jennifer.

'Mine,' says PG, remembering the Jag is in a body shop, and the other too damaged for him to want to drive.

'I'll leave now,' she says.

-

'What the bloody hell you got there, Derek?' asks a worried looking Marion as the waitress brings his drink to the table. 'It's all murky.'

'All that talk o' scrumpy, I thought I'd have a change,' he says, taking a swig. 'Bloody luvverly!'

'Stop it, Dekko! They don't sell rough cider here!' says Marion, disbelieving. 'Not in a place like this!'

'You taste it then,' Derek continues, trying to keep a straight face. 'Put hairs on your chest, this stuff.'

Marion picks up the glass, smelling it, then taking a small sip. 'That's squash!' she says.

Derek laughs. 'No flies on you,' he says.

'What, turned over a new leaf? Gone TT?'

'Well, if we're all going to Norton St Philip, I thought I'd save meself for a pint o' the real stuff.'

'I hadn't planned on going to the pub, Derek,' says Detlef. 'There's your mother to think of too.'

'Oh, I don't mind,' she chips in. 'Would be nice altogether.'

'I don't want you tiring yourself out, Ellen,' warns Margaret. 'And we have to be back in good time. I don't want to lose my job.'

'We'll get back alright,' the old lady insists. 'Besides, you only live once,' she says.

-

'I'll put you in for an X-ray,' the nurse tells Phil.

'Will it take long?'

'It's a bit busy at the moment, unfortunately. Always the same on a Saturday.'

'Bloody hell!'

'And you'll have to be seen by a doctor after they've had a look.'

'But I've got to get back.'

'What's more important? It looks like a bad break or fracture and close to the elbow.'

'Can't you just strap it up? I've done worse.'

'That's not a good idea, now is it, Mr Vincent? You want it to repair properly, don't you?'

'Well, yeah, course I do.'

'Then the X-ray department is down the corridor on the right. It's easy. Just follow the signs.'

-

'I can take you in me Roller, if ya like?' Derek suggests. 'Just bought meself one.'

'You have a Rolls-Royce?' reacts Maciej, excited by the idea.

'Yeah, I 'ave. It's a beauty.'

'Wow! A real Rolls-Royce,' repeats Maciej.

'Have you, son?' asks Ellen, equally impressed.

'But Maciej is driving us,' says Detlef.

'Why? I got plenty of room for the pair o' ya. Wheelchair an' all. It's huge.'

'That's OK, Detlef,' says Maciej, understanding. 'Your son is proud.'

'But what about Ellen?' questions Margaret.

'I can help her,' says Marion.

'But what if anything goes wrong, I could get shot.'

'It won't,' insists Derek.

'What do you think, Ellen?' Marion asks her. 'Mum?'

'Oh, I don't know,' she says, uncertain and not wanting to offend. 'I don't mind.'

'I shall have to tell them,' says Margaret. 'Let them know.'

'Don't worry,' Marion tries to allay her fears. 'I'll keep her safe.'

'I can take you to the airport tomorrow too,' Derek suggests to his father.

With that, Detlef looks very uncertain and like he is to insult young Maciej.

'Really, I understand, Detlef,' he repeats. 'It's why you came to England, to find each other. Father and son.'

Derek seizes the opportunity. 'Right, great, that's that sorted then,' he says. 'Let's get some nosh in, shall we?'

'I'll go an' get me motor then, shall I?' says Derek after they'd all finished eating and Detlef is about to settle the bill. 'Be easier. I'll bring it outside.'

-

Phil, his arm in plaster and a sling, returns to the waiting room to find a very anxious and tetchy looking Jimbo.

'Wondered where you'd bloody got to?' he squeals under his breath. 'You been friggin' ages.'

'Bad break, Jim. Sorry.'

'You could o' at least asked someone to let me know! I been waitin' 'ere like piffy!'

'I said, I'm sorry. Looks like I'm gonna need bloody physio.'

Jimbo then leans in closer. 'An', look,' he whispers, 'there's coppers all over the friggin' place! Freakin' me out, it is!'

'Did you hear what I said?'

'Yeah! So, I'm still drivin' then! Brilliant!'

'Come on, let's go. I need a bloody pint.'

'But didn't they give you any painkillers?'

'Yeah.'

'Then you're not supposed to drink.'

'Gi' me a break, Jim!'

'Comedian too! Funny.'

'Not for me. You still got the keys?'

'Course, but I'm bloody worried, mate.'

'Well, don't be. Let's get out o' 'ere.'

-

'I shall need the amounts and dates,' Jennifer is telling him.

PG opens his most recent notebook, flicking through the pages.

'No, not that. I want to see your actual bank statements. Do you have a copier?'

PG appears highly reluctant, suspicious even. 'I have all the information you need in here,' he tries again.

'PG, please,' his solicitor implores him. 'After all these years, I know *exactly* what you're all about. Just get them, will you?'

-

Margaret gives Ellen a kiss on the cheek as they see the Rolls-Royce pull up outside. 'I'll see you tomorrow morning for breakfast, love,' she says. 'I'm on earlies.'

'Yes. God willing. Don't know what I'd o' done without you. Thank you everso much, Margaret.'

'Nonsense. My pleasure. You can tell me all about it over your eggs and bacon, can't you?'

'Pity you can't stay.'

'You've got all your family now,' says Margaret but still feeling a little unsure about it. 'I'm sure it will be alright,' she adds whilst releasing the brake on the chair. 'You've got Marion to look after you now, haven't you?'

'Yes, I have,' Ellen agrees. 'I've missed her, since she and my Derek got separated.'

'Course, you did, but it looks like they might be getting back together, bickering like an old married couple.

'Yes,' says Ellen, smiling. 'I noticed that too.'

PG goes into his library, running his fingers along the spines of a row of his precious antiquarian books and towards the corner where he keeps his office. Quickly, easily, he pulls out a clearly marked box file and puts it under his arm.

Derek jumps out onto the pavement as they all appear at the top of the steps of the hotel. 'Mother! Father! Your chariot awaits,' he gleefully shouts up to them and performing one of his elaborate Shakespearian style bows. 'Wha' d'ya think? A beauty, eh?'

Maciej raises his thumbs instantly. 'Amazing! A real Rolls-Royce!' he calls back down as Detlef turns to him, holding him by his sleeve. 'I cannot thank you enough, Maciej,' he says, the emotion clear in his voice.

'You're welcome, my friend,' says Maciej, equally touched and throwing arms around the old man's shoulders. 'I shall never forget you!'

'But, please, we must keep in contact.'

'I'd like that, Detlef. Give me your address and I'll send you a Christmas card,' says Maciej, trying to soften the blow.

'I will write it down,' says Detlef, fumbling in his pocket for a piece of paper.

'You'll need mine too,' says Maciej, taking out one of his business cards. 'Do you have a pen?'

'I've got one,' says Derek, bounding up the steps to join them.

'Beautiful car, son,' his father tells him.

'You'll be in it in a minute. Will you sit up front with me, dad?'

'I'd love to,' he says, 'but first, I must settle up. How much do I owe you Maciej?'

'Nothing,' the young man says. 'You have paid me enough.'

'No, please,' insists Detlef. 'I must.'

'Let me,' Derek interjects, 'the least I can do as you wouldn't let me pay for the food just then.'

'But …'

'But nuthin',' Derek stops his father this time, pulling out his pen together with a huge bundle of twenty pound notes and roughly splits it in half. 'Here you go, you two,' he says, thrusting one wad into Maciej's hand, the other into Margaret's.

'Oh, Dekko, I can't accept this,' she says, refusing to accept it. 'There must be hundreds there!'

'An' plenty where that came from,' says Derek. 'Put it into your bag an' shut up. The pair o' ya 'ave helped me mum an' dad out no end, and me as a result.'

Still, Margaret refuses to take it.

'I'm not going to accept no for an answer,' repeats Derek, pushing the money into the top of her handbag and backing away.

-

'Now, this Sir Alun Tate. What do you know of him? How did you meet?'

At an art exhibition in Clifton,' says PG as if it qualifies his status. 'I've even been to his house. Magnificent place, just outside of Bath.'

'Really? Where exactly? What's his address?'

-

As the Rolls-Royce begins to pull gently and quietly away, Detlef speaks to Maciej through the open window, his eyes misting up. 'If ever you come to Germany,' he says, 'you must come to see me.'

'I will, Detlef. No problem!' calls out Maciej after him. 'Safe journey, my friend! *Sichere Reise!*'

'Bye, Margaret, bye,' says Ellen, joining in and waving to her like the Queen on her way to a Royal Variety Performance. 'See you tomorrow.'

Chapter 41

'There it is!' shouts Derek, gesticulating wildly. 'Straight ahead, sat down there all on its own!'

'Where? What?' sputters Marion, shaken awake after having drifted off in quiet and comfortable backseat of the Roller.

'Back in the land o' the livin', then?' observes Derek, laughing and looking in his rear view mirror.

'Leave me alone, Dekko,' she bites back. 'You know how I get.'

'OK, spikey! This is it, Pops, innit?' he asks.

Detlef doesn't answer. He's miles away and back in time.

'Zonks me out,' explains Marion, 'eatin' in the middle of the day.'

'Never mind 'bout that,' Derek continues excitedly. 'Look! It's that Tucker's Grave we were talking about! Definitely!'

Marion raises her head and peers bleary eyed. 'Oh, yeah. Think so,' she says. 'Maybe. I don't know.'

'You must remember! We got slaughtered there years back. Wha' d'ya reckon, Pops?' Derek asks again. 'That's it, isn't it?'

Detlef remembers it all too clearly. He'd already spotted it. 'It is,' he confirms. 'I know where I am now.'

'Ha! Strange ol' world, innit?' says Derek, shaking his head. 'That bein' your ol' waterin' 'ole an' me not knowin' about it.'

'This is where you lived, Detlef?' Ellen then asks, looking out at the vast expanse of countryside on either side.

'It is, Ellen,' he answers. 'Over there, on the right. Brock Farm. There was a turning. A gate.'

'Just imagine,' she then says. 'We could have all lived here together, couldn't we?'

'Yes, we could,' he answers a little ruefully. 'The offer was always there.'

'Silly me,' says Ellen, instantly reprimanding herself. 'I'm sure I could have got used to it, in the end.'

'What? Me too?' Derek then asks, pretending to be aghast. 'Livin' out 'ere all in the middle o' bloody nowhere? You're jokin' ain't ya?'

'Of course, you too!' chuckles his mother.

'So, this could o' been me local?' he says as they are almost upon the old Cider House, laughing in disbelief. 'Funny little place, innit? Can we pop in for one after?'

'Looks shut to me,' says Marion.

'You go around the back,' recalls Detlef, now more than a little intrigued himself, 'but, please, I'd like to find the farm first.'

'Deal!' agrees Derek enthusiastically. 'Point me in the right direction, Pops.'

-

Phil and Jimbo are virtually home and onto the estate.

'Now, don't forget,' warns Phil as the Traveller's comes into view. 'Not a bloody word to anyone, d'you hear me?'

'I know.'

'If it gets out, we're fucked.'

'I said, I know.'

'Not even Reenie.'

'No, definitely not!'

-

PG's mobile phone rings. It's a withheld number but, intrigued, he answers it.

'Hello,' says a woman's voice. *'This is the Avon and Somerset Constabulary here. My name is Detective Inspector Davies.'*

'The police?' answers PG and in order to alert Jennifer.

'Yes. DI Davies,' she repeats.

'What can I do for you?'.

'Am I speaking to Peter Green?'

'Yes.'

'Great. Nothing to worry about, but I wonder if you would be kind enough to come in to speak to us?'

'Why?'

'We have been given your name and hope you might be able to help us with some ongoing inquiries?'

'What about?'

'There's nothing to worry about, Mr Green,' repeats DI Owen. *'It's to do with Tate Holdings and I believe you have had dealings with them?*

'What if I have?'

'I can arrange to have someone pick you up and return you home if you like?' the inspector offers.

-

'It's there, I think,' says Detlef pointing to what is little more than a gap in the hedgerow.

'Can't see a sign,' says Marion and now feeling decidedly outside of her comfort zone. 'Are you sure?'

'No probs, Pops,' says Derek, ignoring his ex's concerns and driving the heavy Rolls-Royce into the heavily rutted track. 'Let's give it a whirl, shall we? Find out. Hold on to yer 'orses!'

-

'What have you done, Phil?' asks Reenie from behind the bar as they walk in.

'Bloody tripped, didn't I!' says Phil, laughing, and as if it was one big joke. 'Smacked me elbow on a kerb. Bloody idiot!'

'Nasty things, elbows. Is it going to be alright?'

'Will be when you've poured me a pint,' he says.

-

Some half a mile down the increasingly narrow and furrowed track, a farmhouse and outbuildings finally appear in front of them - slate roof, painted white - a rusty open sided barn towering to the left, still there and where it had always been.

'This the one?' asks Derek.

'What a terrible stink!' says Marion, holding her nose. 'It pongs to high heaven!'

'It's the cattle,' explains Detlef. 'It was always the same.'

-

'Do you want me to come with you?' asks Jennifer.

'No,' says PG. 'It will look as if I have something to hide, which I haven't.'

'Your choice, but be careful.'

'I will, but you can give me a lift, if you be so kind,' he requests.

'Yes, I was meaning to say. What happened to the Range Rover looks like it's been through the wars.'

'Don't ask,' says PG. 'Don't ask.'

-

The Rolls-Royce purrs and squelches its way into the wet and cow shit muddy farmyard.

'I shall 'ave to go to the bloody car wash after this,' says Derek, but not at all bothered. 'It's like a bloody quagmire!'

'I don't like it,' worries Marion and looking immediately very apprehensive. 'There's no-one about. Not a soul!'

'Stop frettin', Mar,' Derek tells her. 'Well, has it changed much, Pops?' he then asks and as a pair of dogs run up to them, barking furiously.

'I think we should go!' Marion now screeches.

'Can we wait? Just for a short while?' asks Detlef, his memories flooding back. 'I'd like to look for a little longer.'

'Sure, but don't get out!' Derek reacts, 'they'll 'ave your legs off, tha mad bastards!'

-

'Did you find them?' asks Reenie, handing Phil a very frothy beer.

'Yeah, we did,' answers her husband.

'That's good then,' she says. 'And they're all together?'

'Think so. I had to get Phil to the A&E.'

'Did you have to drive his car?'

'No choice, Reen,' Phil interjects, reminding her of his arm.

'Yes, I suppose,' she acknowledges, but tutting. 'Now, are you going to get back behind this bar, Jim,' she then asks. 'I've got stuff to do.'

'Gi' me a break. I've only just walked in,' he says, but still, lifting the hatch and taking up his usual station.

'Good,' comments one of the regulars and rather snidely. 'Your missus can't pull a pint for toffee. I'll 'ave another now you're back.'

-

After some minutes, an ATV, a small 4x4 agricultural vehicle, pulls up noisily in front of them and a man leaps out dressed in a battered waxed jacket and accompanied by two more dogs, fox terriers, who immediately join in with the barking and growling mayhem. 'Shut up!' he yells at them. 'Bloody dogs! What can I do for yoos?' he then asks, suspiciously, aggressively.

Derek lowers his window. 'It's me dad,' he begins to explain. 'He used to work 'ere.'

'Tha' roight, is it? Who moight tha' be then?'

'Me,' answers Detlef, leaning forward, showing his face. 'I was here in the 1950's. The Ogden family were here.'

'An' you are?'

'My name is Otto. Detlef Otto.'

The farmer drops his head, peering at Detlef intently. 'You better wait 'ere,' he says before turning around to head his way over to the farmhouse, followed by three of the four yapping dogs.

-

'What you done to yer arm then, Phil?' chortles the same man. 'Been beatin' the meat a bit too ferocious, 'ave ya?'

'I'll beat the meat outa you, if ya don't shut it, ya stupid ol' bastard,' Phil threatens him before precariously taking up his glass in his left hand. 'You just wait, when this damn thing's gone.'

-

Instantaneously, Detlef recognises the older man ambling over towards them from behind the farmhouse. 'It's Dick,' he says, his throat catching at the sight of him.

'Wasn't he one of the ones at our wedding?' asks Ellen, connecting.

'Yes, he was. The son,' Detlef replies, partially opening the door despite the mud and the remaining growling dog.

'Lovely people,' Ellen recalls. 'You remember that orange sugar bowl, Derek?' she asks.

'Yeah. What of it?'

'His mum and dad gave us that.'

'Did they?'

'Yes, and your baby's shawl. I've still got that too.'

'And the bonnet I gave you,' reminds Detlef.

'What? It all came from here?'

'Yes, son,' says Detlef as he cautiously looks for somewhere to place his feet. 'It did.'

'Bugger me!' exclaims Dick, stopping dead in his tracks as he sees Detlef emerge from the Roller. 'Now there's a soight fer sore eyes!'

'Dick,' Detlef greets him, stepping carefully to take his hand. 'You look just the same,' he lies.

'Ha! Oi wish, Detlef! Done alroight fer yerself then?' he says, admiring the car.

'It's my son's,' explains Detlef, 'Derek,' he introduces him, 'this is Dick.'

'Ah, hallo, Derek. That wuz mine you just met. Mike. A good lad.'

'And you remember Ellen?' Detlef asks.

She leans forward, waving politely.

Unsurprisingly, Dick doesn't recognise her but waves in return. 'Hallo, love,' he says, 'must be fifty odd years or more. My memory ain't so good as it used to be.'

'Yes, I know the feeling,' says Detlef, smiling wryly. 'Your dad? Nancy?' he then asks but only out of politeness and knowing the answer.

'Dad's long gone now, Detlef, mother comin' up five years. Shame, they 'ad quite a soft spot for yoo, they did. Often mentioned ya, time to time..'

'Did they?' says Detlef, genuinely touched and flattered to hear it.

'Yeah, they did. They'd o' liked to o' seen you again.'

'I'd never forgotten them either - or you.'

'Shut up, ya soppy bugger,' Dick dismisses him with a laugh.

'Frankie?' Detlef then asks after his old friend.

'Frankie? Yeah, he's still about. Long retired now. I still see him. I'll give him a call if ya like. He's not far,' says Dick before adding, 'I can't bloody believe it, Detlef! Never thought I'd see you ever again!'

'Can we all have a drink together?' Derek seizes the opportunity. 'Thought we might go to the pub back there.'

'Wha'? Tucker's?' says Dick, thinking. 'Shouldn't really, but all things considered, don't see why not, as it's a special occasion. I'll follow you down, get me boy to pick up Frankie if he's about. He'd hate it if I told him he'd missed ya.'

'Would you? I'd enjoy that very much,' says Detlef.

'Moight cost ya though,' says Dick, grinning broadly.

Detlef looks momentarily confused.

'There's tha milkin' to be done 'fore you go!'

Detlef laughs, smiling at the memory. 'I used to enjoy it,' he says.

'Well, you know where it is! Still there!'

'You milked cows, Pops?' asks Derek in astonishment.

'He did,' confirms Dick, 'good at it too, oi remember. An one more thing, Detlef,' he adds.

Detlef looks at him, confused once again.

'When you get in the pub, keep yer trap shut!' says Dick, now laughing uproariously. 'We don't want you gettin' banned!'

Detlef laughs along, recalling all those evenings just after the war had finished where he was forced to stay silent for fear of upsetting the locals.

'Let's get down the road then, shall we? 'Ave a little celebration together.'

'Ready when you are,' says Derek, firing the Roller up.

'Bit keen, your boy,' observes Dick with a knowing wink. 'Seems loik he's got a bit of a thirst on.'

Chapter 42

The narrow doorways and twisty corridors of the ancient old pub prove hard to negotiate with Ellen in her wheelchair. 'I can still stand, you know,' she tells them. 'Let me try.'

And she does, successfully so in fact.

Ably supported by her son with Detlef guiding and clearing the way ahead of them, she manages to walk into one of the rooms and sit herself down in front of a blazing and open wood fire.

'See,' she says triumphantly. 'I told you I could do it. I've been telling people for ages.'

'Well done, Ellen,' Marion congratulates her. 'Now, I wonder if they've got a cushion you can have? That chair looks a bit hard.'

'No, I'm quite happy,' she warbles, inhaling the sweet smell of woodsmoke. 'I could stay here all day long,' she says. 'It's smashin'. Just like Christmas.'

'So, wha's it to be then?' Dick then poses the question, already laughing at what he is about to say. 'No frills 'ere. You got a choice o' scrumpy, scrumpy, or some silly little things in bottles. Tha's yer lot.'

'I'll get these,' Derek offers.

'Oh no you won't, young un,' Dick gently chastises him. 'You're in moi territory now. I'll get 'em.'

'OK, fair enough, I'll get the next,' Derek concedes. 'I'll 'ave a pint o' cider, please.'

'Will ya now?' says Dick, grinning knowingly. 'Ain't any ol' cider, ya know. We tend to drink it in 'alves in these neck o' the woods,' he advises. 'Potent stuff.'

'I'm sure I can manage a bloody pint!' insists Derek, feigning insult and tapping his stomach. 'Look at me.'

Dick nods approvingly. 'OK, but on your 'ead be it,' he says. 'So then, girls, wha's yours to be? An' you, Detlef? A small un?'

'Anything will do for me,' says Ellen. 'It's just nice to be out of that damn chair, if you'll forgive my expression, and able to stretch these legs of mine. It's lovely.'

-

PG had gone upstairs to spruce himself up.

'I've done a little research,' says Jennifer as she hears him come back down and looking at her laptop.

'What research?'

'Tate Holdings. Unfortunately, all is not quite as it seems, I'm afraid.'

'Shit!' he says, already fearing the worst. 'How? What?'

'It's under an umbrella company, and one that has had severe financial problems in the past. Did you not know?'

'Does it look like I fucking knew?' he snaps.

'Unlike you, PG. Losing your cool.'

'Wouldn't you? Who are they?'

'Unsure, there's been a couple of name changes, and there don't appear to be any common directors, but, strangely, there is a Lord Alan Lyle.'

'You're kidding me! A lord named Lyle?'

'I can't sugar coat it for you,' says Jennifer, unable to resist.

'Remember who's paying you,' snaps PG, unwilling and unable to see the funny side of it.

'What do you mean?' she says, acting all innocent. 'It might just be an extraordinary coincidence.'

-

There is no actual bar in Tucker's Grave to stand or sit at, just an old Tap Room with two or three barrels lodged high in the window secured by wedges and with bottled drinks of various sorts stored underneath. Dead opposite, there's a well-used and scrubbed table with fixed and painted wooden bench seats either side. Sat on them, opposite each other, are a pair of regulars, one inspecting a brace of partridge he'd just this minute bought from a shooter in off the fields, the other pinching a peck of snuff onto the back of his left hand before snorting deeply.

'When you're ready, Glenda,' says Dick, ambling his way through. 'I shall need a tray, reckon.'

-

PG snatches up his phone to call Piers but only to be greeted with a monotonous and continuous dialling tone. He yells out loud 'Idiot!' he screams, berating himself.

-

'I was wondering, why is it called Tucker's Grave, Dick?' enquires Ellen as he returns with the sloshing tray of drinks - a single pint, two halves (his in his own half pint enamelled mug complete with chips and dings) a couple of soft drinks for the ladies, and several packs of plain and cheese and onion crisps.

'Everyone asks tha' when they first come in,' he says. 'Sad story. Edward wuz his name, Edward Tucker, a farm hand. He 'ung himself in a barn not far from 'ere.'

'Oh, how terrible. When? Not recently?' asks Ellen.

Dick chuckles. 'No-oh! Hundreds o' years back. 1740's, I seem to recall,' he tells her. 'It wuz custom, back then, to bury people who took they's own lives at a crossroads an' on unhallowed ground. A sin, ya see.'

'Wha's that?' asks Derek. 'Unhallowed?'

'Unconsecrated.'

'Ah,' says Derek, but still none the wiser.

'But why?' says Ellen.

'Why? So as their spirit don't know which way to go at the crossroads.'

'Terrible,' she repeats. 'How cruel.'

'Rumour has it, on our farm too.'

'No!'

'Anyway, 'nuff o' that, on an 'appier note,' says Dick, lifting his mug. 'Cheers! Here's to all of you, particularly to long lost friends. Good to see you again, Detlef. Very good indeed.'

-

'Right, you can do one thing for me. You can take me to the Police Station,' demands PG. 'I need to get to the bottom of this.'

-

'Bu', what about his car, Phil?' asks Jimbo during a lull in demand at the bar.

'Hopefully, he'll take it steady and not prang it already.'

'Not Dekko!'

'Whose then?'

'Brian's. Who d'ya think? It's gonna get noticed eventually, a big black Beemer sat there for days doin' nuthin'.'

-

As Derek drains his glass well before everyone else and is already feeling its powerful effects, another familiar face appears at the door, his body entirely filling the frame, his head stooped to get under it. 'Bloody Detlef, you ol' scoundrel, you!' booms Frankie, a mountain of a man, despite his years and dressed in his time honoured and ragged poacher's coat. 'You could o' knocked me down with a bloody feather when young Mike just told me!'

Detlef stands to greet him, the offer of his hand gently pushed aside only to be replaced with a great big bear hug. 'Frankie, my old friend,' he sputters, but happily, the air all but expelled from his lungs.

'Put 'im down, Frankie,' Dick jokes. 'Where's me boy, getting the drinks?' he then asks.

'No. Just dropped me off. 'Ad to get back he said, might come later, say hello,' explains Frankie. 'So, looks like I'm in the chair. Wha's everyone 'avin'?'

'I'll get 'em,' Derek offers again, but feeling decidedly unsteady as he stands, a slur clear in his voice.

'I think you already 'ad some, ain't ya?' says Frankie, laughing. 'But as your askin' I won't say no,' he accepts. 'Just a poor ol' retired farm worker, me. I'll 'ave an 'alf, thank-ee, an' a packet o' them there pork scratchin's, if you wouldn't moind?'

-

Jimbo comes up to Phil again, leaning in far too close.

'What now Jim?' he asks. 'Chill out an' act normal, will ya?'

'Not that. Just wonderin', d'you think Dekko'll be back later?'

'No idea. I'm not a bloody mind reader,' says Phil.

'What you gonna tell 'im? You said it was cramp.'

'Forget it! I'll think o' summat, besides, if he does come back, I guarantee he'll be off 'is face.'

'Yeah, prob'ly,' says Jimbo, managing a smile. 'I think his dad's a bit pig sick of it, to be honest.'

'What, Detlef?'

'Yeah, you can see it in his face.'

'You were Detlef's best man?' connects Ellen as he is introducing everyone.

'I wuz, Ellen. Indeed, I wuz! Bloody years back!'

'Oh, how funny,' she says. 'I remember you now.'

'Tha's my problem,' says Frankie with a laugh, 'no-one forgets me! Gets me into a lot of trouble!'

'Oh, how funny,' Ellen repeats.

'So, wha' actually 'appened, Detlef?' asks Frankie, pulling up a particularly wide carver chair to take his girth. 'We read about it in the Post. We 'ad no idea.'

Detlef looks red faced and slightly taken aback by the speed and directness the question.

'Gi' the poor man a minute, Frankie,' complains Dick. 'You've only just walked in.'

'Sorry, Detlef' apologises his old friend. 'You know me, I never did no pussyfootin' about. Nosey bugger, I am.'

'It's a long story, Frankie,' says Detlef, seemingly unwilling to delve into the past.

'No problem,' he persists. 'We got all arter-noon, ain't we?'

'You don't never give up, do you?' Dick rebukes him again.

'Money was very short,' Detlef offers them the briefest of explanations, 'and I was desperate and stupid.'

'Bu' we would o' 'elped you out!' says Frankie. 'All you needed to do wuz ask.'

'I was too embarrassed,' admits Detlef as Derek returns with the drinks.

'Embarrassed about what?' Derek asks, somehow thinking it might be about him.

'About me, Derek,' his father tells him.

'Ah,' he says, quietly relieved, 'I'm all ears, an' 'ere's your drinks.'

'Very kind of you,' thanks Frankie, taking his but noticing another full pint glass on the tray. 'Is tha' your second pint already?' he asks.

'Yip,' answers Derek. 'Lovely stuff.'

'Then you wanna go careful, young un. You'll be flat on your back 'fore you know it. Tis strong stuff fer the uninitiated.'

'I tried tellin' 'im,' says Dick.

'I've 'ad it before!' says Derek.

''Ave ya now?'

'Yeah.'

'And remember what happened,' Marion reminds him. 'Please listen, Dekko. Don't forget you've got to drive? You've already had two in Weston.'

With that, Frankie pulls a face. 'You 'ad two already?' he says. 'Tha's not your gert big Roller outside, is it?' he then asks.

'Yeah, it is,' says Derek proudly, pulling out his keys to prove it. 'Beauty, ain't she? I just bought it. I won the jackpot on the lottery.'

'Did ya now? Lucky lad,' says Frankie, but snatching them from him and quickly shoving them into his oversize pocket. 'Then you can afford a taxi then, can't ya? I'll leave 'em wi' the landlady for safe keepin'.'

'But ...'

'But nuthin',' Frankie stops him. 'You understand, Detlef, duncha? Only lookin' after ya.'

'Yes, I do,' he says. 'I wish Derek would slow down.'

'See, yer dad agrees wi' me too. I seen too many bad accidents along this road,' explains Frankie, 'an' you're not gonna be tha next, not least wi' yer family and my dear ol' friend in the car, yer not - an' there's an end to it. Now, where wuz we?'

But Derek can't let it go and begins to look very angry. 'Give 'em back!' he demands.

'No. You can pick it up tomorrow,' repeats Frankie. 'You'll thank me for it in the end. So then, Detlef?'

'Who, d'you think you are?' Derek then begins to rage, trying to reach into Frankie's pocket. 'I only just bloody met ya, tellin' me want I can or can't do!'

'Stop now, Derek,' reprimands his father. 'I knew Dick and Frankie long before you were born.'

'I'm still drivin' my car,' Derek insists.

'No, you're not. Not if you are going to carry on drinking. I can call Maciej. He will help us.'

'It's the scrumpy, see,' Dick explains. 'We see it wi' grockles all the time,' he says. 'They must think it's apple squash. Some can get right nasty.'

'Please don't ruin it, son,' his mother then pleads with him. 'It's been such a lovely day.'

'I'm not ruinin' nuthin'!'

'You are!' Marion joins in. 'Listen to the state o' ya!'

'Gi' me a break! I jus' want me keys back!'

'No,' Frankie continues to refuse.

'You could always stay at mine,' Dick then offers. 'It's not as if I ain't got plenty o' space.'

'What about your wife?' asks Detlef, assuming. 'What would she have to say?'

'Oh, she up an' left years back, Detlef. She wuz a right townie. She couldn't hack it. My mistake for pickin' a wrong un. Lovely woman, mind. Beautiful.'

'I'm sorry to hear it,' says Detlef, exchanging knowing glances with his Ellen. 'It's a very kind offer,' he then adds, 'but we need to get Ellen back to her nursing home.'

'But not for much longer!' says Derek, overloud, and greedily slurping more of his drink. 'I'm buying her a nice little flat, ain't I Mu

'You are, Derek,' she says, trying to placate him.

'And I need to pack,' adds Detlef. 'I'm flying home to Germany tomorrow.'

'Ah, I see,' says Dick. 'Shame.'

'An' I'm drivin' 'im to the airport, so I need me fuckin' motor!' Derek shouts again.

Detlef has finally heard enough. 'Then you should have thought of that!' he admonishes, atypically raising his voice.

'What?!'

'I'm sorry, Derek, but we are not getting into a car with you, and no-one else can drive it. So, stop! Now! You're embarrassing me in front of my friends. I will not have it. Do you hear me?'

-

'I'll put on the local news, shall I?' says Jimbo, reaching for the remote control and about to change the channels.

'Oi, fuck off, Jim. We're watchin' this!' complains one of the many at the other end of the bar. 'The results will be comin' up in a minute!'

'Jim! Leave it!' Phil instructs him. 'Just bloody leave it!'

-

Even in his increasingly befuddled brain, hearing those stern words from his father and the inherent disapprobation in them, the disappointment, Derek looks momentarily stunned and belittled.

Deep down, it dawns on him that there is no-one else in this world that could speak to him in such a way and to such great effect - not his friends, not his children, not even his mother, and in front of people too. Again, he understands what has been sadly lacking all his life - the firm voice of authority, the voice of reason. In short, a father figure.

'I'm sorry, Dad,' he apologises. 'I only wanted to make you proud, take you to the airport in me new motor, tha's all.'

'Well, stop drinking. That would make me proud.'

'What time are you flying? I'll be fine by then. I'll take it easy. I promise.'

'We shall see,' says his father, not fully accepting his apology and certainly not letting him off the hook as yet.

'What time *are* you flying, Detlef,' Ellen enquires, but not really wanting to know the answer.

'*Drei Uhr vierzig*. Twenty to four,' says Detlef, correcting himself. 'I must be there two hours before.'

'I'll tell you what then, Detlef,' starts Dick, and offering another solution. 'If your son 'ere sticks to 'is promise, I'll get my lad to drive you all back a bit later. He's insured for anythin'. I can follow on, drive 'im back.'

'That's very kind of you,' gushes Marion, 'very kind indeed.

'Are you sure?' says Detlef.

'Course, I'm sure, S'what friends are for, Detlef. Your lad will 'ave his car for the airport then, won't he?'

'Tha's nice o' ya. Thank you,' acknowledges Derek, his tail still between his legs..

'But will you stick to your end o' the bargain, Dekko?' Marion then asks him. 'We don't want any more of your silly nonsense now you ain't got to drive.'

'Course I will,' he says but immediately considering whether he might be able to squeeze in one more. 'All calm an' gentle.'

-

'Are you sure you don't want me to come in with you?' Jennifer asks him outside.

'No,' repeats PG. 'But keep your phone on.'

'OK. Will do.'

'And try not to rack up your fees too much for the convenience. I fear this whole exercise is already going to prove highly expensive as it is.'

-

'Roight, now we got that all sorted, it were out near Chew Valley, weren't it?' Frankie turns the conversation back around once again.

Again, Detlef looks reluctant to answer.

'Leave it, Frankie,' says Dick, 'if he don't wanna talk about it. It's up to 'im.'

'No, it's alright, Dick,' says Detlef. 'Perhaps it would be better, after all this time.'

'Only I met the daughter once,' reveals Frankie.

'Did you?' says Detlef, looking horrified.

'I did. Only twelve when her mum got killed.'

'I didn't realise they had a gun, Frankie. I had no idea.'

'I know, Detlef,' he says. 'I know it weren't you tha' pulled the trigger. Married her in the end, see.'

-

'But what about my money?' PG is asking. 'I've invested over six hundred fifty thousand pounds, and I want it back. I need it back!'

'That's not possible, I'm afraid,' says DI Davies. 'The accounts have all been frozen, not to mention there are a significant number of other people in a similar situation as yourself – contractors, investors.'

'Other investors?' PG asks incredulously.

'Oh, yes,' reveals the inspector. 'Quite a number.'

-

With Detlef looking dumbstruck, Dick suddenly calls out. ''Ere he is!' he says as his son appears, conveniently stopping the conversation. 'You met him earlier. His name's Mike. Mike, this is Ellen, Marion, my old friend, Detlef, this is Derek or Dekko, his son.' he introduces them each in turn.

Mike waves politely and looks entirely unlike the gruff man they'd met earlier, dressed smartly. 'Nice to meet you all,' he says. 'Just dropped in to say hi.'

'Are you not stoppin'?' asks his father, noticing his change of clothes.

'Can't, Dad. I told you. I'm off out.'

'Did you?'

'Yeah. Down to Bridgwater. You know?' says Mike, looking a trifle embarrassed and like it was a secret.

'Ah, yeah. Sorry. Forgot,' says his father, remembering and a little disappointed not to have his son with him. 'Thought you looked a bit diff'rent. Don't go spendin' too much money on her, d'ya 'ear?'

'Wha? Did someone mention money?' says Derek, perking up and swaying unsteadily on his stool. 'I got loads 'ere! 'Ave some!' he says, pulling out a bundle of notes and accidentally scattering them to the floor.

-

'We'll be in touch,' says the DI as she escorts PG back out to the entrance.

'So, can I ask, where is Sir Alun Tate?'

The DI thinks for a moment. 'I'm not at liberty to say,' she says.

'Yes, and I hope he loses his!' says PG.

-

'Well, that changes things a bit,' says Dick after his son bids them all farewell to go on his date.

'I would like to apologise to her,' says Detlef, and looking close to tears

'No, I don't think tha' would be a good ideal,' says Frankie. 'Let sleepin' dogs lie, eh? Just 'ad to tell ya, tha's all.'

'I have a taxi driver. I will call him,' says Detlef.

'You don't 'ave to go yet!' says Dick. 'The offer's still there. As I say, I got plenty o' space - an' wi' me son gone on a promise, you'll be keepin' me company. I'd like it.'

'I don't know,' says Detlef, still shaken by Frankie's revelation. 'What do you think?' he asks Ellen and Marion.

'I don't mind,' says Marion. 'I shall have to make a call though,' she adds cautiously.

'I'd like to,' says Ellen, not wanting to return to the nursing home and not at all keen for the day to end at all. 'I'd love to really see where you used to live, Detlef,' she adds.

'Think we might manage to do somethin' a bit better than tha' ol' room behind the milkin' parlour,' remembers Dick. 'You can 'ave a proper bedroom this toime! Ha-har!'

'Yeah, you must o' been bloody freezin' in the winter!' says Frankie, laughing and clapping his old friend Detlef on the back. 'Not tha' we cared,' he says before adding, 'an' I don't want you to go worryin' yerself 'bout it neither. Wha's done is done.'

'That mean we're stayin'?' connects Derek, perking up. 'Can I 'ave another then? Jus' one more?'

'No!' comes the chorus from around the table.

'Can they do him a cup of coffee? asks Marion.

'Not sure,' says Dick, 'I can only ask.'

Chapter 43

After they'd left Tucker's Grave, and kindly assisted by a local man in his minibus such that they could move Ellen, they are soon back at Brock Farm and all sat around the table in the overly large and typical farmhouse kitchen.

There, with heavy coats crowding the backs of doors, dogs settled on their filthy but warm and familiar bedding, and an old cream coloured oil fired AGA belting out heat like billy-o, Dick is standing at it and preparing them something simple to eat. 'I'll show you the rooms when I've done,' he's saying, lifting his frying pan to melt the lard. 'You moight wanna open the windows fer a bit though, they ain't been slept in since I can remember.'

'Bit chilly!' says Derek.

'Wha's wrong wi' ya?' jokes Dick. 'Tha's wha' all you city types miss out on, good clean fresh air! Which reminds me, you'll find fresh linen in the airin' cupboards at the top o' the stairs, all nice an' clean.'

'I'm happy to do all that,' offers Marion. 'Just point me in the right direction.'

'Thank you, Marion, you're a star,' says Dick, now selecting eggs from a full wire basket of them and cracking them into a bowl. 'I will when we've 'ad this bit o' scrunch. Filled our guts. I'm not very good at that, makin' beds,' he laughs.

'Ooh, isn't this lovely, Detlef?' says Ellen. 'A big old farm like this. Just to think, it could have been me and you here had I not been so silly and wanted to stay close to mum and dad, for all the good it did me - terrible man.'

Detlef, too, is looking around. Despite all his years spent on the farm, he'd rarely been invited into the main house and is amazed by it. Despite the odd modern gadget here and there, the microwave, the under cabinet lighting, he can't imagine it had changed much at all.

'Don't you believe it, love. It's 'ard work,' says Frankie. 'It ain't like the bloody Archer's, I can tell 'ee. Early to bed it is, early to rise, an' seven days a week too!'

'I've never been frightened of hard work,' she says.

'I'm sure you haven't,' he says, laughing. 'Tough ol' bird like you. You got years on us yet! I can tell.'

'Is it alright if I smoke?' Derek then asks, looking a bit jittery and at last coming down.

'Outside, if you don't mind,' says Dick. 'We stopped all that when mother passed.'

'Don't s'pose you got any booze in the 'ouse, 'ave ya?' he chances.

'Derek!' admonishes his mother.

'Anythin'll do. Just to take the edge off?'

'I dunno,' says Dick cautiously. 'I got a bit o' whiskey. You alright wi' that, Ellen, Detlef? Fer a nightcap. He has behaved himself since, I s'pose.'

Detlef nods his assent. 'Just a small one,' he allows.

-

'An unidentified man's body has been found on the beach in Brean' the local news is saying on the television. *'The police are looking for information.'*

Hearing that, Jimbo drops a pint glass, smashing it to the floor, only to be greeted by a huge and raucous cheer from the pub.

'Fuckin' butterfingers!' they shout. 'Wha's that, Jim? Someone you know?'

-

Taking a slurp from a ceramic mug a third full of whiskey, his hands trembling, Derek manages to roll himself a cigarette before heading out into the dark and chill weather outside.

'Wait a minute, Derek,' says Detlef, standing. 'I will join you.'

'Wha'? D'you want one? D'you wanna puff?'

'No, Derek, I haven't smoked since leaving prison,' he reveals. 'I'd just like to talk.'

'Why don't I like the sound o' this?' he says. 'Come on then. It's out this way I think.'

-

'Jim!' Phil orders him over. 'Ask Reenie to come down an' cover for you,' he tells him. 'You need to take a chill pill. I think you best go upstairs, don't you?'

'She won't,' he answers. 'Not twice in a day she won't.'

'Tell her you're ill.'

'I feel bloody ill!'

'Then call her.'

-

'I'd like to talk about Jez,' says Detlef as they both stand outside under the porchlight, the soft and drifting drizzle illuminated like fairy dust beneath it.

'Wha' about?' says Derek almost dismissively. 'Nuthin' we can do until Tuesday, an' you'll be long gone by then, lucky ol' you.'

'I want you to call me. I want to speak to Jez before he goes into court, and after.'

'OK, fair enough, if you think it'll do any good.'

'He needs support, Derek. He needs to know he has people on his side.'

'Don't you think I know that? I'm doin' me best!'

Detlef turns to look his son squarely in the face, pulling his hand holding the cigarette away. 'Then stay sober for him,' he says, almost aggressively. 'He needs his father more than ever right now.'

'Yeah! Right! Tell me about it!' counters Derek. 'Where were you, eh?'

Detlef acknowledges this, his hands up in surrender. 'That was very clumsy of me,' he apologises. 'I'm sorry. I didn't mean it that way.'

Derek then takes a deep draw on his roll-up, exhaling huge plumes into the cold night air. 'You were goin' to tell me somethin' yesterday,' he recalls. 'Outside Jefferson's office? Remember?'

Detlef feels uneasy with this unwelcome reminder of his condition. 'It was nothing,' he says.

'Don't gimme that. Tell me.'

'Not now. It's unimportant, but I have been thinking,' says Detlef, swiftly moving the conversation along.

'Oh yeah? Wha' about?'

'I would like you to meet your sister and her family,' says Detlef. 'She would like to meet you too.'

'Would she? Really?' says Derek feeling almost unworthy. 'The girl in the photo?'

'Yes, the girl in the photo. Renata, and my wife too, Gisella.'

'Wow! Never thought. I bet you miss 'em, duncha?' asks Derek as he senses the catch in his dad's voice as he mentions their names.

'I do, son. Very much.'

'But you'll be seein' 'em tomorrow,' Derek tries to comfort him. 'Not long to wait.'

'No, but please hear this,' Detlef continues, 'I want you to know I am very pleased to have found you, Derek. You and all your family. It was something I needed to do while I still have life left in my body.'

'There you go again! Wha' d'ya mean by that? You ain't gonna die! You're my dad!'

'I am,' says Detlef, 'and don't you forget it, but none of us are getting any younger, don't forget that either.'

-

PG is trying to settle down for an early night, but he simply cannot relax, despite a glass or two of a very good red.

Sat in his Chesterfield, he cannot help but flick through the pages of his notebook to remind himself of the colossal sums he had paid to that bastard Sir Alun Tate, or was he Lord Alan Lyle, he now wonders.

-

Standing in silent and mutual acknowledgment for just a few seconds, Derek breaks their moment. 'Tell ya what, Pops! We can *all* go on 'oliday together!' he suggests. 'I'll pay! I can pay for everyone!'

Detlef pauses for a second. 'Maybe, but I thought you might like to come to Germany first, so you can get to know them.'

'What? Me? Come over to Germany. You're jokin', ain't ya?' says Derek but looking flattered and not a little taken aback by the idea.

'But there is a condition,' cautions Detlef.

'I knew it. I know,' says Derek in a moment of lucidity and realisation. 'You want me to stop drinkin', don't ya? Go tee-total.'

'I do, Derek. You will end up killing yourself like this, and what good will that do? With your recent good fortune, think of what you could do to improve the lives of others?'

'S'pose.'

'Remember, you will not make any good decisions in the pub and under the influence of alcohol.'

'I get it.'

'But, most importantly of all, whilst you're there, you are not giving of your time to your family, and that costs nothing.'

'I know,' repeats Derek. 'I'm not an idiot, ya know.'

'I know you're not.'

'Everyone's tellin' me the same,' he admits, 'my little Julie, even Jimbo down the pub.'

'And they are right. No-one wants a drunk for a father, son,' emphasises Detlef, 'or a husband.'

'Husband?' says Derek, laughing at the thought. 'Shut up!

'Well, you do seem to be getting on, you and Marion.'

-

After Dick had shown her the bedrooms and the whereabouts of the airing cupboard, Marion is soon sorting out the bed sheets and pillowcases but is wondering as to who is going into which room. She goes back down to the kitchen. 'Right,' she says, 'who's sleeping where? There's a room with a double bed and one with two singles.'

'Ellen and I can take the two singles,' Detlef suggests and out of the blue. 'Ellen?'

'Blimey, hadn't thought,' says Derek, suddenly looking very nervous. 'I hope you ain't still got cold feet?' he says.

'And you better not snore like you used to!' says Marion, giggling.

'Ellen?' repeats Detlef. 'Are you OK with that. Please say? I thought we might talk each other before we fall asleep, remember the good times together.'

The old lady nods in welcome astonishment and somehow looking like a young girl smitten all over again.

'Let's get you to the loo then,' Marion says to her, 'an' we haven't got any toothbrushes.'

'Jus' use your finger,' says Derek, showing them the actions. 'Ain't gonna hurt for one night, is it? I do it all the time.'

They'd needed an early start, the following morning, such that Derek could get his dad back to the hotel, gather his stuff, then make the mad dash to the airport to make sure he didn't miss his flight. However, despite setting off in good time, and having said their goodbyes to Dick and Frankie, the journey back home had not been without its awkwardness, its pain, its heartbreak - far from it in fact.

First of all, despite their passionate reunion last night (aided and abetted by the fact that Derek had not been totally pissed as per usual) Marion, the scent of sex still noticeable on her body and wishing she'd had time for a bath, was racked with guilt and had been noticeably jittery and anxious for the entire trip home. She was worried about the reception she would likely receive - the concern of how she would explain her absence to dear Nigel and what she would ultimately have to say to him. He would be devasted, the poor man. He didn't deserve it, not really.

For his part, Derek was feeling in two minds about it all. Sure, he hadn't been with another woman, not since Roxxii, not properly, and since he and Marion had separated, but as enjoyable and nicely familiar as it had been, he knew that it meant many changes were afoot and wondered whether he could step up to it, not least his promise to his dad that he would cut his drinking dramatically.

But most significantly of all, the epicentre of the mood in the car was around Detlef and Ellen. They were sat in the back together, hardly saying a word, but holding each other's hand. Tacitly, both of them understood that this was literally the end of the road for them and likely the last time they would ever see each other again. Last night, face to face and across the divide in between the two single beds, he'd told of his illness, sworn her to secrecy. She asked him to pray with her, as she'd done throughout her life. Detlef agreed, and, with some difficulty had even knelt by her bedside. She'd recited the Lord's Prayer, they'd said Amen together. Through his shirt, she'd touched his chest before he'd got back into bed, caressed it. He'd kissed her on the cheek in return, smoothing her hair.

Derek, sensing the vibe and had tried to lighten things up - they'd all keep in contact he'd said, reminded them that he was planning a big family holiday, that he'd get his mum out of the home and living much closer to her family. He'd get onto that this very week he'd assured her, see an estate agent - but all to little or no avail. There were precious little smiles, no laughter.

Then, heading ever closer to the New Horizons Nursing Home in Ashton Gate, came the moment that Ellen was dreading most of all.

It had been a terrible and upsetting experience for all concerned. Excruciating, in fact.

Outside the vehicle and in her wheelchair, Ellen found herself unable to let go of him, her beloved Detlef. She couldn't stop herself, couldn't help it, clinging to his arm, his leg, weeping and inconsolable, even when Margaret appeared and tried to gently calm her and coax her inside.

Now at last back on home territory himself, red-eyed and feeling emotionally drained like never before, Derek's body is screaming out for another drink, despite the promises he'd made to his long lost father and which he'd repeated to him at the airport. He'd come to see him in Germany, he'd told him, couldn't wait see his sister, the whole family. Detlef had at least smiled at that, hugged him and been hugged back in return.

Added to that, as hard as he might try, he can't seem to get the sound of his mum's pitiful crying out of his head, the sight of his dad disappearing into Departures, obviously traumatised and looking older somehow.

Derek parks his Roller around the back and next to his previous decaying old heap, tapping it affectionately as he walks past and, innately, heads in towards the precinct - he's got to get himself some more tobacco at least. He'd die otherwise.

Outside Bombay Nights and the now locked and shuttered bookies, Derek double takes as he recognises the little girl in the fur rimmed hood from the previous weekend, albeit it now feels more like a month to him. 'Hello, you,' he says. 'Did you get your Monster Munch in the end?' he asks her.

She backs away from him, instantly fearful.

'Don't be scared, I ain't gonna bite your 'ead off,' he says before reaching into his pocket to grab some money. 'Look, 'ere, you can buy yourself whatever ya like now,' he says, counting out over a hundred pounds in ten and twenty pound notes and giving her a handful of coins too.

'Not you a-fuckin'-gain!' shouts her mother as she appears from around the corner. 'Get away from him, Aisha!' she orders her. 'Get away!'

Still, the girl takes the money, snatches it in fact, and runs back to her mum, showing her, spilling some of the coins in her excitement. Her mother takes the notes, fingering them in obvious amazement and not a little relief. Still, she shouts at him again. 'Are you some sort o' fuckin' paedo, ya wankah?' she yells. 'I should get the bastard cops on ya! You need bangin' up!'

'Please yerself!' he calls back after them as he sees them turn on their heels head in the opposite direction. 'See if I care!'

And right at that very moment, he doesn't.

Detlef is swallowing hard as the aeroplane makes its descent into Hannover airport.

Naturally, he cannot wait to see his family again, all their joyous faces eagerly awaiting him in Arrivals, to hug them and to kiss each of them in turn. But he is torn. He cannot help it. During his whole helter-skelter of a quest, something has backfired on him. Something he could never have considered. It had something to do with where he was needed the most.

-

The mini-mart is virtually empty this early on a Sunday evening with most people now tucked up warm and safe at home such that there is no queue at all. 'Fifty grams o' Golden Virginia, please,' says Derek to the young black girl behind the tills, 'and give us half a dozen Lucky Dips for next Saturday's Lotto too, yeah?' he asks as an afterthought.

She presses the appropriate buttons on the machine, rasping it into life and spewing out his ticket. She hands it to him, along with his tobacco. 'No, they're for you,' he says. 'Good luck, yeah?'

-

Ellen's room is eerily silent when Margaret goes in to check on her once again and bring her a cup of tea. 'Ellen,' she calls her. 'Ellen?'

At first, Margaret thought she was just sleeping, but she wasn't.

Next to her hand is a piece of paper on which she'd written 'I love Detlef' multiple times and framed with hundreds of small kisses - xxx.

Underneath, on a separate sheet altogether, she'd drawn a stick picture of the hangman's game together with the initials ET and a double lined cross with arrows pointing in each direction.

-

Outside, Derek peels the cellophane from his fresh pouch and rolls himself a cigarette. He hears a text message come in on his phone and looks at it. It's Phil. *'Where are ya ya fuker,'* it reads. *'Pint'*

Thinking hard, Derek shields himself in his jacket and lights up.

It's decision time - Left, home to his poxy little flat. Right, to the fun and banter of the 'Raveller's, or, just a few minutes further on, back to his matrimonial home and to Marion and his kids.

It's a no brainer, and, deep down, he knows it.

So, making his way slowly past the boarded-up ironmongers, opposite Rub-a-Dub-Dub, the launderette, he can't help but notice movement from within the covered doorway, amongst the litter and cardboard boxes strewn in there. A familiar voice then calls out his name.

'Dave?' asks Derek but just as his phone begins to ring.

He looks.

This time, it's Margaret.

'Wha's she want, I wonder?' Derek says to himself.

Printed in Great Britain
by Amazon

35935086R00205